The Lessons of Modern War

Volume I: The Arab-Israeli Conflicts, 1973–1989

Anthony H. Cordesman and Abraham R. Wagner

Westview Press
BOULDER AND SAN FRANCISCO

Much of the research presented in this volume was supported by the Defense Advanced Research Projects Agency (DARPA). The views expressed are, of course, those of the authors and are not intended to reflect any position of DARPA or the U.S. Department of Defense. The authors are deeply indebted to Dr. Craig Fields and Dr. Anthony Tether of DARPA for their continued support and insight.

Copyright © 1990 by Anthony H. Cordesman

Published in 1990 in the United States of America by Westview Press, Inc., 5500 Central Avenue, Boulder, Colorado 80301, and in the United Kingdom by Westview Press, 36 Lonsdale Road, Summertown, Oxford OX2 7EW

Reprinted in March 1991

Library of Congress Cataloging-in-Publication Data
Cordesman, Anthony H.
   The lessons of modern war / Anthony H. Cordesman and Abraham R. Wagner.
      p.   cm.
   Includes bibliographical references.
   Contents: v. 1. The Arab-Israeli conflicts, 1973–1989.
   ISBN 0-8133-0954-9 (v. 1)—ISBN 0-8133-1329-5 (pbk.)
   1. Military art and science—History—20th century.   2. Military history, Modern—20th century.   I. Title.
U42.C59   1990
355.4'8—dc20   89-16631
                                                                                   CIP

Printed and bound in the United States of America

The paper used in this publication meets the requirements of the American National Standard for Permanence of Paper for Printed Library Materials Z39.48-1984.

10   9   8   7   6   5   4   3

The Lessons of Modern War

Volume I

*To Alex, Andrea,
Bridget, and Justin*

CONTENTS

TABLES AND FIGURES

PREFACE

This is the first in a series of three volumes that the authors have written with the assistance of Raymond J. Picquet, W. Andrew Terril, and Carol K. Wagner and with the support of the Royal United Services Institute. These volumes cover five major wars: the Arab-Israeli conflict of October 1973, the Israeli invasion of Lebanon in 1982, the Iran-Iraq War, the Soviet invasion of Afghanistan, and the Falklands conflict with Argentina. Volume I covers the lessons of the Arab-Israeli arms race between 1973 and 1989 and of the Arab-Israeli conflicts of 1973 and 1982. Volume II in this series covers the Iran-Iraq War. Volume III covers the Falklands and Afghan conflicts and provides the general conclusions of the study.

Each of the three volumes is written as an independent work, but the analysis of the wars in question is standardized as much as possible. The analysis of major conflicts is divided into sections that analyze the forces involved, the history of the conflict, key aspects of the operational art of war, and the impact of major types of forces and weapons. Where the source data permit, these sections are as comparable as possible.

The analysis in each volume focuses on military events and lessons and treats the politics of each conflict only to the extent necessary to understand military events. Only summary histories are provided of given battles, except where a description of military action will help the reader understand the broader lessons involved. Where possible, key events and data are described in a way that will allow the reader to draw his or her own conclusions. A deliberate effort has been made to avoid oversimplifying the complex nature of modern war.

The sources and methods used in each volume are described at its end, and a research bibliography is provided for each conflict. Frequent use is made of tables and charts to allow comparisons of forces, portray force shifts over time, and show the key performance features of major weapons. In most cases, the data are shown as provided in the original source rather than standardized or altered to eliminate minor conflicts. This is done to allow the reader to see the original data on which the analyses are based.

Anthony H. Cordesman

xv

ACRONYMS

AA	anti-aircraft
AAA	anti-aircraft artillery
AC&W	air control and warning
ACDA	Arms Control and Disarmament Agency
ADAM	artillery-delivered area munitions
AEW	airborne early warning
AFS	Armor Forces Sinai
AFV	armored fighting vehicle
AGM	air-to-ground missile
APAT	anti-personnel, anti-tank
APC	armored personnel carrier
APFSDS	armored piercing fin-stabilized discarding sabot
ARM	anti-radiation missile
ARPS	advanced radar processing subsystem
ASM	air-to-surface missile
ASW	anti-submarine warfare
ATBM	anti-tactical ballistic missile
ATGM	antitank guided missile
AWACS	airborne warning and air control system
BM	battlefield management
BVR	beyond visual range
C^2	command and control
C^3	command, control, and communications
C^3I	command, control, communications, and intelligence
CAS	close air support
CBU	cluster bomb unit
CEP	circular error of probability
COMSEC	communications security
EAF	Egyptian Air Force
ECCM	electronic counter-countermeasures
ECM	electronic countermeasures
ELINT	electronic intelligence
EPLF	Eritrean People's Liberation Front
ESM	electronic support measures
ESSM	electronic systems support measures

EW	early warning
FAC	forward air controller
FEBA	forward edge of the battle area
FFC	Field Forces Command
FGA	fighter ground attack
FLIR	forward-looking infrared
FMS	foreign military sales
FRG	Federal Republic of Germany
GCI	ground-controlled intercept
GCS	ground control station
GDP	gross domestic product
GSR	ground surveillance radar
HI	harassment and interdiction
HUMINT	human intelligence
IAF	Israeli Air Force
IAI	Israel Aircraft Industries
ICBM	intercontinental ballistic missile
ICM	improved conventional munitions
ICV	infantry combat vehicle
IDF	Israeli Defense Forces
IDS	interdictor-strike
IFF	identification of friend and foe
IMF	International Monetary Fund
IMI	Israeli Military Industries
IOC	initial operation in combat
IR	infrared
IRBM	intermediate-range ballistic missile
ITOW	improved TOW
JSTARS	joint surveillance and target attack radar system
LAV	lighter armored vehicle
LAW	light antitank weapon
LCU	landing craft-utility
LSM	landing ship-medium
LST	landing ship-tank
MICV	mechanized infantry combat vehicle
MNF	Multi-National Force
MRL	multiple rocket launcher
MSIP	multi-stage improvement program
MTI	moving target indication
NBC	nuclear-biological-chemical
NMH	nautical miles per hour
NUMEC	Nuclear Materials and Equipment Corporation
OAFV	other armored fighting vehicle

OAV	other armored vehicle
OCU	other combat unit
PCS	personal control station
PDRY	People's Democratic Republic of Yemen
PFLP	Popular Front for the Liberation of Palestine
PGM	precision-guided munition
PHOTINT	photo intelligence
P_K	probability of kill
PLA	Palestine Liberation Army
PLO	Palestine Liberation Organization
POW	prisoner of war
PRC	People's Republic of China
R&D	research and development
RF	radio frequency
RPG	rocket-propelled grenade
RPV	remotely piloted vehicle
SAM	surface-to-air missile
SAR	search and reconnaissance
SDIO	Strategic Defense Initiative Office
SHORADS	short-range air defense systems
SIGINT	signals intelligence
SLA	South Lebanon Army
SLAR	side-looking airborne radar
SP	self-propelled
SSM	surface-to-surface missile
STOL	short takeoff and landing
TEL	transport-erector-launcher
TISEO	target identification system—electro-optical
TOW	tube-launched optically tracked wire-guided
UAE	United Arab Emirates
UNIFIL	United Nations Independent Force in Lebanon
USCENTCOM	U.S. Central Command
VSTOL	vertical and short takeoff and landing
YAR	Yemen Arab Republic

1

INTRODUCTION

The Changing Importance of Third World Conflicts

The United States and its Western allies have used military force 220 times since the end of World War II. About 80 of these uses have involved low-level conflict, while 15 have involved major task forces or extended and fairly intense conflict, and all 15 have occurred in the Third World (see Table 1.1).[1] At the same time, the West has become steadily more dependent on imports of oil, minerals, and raw materials from Third World states, and it has encountered a growing military challenge from radical Third World states. The resulting Western involvement in the Third World is symbolized by the fact that the United States alone has defensive alliances and treaties with 26 Third World nations and informal agreements with many others.[2]

Western technology transfers are also steadily changing in character and volume. The U.S. is selling F-15, F-16, E-3A, and E-2C aircraft and Improved Hawk missiles to the Third World. Britain is selling Tornado fighters and Chieftain tanks. France is selling virtually its entire inventory of advanced fighters and missiles, and the Soviet Union is selling "first-line" systems, such as the SS-21 and MiG-27. Iraq has manufactured and used its own chemical weapons, and other Third World states are now making tanks, jet combat aircraft, and surface-to-air missiles. In fact, Third World states now account for an increasingly significant share of world arm sales to the Third World. Their arms exports rose from $470 million in 1973 to over $6 billion annually in the mid-1980s. Military technology transfers continue to proliferate, and a steadily larger percentage of Third World arms purchases have technology equal to the deployed technology in Western forces. This is particularly true in the Near East and southwest Asia, which received over 70 percent of all major weapons and military technology transfers to the Third World during 1980 to 1985.

The pace of technology transfer is also reflected in the massive weapons shipments shown in Table 1.2. During 1980 to 1987, these

TABLE 1.1 Significant U.S.–Third World Military Incidents Involving Combat

1950–1953	Korean War[a]
1958	U.S. Marine intervention in Lebanon to support conservative government of Camille Chamoun
1961–1973	Vietnam intervention
1961	Bay of Pigs invasion of Cuba (supported by U.S. training and airpower)
1962	Cuban Missile Crisis (U-2 shot down)
1965	U.S. invasion of the Dominican Republic
1967	USS *Liberty* accidentally attacked by Israeli aircraft
1968	USS *Pueblo* seized by North Korea
1969	U.S. EC-121 aircraft shot down over North Korea
1975	*Mayaguez* incident in which U.S. Marines recover American merchant ship seized by Cambodia
1981	Two U.S. F-14s shot down two attacking Libyan aircraft over the Gulf of Sidra
1982	U.S. Marine intervention in Lebanon to evacuate the PLO and then to serve as a peacekeeping force
1983	U.S. invasion of Grenada
1987	U.S. and West European intervention in the Gulf
1987	U.S. air strike against Libya from England

[a]Involves a variety of separate combat events or battles.

shipments involved over 3,500 supersonic jet fighters, 11,000 modern main battle tanks, 20,000 artillery weapons, 500 combat ships, and 37,000 surface-to-air missiles. As Tables 1.3 and 1.4 show, Third World nations acquired an average of over $37 billion annually in major arms and military technology from 1981 to 1988 and probably acquired some $10 to $15 billion more in imports of advanced civil technology applied to military uses. These arms do not simply fuel a struggle for prestige or political power. At this writing one out of every seven nations in the world is at war.[3]

It is essential, therefore, that both the West and its allies make proper use of the lessons that can be learned from "limited force engagements" and other conflicts in the Third World. These conflicts

TABLE 1.2 Numbers of Weapons Delivered by Major Suppliers to the Third World[1]

Weapons Category	United States	U.S.S.R.	Major Western European[2]
1981–1984			
Tanks and Self-Propelled Guns	2211	4320	660
Artillery	1691	9420	1790
APCs and Armored Cars	4179	7085	2390
Major Surface Combatants	17	27	51
Minor Surface Combatants	31	84	121
Submarines	0	6	10
Supersonic Combat Aircraft	344	1610	250
Subsonic Combat Aircraft	236	70	155
Other Aircraft	108	345	375
Helicopters	116	785	330
Guided Missile Boats	0	26	31
Surface-to-Air Missiles (SAMs)	3003	14920	3140
1985–1988			
Tanks and Self-Propelled Guns	950	3055	145
Artillery	1014	5690	750
APCs and Armored Cars	772	6095	480
Major Surface Combatants	0	17	18
Minor Surface Combatants	6	72	69
Submarines	0	10	7
Supersonic Combat Aircraft	193	570	145
Subsonic Combat Aircraft	13	95	50
Other Aircraft	206	300	210
Helicopters	130	760	280
Guided Missile Boats	0	0	1
Surface-to-Air Missiles (SAMs)	697	14495	925
1981–1988			
Tanks and Self-Propelled Guns	3161	7375	805
Artillery	2705	15110	2540
APCs and Armored Cars	4951	13180	2870
Major Surface Combatants	17	44	69
Minor Surface Combatants	37	156	190
Submarines	0	16	17
Supersonic Combat Aircraft	537	2180	395
Subsonic Combat Aircraft	249	165	205
Other Aircraft	314	645	585
Helicopters	246	1545	610
Guided Missile Boats	0	26	32
Surface-to-Air Missiles (SAMs)	3700	29415	4065

[1]Third World category excludes Europe, NATO nations, Warsaw Pact nations, Japan, Australia, and New Zealand. All data are for calendar years given.
[2]Major Western European includes France, United Kingdom, West Germany, and Italy totals as an aggregate figure.
SOURCE: Richard F. Grimmett, *Trends in Conventional Arms Transfers to the Third World by Major Supplier, 1981–1988,* Washington, D.C., Congressional Research Service, Report 89-434-F, July 31, 1989, p. 57.

TABLE 1.3 Arms Deliveries to the Third World, by Supplier (in Millions of Current U.S. Dollars)*

	1981	1982	1983	1984	1985	1986	1987	1988
Non-Communist								
Of which:								
United States	5,978	8,084	9,438	5,603	5,397	6,120	7,316	4,865
France	3,950	3,780	3,770	4,060	5,050	4,230	1,600	630
United Kingdom	2,510	1,600	1,360	1,190	780	890	1,550	280
West Germany	1,160	490	1,230	2,460	570	240	550	190
Italy	1,140	1,050	1,220	1,170	990	500	240	240
All Other	3,080	4,740	13,900	5,330	3,220	2,440	3,300	2,530
Total non-Communist	17,818	19,744	30,918	19,813	16,007	14,420	14,556	8,735
Communist								
Of which:								
U.S.S.R.	14,470	16,010	16,380	16,100	13,500	14,980	18,900	18,710
China	400	1,250	1,570	2,040	670	1,240	2,310	3,070
All Other	2,300	3,010	2,360	3,340	3,620	2,700	2,810	2,480
Total Communist	17,170	20,270	20,310	21,480	17,790	18,920	24,020	24,260
GRAND TOTAL	34,988	40,014	51,228	41,293	33,797	33,340	38,576	32,995
**Dollar inflation index (1988=100)	.7704	.8284	.8585	.8841	.913	.9368	.9656	1

*Third World category excludes Europe, NATO nations, Warsaw Pact nations, Japan, Australia and New Zealand. All data are for the calendar year given. All amounts given include the values of weapons, spare parts, construction, all associated services, military assistance and training programs. Statistics for foreign countries are based upon estimated selling prices. U.S. commercial sales delivery values are excluded.

**Based on Department of Defense Price Deflator.

SOURCE: Richard F. Grimmett, *Trends in Conventional Arms Transfers to the Third World by Major Supplier, 1981–1988*, Washington, D.C., Congressional Research Service, Report 89-434-F, July 31, 1989, p. 43.

TABLE 1.4 Percentage of Supplier Deliveries Value by Region, 1981–1988

	East Asia/Pacific		Near East/So. Asia		Latin America		Africa (Sub-Saharan)		TOTAL	TOTAL
	1981–84	1985–88	1981–84	1985–88	1981–84	1985–88	1981–84	1985–88	1981–84	1985–88
Non-Communist										
Of which:										
U.S.	13.49%	18.74%	82.54%	74.04%	2.67%	5.58%	1.30%	1.64%	100.00%	100.00%
France	1.93%	1.56%	85.54%	87.84%	6.81%	5.73%	5.72%	4.87%	100.00%	100.00%
United Kingdom	7.52%	8.86%	79.25%	80.57%	4.06%	3.14%	9.17%	7.43%	100.00%	100.00%
West Germany	9.36%	13.55%	37.83%	65.16%	43.63%	16.77%	9.18%	4.52%	100.00%	100.00%
Italy	5.03%	15.15%	61.49%	58.59%	24.07%	5.05%	9.41%	21.21%	100.00%	100.00%
All Other	13.53%	22.82%	68.30%	64.46%	12.59%	6.62%	5.58%	6.10%	100.00%	100.00%
Total non-Communist	9.87%	15.00%	75.58%	74.55%	9.78%	5.98%	4.78%	4.47%	100.00%	100.00%
(Major West European)*	4.76%	5.39%	72.88%	81.45%	14.82%	6.09%	7.53%	7.07%	100.00%	100.00%
Communist										
Of which:										
U.S.S.R.	11.35%	16.58%	63.49%	57.64%	11.16%	12.02%	13.99%	13.76%	100.00%	100.00%
China	4.94%	3.58%	90.49%	93.95%	.00%	.00%	4.56%	2.48%	100.00%	100.00%
All Other	3.45%	2.36%	87.47%	76.38%	2.36%	13.82%	6.72%	7.44%	100.00%	100.00%
Total Communist	9.83%	13.55%	68.61%	63.27%	9.20%	11.24%	12.35%	11.94%	100.00%	100.00%
GRAND TOTAL	9.85%	14.12%	72.05%	67.64%	9.49%	9.20%	8.62%	9.05%	100.00%	100.00%

*Major West European category includes France, United Kingdom, West Germany, and Italy.
SOURCE: Richard F. Grimmett, *Trends in Conventional Arms Transfers to the Third World by Major Supplier, 1981–1988*, Washington, D.C., Congressional Research Service, Report 89-434-F, July 31, 1989, p. 47.

not only shed light on the possible character of future struggles involving Western forces; they often provide important lessons regarding current weapons systems and modern tactics for conflicts involving Europe or northeast Asia. They demonstrate the impact of such weapons and tactics under actual battlefield conditions. Although it is not possible to draw sweeping conclusions from such conflicts, it is obvious that each conflict can provide important lessons and insights.

The Conflicts Under Study

The specific conflicts examined in this study are the 1973 Arab-Israeli War, the Soviet military operations against Afghan mujahideen since December 1979, the Iran-Iraq War since September 1980, the Israeli military operations in Lebanon that began in June 1982 (Peace for Galilee operation), and the Falkland Islands War. These five conflicts involved several types of warfare which were carried out in a variety of different settings. The types of warfare ranged from primitive guerrilla combat to modern tank, air, and naval exchanges. The settings include urban warfare, mountain warfare, marsh and amphibious warfare, desert warfare, naval warfare, and arctic warfare.

While all five conflicts varied in terms of their objectives, tactics, force structures, weapons employed, training, support, and in many other aspects, each provides insights into several combat situations of interest to the West. These areas of interest include:

- the overall value and impact of technology in low-level and Third World conflicts;
- the impact of weather, terrain, distance, urban warfare, and other special conditions of combat;
- the role of warning, threat assessment, intelligence, and tactical command, control, communications, and intelligence (C^3I) systems;
- the relative impact of force numbers, tactics, and technology;
- the value of given elements of combined arms, joint operations, land-air battles, and sea power;
- the capability of Third World states to absorb technology transfer and operate advanced weapons and support systems;
- the impact of training, support systems, and logistics in shaping the ability to use advanced weapons and military technology;
- the utility or disutility of relatively "sophisticated" military technologies; and
- the importance of support technologies versus major weapon systems.

The 1973 Arab-Israeli conflict is the war that has received the greatest analytical attention. Many prominent analysts have evaluated and reevaluated the "lessons" of this war, and many of the participants have written military memoirs. Still, the 1973 war remains important because it provides a baseline for the analysis of later wars. The data on the 1973 war furnish a relatively firm body of knowledge that can be augmented and refined by insights gained in later conflicts.

The four more recent conflicts—the Soviet invasion of Afghanistan, the Iran-Iraq War, Israel's 1982 invasion of Lebanon, and the Falklands War of 1982—have so far received only limited study, and little of that study has been comparative. All of these conflicts involve some of the technologies and tactics that shaped the 1973 Arab-Israeli conflict. At the same time, each conflict involves different terrain and/or weather conditions, different force mixes, significant advances in weaponry and technology, and different patterns of combat.

The Soviet invasion of Afghanistan, and the resulting Soviet struggle with the Afghan rebels, took on massive dimensions after its beginning in December 1979. This war is significantly different from the other conflicts for a variety of reasons. It was the only conflict dominated by counterinsurgency warfare, and it was the only recent conflict involving Soviet forces and Soviet use of first-line military technology. Although the Lebanon conflict involved some elements of counterinsurgency warfare, this was not the predominant mode of fighting, and the Soviet weapons involved in the other conflicts have often been export weapons involving a very different force mix from Soviet forces.

The Iran-Iraq War, which began in September 1980, yields interesting insights for a variety of reasons, including Iraq's extensive use of modern Soviet and West European weaponry and a level of intensity that rivaled any conflict since World War II, producing more than twice the casualties of all the Arab-Israeli conflicts combined. In addition, the highly sophisticated American-made weapons initially used by Iran, and the problems that were associated with Iran's efforts to support these weapons, yield valuable insights into the problems U.S. forces may face using high-technology weapons in a future conflict. Iraq's efforts to improve its forces and weapons during more than eight years of conflict are of considerable interest, as are Iran's attempts to compensate for its gradual loss of U.S. weapons and its attempts to overcome technological shortcomings through the application of manpower resources. Finally, the latter years of the conflict provide useful lessons about naval warfare.

Israel's 1982 invasion of Lebanon began with the Peace for Galilee operation and was followed by a low-intensity war of attrition which has characterized Israel's post-invasion occupation of south Lebanon. The conduct of operations during Israel's invasion of Lebanon and the siege of Beirut provide good insights into air combat, air defense suppression, C^3I and joint operations, tank warfare, artillery, and infantry combat. The initial phase of Operation Peace for Galilee was the most intense period, the time when Israel's adversaries (i.e., Syria and PLO troops) were most formidable in terms of strength and weaponry. Nevertheless, almost 300 Israeli soldiers have died in Lebanon since September 1982 (after the Palestine Liberation Organization [PLO] evacuation from Beirut and the last major Syrian-Israeli battles), and the U.S. has already learned that it too may be involved in similar types of combat conditions.

Finally, the Falkland Islands War of 1982 is of special interest because it involved modern naval, air, and ground forces. It is also of considerable interest to U.S. Central Command (USCENTCOM), and the other Western states that might contribute to NATO out-of-area[4] operations, because it involved a sea-based projection of power by a Western state into a distant theater of war. While British military forces were forced to improvise and operate rapidly under extraordinarily difficult basing, weather, and logistics conditions, this improvisation is characteristic of most past Western interventions in the Third World and seems likely to be characteristic of the future.

Categorizing the Lessons of Recent Conflicts

It is not easy to categorize the key insights or "lessons" that can be drawn from these five conflicts, but each conflict provides important lessons regarding combined arms, technology, and tactics. While any list can only include part of the lessons to be learned, it is clear that significant lessons emerge in each of the following areas:

1. *Threat Assessment Technologies and Warning and Surveillance Systems:* All five conflicts involved tactical and/or strategic surprise in spite of the presence of ample warning indicators. All involved major problems in human intelligence (HUMINT), targeting, damage assessment, and the coordination of intelligence and operations. While very different levels of intelligence and surveillance technology were involved in the five wars, all exhibited serious limitations in the ability of current technology to cope with the pace demanded by modern combined arms and joint operations.

Each war also demonstrated the actual or potential value of theater intelligence assets, targeting systems, and damage assessment capabilities that could look far beyond "line of sight" and do so at night and/or under poor weather conditions. Several wars illustrated the need for major improvements in threat-assessment technologies and tactics for urban warfare, counterinsurgency warfare, or rough terrain or mountain warfare.

2. *Effective and Secure Command, Control, and Communications (C^3):* All five wars showed the need for effective and secure command and battlefield C^3 technology and systems, as well as reliable identification of friend and foe (IFF) capabilities. These become critical when reaction times are reduced and the geographic parameters of the conflict environment necessitate optimal use of available manpower through coordination of offensive movements and defensive measures.

3. *Combined Arms:* No force on any side of the five conflicts under study was able to meet its own expectations regarding its technical and operational ability to integrate combined arms, although Britain came close in the Falklands, and Israel did reasonably well in June 1982. The failure of combined arms was more the rule than the exception. This was partly a result of overcompartmentalization of key elements, tactics, and training. It also, however, was the result of basic problems in technology involving targeting, communications, weapons lethality, intelligence, and data processing as support. The excessive reliance of a variety of forces on armor and mechanized infantry was also a recurring problem in many of the conflicts being considered. A related problem for these forces involves the continuing failure of mechanized troops to fight in a dismounted mode when the tactical situation called for this type of action.

4. *Infantry:* Infantry combat was a critical feature of each conflict. While mechanized infantry played an important role in every conflict except the Falklands War, it is important to note that much of the other four wars was fought by dismounted infantry fighting in built-up areas, mountains, marshes, and deserts. No single area of tactics, technology, and readiness ultimately had more critical overall impact than infantry combat. If these wars are at all typical, Western nations may be underestimating both the need to improve the equipment of their infantry forces and the need to make C^3I armor, artillery, and air power more effective in supporting infantry forces.

5. *Tanks and Armored Vehicles:* Four of the five wars involved tank warfare. In each war, the C^3I, maneuver, and support issues affecting tank warfare were more important than tank technology per se. The Afghan and Iran-Iraq conflicts also suggest that tanks may not be as important under some limited-war conditions as a lighter armored vehicle (LAV), designed for the specific terrain and combat conditions that are likely to be encountered, might be. The 1982 Israeli invasion of Lebanon provides some particularly important lessons regarding the

vulnerability of modern armored personnel carriers (APCs). The Iran-Iraq War and the Afghan conflict also suggest that the impact of modern antitank weapons may be more important in limiting the utilization of APCs and mechanized infantry combat vehicles (MICVs) than in limiting the utilization of tanks.

6. *Precision-Guided Land Weapons and Specialized Munitions:* The various wars have shown that air- and ground-launched precision-guided munitions (PGMs) may offer high accuracy and may significantly alter the course of combat under certain conditions, but much also needs to be done to improve sensors, targeting, ease of operation, IFF, and "launch and leave" capability. PGMs and specialized munitions were generally far less effective than might have been expected.

7. *Tube Artillery and Multiple Rocket Launchers:* Each war has shown that major advances are needed in C^3I and targeting and area fire lethality to make artillery weapons more effective.

8. *Surface-to-Surface Rockets and Missiles:* These systems were employed in the 1973 Arab-Israeli conflict and the Iran-Iraq War, although they served more as terror weapons than as weapons to strike at enemy combat power.

9. *Mines and Barriers:* Mines theoretically provide the capability for a smaller defensive force to impose high attrition rates on an invasion force and require the attacking forces to concentrate in high-density formations. In general, however, it was physical barriers that proved most effective. Extensive mining efforts affected maneuver but rarely affected the overall pace or outcome of a conflict to the same degree as passive barriers.

10. *All-Weather and Night Target Acquisition Systems:* All five wars showed that the ability to accurately deliver firepower and the ability to detect, identify, and position enemy targets can be critical in overcoming an imbalance in forces. Such capabilities dramatically increase the relative effectiveness of general purpose forces, enabling those forces to take advantage of natural terrain features, man-made barriers, and other advantages of combined arms operations.

11. *Anti-Aircraft (AA) Artillery:* Recent wars suggest AA guns are still an important element of air defense and can play a vital infantry role as well.

12. *Surface-to-Air Missiles (SAMs):* SAMs played very different roles in the five wars under study, and C^3I and IFF generally proved more important than the lethality of individual SAMs. Light SAMs and short-range air defense systems (SHORADS) generally had as much or more impact on combat as medium and heavy SAMs.

13. *Air Suppression of Ground- or Sea-Based Air Defenses:* Every

conflict under study involved a major struggle between air forces and ground- or sea-based air defenses, although the results were very different in each conflict. In 1973 Israeli ground forces had to open gaps in the Egyptian SAM belt before air suppression became effective. In Afghanistan, the Soviets only had to deal with a relatively minor threat from mujahideen guns and SA-7s. Israel fought the most successful SAM suppression battle in modern history in 1982 in Operation Peace for Galilee. In spite of massive medium and heavy SAM defenses on both sides, Iraqi and Iranian forces only faced serious threats from light SAMs and AA guns. Argentina and Britain fought the first major battle between an air force and modern shipborne air and cruise missile defenses with mixed results. Each case illustrates the delicate balance technology, training, and systems integration create between dominance by air power and by ground- or sea-based defenses, as well as the critical impact of tactics, C^3I, and training.

14. *Air-to-Air Combat:* The Soviet invasion of Afghanistan is the only conflict that did not involve air-to-air combat. The others revealed the critical importance of advanced air-to-air missiles, avionics, C^3I, tactics, and training.

15. *Close Air Support:* All five conflicts involved extensive close air support (CAS) activity. In each case, however, CAS activity had far less impact on the ground battle than either the participants or outside observers anticipated. This was partly the result of fighter- or ground-based air defenses, but it was also the result of inadequate target acquisition, C^3I, training, and munitions lethality.

16. *Interdiction and Long-Range Air Attack:* Each conflict reveals slightly different lessons about air interdiction and long-range bombing attacks. All, however, reveal significant targeting, munitions lethality, damage assessment, and tactical problems. In general, long-range bombing rarely had the anticipated effectiveness.

17. *Air Reconnaissance, C^3I, IFF, and Air Control and Warning (AC&W):* Many of the issues regarding reconnaissance, C^3I, IFF, and AC&W are subsumed in the previous operational categories. At the same time, each conflict reinforces the need for advanced integrated C^3I, AC&W, and IFF systems.

18. *Helicopters:* In every conflict, extensive use was made of combat and support helicopters. It was indicated in each, however, that the impact of the helicopter is highly dependent on both tactics and the availability of advanced helicopter technology and munitions. The race between helicopter effectiveness and countermeasures is and has been a close one.

19. *Combined Operations:* Britain was the only power out of the twelve forces involved in all five conflicts to make effective use of

combined land, air, and sea operations. For a variety of reasons, no other power was able to effectively unite land and air operations. The USSR, however, steadily improved its land/air operations, starting in 1981. The inability of the land and air arms to function in unison and the unraveling of combined operations once they are initiated are examined in this work so that we can identify the ways mistakes occurred.

20. *Logistics and Support:* Adequate logistics, combat and service support, and strategic and theater mobility proved critical in several conflicts and often had as much impact as tactics and technology. C^3/battlefield management (BM) proved to be as critical a problem in these areas as in the allocation of combat forces.

21. *Naval Systems:* Although the Falklands War and Iran-Iraq War were the only conflicts involving the extensive use of modern naval weapons, they still provide important lessons about airborne early warning (AEW), ship defense, ship vulnerability, submarines, anti-submarine warfare (ASW), and light carrier/vertical and short takeoff and landing (VSTOL) operations.

22. *Chemical/Biological Weapons and Defensive Systems:* Iraq and the USSR used chemical warfare with indifferent results. The key problems were a mixture of targeting, terrain, delivery means, and tactics.

23. *Nuclear Weapons:* Nuclear weapons might conceivably have been used in the 1973 Arab-Israeli conflict and in the fighting in the Falklands to provide the force leverage unavailable from conventional technologies. There is little indication, however, that such escalation was ever likely or imminent.

The Broader Lessons of War

It is tempting to go beyond these lessons and to try to deal with the broader lessons of war. Each conflict did provide new lessons regarding the risks of initiating a conflict, the problems of controlling escalation, the complications of trying to implement a grand strategy in the face of the "friction" of conflict, and the difficulty of making war an "extension of diplomacy by other means." These lessons are so subjective, however, that it seems better to concentrate on those areas where it is possible to make relatively simple judgments and a wide range of supporting data are available.

Tactics, technology, training, and military organization are uncertain enough. It has become apparent that far more data are available than "facts." The reporting on recent wars may be far more detailed than the reporting on past conflicts, but this reporting is filled with subjective judgments. This is true even when reports appear to be based on direct observation before or after the conflict. Far too often such reports do not hold up under careful examination. In other cases, key data are missing or cannot be verified. This is particularly true when the impressions of one side dominate reporting on the conflict or when some dramatic "lesson" captures public attention early in the conflict and shapes all following reports and analyses. War may change its character, but truth remains its first casualty.

It seems best, therefore, to concentrate on providing the available data in well-established areas. Even so, each reader must bring his or her own experience to bear in judging the reporting now available. It is not possible to caveat each comment or conclusion, but it is necessary to provide an overall statement that no country involved in any of the five wars under study was able to report objectively on its own performance and that most lacked the ability to conduct serious operations research before or after the combat.

It is also important to note that war is an incredibly complex process and that no one can be an expert on all the factors involved. This study tries to examine the interactions between a wide range of different factors and to draw conclusions regarding how detailed aspects of the fighting on each side interact with battle management and combined operations or combined arms. The fact remains, however, that war continues to defy simple description or analysis. No one can easily weigh the relative importance of human factors and technology or tactics and training. It is dangerous not to learn from past wars, but it is equally dangerous to assume one can learn enough to properly fight the next war. The most this study is intended to accomplish is to provide military officers, planners, technologists, and strategists with helpful insights and a means of challenging their own ideas and conceptions.

Notes

1. These statistics are adapted from Phillip D. Zelikow, "Force Without War," *Journal of Strategic Studies*, Vol. 7, No. 1 (March 1984), pp. 29–54, and Barry M. Blechman and Stephen S. Kaplan, *Force Without War* (Washington, D.C.: The Brookings Institution, 1978), pp. 547–553.

2. John W. Sewell and John A. Mathieson, *The Third World: Exploring U.S. Interests* (Washington, D.C.: Foreign Policy Association, 1982).

3. Secretary of Defense Caspar W. Weinberger, Conference on Low-Intensity Warfare, Fort McNair, January 14, 1986.

4. "Out-of-area" is defined as a contingency falling outside then-current NATO or bilateral/multilateral plans and arrangements.

2

THE LESSONS OF THE 1973
ARAB-ISRAELI CONFLICT:
THE OCTOBER WAR

An overview of the major lessons of the October 1973 fighting between the Arabs and Israelis is an essential background to understanding the wars that have followed. Such an analysis also lays the groundwork for understanding many of the controversies which have developed around given tactics and technologies in succeeding conflicts.

The Combatants

The 1973 war between Israel, Egypt, and Syria marked the fourth major encounter between Arab and Israeli forces. The previous conflicts were the 1948 War of Independence, the 1956 conflict which grew out of Britain and France's invasion of Egypt in an effort to seize the Suez Canal, and the 1967 Six Day War, in which a preemptive Israeli attack destroyed Arab airpower on the ground and the Israeli Defense Forces (IDF) seized the Sinai, the West Bank of the Jordan, and the Golan Heights.

Each conflict resulted in massive military buildups on each side and in a progressive improvement in the rate of technology transfer. By 1973, the IDF was comparable in deployed tactical technology to most Western armies and air forces, and Arab forces had technology roughly comparable to Soviet forces. This pattern of military buildup is shown in Tables 2.1 and 2.2. These figures show that the term "low-level conflict" can be highly misleading as a generic description of wars in the Third World. By 1973, the forces engaged on the Sinai and Golan fronts often exceeded the maximum force densities of armored vehicles normally used in NATO–Warsaw Pactwar games.

These conflicts did not, however, follow any clear pattern:

TABLE 2.1   Patterns in the Arab-Israeli Military Buildup: 1947-1973

	1947-1949		1956		1967		1973	
	Arab	Israel	Egypt	Israel	Arab	Israel	Arab	Israel
Ground Forces	22,500	70,000	88,000	60,000	522,000	289,000	350,000	350,000
Tanks	some	145	500	305	2,250	800	3,000	2,120
APC							3,250	3,145
Naval Forces	7,000	2,000	7,300	3,200	16,100	4,000	20,000	8,000
Ships/Craft			45	5	172	25	165	85
Air Defense Forces		3,000			39,500	8,000	93,000	17,000
Aircraft	45	80	340	150	940	340	1,280	625

INCREASE IN FORCES: 1967-1973

	Ratio of Egyptian and Syrian Forces to Israel			Israel			Egypt, Syria		
	1967	1973	% of Change	1967	1973	% of Increase	1967	1973	% of Increase
Mobilizable Manpower	1.4	1.4	0	225,050	373,000	65	321,975	540,360	70
Main Battle Tanks	1.7	2.2	30	1,000	2,120	110	1,700	4,150	145
Artillery (100-mm+)	4.5	3.7	20	200	570	180	925	2,085	125
Jet Combat Aircraft	1.7	2.2	30	260	475	80	40	40	40

SOURCES: IISS, *Military Balance,* various editions (London: International Institute for Strategic Studies); Trevor Dupuy, *Elusive Victory* (New York: Harper and Row, 1978); *Born in Battle,* various editions.

- The 1948 conflict was essentially an infantry/artillery battle of attrition. It was the least well armed and lowest technology war, but as Table 2.3 shows, it involved the highest casualties.
- The 1956 fighting between Israel and Egypt was a sideshow to the much broader conflict involving Egypt, Britain, and France. In 1956, Egypt had roughly 150,000 men in its field forces, some 430 tanks, 100 Su-100 assault guns, 200 armored personnel carriers, 500 artillery pieces, 50 self-propelled antitank guns, and 255 combat aircraft. Israel had roughly 100,000 men in its mobilized field force, some 300 medium tanks, 100 AMX-13 light tanks, 450 half-tracks, 150 artillery pieces, and 155 combat aircraft. Egypt had withdrawn all of its forces from the Sinai, with the exception of one brigade. Egypt committed only 50,000 men to its defense against Israel, and Israel committed only about 45,000 men in its attack on Egypt. While Israel scored major advances against the weak Egyptian defenses, Egypt had to deploy its forces to deal with the fact that Britain and France deployed virtually all of the power-projection forces they had available in their attack on Suez and were able to destroy over 200 of Egypt's aircraft—

TABLE 2.2   The Arab-Israeli Balance in October 1973

	ISRAEL	EGYPT & SYRIA	EGYPT	SYRIA	JORDAN	IRAQ
A. TOTAL MILITARY MANPOWER						
1. War Authorized	373,000	621,000	350,000	271,000	69,360	
2. Peacetime Active	113,000	571,000	350,000	221,000	69,060	
B. GROUND FORCES						
1. War Authorized	350,000	500,000	250,000	250,000	64,300	95,000
2. Peacetime	90,000	450,000	250,000	200,000	67,000	-
3. Combat Divisions:						
Armored	7	4	2	2	2	2
Infantry/Mechanized	0	11	8	3	3	4
Separate Combat Brigades	18	24	17	7	1	?
4. Medium Tanks	2,100	3,742	2,100	1,642	540	'1,200
5. APC/Half Tracks	3,450	3,515	2,300	1,215	470	1,500
6. Artillery (100-mm+)1/	570	1,955	1,280	675	130	600
7. Mortars (100-mm+)	750	615	280	335	65	?
8. Antitank Guns and Missile Launchers 2/	650	1,575	890	685	-	?
9. Free Rockets and SSMs	0	36	12	24	0	?
10. SAM Launchers	95	1,630	1,280	350	0	?
11. Air Defense Guns	1,000	4,650	2,750	1,900	290	?
C. AIR FORCE						
1. Total Manpower (less ADA Personnel)	17,000	32,000	23,000	9,000	4,900	-
2. Jet Combat Aircraft	476	981	627	354	55	306
3. Jet Pilots	650	735	540	195	65	-
4. Air Bases	12	56	38	18	7	-
5. Shelters (Hangarettes)	400	780	546	234	52	-
6. Helicopters	92	261	194	67	6	-
7. Transport Aircraft	48	85	77	8	11	-
8. ADA Total Manpower	2,000	70,000	60,000	10,000	0	-
9. Early Warning Radars	20	445	360	85	1	-
10. Reconnaissance Aircraft	6	10	6	4	2	-
D. NAVY						
1. Total Manpower	4,000	19,000	17,000	2,000	160	-
2. Destroyers and Frigates	0	5	5	0	0	0
3. Missile Boats	14	25	17	8	0	4
4. Submarines	1	12	12	0	0	0

1Includes AT Guns 100-mm and over.
2Includes AT Guns under 100-mm.

SOURCES: IISS, *Military Balance, 1973–1974* (London: International Institute for Strategic Studies, 1973); Trevor Dupuy, *Elusive Victory* (New York: Harper and Row, 1978), pp. 608–9; "The Yom Kippur War," *Born in Battle*, No. 3, 1978; and various editions of the *Born in Battle* series.

largely on the ground. The total British and French task force involved some 100,000 men. There were approximately 13,500 men, 400 tanks and other armored vehicles, and 70 combat aircraft in the British task force. The French task force had roughly 8,500 men, 200 tanks and other armored vehicles, and 45 aircraft.

- The 1967 conflict saw Israel achieve almost complete tactical surprise when it executed a brilliant preemptive air strike that nearly destroyed the unsheltered Egyptian, Syrian, and, later,

Jordanian air forces. The IDF executed rapid armored thrusts across the Sinai and reached the Suez. It then launched armored and infantry assaults that seized the Golan, Jerusalem, and West Bank. Unlike the 1948 and 1956 fighting, the result was a decisive Israeli victory and one against Arab forces with more than twice as many tanks and aircraft. In the 1967 War, Israel had roughly 250,000 men in its mobilized field force, some 850 main battle tanks, 150 AMX-13 light tanks, 1,500 half-tracks and APCs, 200 artillery pieces, 50 surface-to-air missiles, 550 anti-aircraft guns, and 286 combat aircraft. Egypt had roughly 210,000 men in its field force, some 1,300 main battle tanks, 1,050 armored personnel carriers (APCs), 575 artillery pieces, 160 surface-to-air missiles, 950 anti-aircraft guns, and 430 combat aircraft. Syria had roughly 63,000 men in its field force, some 750 main battle tanks, 585 APCs, 315 artillery pieces, 1,000 anti-aircraft guns, and 127 combat aircraft. Jordan had 55,000 men in its field force, 288 main battle tanks, 210 APCs, 263 artillery pieces, 143 anti-aircraft guns, and 18 combat aircraft.

- The 1969–1970 Canal War, or War of Attrition, was essentially a high-technology air war between the Israeli Air Force (IAF) and steadily improving Egyptian SAM defenses—largely SA-2s and SA-3s.
- No clear correlation emerged between losses and casualties and the size of forces or technologies involved. As Table 2.3 shows, the first Arab-Israeli conflict, with the lowest level of technology and forces, produced the most casualties.

Each Arab-Israeli conflict led both sides to draw new lessons, create new force mixes, and use new technologies. Each side, however, drew different political, strategic, tactical, and technical conclusions. By 1973, the IDF was armor oriented, air defense oriented, and politically over-confident. Egypt was preparing for a secret attack, using a carefully planned crossing of the Suez Canal, with the limited objective of securing the southern Sinai and possibly the key passes with air protection from heavy SAM and air defenses. A much weaker and less well prepared Syria was forced to improvise an attack with significantly fewer ready and well-equipped forces.

The Lessons and Mistakes of 1967–1973

The Israeli victory in 1967 was so sweeping that it is understandable that Israel did not follow its victory with a searching examination of its remaining military weaknesses. Israel tended to treat Arab weaknesses as if they were cultural and almost inevitable in the Arab

TABLE 2.3   Losses in the Arab-Israeli Wars: 1948–1973

A. Overall Trend: 1948–1973 Wars

	1948		1956		1967		1973	
	Arab	Israel	Arab[1]	Israel	Arab	Israel	Arab	Israel
Casualties[2]								
Killed	4,800	4,500	1,000	189–210	4,296	750–983	8,528	2,510–2,838
Wounded	25,000	15,000	4,000	899	6,121	4,517	19,549	7,500–8,800
Total	40,000	21,000	5,000	1,088–1,109	10,417	5,267–5,500	28,077	11,310–11,638
Equipment Losses								
Main Battle Tanks[3]	—	—	30	40	965–1,000	200–394	1,850	400–850
Aircraft	—	—	215–390	15–20	444–500	40	392–468	102–103
Combat Vessels	—	—	2	0	?	0	19	0

B. Land, Air, and Naval Losses: 1973 War

	Israel	Total Arab	Egypt	Syria	Jordan	Iraq	Other Arab
Casualties							
Killed	2,838	8,528	5,000	3,100–3,500	28	218–260	100
Wounded	8,800	19,549	12,000	6,000	49	600	300
Prisoners/Missing	508	8,551	8,031	370–500	—	20	?
Equipment Losses							
Main Battle Tanks[4]	840	2,554	1,100	1,200	54	100–200	?
Other Armor	400	850+	450	400	—	?	?
Artillery Weapons	?	550+	300	250	—	?	?
SAM Batteries	—	47	44	3	—	—	?
Aircraft	103	392	223	118	—	21	30
Helicopters	6	55	42	13	—	?	?
Naval Vessels	1	15	10	5	—	—	—

[1]Includes only Egyptian casualties in fighting with Israel. Equipment losses include total Egyptian losses, including those to France and the United Kingdom.

[2]Prisoner of war and missing data are too unreliable to be included.

[3]Lower end of range often reflects losses that could not be returned to combat by the end of war. Higher end shows "kills" that put tank temporarily out of combat.

[4]Lower end of range often reflects losses that could not be returned to combat by the end of war. Higher end shows "kills" that put tank temporarily out of combat.

SOURCES: Estimates differ widely from source to source. The figures shown are adapted from Trevor Dupuy, *Elusive Victory* (New York: Harper and Row, 1978); Chaim Herzog, *The Arab-Israel Wars* (New York: Random House, 1982); and from various editions of the *Born in Battle Series,* Tel Aviv, Eshel Drammit.

approach to the art of war rather than the result of poor organization and leadership. Israel was also distracted by the problem of absorbing its occupied territories, by the emergence of the Palestine Liberation Organization, and by a long war of attrition with Egypt.

It is difficult to date the first step in this war of attrition, but an Egyptian missile boat scored a major victory on 1 October 1967 when it launched a ship-to-ship missile that sank the Israeli destroyer *Elath (Eilat)* and provided the first demonstration in combat of the missile developments that were revolutionizing naval warfare. In September and October 1968, Egypt evacuated many of its citizens from the Canal Zone and launched brief artillery bombardments from some 150 artillery positions. Roughly 5,000 rounds per hour fell on Israeli positions in the canal area on two separate occasions. The Egyptian bombardments then halted, but they led Israel to fortify its canal positions and to create bunkers in the forward area. Israel created an extensive system of military roads, crossing points, and defense positions, although its ability to man this system depended on prior warning and mobilization.

The Egyptians, in turn, built up their defenses along the canal. They built up a sand ridge along the entire western bank of the Suez Canal to protect Egyptian positions against Israeli fire and conceal Egyptian forces from observation. They established a road network of roughly 2,000 kilometers to allow rapid reinforcement of the canal area and lateral movement along the western bank. They built twenty new sheltered air bases and an extensive network of surface-to-air missile sites.

Gamal Abdel Nasser declared the formal beginning of the War of Attrition on 8 March 1969. Egypt launched a new and even more massive bombardment which went on for nearly 80 days. Israel responded with artillery and commando attacks and air attacks. Egypt responded by building up a crude net of SA-2 and AA gun defenses. Israel was able to seize some of the key equipment involved and launched one sweep across the canal and up the coastal road. In general, however, Israel relied on airpower, and this led to a struggle between Israeli fighters and Egyptian ground-based air defenses.

The Egyptians also began to raid across the canal, beginning on 10 July 1969, when Egyptian forces raided an Israeli position on the Port Tawfik Isthmus. These Egyptian raids started with a series of limited attacks by small groups and ended with company-sized raids that took a number of Israeli prisoners of war (POWs). The raids escalated from attacks on individual targets to assaults on fortified positions. Egyptian forces raided Elath (Eilat) harbor on 16 November 1969 and destroyed three Israeli vessels. They repeated these raids on 6

February 1970 and destroyed two Israeli ships filled with military equipment and ammunition. While Israel viewed these raids largely as harassment attacks, they had a major impact on Egyptian morale. They demonstrated to Egypt both that the Israelis were vulnerable and that they could breach Israeli defenses.

Egypt also flew air sorties over the canal area and tried to penetrate into the Sinai airspace. An Egyptian MiG-21 shot down an Israeli Phantom for the first time on 9 December 1969. In general, however, Egypt was not successful in air-to-air combat. It lost some 60 fighters between 1967 and January 1970. The main battle, however, was between Israeli fighters and the SA-2. Since the Israeli fighters could generally detect and outmaneuver the missile, as well as fly under it, they had a decisive edge. Israel lost only six fighters to all causes between the end of the 1967 war and January 1970, and it succeeded in virtually destroying the SA-2 net. It then shifted to deep preventive raids which proved so successful the Soviets were forced to give Egypt massive numbers of SA-3s and sharply increase their military presence.

Some 55 SA-3 sites were in place by June 1970, and Soviet-flown MiG-21Js began to appear in the air. Egypt's growing strength rapidly increased Israeli losses, and some 20 IAF aircraft were lost in the course of the next six months. The Soviets kept the missiles 30 kilometers from the canal and suffered their own losses—including five MiGs and pilots in a single day on 30 July 1970. Nevertheless, the U.S. responded by supplying more Phantoms, more Hawk missiles, and advanced electronic warfare gear.

The risks then became too high for both sides. In August 1970, a U.S.-Soviet sponsored cease-fire brought an end to the fighting before Israel fully came to grips with the problem of suppressing the SA-3 or realized the potential implications of the improvement in Arab ground-based air defense.

This end to the 1969–1970 conflict helps explain why the War of Attrition failed to correct a broad Israeli overconfidence in air power and particularly in Israel's ability to win immediate air superiority and then to provide close air and interdiction support to Israeli ground troops. Israel continued to act as if its air force would have virtual freedom of action in war.

Israel did not seek out more advanced air-to-ground weapons, did not carry out advanced attack mission training, did not keep up its still nascent SAM suppression and electronic countermeasure (ECM) effort, and left mission planning largely to armed reconnaissance and the ground force calls for close support. Israel concentrated on air-to-air combat and did not even develop a central staff to manage attack missions and coordinate reconnaissance data and attack mission planning.

The other problems that developed in Israel's art of operations may be summarized as follows:

- *Israel's superb tank forces and air-to-air combat capabilities disguised the need for more balanced combined arms.* Israel was particularly weak in artillery strength and mobility and antitank forces.
- *Israel failed to preserve a proper balance of advanced technology.* It did not buy badly needed improvements in its communications, modern antitank guided missiles, night vision devices, advanced artillery fire-control systems, added armament for its APCs, off-road supply vehicles, or a host of other technical aids to military operations.
- *Israel never came to grips with the need for positioned or fixed defenses.* It left its defenses on the canal and in the Golan Heights at the level of isolated strong points. It came to rely completely on warning and prior mobilization for forward defense.
- *More generally, Israel never developed effective plans for a surprise attack or mobilization in response to an Arab attack.* Its whole reserve structure assumed sufficient time to become ready before a war began. It was not structured to put balanced forces on line in sequence, and key positions such as artillery spotters and forward air controllers (FACs) were left for the final state of mobilization.
- *Israel let its reserves slide in readiness for financial reasons.* It cut its defense budget to fund civilian programs. As a result, it never developed adequate tank transporters and failed to maintain its reserve equipment.
- *Israel failed to build up munitions stocks and war reserves in preparation for further serious conflict.* It assumed it could determine the length of the war.
- *Israel did not come to grips with its lack of a true central command structure.* It lacked the ability to manage the overall conduct of war and to force coordination between its independent and feuding major combat unit commanders in the field. If anything, the 1967 war seemed to validate the need for battle leaders who acted independently and disregarded orders in showing initiative. Israel went into the 1967 war fighting with an army and emerged with a series of decentralized units.

Israel also failed to pay proper attention to the changes in the Arab world. This may be in large part because Israeli military intelligence had become steadily more tactical rather than politico-military in character, and it was ill suited to gather data on intentions as distinguished from capability. The quality of Israeli intelligence slid from a balance of collection and analysis to an emphasis on providing data directly to commanders. Moreover, Israelis who had grown up in the Arab world and understood its thought patterns and goals were being replaced by a steadily more xenophobic group of "experts" with limited practical experience with their enemy. Israel also committed the sin of overconfidence. Israeli commanders and political leaders simply began to feel they had nothing to fear.

The evidence is conclusive that Israel never was able to develop a full understanding either of the meaning of President Sadat's ascent to power upon the death of Nasser on 28 September 1970 or of the rise to power in Syria of Hafiz al-Assad on 18 October 1970. This lack of understanding was to prove critical in shaping the Arab success in achieving strategic surprise in October 1973.[1] Virtually all sources show that Israel had all the proper warning indicators but failed either to monitor properly the meaning of the detailed changes in Arab force structures between 1970 and 1973 or to understand Sadat's and Assad's intentions in spite of several exercises that were near rehearsals for their later attacks.[2]

This failure to heed the warning indicators is further illustrated by the fact that the Israeli government decided before the war to reduce the proportion of the GNP being spent on defense. This decision was accepted by the Ministry of Defense, in part because of the argument that the risk of war was sufficiently low so that an emphasis on economic growth was necessary to build up Israel's economy and longer-term ability to support a strong defense. Even when Israel stood on the edge of war, it left the Bar-Lev Line in the Sinai, as well as the Golan Heights, virtually unmanned. Further, although junior Israel intelligence officials correctly predicted the Arab attack roughly 48 hours in advance, more senior officers held their reports back until the last minute. Even then, the Israel cabinet delayed mobilization and refused to give the Air Force authority for a preemptive strike to try to break up the developing Egyptian and Syrian attack.

Full credit must also be given to the Egyptians for one of the most brilliant deception plans in military history. From 1971 to 1973, Egypt was gradually able to build up the capability to launch a surprise attack that involved hundreds of thousands of men. They did this by exploiting Israeli overconfidence and making a repeated series of Egyptian mobilizations and buildups in the area seem little more than a routine exercise in political posturing and propaganda. The Egyptian plan took advantage of three basic principles: Conceal all military operations as training or political acts, hide all evidence that Egypt had a concept of operations for crossing the Suez Canal and seizing the southern part of the Sinai, and hide all information relating to the timing of the attack.

This success was particularly impressive, given the fact that Egypt normally found it exceedingly difficult to keep *any* kind of secret. It was achieved by keeping the plan secret except for a very small number of advisors close to Sadat. Most senior Egyptian ministers and officers were kept in the dark until five to six months before the war, when large-scale coordination between ministries became necessary. The number of officers and planners involved then slowly expanded, but most Egyptian officers and troops had no idea war was imminent until the very last moment. This secrecy and deception kept the Israeli government from mobilizing when it finally did detect the signs of an Egyptian and Syrian attack, led the Israeli prime minister to deny authority to carry out preemptive attacks to break up the coming offensive on the day the war began, left the Israeli command structure poorly informed and confused when the war began, and greatly reduced the initial number of Egyptian and Syrian casualties.

The History of the Conflict

The details of the forces engaged during the 1973 conflict are discussed throughout the following analysis. It is important to note, however, that Israel faced major problems at the start of the war because of the Arab success in achieving surprise. This is reflected in the force ratios shown in Table 2.4.

As the war went on, however, the Israelis achieved numerical superiority in many tactical encounters because they had:

- a superior mobilization system;
- superior intelligence and C^3I;
- much greater field mobility for their ground forces; and
- an air command and control system that allowed them to rapidly shift air defense assets from one front to another.

The fighting does not lend itself to a single simple chronology because it rapidly became two major series of battles: one on the Syrian front and one on the Egyptian front. The chronology of the fighting on the Syrian front is summarized in Table 2.5. The chronology of the fighting on the Egyptian front is summarized in Table 2.6. These chronologies show that the Arabs dissipated their initial

TABLE 2.4 The Impact of Surprise on the Initial Arab-Israeli Force Ratios

	Israel	Egypt	Arab/Israeli Force Ratio
A. Israeli-Egyptian Force Ratio, D-Day at Sinai			
Major Combat Units	One Regular Armored Division	Five Infantry Divisions, Five Armored Brigades, Five Commando Battalions	7–11:1
	One Extra Reserve Armored Brigade?	Two Armored and Two Mechanized Divisions in Reserve	
	15 Strong Points of 20–40 Men Each	One Infantry and Marine Brigade	
Manpower	12–15,000	120,000	8–10:1
Tanks	270	1,650–1,700	6:1
Artillery	45	1,330–1,415	30:1
Antitank Weapons	70	6,350–6,400	90:1
AA Guns and SA-7s	0?	1,370–1,620	NA
SAMs	3 Hawk Batteries	250–260 SA2/3 40 SA-6	NA
B. Israeli-Syrian Force Ratio, D-Day at Sinai			
Major Command Units	One Division Regular Armored Brigade Regular Infantry Brigade Some Infantry 12 Strong Points	Three Infantry Divisions with 2–3 Extra Armored Brigades - plus - Two Armored Divisions, One Armored Brigade, Para Battalion	4–7:1
Manpower	6,000	60,000+	10:1
Tanks	180	820–930 on line 1,260–1,600 total	7:1
Artillery	20–45	1,020	25:1
Antitank Weapons	70?	3,650–4,250	50:1
AA Guns	0?	690	NA
SAMs	1 Hawk Battery? (3 assigned on mobilization)	120 SA-7 84 SA-2 32 SA-3 60 Tel	NA

SOURCES: Rough estimate based on the work of Trevor Dupuy, *Elusive Victory* (New York: Harper and Row, 1978), the *Born in Battle* series, and various writings by Chaim Herzog and Zev Schiff.

TABLE 2.5 The Syrian Front

April–September (1972–Prewar)	-	Syrian Army conducted the training cycle normally carried out during the winter. Training doubled over previous years.
June 1973	-	Tensions between Syria and Jordan relaxed.
August	-	SAM units were reorganized and redeployed south of Damascus.
10 September	-	Arab "Summit" was held in Cairo.
11 September	-	Israeli aerial photography revealed a buildup of strength in Syrian forward area.
13 September	-	IAF shot down 13 Syrian fighters in a major incident.
28 September	-	Arab terrorists attacked train in Austria bearing Jewish emigres from USSR.
1–7 October	-	Syrian "maneuvers" were underway.
3 October	-	IAF photography revealed Syrian armor division artillery deployed in 2d defensive zone. First elements of Israeli 7th Armor Brigade arrived to reinforce the Golan defenses.
4 October	-	Two Syrian independent armor brigades were deployed into infantry division Area of Operations.
5 October 1973	-	Syrian artillery located only 5 km from front instead of the usual 15 kms.
Night of 5– 6 October	-	Israeli intelligence received strong indication that war was imminent.
6 October	-	0940–1000: Israeli units received mobilization notification.
	-	Israeli 36th Division Headquarters was established in Golan (without maneuver units).
	-	1100: Remainder of Israeli 7th Armor Brigade in Golan; Israeli 188th Armor Brigade redeployed elements from northern sector of front to south.
	-	1400: Three Syrian infantry divisions attacked all along the front. Air strike and artillery preparations began. About this time (possibly a little later) Syrian air-mobile and overland attack of Mt. Hermon strongpoint began. Syrian 1st Armor Division moved south.
	-	1455: Syrian artillery preparation ended; fires shifted in depth and on-call.
	-	1600–1700: Israeli Mt. Hermon strongpoint fell.
	-	About 2000 or 2100: Syrian infantry division's armor and mechanized brigades were committed.

(continues)

TABLE 2.5 *(continued)*

---

6 October 1973 *(continued)*	- 2200: First mobilized Israeli reinforcements arrived on Golan. Mobilizing units were moved piecemeal to the front. - 42 total Syrian air-strike sorties in north; 25 to 26 IAF air-strike sorties against Syrian troop concentrations.
7 October	- Syrian armor and mechanized brigades of infantry divisions continued their attacks into the morning. Syrian 43rd Armor Brigade ambushed southeast of Kuneitra either early morning (during dark) or during the night of 7–8 October. Some Syrian tanks reached (or penetrated) Kafr Naffakh, a point 3 to 4 km from Jordon River, and to within 2 km north of El Al. - About noon, 2 brigades of the Syrian 1st Armor Division crossed the front and continued the attack, stopping at night not far from Kafr Naffakh. Syrian 47th Independent Armor Brigade committed in attack in south. - 1,000 Syrian tanks (including losses) were "on the Golan." - The Israelis continued to reinforce; elements of 210th Division began arriving about mid-day and CG took command of southeast sector. 36th Division elements concentrated in the north. 146th Division, enroute from Central Area Command, received orders to attack on 8 October. - Israeli infantry made an unsuccessful attempt to recapture Mt. Hermon position. - Israeli 188th Armor Brigade down to 13 tanks by noon. - 20 Syrian Air Force (SAF) and 271 IAF air-strike sorties (98 against troop concentrations).
8 October	- Syrian armor attacks continued unsuccessfully along Hermonit approach to northern Golan. Attack in south generally stopped and/or ran into Israeli counterattacks. - Two-division Israeli counterattack in southern and south central Golan. Israeli 146th Division made a main effort attack in El Al area at 0630—initially with two brigades. Two additional brigades were committed, and the division reached the "Violet" line in the vicinity of Tel Saki and Tel Jukhdar. Israeli 210th Division supported with counterattack in south central area. - Another Israeli infantry attack failed to recapture the Mt. Hermon strongpoint. - 188 IAF air-strike sorties. SAF sorties flown were large, but number was not reported.
9 October	- Last major Syrian offensive effort. 91st Armor Brigade (1st Armor Division) repulsed in attack toward Kafr Naffakh. 81st Armor Brigade (3rd Armor Division) made intensive attack at about 0800 in the north and was turned back with heavy losses at about noon as Israeli 7th Armor Brigade (defending) was almost ready to withdraw.

(continues)

TABLE 2.5 *(continued)*

---

9 October 1973 *(continued)*	- Syrians lost about 650 tanks in northern Golan from 6 through 9 October. - Israeli 146th Division counterattack in the south reached Rafid junction and threatened to roll up Syrian southern flank. - Initiative passed to IDF. - 168 IAF air-strike sorties. 85 SAF sorties reported for the morning but that was not the total count.
10 October	- Syrian local counterattack(s) in Kushinaya triangle to relieve pressure on withdrawing 1st Armor Division forces. - Israeli counterattack restored "Violet" line (except for Mt. Hermon); preparations started for offensive into Syria. - 230 IAF and probably about 80 SAF air-strike sorties.
11 October	- 1100: After heavy artillery preparatory fires, Israeli 36th Division launched offensive into Syria on an axis north and parallel to Kuneitra-Damascus Road against limited opposition. - 1300 or 1400: 210th Division launched offensive on axis south of Kuneitra-Damascus Road and met strong initial opposition on front line of defenses. - 353 IAF and no SAF air-strike sorties reported.
12 October	- Israeli offensive continued into Syria. 210th Division was overextended and made minor withdrawal during evening. - Israeli commando raid 100 km north of Damascus ambushed Iraqi forces. - Two brigades of Iraqi 3rd Armor Division arrived on line (precipitating the 210th Division limited withdrawal). - Syrian helicopter raid at Kafr Naffakh resulted in the loss of 9 helicopters and all troops. - 158 IAF air-strike sorties. SAF attacked IDF ground forces, but sortie numbers were not reported.
13 October	- 0300: Israeli 210th Division met the Iraqis head on and destroyed 70 tanks without losing any. - Jordan announced sending a force to Syria (40th Armor Brigade). - 2200: Israeli paratroopers captured Tel Shams after antitank defenses there had driven off Israeli armor attacks. Both IAF and SAF were active but exact number of sorties was not reported.
14 October	- Israeli Northern Command told to hold on-line and that IAF support priority would be shifted to the southern front. - Arab local counterattacks probably conducted (information received was incomplete and inconclusive). - 36 IAF ground-support sorties. SAF sortie numbers not reported.
15 October	- Possible unsuccessful local counterattacks by Iraqis and Jordanians.

(continues)

TABLE 2.5 *(continued)*

---

15 October 1973 *(continued)*	- Elements of Israeli 146th Division may have started moving to the Sinai/Egypt front. - 33 IAF air strikes against troop concentration. SAF was active, but strike numbers were not reported.
16 October	- Joint Jordanian-Iraqi counterattack defeated (apparently piecemeal) with heavy losses. - 30 IAF air-strike sorties. Probably 18 to 20 SAF sorties.
17 October	- Arab local counterattacks apparently continued (but no details provided). - 12 (plus one unnumbered effort) IAF air-strike sorties. SAF was active, but sortie numbers were not reported.
18 October	- Iraqi-Jordanian counterattack stopped without significant gains. - No IAF or SAF air activity was reported for the northern front.
19 October	- Possibly other Arab local counterattacks. - Only 2 IAF air-strike sorties reported. - 2 SAF sorties against IDF units reported. - SAF possibly hit Iraqis by mistake.
20 October	- IAF air-strike sorties not reported. SAF sortie numbers not reported. SAF and Iraqi aircraft apparently hit Jordanians by mistake.
21 October	- Israelis recaptured Mt. Hermon with joint attack by heliborne and ground forces (ground attack may have begun later on 22 October). - 92d Jordanian Armor Brigade joined the 40th in Syria. - 55 IAF air-strike sorties. 24 SAF sorties reported.
22 October	- 22 IAF air-strike sorties. SAF sortie numbers not provided (three separate attacks reported). - 1020: IDF consolidated on Mt. Hermon.
23 October	- Morroccan attack scheduled but not carried out. - 42 IAF air-strike sorties. No SAF offensive activity reported.
24 October	- Cease-fire went into effect.

SOURCES: Col. T. N. Dupuy, *Elusive Victory* (New York: Harper and Row, 1978); A. R. Wagner, *The Impact of 1973 October War on Israeli Policy and Implications for U.S. Defense Policy*, AAC-TR-3396/75 (Marina del Rey, CA: AAC, 1975); A. R. Wagner, *The Middle East Force Balance and Israeli Assistance Requirements: Future Budget Alternatives* (Marina del Rey, CA: AAC, 1976).

TABLE 2.6 The Egyptian Front

1969	- Egypt began construction on vehicle ramps, approaches, etc., to support a potential canal crossing.
1970	- Israeli-Egyptian War of Attrition ended.
1971	- Egypt began to receive T-62s. - Construction began on earthen ramparts overlooking the canal. - Work intensified on preparation to support a potential crossing.
1972	- Soviet advisors expelled. - Ground preparations continued.
Spring 1973	- Ground preparations were greatly intensified. - SA-6 units were located in the vicinity Abu Suwayr and Kutamia. - 6th Mechanized Division moved eastward. - Egypt received SCUDs, BMPs, and BRDM-2 SAGGER launcher vehicles.
10 September	- Arab "Summit" was held in Cairo.
13 September	- Israeli-Syrian air incident.
28 September	- Arab terrorists attacked train in Austria bearing Jewish emigres from USSR.
1–7 October	- Egyptian "field exercises" covered preparations for attack. - Egyptian 23rd Mechanized Division moved to canal area west of Ismailiya. 25th Independent Armor Brigade moved to just northwest of Suez City. - Egyptian 130th Independent Mechanized Brigade (Marines) moved from vicinity of Alexandria to vicinity of Little Bitter Lake. - Egyptian divisional artillery infiltrated forward; 60 additional batteries in place by 4 October.
4 October	- Egyptians secretly opened lanes in their minefield. - Egyptian Frogmen secretly plugged pipes which they expected the Israelis to use to flood the canal with napalm. - IAF photography revealed many tanks on the ramps, additional artillery, and increased crossing equipment in the rear of infantry divisions.
Night of 5–6 October	- Egyptian TIN/ZATUN and FROG units moved forward at night. - SA-6s advanced to within 5 km of canal. - Israeli 460th Armor Brigade deployed to Sinai. - Israeli intelligence received strong indication that war was imminent.
6 October	- 0940–1100: Israeli units received mobilization notification.

(continues)

TABLE 2.6 *(continued)*

6 October 1973 *(continued)*	-	1300: CG, Armor Forces Sinai (AFS), assembled IDF commanders and staff, informed them that war was expected at 1800, and issued instructions for movement.
	-	1400: Five Egyptian divisions attacked all along the canal. Air strikes and raillery preparations began. Israeli 400th Armor Brigade in position east of Kantara (remaining battalion in vicinity of Tasa) and reinforced elements on-line.
	-	1422: First of 12 waves (about 15 minutes apart) crossed the canal in small boats.
	-	1453: Egyptian artillery preparation ended, fires shift in depth and become on-call.
	-	1600: Egyptian ferries and amphibious transporters crossed the canal.
	-	1630: Israeli 4091st Armor Brigade, 252nd Division, reinforcing elements opposite Egyptian 3rd Field Army, made first contact with enemy.
	-	1730: Egyptian helicopters lifted commando elements to vicinity of Ras Sudar, east of Tasa, vicinity of Tel Farma and north of Abu Rudeis.
	-	1800–1900: First Egyptian medium tanks crossed the canal.
	-	2100: First Egyptian bridge across the canal completed in 2nd Army area. Less than 100 Egyptian tanks were on the East Bank.
	-	Egyptians started jamming operations sometime during the evening.
	-	The Egyptian 135th Independent Mechanized Brigade (Marines) crossed the canal in an effort to secure the left flank of the 3rd Field Army and seized a bridgehead near Kabreet. It launched deep reconnaissance patrols. The Mitla Command Post was besieged and a radar was destroyed. Another company advanced toward the Gidi Pass and nearly reached the Tamada Airfield before being turned back after an attack by the Israeli Air Force. The 135th Brigade continued to hold the Kabreet bridgehead until the end of the war.
	-	Mobilizing Israeli forces started piecemeal movement to front. All but one of ten armor and mechanized brigades designated for the Sinai had 90 percent of personnel arrived at assembly camp by 2400.
	-	130 Egyptian Air Force (EAF) and 197 Israeli air-strike sorties.
7 October	-	0030: 1st bridge (TPP) across canal in Egyptian 3rd Army area; blocked by stuck tank until 0400.
	-	Egyptians built up bridgehead and pushed carefully forward with deepest advances 7 to 10 km (5 km or less in 3rd Army area).
	-	Egyptian FROG firings (no significant result).
	-	8 to 10 Egyptian bridges in place across the canal. Two were broken by IAF at 0600.
	-	Israeli 460th Armor Brigade, with 11 tanks operational, pulled back (from 6 October attack) to a position on Tasa Road opposite Kantara.

(continues)

TABLE 2.6 *(continued)*

---

7 October 1973 *(continued)*	-	"Most" Bar-Lev Line strongpoints lost or evacuated.
	-	Israeli forces continued to mobilize and move to the front.
	-	Headquarters and element of two brigades of Israeli 162nd Division arrived in Romani area.
	-	Headquarters and lead elements of Israeli 143rd Division arrived in Southern/Central Sector; no real contact.
	-	44 EAF and 116 IAF air-strike sorties.
	-	Priority of Israeli air effort shifted to the north about noon.
8 October	-	Egyptian bridgeheads remained virtually at the same size as on 7 October. At least one mechanized brigade attack was launched against Israeli position in the vicinity of Hamatal. Possibly another mechanized force attacked toward Mitla pass. The attacks were driven back with heavy casualties.
	-	Egyptian 3rd Field Army constructed a fourth heavy bridge during the night (one of original three was out of operation due to IAF strikes).
	-	2300: Egyptian commando battalion landed in helicopters between Abu Rudeu and Ras Sudar.
	-	Israeli mobilization and reinforcement continued.
	-	Israeli 162nd Division attacked toward Kantara with two reduced-strength brigades inflicting heavy casualties on Egyptian 15th Armor Brigade and running into large-scale SAGGER attack from West Bank ramparts. 162nd Division's Mechanized Brigade arrived in Romani area where it remained to counter Egyptian commandos.
	-	40 tanks from Armor Forces Sinai were relocated from northern sector to the south.
	-	0630: Israeli 143rd Division had first contact east of Ismailiya.
	-	Israeli 440th Division apparently deployed opposite 3rd Field Army.
	-	Over 100 EAF and 434 IAF air-strike sorties.
9 October	-	Egyptians mounted local attacks to expand bridgeheads. Two field army elements almost reached Phase I objectives in 16th Division area of operation, still 2 km or more short in 2nd and 18th Divisions' area of operation.
	-	Egyptian FROG firings (no significant results) on the night of either 8 or 9 October.
	-	Israeli mobilization and reinforcement virtually completed.
	-	Israeli 162nd Division shifted southward to sector between Kantara and Ismailiya; Task Force "Kalman" had responsibility of sector north to the Mediterranean; 143rd Division Sector was from Ismailiya to the Bitter Lakes; 440th Division continued opposite Egyptian 3rd Army.
	-	442 IAF air-strike sorties. EAF air-strike sorties fell off but number not reported.
10 October	-	Egyptians continued to consolidate and mount local attacks, especially against Israeli 162nd Division defenses.

(continues)

TABLE 2.6 *(continued)*

10 October 1973 *(continued)*	-	Israeli mechanized force relieved strongpoint Budapest.
	-	296 IAF air-strike sorties. EAF activities not fully reported but included at least 12 MiG sorties and 2 KELT launches.
11 October 1973	-	Local attacks by Egyptians (five in Israeli 162nd Division Sector); IDF defended against these attacks.
	-	69 IAF air-strike sorties; EAF activities not reported other than Tu-16 bombing attacks near Abu Rudeis and 8 KELT launches at targets 50 miles east of the canal.
12 October	-	Egyptian local attacks continued the same as previous day.
	-	154 IAF air-strike sorties against Egyptian troop concentrations; EAF air-strikes not reported.
	-	Remainder of Egyptian 21st Armor Division (one armor, one mechanized brigade) and one armor brigade of 4th Armor Division crossed the canal during the night of 12–13 October.
13 October	-	Egyptian operational tank strength on East Bank was about 750.
	-	0830: Egyptian armor brigade attacked Israeli positions (143rd Division) in vicinity of Hamadiya.
	-	Fourteen Egyptian SAM battalions crossed the canal during the night of 13–14 October.
	-	96 IAF and probably 28 EAF air-strike sorties.
14 October	-	Egyptians attacked all along the line, from north to south. The 15th Independent Armor Brigade, 24th Armor Brigade (23rd Mechanized Division), 21st Armor Division (minus), 3rd Armor Brigade (4th Armor Division), and a mechanized force (6th Mechanized Division) attacked on separate axes. The 21st Armor and 3rd Armor elements made the main efforts.
	-	21st Armor Division attacked all day, with losses of about 115–120 tanks, and were repelled by Israeli 143rd Division. The degree of real coordination between attacks was not clear.
	-	3rd Brigade (4th Armor Division) was hit on flank by battalion of Israeli 401st Armor Brigade (reinforced with a parachute element) and lost possibly as many as 64 tanks.
	-	All attacks were repulsed, and total Egyptian losses on 14 October ran between 200 and 300 tanks.
	-	24 EAF air-strike sorties. Exact figures for IAF air-strike sorties not provided but were "heavy."
15 October 1973	-	During night of 14–15 October, Israeli 162nd Division relocated to an assembly area near Tasa. 274th Armor Brigade (reinforced) and Task Force "Kalman" took over the former division front-line sector.
	-	Israeli 143rd Division prepared to attack.
	-	1700: 421st Armor Brigade (143rd Division) attacked west into Egyptian 16th Infantry and 21st Armor Division defenses.

(continues)

TABLE 2.6 *(continued)*

15 October 1973 *(continued)*	-	1800 (or 1900): 14th Armor Brigade (143rd Division) attacked northwest into underside of Egyptian forces fighting the 421st Brigade and opened a corridor to the canal.
	-	Parachute Brigade (143rd Division) moved down Tasa Road to a site near Deversoir and commenced crossing in small boats.
	-	184 IAF and 2 EAF air-strike sorties.
16 October	-	0100: Israel Parachute Brigade had a 600-meter bridgehead on West Bank.
	-	0600: Israeli 143rd Division commenced crossing tanks (600th Brigade?) on mobile assault rafts.
	-	1600: Israeli uniflote bridge was operational across the canal.
	-	Egyptian 2nd Army counterattacked all day in waves from the north. 21st Armor Division, 16th Infantry Division, and possibly 24th Armor Brigade, 23rd Division, elements attempted to close the corridor to the canal. 143rd Division's 421st and 14th Brigade elements, reinforced late in the day by elements of the 162nd Division, kept the corridor open in heavy fighting (battle of "Chinese Farm") extending from the night of 15–16 October well into 17 October. Heavy losses on both sides, especially the Egyptians.
	-	Late afternoon Egyptian 25th Armor Brigade (3rd Field Army) received orders to attack corridor from south.
	-	36 EAF and 383 IAF air-strike sorties.
17 October	-	Egyptian attacks from the north continued into the night but at a lesser intensity than 16 October or the night of 16–17 October.
	-	0600: Egyptian 25th Armor Brigade started moving north to attack Israelis across canal corridor. Israeli's 162nd Division and apparently 14th Armor Brigade, 143rd Division, ambushed and destroyed it.
	-	Remnants of Egyptian 3rd Armor Brigade (4th Division) returned to West Bank in reaction to Israeli penetration.
	-	About 2200: Elements of the 143rd Division began crossing to the West Bank.
	-	165 IAF air-strike sorties in support of ground forces. EAF sortie numbers not fully reported but included at least 7 against the crossing site.
18 October	-	162nd Division forces crossed all day and began pushing south and southwest. 143rd Division continued to consolidate and expand bridgehead north and west.
	-	Egyptians deployed 3rd Mechanized Division elements east from Cairo to contain penetration.
	-	Egyptian 116th Mechanized Brigade (23rd Mechanized Division) moved against the bridgehead from the north; 113th Mechanized Brigade (6th Mechanized Division) moved up the west shore of Great Bitter Lake toward Faid.
	-	1700: Israeli roller bridge arrived at East Bank.
	-	2300: Permission given to launch roller bridge.

(continues)

TABLE 2.6 *(continued)*

18 October 1973 *(continued)*	- -	Significant numbers" of IAF air-strike sorties; EAF sortie numbers "included at least 28 fighters and helicopters striking the bridgehead and crossing site.
19 October	- - - -	0010: Israeli roller bridge was in place across the canal. Israeli 162nd Division advanced south parallel to Bitter Lake's shore. Elements of 14th Armor Brigade (143rd Division) began crossing. 357 IAF and 47 EAF air-strike sorties.
20 October	- - - -	Israeli 162nd Division forces captured Faid air base, moved into Giniefra Mountain area, and threatened northern Cairo–Suez City road. Division Task Force "Kalman" (252nd Division) was either moving toward crossing or began crossing canal. Remnants of Egyptian 1st Mechanized Brigade (6th Division) returned from East Bank in reaction to Israeli penetration. 376 IAF air-strike sorties. EAF sorties (numbers not fully provided) included 8 Su-7s, L-29s, and Tu-16s.
21 October 1973	- - -	Israeli 162nd Division consolidated on Giniefra Mountain. One element began drive toward canal south of Bitter Lake, and other elements evidently cut the northern road between Cairo and Suez City. 252nd Division ("Div Task Force" "Kalman") screened 162nd Western Flank. Egyptian 4th Armor and 6th Mechanized Division remnants opposed the Israeli advance southward. 154 IAF ground-support and 56–62 EAF air-strike sorties.
22 October	- - - -	First cease-fire broke down with both sides claiming violations by the other. Israeli 162nd Division forces drove east to Little Bitter Lake and the shores of the Suez Canal south of the lake and cut off thousands of Egyptians. Other elements cut southern road between Cairo and Suez City. Egyptians fired SCUD missiles with no significant results. 532 IAF air-strike sorties. 40 EAF sorties reported.
23 October	- -	Israeli 162nd Division drove to Gulf of Suez and completed encirclement of the Egyptian 3rd Field Army. 354 IAF air-strike sorties. EAF sortie numbers not provided.
24 October	- - -	Cease-fire went into effect. IAF flew 315 attack sorties. IAF flew 28 interceptor sorties.

SOURCES: Col. T. N. Dupuy, *Elusive Victory* (New York: Harper and Row, 1978); A. R. Wagner, *The Impact of 1973 October War on Israeli Policy and Implications for U.S. Defense Policy*, AAC-TR-3396/75 (Marina del Rey, CA: AAC, 1975); A. R. Wagner, *The Middle East Force Balance and Israeli Assistance Requirements: Future Budget Alternatives* (Marina del Rey, CA: AAC, 1976).

advantage because Egypt and Syria could not coordinate land or air operations—they lacked effective land force maneuver training and C³ capability, coordinated air control and warning and IFF capability, and a flexible high command.

The war began on 6 October 1973 when Egyptian and Syrian forces attacked across the 1967 cease-fire lines on two fronts. The attack benefited from fairly elaborate deception efforts by the Arabs, and the plan was only pieced together by Israel on the eve of the hostilities. The Israelis decided not to initiate a preemptive strike against Arab forces for political reasons.

The first few days of the war were the most critical for Israel. The Israeli regular army and limited numbers of reservists were faced with the unpleasant task of holding back advancing Arab troops while the balance of the Israeli reserve was mobilized and large amounts of war material were airlifted from the United States.

The dominant event of the first few days of the war on the Egyptian front involved the siege of an Israeli set of fortresses known as the Bar-Lev Line. These well-situated and well-entrenched Israeli defenses were attacked by overwhelming numbers of Egyptian troops. All of these fortresses except one were destroyed or captured by Egypt in the initial part of the fighting. The one fort to hold out was code-named Budapest. The Israelis managed to resupply this fort several times during the first part of the fighting.

On the northern front, Syria attacked Israel across the Golan Heights area with special emphasis on the areas just north and south of Kuneitra. The gravity of the situation there required that the main focus of the Israeli reinforcement effort be directed at this front during the first part of the war. Moshe Dayan maintained that the Golan remained "the center of military gravity until October 13" (i.e., the first week of the war).[3]

The Arab advances on both fronts were protected by surface-to-air missiles which were used to help neutralize the Israeli advantages in quality of aircraft and level of pilot proficiency. During the first part of the war, these missiles were especially effective because the most sophisticated U.S. countermeasures equipment had not yet been transferred to Israel. Additionally, Israeli aircraft were forced to fly close-support missions at this time without the benefit of prior SAM suppression.

As the initial center of military gravity, the Golan received the most significant numbers of reinforcements. While the Israelis were badly mauled during the first few days of the war, they were nevertheless able to begin a counteroffensive on 11 October. This began with an Israeli push into the main Syrian defensive zone using four columns of armor. These advancing troops pushed the Syrians back in spite of fierce resistance. The Syrians did not, however, allow their defenses to collapse as the Israelis had hoped would happen. The Syrians withdrew in an orderly fashion, fighting as they went. By 13 October Defense Minister Dayan considered this first counteroffensive to have been successful and directed that the Sinai front be given priority for resupply with troops and material.

On 11 October, the Egyptians received an urgent appeal from the Syrians to help relieve pressure on the Golan front through the launching of an offensive on the southern front. The Egyptians felt a need to respond to this request which would keep their northern ally from collapsing. This resulted in an assault on the morning of 14 October, which went very badly for the Egyptians. Chief of Staff Lt. General Shazly later (as an exile) published his own harsh indictment of President Sadat for ordering the attack. It also was a total failure since it provided the Syrians with no relief from the Israeli military pressure on the northern front. Military problems, therefore, continued on this front with a series of Arab counterattacks ending in failure. By 21–22 October the Israelis had recaptured Mt. Hermon and were in a good position to threaten Damascus.

The turning point in the war along the southern front occurred on 16 October when Israeli forces crossed the Suez Canal and began establishing a beachhead along its western bank. As part of this effort, the Israelis were able to capture and destroy Egyptian missile batteries on the west bank. In particular the Israelis brought a battalion of long-range 175-mm guns across the canal to destroy the Egyptian SAMs on the west bank of the Suez.

Once the canal had been crossed, Israeli General Sharon broke through Egyptian lines and captured Deversoir. This had been done with the support of the Israeli air force which was able to operate in airspace previously protected by the Egyptian SAMs. From this point onward, the Israelis clearly made great progress exploiting their crossing. Fast-moving Israeli armored columns struck at Egyptian troops behind the Egyptian lines and succeeded in cutting vital lines of supply and communications. They also were facing a much less formidable adversary since Egypt's best troops and most advanced weapons were on the east bank.

The Israelis' most dramatic exploitation of the crossing to the west bank was the isolation of major elements of the Egyptian Third Army. The Israelis were determined to completely cut off supplies and force the surrender of this huge force. This would be a difficult task since the Third Army had large reserves of food and ammunition, and water lines from wells in Suez City were still operational. The Third Army therefore dug in in anticipation of an Israeli attack.

A cease-fire established on 22 October broke down the same day with Israel moving to destroy the isolated portions of the Third Army. In doing this they faced a tough and still very well-armed enemy. Now, however, Israel was able to bring the full weight of its air superiority to bear, sending sortie after sortie to strike at the Egyptian forces.

The Israelis might have been able to inflict a great deal more harm upon the Third Army if it had not been for the political intervention of the United States. The Third Army had not been defeated by the IDF before the cease-fire and continued to improve its defensive barriers and other preparations. It did, however, remain besieged and could not be effectively resupplied. The Israeli Air Force continued to keep up air attacks at the bridgehead after the cease-fire, and the Third Army would probably have had to surrender because of these attacks and lack of supply. U.S. Secretary of State Henry Kissinger did not want to see Egypt totally defeated because it was feared that a post-defeat Egyptian government would be too weak to negotiate. He also felt that such action could severely harm the image of the U.S. within the Arab world, since a wide array of modern weapons had just been delivered to Israel by the U.S. The U.S. correspondingly made a very intensive effort to end the fighting, which did end on 24 October.

Terrain and Defenses

The fighting was shaped by two different terrains. The first was the Suez Canal area and the desert on each side. The second was the Golan Heights.

Terrain: The Sinai. The Sinai Peninsula is a desert area between Egypt and Israel. It is characterized by salt wastes and wadis (sand dunes) in the north and mountainous topography in the south.[4] The Sinai has served as a land bridge for immigrating peoples and invading armies throughout history. More recently it has served as a barrier between Israel and Egypt.

Along the Mediterranean coast, the Sinai consists of 134 miles of salt flats and marshes interspersed with occasional oases and mountains. The west side is bordered by the historic Suez Canal and the Gulf of Suez, a distance of 311 miles. On the east, the Sinai is roughly 155 miles long, incorporating the Gulf of Aqaba and the border of Israel. Major roads link Kantara and El-Arish in the north and Ismailia and Abi Ageila in the center. In the west, roads connect Kusseima, Kuntilla, and Ras El-Naql, and between El-Arish, Bir El-Hassne and Nakhle.

The lower Sinai varies in topography from rugged mountains to massive sand dunes, which render military operations difficult to sustain because of logistical difficulties, impediments to mobility, and a general lack of natural cover for purposes of concealment. Only the road between Suez, Ras Sudar, A-Tor, and Sharm El-Sheikh can facilitate heavy transport.

Because of the harsh nature of the terrain, war in the Sinai has historically been a struggle for strategic roads and passes and the high points above such routes. However, the dominating condition is the desert character of the environment, the major implication of which is that the need to conduct military operations means struggling with the effects of heat and the requirements this condition puts on logistical support trains for water supplies and cooling lubricants. In addition, high temperatures place substantial limitations on military personnel, both in terms of physical performance and as a component of psycho-physical stress.

Modern military operations in the Sinai have emphasized the importance of armored/mechanized units and airpower. This is largely due to the mechanical and military advantages associated with open terrain, where the general lack of vegetation such as trees and bushes does not hamper mobility or conceal military activities. It is simply very difficult to hide in the open desert. The same generalization applies to mountainous regions in the Sinai which are largely barren of natural cover. However, the mountains, especially in the south, are precipitous and rugged enough to restrict armored movement to certain access routes in many strategic areas.

While the openness of desert terrain typically provides the necessary mobility for armored movements, it facilitates vulnerability to air power. This provides another dimension of desert warfare; the tank-against-tank struggle is vastly complicated by the ability of aircraft to strike quickly and repeatedly, with devastating effectiveness, against armored units at considerable distance from their bases. Vast open spaces and clear skies are highly advantageous to air forces, unhampered by the roughness of the terrain below, except where it provides concealment or protection against air-to-ground weapons. What is a distinct disadvantage on the ground, i.e., difficulty of terrain and distance from logistical supply, is often a decisive asset for air power.

Another aspect of the Sinai War structured by terrain features was the vulnerability of static defenses to siege tactics. Cut off from water and food, such sites cannot survive or remain combat effective for more than a very limited time. Unfortunately for the Israelis, such static sites were forced on them by the nature and parameters of the Sinai and their conquests in the June 1967 War. However, these strongpoints played an important role in the early phases of the 1973 war. They were known collectively by the Israelis as the Bar-Lev Line.

Barriers: The Sinai. The Suez Canal is 175 kilometers long, its width varies from 180 to 220 meters, and its depth varies from 16 to 18 meters. The water level is 2 meters below the bank, and the canal has very steep banks, covered by reinforced concrete, which prevented amphibious vehicles from landing and climbing the banks without prior construction and engineering. The current is rapid and strong and reaches 18 meters per minute in the north and as much as 90 meters per minute in the south. It has a tide change of 60 centimeters in the north, increasing to 2 meters near Suez in the south, and the direction of the current changes every 6 hours with the change in the tide. These factors greatly affected the Egyptian crossing plan, particularly the technical problems of establishing ferries and erecting bridges.

The Israelis had spent some $268 million to create a series of fortifications, roads, and rear-area facilities called the Bar-Lev Line to defend the east bank of the canal. These defenses extended over 160 kilometers along the east bank of the Suez Canal from Port Fuad in the north to Ras Misallah on the Gulf of Suez, and their depth to the east extended from 30 to 35 kilometers. These defenses covered a surface area of some 5,000 square kilometers and contained a system of fortifications, shelters, strong obstacles, and antitank and anti-personnel mine fields. The fortified area consisted of several lines, with areas for administration, armored troop concentrations, artillery positions, Hawk anti-aircraft missiles, anti-aircraft artillery, water pipelines, and a 750-kilometer network of roads. The armored troop concentration areas were located 5 to 30 kilometers to the east of the canal. There were 240 prepared long- and medium-range artillery positions, 30 of which were kept fully active. The defenses were backed in the north by the Mediterranean Sea, in the east by the Central Sinai mountains, and in the south by the Egma Mountains and the Gulf of Suez.

The canal thus formed a body of water which had to be physically traversed by thousands of men, which required a massive logistics and planning effort, delays and snafus at crossing points, and, inevitably, casualties due to accidents and hostile fire. Too deep and too wide to be crossed without vehicular support, it provided opportune targets for Israeli gunners during the actual process of crossing, exposing soldiers and military equipment to concentrated artillery, tank, and automatic-weapons fire. Unfortunately for the Israelis, the Egyptian troops did not cross when and where planned.

The Israelis attempted to develop a system designed to ignite the canal as a burning moat. At at least one point, underground tanks and pipelines were emplaced to provide oil which would be sprayed on the canal.[5] This barrier of oil would then be ignited into a barrier of flames from the fortification site(s). However, there is considerable controversy as to the status of its development when the war started. Some Israeli sources claim that the system was unreliable and was abandoned. Others insist that the system had been reactivated and that at least one or two taps were operational. The Egyptians claim to have conducted frogmen operations against the system, plugging the pipelines and rendering them useless.

The first defensive obstacle was the concrete side of the canal, which was constructed to solidify the sand bank. Three feet high at high tide, it is six feet above the water surface at low tide. This barrier limited entrance and exit from the canal to light amphibious craft which can be lifted over the side by external mechanical or human power. In effect, it required the use of mobile, military bridges normally utilized in river crossings. According to General Dayan, the canal was itself "one of the best anti-tank ditches available."[6]

Above the concrete side of the canal, the Israelis created a high embankment, which stood along the entire length of the system, southward from Kantara. In general the embankment averaged more than 10 to 25 meters high. It served to conceal Israeli movements and, by virtue of its steepness, to prevent landings by amphibious vehicles.

This embankment formed the first of three embankments. It had firing positions for artillery or armor roughly every 100 meters. There were 22 fortified positions with a total of 31 strongpoints, each covering 40,000 square meters. These strongpoints were surrounded by up to 15 circles of barbed wire separated by mine fields, early-warning devices, and booby traps. The strongpoints themselves were complicated engineering structures of several stories, built up high enough to reach the top of the ramparts. The facilities at each strongpoint included first-aid equipment, a medical group, bathing facilities, a printing center, a movie house, and a recreation center. Each story of the strongpoints consisted of several concrete shelters, reinforced by railway rails and steel plates and separated from the other shelters by layers of iron rails, reinforced concrete, and sand and stone piles, two to three meters thick. Each concrete pillbox was equipped for both artillery weapons and tanks and had several loopholes to allow fire over a wide frontal arc. The pillboxes were connected by deep communications trenches, lined with steel plates and sandbags. These strongpoints and engineering works could absorb hits by 1,000-pound bombs. Sufficient supplies were available to hold out in the face of major attacks.

The system depended on mobilization, however, and had only limited active manning at the time the Egyptians attacked. General Sharon had reduced the number of active strongpoints during his tenure as commander of Southern Command. Although Major General Shmuel Gonen had ordered the re-activation of some of the posts, this had not been accomplished. When the first wave of the 8,000 Egyptian assault infantrymen stormed across the ten improvised military bridges, they were confronted by an Israeli force of only 436 soldiers spread over 110 miles along the Suez Canal.[7] These soldiers were members of the Jerusalem Brigade, serving their reserve duty. Many of the soldiers had little or no combat experience.

To the rear of the embankment was a minefield system concentrated around strongpoints, but it was not a comprehensive system. These areas could be covered with tank ramps on the main embankment and on a second embankment. The second embankment was designed for defense against attackers who had penetrated the first one. Along major access routes, a third embankment was occasionally utilized to provide additional cover and fire angles for areas of potential tactical value.

Behind these defensive lines were mobile reserves in depth, mostly armored units. Their mobility was facilitated with an extensive road network for quick transfers of men and equipment. The first lateral, called Lexicon, was about 1,000 meters from the canal and was for communication between the Bar-Lev strongpoints. The second road, called the Artillery Road, was for lateral artillery movement. East of the artillery road were six command posts which functioned to provide frontline command coordination to the Bar-Lev strongpoints. These command posts were linked to rear area command posts at Tass, Romani, Bir Gifgafa, and Um Kasheiba.

Tasa was located at the intersection of the main Beersheba-Ismailia road and the Lateral Road. It included an underground command post, divisional support units, an airstrip, and an advanced depot of weapons, equipment, ammunition, and engineer supplies.

Located about 50 kilometers to the east of Tasa was Bir Gifgafa (Refidim to the Israelis) on the Talisman Road. Refidim was an administrative-logistical installation, with a large airfield, an underground command post, and a major supply depot.

The wartime command post of Southern Command was at Um Kasheiba, north of the Giddi Pass and overlooking the West Sinai Plain. This site had a large and complex electronics monitoring facility and excellent visual observation equipment.

Confronting the Israelis on the east side of the canal were Egyptian forces protected and concealed by a system of earthworks. The basic component was a huge embankment of sand about 20 meters high, 15 meters wide, and 120 kilometers long, extending southward from the Kautara area. At various points along the embankment, broad mounds or towers were constructed to provide firing points for tanks against Israeli strongpoints. The Egyptians eventually elevated the banks on the west side to a height of 130 feet, which provided the ability to overlook Israeli ramparts and fortifications and the tank ramps protecting them. In addition, the added height provided observation of the second line of defense along the Artillery Road which was five to eight miles distant.[8] The Israeli response, initiated by General Gonen, was to build earthworks to conceal activity along the second line of defense. In addition, plans were developed to construct tall observation towers, but these plans were not completed by the outbreak of the war.

Antitank missiles and antitank gun batteries were deployed at various points along the embankment. Hard-surfaced roads provided access to the top of the embankment at each of the towers.

Approximately 40 to 60 miles behind this system was a belt of fortifications including both weapons and logistical support equipment. These included artillery, hospitals, airfields, and numerous SAM missile sites.[9]

The Egyptian strategy of surprise attack put the Israelis in a distinctly unfamiliar and uncomfortable defensive position. First, the Israelis had not, since the 1948 war, allowed their Arab enemies to take the initiative. They had consistently attacked first, usually with well-planned and devastating air strikes. Second, the defensive orientation relied, at least initially, on a system of fortifications on both fronts which were stationary and could be outflanked and cut off by the enemy. Unfortunately for the Israelis, the appreciation of this problem wavered according to the strategic bases of commanders in the field, i.e., the Southern Command and the staff headquarters of the IDF. As a result, the concept of barrier defense changed over time, from an initial trip-wire concept with the canal defenses acting primarily as observation posts to the development of strongpoint fortifications. In both cases the concept continued to emphasize the importance of the mobile armored reserve attacking the invaders in the early phases of the assault. However, Generals Bar-Lev, Sharon, and Gonen differed as to the role of the strongpoints in confronting this assault.

According to former Israeli General Chaim Herzog, the fortifications were a failure because of their weak active manning at the time the Egyptians attacked.

> Over the years, they had become a compromise between strongpoints designed to hold the Canal against Egyptian attack, and warning and

observation outposts. As the former, they were too weak and dispersed; as the latter, they were too strongly manned. There is no doubt that the Egyptians would have succeeded in establishing a foothold even if the original concept of the Bar-Lev Line (including the complete Israeli plan to move forces to the front line) had been executed on time, and the quality of the troops on the front line raised (as was envisaged in the event of an emergency). But they would have found their task a much more difficult one, would have incurred very heavy losses, and their attack may conceivably have been beaten back in the final analysis.[10]

The Golan Heights. The Golan Heights is a plateau rising from a height of 600 feet above the Yarmak Valley in the south to the 9,000-foot summit of Mount Hermon in the north. A maze of volcanic hills, wall-like escarpments, alluvial fans, and other geological features limits passage of even modern vehicles from Mount Hermon to the Damascus-Quneitra road. In the south the area is more accessible, but numerous volcanic hills called "tels" offer excellent vantage and observation points.[11]

A line of tels spans the border that was set following the Six Day War, from the Rafid junction toward Quneitra and from that point northward to Mount Hermon. Another complex of hills lies to the southwest. Seen from the northeast, the plateau slopes westward until it drops sharply from a height of 2,000 feet to the Huleh Valley and the Sea of Galilee. South of Kunetira the area to the southeast of Kuneitra is a flat plateau that slopes down to the east until it reaches the hills along the Maskin-Damascus Road.

Five roads ascend the Golan Heights from Israel: the road from Kibbutz Dan to Mas'asla and Mount Hermon; the Quneitra–Nafakh–Benot Yaakov road; the Quneitra–Khushinya–Arik Bride road; the road from Gonen to Wasset; and the Gamla Rise and the El Al Route from the Sea of Galilee. Two roads traverse the Golan Heights from north and south. One runs along the 1967 cease-fire line known as the Purple Line, from Rafid to Mas'adeh. The other road is a maintenance road known as the Tap Line Road because it runs alongside the oil pipeline emanating from Saudi Arabia. Other roads connect these main routes, but few can withstand heavy use.

The Defenses Along the Golan Heights. Since the Golan Heights present a narrower frontage than the Bar-Lev Line, it represented a smaller area in which to make use of obstacles although it didn't have the Suez Canal serving as "the world's largest tank ditch."

The Israelis used the period between 1967 and 1973 to make their defensive position as impenetrable as possible since they were obviously concerned about the possibility of a Syrian attack across the heights. This effort involved the construction of a series of obstacles and fortifications throughout the area but especially along the eastern edge of the plateau.

The Israeli barriers began just west of the cease-fire line with an antitank ditch which was approximately 4 to 6 meters wide and about 4 meters deep. The earth from the ditch had been used as an embankment on the Israeli side of the ditch. As such, it served as an additional obstacle. Beyond the embankments the more sophisticated Israeli defenses actually began. This involved a complicated series of observation/listening posts as well as seventeen larger forts which had garrisons of between ten to thirty men. These posts were equipped with modern electronic monitoring devices including a variety of sensors.

Minefields also made up an important part of the Israeli defenses along the Golan Heights. Minefields were placed both in front of and behind the antitank ditch along key avenues of advance. They were also used to provide protection for the strongpoints.

In order to penetrate these obstacles, the Syrians, like the Egyptians, had planned to make considerable use of aggressive combat engineering and commando assaults. The basic task was to breach the minefields, cross the tank ditch and embankments, and then proceed along the avenues of advance. Strongpoints were to be either captured by commandos or surrounded and bypassed. The commandos had only one real success in capturing an observation post/fort but this was a significant action. It involved the seizure of the Israeli fortified observation post on Mt. Hermon by Syrian heliborne commandos. These commandos approached the post from the north and then surprised and wiped out the garrison.

The breaching of these Israeli defenses by Syria was a difficult task which was not always carried out according to plan and was, therefore, characterized by mistakes. Extensive use of mine-destruction equipment and artillery characterized the operation while the anticipated use of bridging tanks for crossing the antitank ditch was a failure. The reason for this latter problem was that the bridging tanks were left behind as the maneuver combat units advanced. This meant that these same combat troops had to dismount their vehicles and begin filling in the ditch with shovels while they were under intensive fire from the Israelis. The situation improved for these troops later during the assault when some bulldozers were able to move up to the front and assist in the task of filling in the ditch. Bulldozers were also used to clear away the embankment on the Israeli side of the tank ditch.

Threat Assessment Technologies

Israel had adequate threat assessment technology in 1973 but failed to cope with Arab deception. Egypt's political leadership was able to persuade Israel's political leadership that Egypt was not ready for war and would not be ready for at least a year. Prior to their successful crossing of the Suez Canal, Egyptian forces managed to deceive Israel's intelligence into believing that Egyptian units were engaged in military maneuvers rather than actual preparations for an invasion. This led to a major strategic surprise of the Israeli forces and is generally considered to be the result of shrewd Egyptian planning and Israeli overconfidence. There is some possibility that more Israeli attention to SIGINT could have resulted in an unraveling of the Egyptian deception plan, but this plan was based on a careful analysis of the preconceived ideas of Israeli political and military leaders. The problem was not the input data but a failure of intelligence analysis.

Israel had, in fact, reduced its readiness in 1972–73 to save military expenditures. This produced the following problems in Israeli forces, all of which increased Israel's dependence on warning:

- reduced manning levels and forward deployments;
- resources and manpower limited;
- reduced air-defense-suppression planning and training;
- limited funding of reserve readiness and activity;
- reduced spending on command and control systems;
- limited artillery and infantry armament;
- little funding of barrier crossing and assault capability; and
- combat consumable stock levels left at 6 to 7 days.

Numerous studies have shown that Israel had the warning indicators necessary to execute its mobilization and deployment plans in time to have been prepared for the Egyptian and Syrian attack. They have documented the fact that the failure to execute such mobilization was a combination of: political fear of being seen as rushing to war; a failure of Israel's senior intelligence officials to appreciate the risks; an Israeli mind-set focused on Egyptian and Syrian weaknesses; and superb Arab timing in attacking Israel during a national holiday.

One additional reason for the Israeli intelligence failure was Israel's intelligence methodology. The Israelis focused too myopically on Arab intentions and ignored Arab capabilities.[12] There is obviously some truth in this observation, but it tends to gloss over some significant problems with the way the Israelis had been assessing capabilities. A particular problem was the Israelis' belief that the Arabs could not present a clear challenge to Israel while the Arab air forces remained so patently inferior to the IAF. These biases were reflected in briefings presented to Israeli Defense Minister, Moshe Dayan, several days prior to the war. According to Dayan:

> The chief of staff, the Air Force commander, and the acting head of intelligence gave their reports, presenting the activities of the enemy and of our own forces. The Intelligence representative emphasized that the Syrian and Egyptian armies were so deployed along the fronts that they were able at any moment to launch an attack, but he did not think they were about to do so. In his judgment, what was happening on the Egyptian side of the line was annual maneuvers.[13]

In contrast, Egypt provided virtually all the threat assessment for Egyptian and Syrian forces. Egypt combined its own political and military insights with a limited use of Soviet-made electronic intelligence (ELINT) and photo reconnaissance systems and access to equipment and Soviet satellite reconnaissance. According to Egyptian Chief of Staff Shazly:

> We used to complain we did not see enough [Soviet satellite] photographs; but from time to time we would be shown new film to study, though never to take away or copy. To my personal knowledge, Sadat himself saw those pictures at least twice before the war and once during it. After the cease-fire of October 24, Soviet satellite photographs were our main source of information about enemy activity.[14]

Shazly has also pointed out that the Egyptians themselves had no MiG-25 reconnaissance aircraft and that they had to depend on four Soviet MiGs that were stationed in Egypt for air reconnaissance. He further claims that on 15 October 1973, Egyptian radars detected the presence of U.S. reconnaissance aircraft in the form of nine SR-71A flying faster than Mach 3.[15] He notes, however, that once the SR-71As were discovered there was nothing that the Egyptians could do to neutralize it.

After the initial Egyptian and Syrian attack, however, the pattern of threat assessment reversed itself. The Arab forces were not prepared to deal with the course of combat objectively. They overestimated their own successes and failed to honestly report their failures. Egypt and Syria failed to coordinate effectively and attempted to use each other. Syria exaggerated its own problems to get Egypt to advance on Israel and manipulated reinforcing Iraqi troops so they took the brunt of an IDF attack (without warning) that would otherwise have been directed against Syria.

The Egyptian command and intelligence systems reinforced each other's failures at every level of command. Units either failed to report bad news, failed to execute plans, or grossly exaggerated failures and the IDF threat. For example, Egypt grossly exaggerated the success of its SAM firings, air operations, and commando helicopter raids; initially failed to admit the IDF had crossed the Suez; and then failed to properly counterattack IDF forces during the period IDF forces were too weak to survive because Egypt exaggerated the size of IDF success.

Even today, the Egyptian analysis of the 1973 war grossly exaggerates the same aspects of Egyptian success it exaggerated during the war, particularly air and commando operations. At the same time, it blames the U.S. resupply effort to Israel for shifts in the course of the fighting that U.S. records show were impossible since major deliveries of the tanks mentioned in Egyptian studies did not occur until the war was over. Egyptian and Syrian forces politicized both command and threat assessment at every level from the battalion to the supreme command. This "web of lies" was a major factor making effective C^{3}I impossible and allowing Israel to turn defeat into victory.

In contrast, Israeli field commanders reacted realistically to both failure and success. They analyzed both their capabilities and those of opposing forces. They accepted honest reporting of failure, learned from it, and reacted to it. They could exploit their maneuver capability because they could trust their tactical intelligence and command net. This gave them a major advantage once active combat began.

Even Israel, however, suffered from major failures in threat assessment once the war began. The IDF high command did not have an effective system for analyzing and managing the overall course of the war. It relied on the conflicting views of the ground commanders and lacked the sophisticated intelligence sensors, processing, and analysis capability to analyze a dynamic threat.

The IDF lacked an effective ELINT and SIGINT capability. In fact, IDF communications discipline was terrible, and Egypt obtained far more SIGINT than Israel. The IDF obtained considerable intelligence input from the U.S. but generally did not know how to use it for tactical or targeting purposes. Its own air-photo reconnaissance effort was poorly trained and organized for large-scale war. The IDF had to rapidly improvise its management of the reconnaissance and ground-support effort. Photographic data took far too long to process and could not be used to target air attack sorties because the units found in photos had generally dispersed. There was no real night coverage although many Arab movements took place at night. The system only really worked against fixed defenses and SAM sites, and even here the IDF lacked an effective fusion capability to blend ELINT and PHOTINT. In several cases, SAM defenses were assumed to be absent because photos failed to show SA-6 deployments, although these had been detected by ELINT. Further, the IDF was often poorly prepared to provide qualitative data from HUMINT or past analyses when it detected an enemy unit. The IDF's success at threat assessment was primarily at the battlefield and front level and virtually every Israeli account of the war shows that front and theater commanders often disregarded higher-level intelligence data.

This experience sets a pattern exhibited by one or more sides in each of the four following wars under study. The side that could not objectively report on tactical developments in near real time— reporting honestly on the success and failure of both its own and enemy forces—suffered a serious loss of effectiveness and maneuver capability. The politicization of command and intelligence before the war either led to unrealistic attack plans and expectations on the part of the attacker or to strategic and tactical surprise against the defender.

The primary threat assessment failures on all sides in all five wars were failures in policy and command and not failures in intelligence. The failures that did occur in intelligence were primarily failures in analysis and in the fusion of diverse intelligence sources—dictated in part by the ideology or preconceptions of senior policy makers—and not failures in intelligence collection. In fact, only direct HUMINT on, or "bugging" of, senior policy-level discussions of the enemy in a form that provided firm, unambiguous intelligence on enemy actions and intentions could probably have overcome the sheer inertia imposed by the politicization of intelligence. No improvement in optical or electronic sensors or national technical means would have been able to overcome the combined bias, delay, and lack of integration in the command-intelligence system.

At the same time, however, it is obvious that all sides in the 1973 fighting could have benefited greatly at the tactical level from adequate airborne or remote intelligence sensors capable of near real time analysis and processing. Systems like Forward-Looking Infra-Red (FLIR), Search and Reconnaissance (SAR), Side-Looking Airborne Radar (SLAR), electro-optics, moving target indication (MTI) radars, Electronic Systems Support Measures (ESSM), and modern ELINT sensors and processors would have enabled either side to avoid tactical surprise after the initial attack, monitor the opponent's maneuvers, improve SAM suppression, and improve beyond visual range (BVR) targeting—a critical deficiency for Israeli and Arab alike. The 1973 war was fought by large, easily characterizable armored and mechanized units. The fact that most land units could generally operate without adequate BVR detection and characterization—even in terms of adequate day/night photo reconnaissance—sharply affected every aspect of the fight. There is no question that the kind of advanced targeting and intelligence systems being introduced to U.S. and other Western and friendly forces will be of immense benefit in future wars. Israel demonstrated this during its 1982 invasion of Lebanon.

Effective and Secure C³I

Neither side had a fully effective C^3 system during the 1973 war and neither had modern secure communications. Israeli C^3 experienced severe problems. Assets were not well organized, secure, or given proper regional or central battle management. The communications gear was of moderate quality at best, often supplied in insufficient numbers, and in some cases was missing or poorly maintained. On a number of occasions, communications broke down and senior commanders lost track of what their subordinate units were doing. On the southern front, one Israeli division commander described his situation in the following manner:

> Communications were terrible. The Egyptians were apparently jamming our nets. I could have overcome this because of my proximity to the brigade commanders, but Southern Command kept bursting into my net. Because we were far from the Southern Command HQ, the jamming of that net was more effective. The Command's intermediate stations would override my division command net, trying to relay messages. The intermediate communication procedure was time consuming, and meanwhile the net was occupied.[16]

It is also noteworthy that the Israelis paid relatively little attention to communications security throughout the war. They lacked training in this area, showed insufficient respect for the Arabs, and often had to break security to force links through a badly organized chain of command.

It also became rapidly apparent that Israel had no effective C^3I system for managing and coordinating air attack missions, large-scale, land, combat unit movements, or even combined arms operations on a narrow tactical front. Israel's system for coordinating air missions had to be improvised after the war began. Its land combat C^3I system depended almost totally on full-scale mobilization before a conflict to provide proper organization and assets. When Israel had to mobilize in a state of near chaos, its command and communications structure broke down. Not only did its chain of command break down, but key personnel, like artillery observers, never reached their proper unit and "blinded" an army C^3I system that was almost entirely dependent on the human eye.

This lack of effective C^3 helps account for many of Israel's early losses in the war. One particularly serious mistake involved an early Israeli counterattack against the Egyptian bridgeheads on the east bank of the canal. While the attack was meant to be directed against the Egyptian flank, it ended instead by pushing against the well-defended Egyptian center.

Israel had virtually no advanced targeting aids, relatively poor land-based sensors, and lacked effective regional and central C^3I data nets. As virtually every Israeli report on the October War makes clear, Israel won in spite of its high command and C^3I system and not because of it. Israeli forces fought and won because of the individual excellence of Israel's pilots and squadrons, individual land combat units, and front commanders.

As has been discussed earlier, Israeli ground forces relied on line-of-sight, armored reconnaissance, and slow arriving air reconnaissance. There was very poor flow of data among command elements and from the air force to the ground. No assets existed to adequately track Arab infantry forces, mobile SAMs, and radar-guided AA guns. The IDF lacked modern artillery and counter-battery targeting systems. There were no tactical centers above the brigade level trying to organize targeting data and no real artillery fire control centers. Forward air controllers were lacking and poorly trained and equipped.

More importantly, Israeli air forces had no real air attack operations center until one was improvised during the war. The IAF could not conduct effective night reconnaissance missions, although many Egyptian and Syrian movements occurred during this period. The IAF also failed to make adequate use of armed reconnaissance, track Arab SAM positions properly, and process day reconnaissance data. Many recce aircraft found high value targets, but the IAF could not process and act on the data rapidly enough to be effective.

This weakness in the IAF contrasts sharply with its readiness and organization for air-to-air combat and even SAM suppression and sets a pattern followed in several of the other wars under study. Regardless of peacetime exercises, it is all too easy for even sophisticated air forces to forget that C^3 for combined operations is almost inevitably as important as C^3 for air superiority. Most air forces reinforce this bias by emphasizing service- or branch-oriented C^3 organization and assets and the fighter mission. The end result is often to severely weaken, if not cripple, the ability of air power to directly influence the land battle.

Syria lacked anything approaching a C^3 system to match the size of its forces. It began the 1973 war without having conducted a single significant armored exercise above the division level, and its land offensive had such poor C^3I capabilities that many key units advanced out of order. The bridging and assault engineer units necessary to allow Syrian tanks to cross Israeli tank ditches were, for example, stuck at the rear of advancing Syrian armored forces. While individual Syrian units often fought courageously and well, this cost Syria much of its advantage in surprise and gave Israel critical time in which to organize its defenses. At the same time, Syria fought without an effective air C^3I system, had no real air recce capability and mission planning, had no real FAC capability, and committed its aircraft to combat using poorly controlled attack sorties and simple ground controlled intercept (GCI) methods that virtually threw its fighters away in the face of a far better-trained and organized Israeli fighter force.

Egypt was considerably better prepared. It could operate the equipment the USSR had installed when it deployed Soviet SAM and C^3I units during the 1969–1970 Canal War/War of Attrition. It had extensively tested its C^3 system and had conducted large numbers of field- and command-post exercises before the war began. However, it lacked the discipline and organization to integrate its C^3 assets effectively, to properly operate many systems, and to adapt other key items of Soviet equipment to new tactical needs once Egypt had to depart from its original plans to limit its attack to the area covered by its Soviet installed C^3I facilities and SAM systems.

Egypt, like Syria, also had only a limited number of effective or lethal land-based air defense systems and no fighters with modern avionics and radars. Egypt had nearly 700 SA-2/3/6 launchers, but less than 50 of these were SA-6 launchers. This compares with 75 modern Hawk launchers in Israel which made comparatively limited use of its SAMs. While Egypt had nearly 1,000 radar-controlled AA guns (and nearly 3,000 more unguided guns), only about 20 were ZSU-23-4s, or less than half the total in Syria. Ironically, Israel had about 200 modern short-range, radar-guided AA guns. Although land-based air defenses were Egypt's only advanced C^3I capabilities, it was again its SA-7s and unguided AA guns that did most of the killing. Egypt's heavier SAMs had more impact in breaking up Israeli air attacks and in forcing Israeli fighters to fly low in areas defended by short-range air defense systems (SHORADS) than in shooting down Israeli fighters.

Like Israel, Egypt lacked the key elements of an air C^3 system for support of the ground battle. It did formulate a detailed air-strike plan for the initial phase of the conflict, but in retrospect, Egypt seems to have conceded the IDF so much of an edge in airpower that it did not give this aspect of C^3 sufficient priority. Egypt attacked without an effective air recce, targeting or damage assessment capability to support air operations, and had a weak and inadequate FAC system.

At another level, both sides had problems in the identification of friend and foe (IFF). For Israel, those problems largely affected ground combat. While Israel lacked the advanced IFF systems needed for head-on BVR combat, its air combat training and excellent air control and warning systems largely eliminated IFF problems in air-to-air combat. With a few exceptions, Israel's air superiority also eliminated the problems its ground forces had identifying attacking aircraft, and the IDF's lack of forward air defense largely eliminated the threat its forces posed to aircraft. Standard communications techniques and clearly defined battle lines also eliminated the problem aircraft faced in identifying ground targets.

Israel did, however, have problems in identifying distant armored forces and instances occurred where IDF tanks destroyed each other. This led the IDF to consider narrow-beam laser communicators and binoculars as a means of establishing a simple IFF link for ranges up to 10 kilometers.

In contrast, both Syrian and Egyptian forces experienced serious IFF problems. Egypt attempted to establish clear zones to separate its SAM and air operations, but found it could not use its air control and warning and GCI systems to establish the identity of aircraft entering the airspace covered by its SAMs. It shot down a significant number of its own planes, perhaps as many as sixty. Syria lacked the sophistication to properly manage its own airspace, and its IFF systems did not have frequency compatibility with those of the Iraqi aircraft that came as reinforcements. Although this C^3 problem did not materially affect the outcome of the air war, it led to some Iraqi planes being lost to Syrian fighters. Further, Syria also seems to have lost some fighters to its own SAMs.

Combined Arms

As Table 2.7 shows, Israel's emphasis on armor deprived it of many of the elements of combined arms present in Arab forces both at the outset of the war and once the forces on each side were fully mobilized. Israel's initial failure to mobilize before the Arab attack prevented Israel from achieving even a minimal combined arms balance during

TABLE 2.7   The Combined Arms Balance in the October 1973 Conflict

BALANCE OF COMBINED ARMS WITHIN THE TOTAL INVENTORY OF ARAB AND ISRAELI GROUND FORCES

	Major Weapons as Percent of Tank Strength		
	ISRAEL	EGYPT	SYRIA
A. Tanks	100%	100%	100%
B. APCs and Halftracks	200%	100%	65%
C. 100mm and Above Artillery	15%	90%	80%
D. Mortars Above 100mm	20%	15%	20%
E. Anti-Tank Weapons	15%	220%	115%
F. AA Guns and SA-7	30%	60%	55%
G. HAWK, SA-2, SA-3, and SA-6 Launchers	7%	20%	15%

BALANCE OF COMBINED ARMS WITHIN THE ARAB AND ISRAELI GROUND FORCES ENGAGING ON EACH FRONT

	Major Weapons as a Percent of Medium Tank Strength			
	Sinai Front		Golan Front	
	Israel	Egypt	Israel	Syria
A. Tanks	100%	100%	100%	100%
B. Artillery	15%	80%	20%	115%
C. Anti-Tank Weapons	20%	380%	25%	400%
D. AA Guns and SA-7	?	85%	?	85%
E. HAWK, SA-2, SA-3, and SA-6	10%	20%	10%	20%

SOURCES: Trevor Dupuy, *Elusive Victory* (New York: Harper and Row, 1978); Chaim Herzog, *The Arab-Israeli Wars* (New York: Random House, 1982); and various editions of the *Born in Battle* series.

the initial period of the attack and forced the IDF to improvise its force structure throughout the rest of the war.

An even more serious effect of the mobilization delay, however, was to force the ready units in the forward area into combat at a rate that left Israel virtually without armor on either front by the night of 7 October. Israeli casualties, armor losses, and aid requests were determined to some degree by the result of this crisis. Israeli attempts to use tanks and air power without strong support from the infantry or artillery branches of the army led to many of its problems during the 1973 war and showed the IDF the need for a more balanced combined arms approach. The Israeli emphasis on tanks derived from the tactical success that the Israelis achieved in 1956 and 1967. During these wars, and especially in 1967, fast-striking Israeli armored columns attacked relatively static Arab formations. The half-tracks containing Israeli infantry were often left behind by faster tank units in 1967, and many infantry units never saw combat. Armored officers were then promoted more rapidly in the postwar environment, and this led to an increasing interest in armor as the main form of combat power.

Israel's lack of artillery was rationalized in terms of the effectiveness of the IAF as "flying artillery." This philosophy led to considerable neglect of the army's artillery arm. In 1973, Israel only had around 300 artillery pieces, few of which were self-propelled. It was very definitely a tank-oriented force.

The end result was that Israel lost several encounters with Egyptian infantry equipped with antitank guided missiles (ATGMs) and was not properly prepared for urban warfare once it crossed the Suez. Israel also took much heavier casualties on the Golan than it would have taken if its defending infantry forces had been properly equipped with modern ATGMs; it experienced far more serious problems in penetrating Syrian defending forces stationed in the rough volcanic terrain on the Golan than it would have if its tanks had had proper artillery and infantry support. This was a major factor shaping the restructuring of Israel's ground forces after 1973 and triggered renewed interest in combined arms operations in many Western armies.

Egypt and Syria, in contrast, had all the proper elements of combined arms but were crippled by weaknesses in tactics, training, and technology which were a mix of Soviet-derived problems and the politicization and bureaucratization of both forces.

Two particularly serious problems emerged in combined operations. The first stemmed from the fact that armor, infantry, and artillery were trained and organized as separate branches. This did not lead to major problems as long as each branch carried out well-exercised attack plans, but coordination between the branches tended to break down the moment follow-on attacks had to be organized or Arab defenses were penetrated. It also compounded C^3, training, and support problems in armored combat and the problems Arab forces faced in using their artillery.

The second grew out of the lack of adequate artillery C^3 and targeting systems. The Egyptians did well in their initial preplanned barrages and in exploiting captured Israeli maps to target fixed artillery and mobilization assembly areas. Syria also did well in firing from presurveyed positions against known target areas or line-of-sight targets. Neither Egypt nor Syria, however, could rapidly deploy or maneuver artillery or shift fires, and both relied far too heavily on the value of prolonged or mass artillery fire. Coupled to the slow processing of orders along branch lines and gross overcentralization of command, this deprived Arab forces of much of the potential value of their artillery forces.

Infantry

Israel should have had an advantage in infantry. As Table 2.8 shows, it was spending far more per man than its Arab neighbors. This money, however, went to other branches of combat arms.

Israel's bias in favor of armor and against infantry stemmed from a belief (almost a dogma) that infantry would find it increasingly difficult to survive and fight on the battlefield. This bias grew out of the IDF's experiences in 1956 and 1967 when Israeli tanks proved effective against poorly trained and commanded Egyptian troops. It was reinforced by an Israeli emphasis on highly mobile wars of maneuver. One analyst has gone so far as to call infantry "the bastard child of the IDF."[17]

As a result, the IDF found itself critically short of infantry. Further, those infantry troops that were available were not well trained in combined arms operations. This meant Israel was not properly prepared to suppress the much better led and trained Arab infantry which had evolved after 1967 and was well-equipped with anti-armor PGMs and RPGs. When Israeli tanks moved against Arab forces, they often did so without adequate infantry support. In some cases they even attacked without infantry support although the IDF tank forces lacked the ability to detect and suppress all those Arab troops who were capable of knocking out Israeli tanks.

The Israelis recognized that part of their tank losses was attributable to this lack of infantry support for armor after 1973, but they chose to emphasize artillery over infantry. They made this

TABLE 2.8 Comparative Arab and Israeli Defense Expenditures per Man in Arms (in SUS/IISS Data)

	1972		1973		1974	
	Peacetime Active	Wartime Mobilized[a]	Peacetime Active	Wartime Mobilized	Peacetime Active	Wartime Mobilized
Israel	20,276	4,535	12,817	4,913	25,347	9,220
Egypt	4,646	3,552	5,830	1,864	9,650	3,257
Syria	1,847	1,702	1,636	626	3,345	1,312
Jordan	1,305	846	1,636	1,038	1,897	1,215
Lebanon	4,975	3,683	4,918	3,896	8,721	6,568
Iraq	2,330	1,967	3,320	890	7,138	2,008

[a]Mobilized or reserve manpower includes paramilitary manpower and gendarmerie funded under defense budget.

SOURCE: Data taken from IISS, *Military Balance*, 1972–73, 1973–74, and 1974–75 (London: International Institute for Strategic Studies).

decision partly because they concluded that artillery could keep up with armor and partly because they feared casualties. They estimated that Arab artillery fire would have extracted substantially higher casualties had they placed significantly greater reliance on infantry. As will be discussed later, the IDF paid dearly for this decision during the war in Lebanon.

In contrast, Arab infantry played a key role in opposing Israeli armor. According to Egyptian President Sadat:

> For the first time in history the Egyptian military planning was changing certain concepts that had been considered, until October 1973 War, more or less immutable. The rule was that only armor should deal with enemy armor. We were taught, as every soldier everywhere was taught, that the infantry whatever their level of training or armaments—should never engage armor, because the infantry are, to use the military jargon, "soft." However, in the October War our Special Service forces and highly trained infantry forces did cross into Sinai, anti-tank missiles in hand, to confront the Israeli tanks. They engaged them in bitter fighting and hit large numbers of them before our tanks joined them to engage in the big tank battle.[18]

While Sadat's remarks are somewhat exaggerated, there is no

question that both Egyptian and Syrian infantry fought well and fought well against armor as long as they could fight defensively in prepared or natural defense positions.

Tanks and Armored Vehicles

As Table 2.1 indicates, all sides had large armored forces and put great faith in the tank. Ironically, Israel's initial combined arms failures triggered a great deal of speculation about the future of the tank early in the fighting. On the third day of the war, the Israel Defense Minister, Moshe Dayan, briefed the editors of the Israeli press in a talk which "exuded pessimism." Israel had already lost fifty combat aircraft and hundreds of tanks, and the tank losses were totally unexpected.

These losses did not come, however, from some decisive shift in the balance of armor and anti-armor technology or in the tank performance characteristics shown in Table 2.9 but from the tactical misuse of armor. This was particularly true of the Israelis on the Sinai. Tank commanders reacted to the Egyptian attack on the Bar-Lev Line by charging to the scene to help their besieged comrades.[19] They counterattacked, however, as an unbalanced force, without infantry or artillery support and proper reconnaissance. They thrust directly into well-positioned Egyptian infantry with ATGMs and RPGs. This led to a dramatic increase in the effectiveness of antitank weapons and particularly of Soviet-made rocket launchers. The Arabs had planned much of their strategy around infantry resistance to tank attacks and had created effective antitank barriers and firing positions across the Canal. The Israelis were also dealing with serious mobilization and C^3 problems, and this created an atmosphere of confusion within the IDF which hurt the effectiveness of Israeli counterattacks. Lt. General Shazly describes the result in his war diary entry for 9 October:

> The enemy has persisted in throwing away the lives of their tank crews. They have assaulted in "penny packet" groupings and their sole tactic remains the cavalry charge. In the latest manifestation, two brigades have driven against the 16th Division. Once again, the attack has been stopped with heavy losses. In the past two days the enemy has lost another 260 tanks. Our strategy always has been to force the enemy to fight on our terms; but we never expected them to cooperate.[20]

The Israelis initially gave ATGM technology the credit, rather than Egyptian organization and tactics and the weaknesses of the IDF. While Soviet ATGMs did prove effective, they did not account for the majority of the IDF tanks destroyed during the war. More were

TABLE 2.9 Performance Characteristics of Main Battle Tanks

Characteristic/Item	Israeli Tanks			Arab Tanks	
	M.48A3 (US)*	MCOAT (US)	Centurion (UK)**	T-55 (USSR)	T-62 (USSR)
Primary armament-cannon	105mm (rifled)	105mm (rifled)	105mm (rifled)	100mm (rifled)	115mm (smoothbore)
Secondary armament-machine guns	two 7.62mm	one 7.62mm & one 50 caliber or two 7.62mm	two 30 caliber	two 7.62mm	one 7.62mm & one 12.7mm
Combat weight (tons)	52	54.8	56.2	39.7	41.3
Cruising range (miles)	310	300	Not Available	310 w/integral tanks; 444 w/aux. tanks	404 w/auxiliary tanks
Height (inches)	107	109	118	91.5	54.5
Engine (horsepower)	750 (diesel)	750 (diesel)	635 (gasoline)	580 (diesel)	572 (diesel)
Number of gears forward/reverse	2/1 (automatic)	2/1 (automatic)	5/2 (manual)	5/1 (manual)	5/1 (manual)
Pull/replace power pack (hours)	3.5	3.5	Not Available	8.5	8.5
Protection on turret front (inches of armor)	4.4	6.3	5.93	8.07	9.0
Ammunition***	18.20 AP 12.13 HEAT 25-26 HEP 3 WP	18.20 APDS 12.13 HEAT 25-26 HEP 3 WP	28.30 APDS 12 HEAT 28-29 HESH	8 APDS 6 APHE 6 HEAT 23 HE	20 HVAPFSDS 6 HEAT FS 14 HE
Ammunition storage capacity (rounds)	62	63	70	43	40

(continues)

TABLE 2.9 *(continued)*

Characteristic/Item		Israeli Tanks			Arab Tanks	
		M.48A3 (US)*	MCOAT (US)	Centurion (UK)**	T-55 (USSR)	T-62 (USSR)
Fire control:	*Rangefinder*	coincidence	coincidence	ranging mach. gun	stadiametric	stadiametric
	Computer	mechanical	mechanical	no	no	mechanical
	Stabilization	no	no	yes	yes	yes
	Night Vision	active IR	active IR	commander IR in	active IR	active IR
		(1,000 meters)	(1,000 meters)	some models	(800 meters)	(800 meters)
Gun depression/elevation limits (degrees)		-R4/+19	-10/+20	-10/120	4/+17	-4/+17
Max. rate of power traverse (degrees/sec.)		24	24	14	17	17
Suspension		torsion bar, suspended live track	torsion bar, suspended live track	horizontal coil springs	torsion bar, flat dead track	torsion bar, flat dead track
Fording depth (feet)		4.0	4.0	4.75 (15 w/snorkel)	18 (snorkel)	18 (snorkel)

AP *Armor Piercing*	HEAT(-FS) *High-Explosive Anti-Tank (Fin-Stabilized)*	HVAPFSDS *High Velocity Armor Piercing Fin-Stabilized Discarding Sabot*
APDS *Armor Piercing Discarding Sabot*	HEP *High-Explosive Plastic*	
APHE *Armor Piercing High-Explosive*	HESH *High-Explosive Squash Head*	WP *White Phosphorous*
HE *High-Explosive*		

* M.48A3 armament retrofitted by Israel.

** The Centurion employed by the Israelis is said to have 2,000 modifications to the original model, including a WS AVDS 1970 diesel engine, a CD 850-6 transmission, and an additional fuel tank across the rear of the chassis.

*** Israeli tank ammunition distribution is a composite of the most frequent distribution by main gun round as reported by Israeli tank commanders in the WSEG armor Questionnaire.

SOURCES: *Jane's Weapons Systems, 1981 - 1982* (London: Jane's) and von Senger and Etterlin, *Tanks of the World, 1983* (NY: Nautical and Aviation Publishing Co., 1983).

destroyed by RPG-7s or the guns of other tanks. Many of those tanks which were destroyed by ATGMs were lost early in the war because of the IDF's flawed tactics.

For example, IDF tank forces charged unsupported into well-positioned Egyptian infantry on 8 October in an attempt to drive back the Egyptian beachhead. No suppressive fire was provided by artillery, air, or tank units, and the IDF tanks were clearly exposed the moment they came within range of the Egyptian Saggers and Swatters. Although most of the first generation Soviet systems missed—IDF tank commanders later referred to tanks being covered in ATGM guidance wires—enough hit to break the momentum of the attack. The Israeli tanks then came within range of Egyptian RPGs and the area turned into a killing ground.

In contrast, later IDF attacks outflanked Egyptian infantry positions, used heavy suppressive fire from tanks and artillery, and often used Israel's limited infantry or paratroop forces in assaults or infiltration attacks against Egyptian forces. Tanks generally performed well in such attacks and had a high rate of survival. The IDF did, however, greatly increase its rate of tank gunfire for suppressive purposes and would have benefited from more and better anti-personnel rounds, a problem Iraqi forces also experienced in the Iran-Iraq War.

One insight that also emerged from the IDF experience with tanks was the comparative indifference many IDF tank commanders showed toward the differences in tank type after the war. They generally concluded that both Western and Soviet tanks had a balanced set of strengths and weaknesses, although it should be noted that the Soviet T-54/T-55 in IDF hands had generally been under-gunned and had modern rangefinders. The key points emerging from the fighting were:

- U.S. tanks had too high a profile, an exposed commander's position, and inadequate machine guns.
- Soviet tanks were more difficult to operate and had inferior fire control and sighting capability.
- U.S. tanks were easier to drive and less fatiguing to ride in, but were less reliable.
- The majority of hits taken did not permanently kill the tanks hit, even if the armor was penetrated. Many tanks could be recovered and repaired within days.
- Tank gunnery ranges expanded to over 500 meters in most cases, and kills occurred at ranges of over 2 kilometers in the Sinai. The superior long-range sighting capability of U.S. tanks did not prove important.

- Contrary to expectation, hits were widely distributed on different areas of the tank. The value of heavy front armor was more limited than expected.
- Inadequate escape capability and burn-proof clothing greatly increased Israeli casualties. Few tank hits produced an immediate catastrophic crew kill.
- Most IDF tank commanders took the risk of fighting "hatch-up" because the increased visibility and ability to coordinate with other tanks outweighed the loss of protection. Iraqi and Soviet experience with problems in closed-tank visibility reinforces this lesson.
- Adequate forward recovery and repair proved absolutely critical to the IDF. So many repairs and recoveries occurred, particularly on the Sinai front, that it was a key factor in keeping IDF tank strength at levels that allowed it to sustain the crossing of the Suez.
- Cooperation among tanks, with some covering other tanks or providing suppressive fire, proved absolutely critical.
- The IDF's high prewar training levels and the independence of small units proved far more critical in the long haul than tank technology or performance. At the same time, the Israeli major combat formations proved too small to mass quickly or effectively and had to be increased after the war.

Light tanks were also used in the 1973 war but failed to play a significant role. The Soviet PT-76 reconnaissance vehicles/tanks were used by both the Egyptians and the Syrians. On the first day of the war, the Egyptians attempted to mount a special operation with the PT-76 which used their amphibious capability. This involved a crossing of the Great Bitter Lake and a thrust toward the Giddi and Mitla passes. The operation ended in failure when the lightly armed, poorly armored, and obsolescent PT-76s encountered Israeli main battle tanks including M-60s and Centurions.[21]

The key fighting vehicles reflected in the buildup shown in Table 2.10 were armored personnel carriers. The performance characteristics of these systems are summarized in Table 2.11. The 1973 war also saw Israel's first large scale use of the M-113 armored personnel carrier. The M-113s had many weaknesses, most of which had previously been exposed in Vietnam. These included its high profile, limited armor, poor firepower, and lack of observation and fire ports. The M-113 also had a tendency to inflict high internal casualties when hit because of the spalling or "burning" of its armor, the difficulty in making rapid exits and entrances, and its inability to keep up with tanks. In 1973,

TABLE 2.10 APC and AFV Strength in Arab and Israeli Forces: 1967–1973

	May 1967	Sept. 1973
Israel[a]	1,500	3,450
Egypt and Syria	1,650	3,235
Egypt	1,070	2,020
Syria	585	1,215
Jordan	210	470

[a]Includes only that part of IDF half-track inventory committed in AFV/APC role. The Israelis had over 500 U.S. M-113 armored personnel carriers (APCs). They liked the mobility, reliability, and overhead protection of the M-113.

SOURCES: IISS, *Military Balance*, various editions (London: International Institute for Strategic Studies), and Trevor Dupuy, *Elusive Victory* (New York: Harper and Row, 1978).

TABLE 2.11 Performance Characteristics of Mechanized Infantry Combat Vehicles

Characteristic/Item	M-113 APC (USA)	BTR-60PB (USSR)	BMP (USSR)
Weight (tons)	12.0	11.3	15.0
Hp/Ton	17.7	14.5	20.0
Fuel Type	diesel	gasoline	diesel
Capacity	9 men (1 driver 8 infantry)	12 men (2 crew, 10 infantry)	11 men (3 crew, 8 infantry)
Armor	aluminum	rolled steel	high strength steel and aluminum
Frontal Portection (inches of armor)	1.5	0.4	0.87
Overhead Protection	yes	yes	yes
Land Speed (mph)	40.	50.	43.
Water Speed (mph)	3.6	6.2	4.5
Range (miles)	350	310	310
Firing Ports	none	none	8
Main Armament	50 calibre MG	14.5 mm MG	73 mm smoothbore gun with automatic loader, SAGGER ATGM
Second Armament	none	7.62 mm MG	7.62 mm MG
Night Vision	active IR	active IR	passive IR (gunner) active IR (driver, commander)
Fording Depth	swims	swims	swims

SOURCES: *Jane's Weapons Systems, 1981–1982* (London: Jane's), and von Senger and Etterlin, *Tanks of the World, 1983* (New York: Nautical and Aviation Publishing Co., 1983).

however, the IDF operated the M-113s or "Zeldas" (the IDF name for the M-113) as a replacement for open-topped half-tracks and trucks. The trucks and half-tracks exposed crews and infantry to artillery and infantry firepower and had poor cross-country mobility. The IDF was forced, for example, to use M-113s to carry artillery rounds because it could not supply its artillery off road with trucks and half-tracks, and the Arabs had captured IDF maps showing the on- or near-road positions where the IDF planned to deploy artillery and shelled them heavily.

This contrast between the Zelda and the inadequate half-tracks and trucks did, however, give the IDF an exaggerated picture of the IDF's capability. For example, General Adan told the IDF's chief armor officer that the M-113 was his key resupply priority from the U.S. airlift: "I want you to know that even though many of our tanks have been hit, our most urgent need is for armored personnel carriers."[22] According to Adan, the M-113 was superior to the half-tracks for the following reasons:

> The half-track was open, hence vulnerable to shelling; the fact that it had two front wheels made it slow or unable to move altogether over rough terrain, especially sand dunes. There was a period when the half-track's slow pace could be coordinated with the IDF's Sherman tanks, which were just as slow and technically unreliable as the half-tracks. However once the Armored Corps began using Centurions and Pattons (M-60s), there was a total mismatch. The Zeldas had a roof that could be left open or in the case of shelling, closed. Its armor also gave the men better protection. Moreover, it moved entirely on tracks, had a stronger engine, greater mobility and speed, and infinitely better maneuvering ability. In fact they were able to advance even faster than our tanks.[23]

The most modern Arab armored personnel carrier used during the war was the Soviet BMP. Although it had just been introduced, it was used in limited numbers and was rarely used effectively in organized maneuver operations. This vehicle mounted a Sagger antitank missile and had the ability to knock out Israeli tanks. The problem for the Arabs was that the Sagger is extremely difficult to operate and is scarcely "a fire-and-forget" missile. It is wireguided and requires around 10 to 15 seconds of flight time during which the target must be in the sights of the operator. It also has to be controlled by the driver using a joystick. The BMP cannot fire on the move, and when it did stop, it was vulnerable to being knocked out by Israeli armor. This feature was also exploited by the Israelis who directed artillery fire at BMPs to prevent them from firing their Saggers.[24]

The BMP was built to be amphibious. This feature required lighter armor than is used on many infantry fighting vehicles that are not designed to be amphibious. As a result, the BMP proved exceptionally vulnerable to heavy artillery.[25]

Precision-Guided and Specialized Munitions

Anti-Armor PGMs

Much of the debate over the usefulness of PGMs versus tanks in U.S. defense literature since 1973 is the result of conflicting interpretations of the lessons of the October War.[26] The destruction of portions of General Adan's armored forces in the early stages of the October War by what appeared to be anti-armor PGMs astounded many observers. This led to some initial predictions that the main battle tank was becoming obsolete.[27]

As Table 2.12 shows, Egypt and Syria did make massive increases in their antitank weapons inventories. Postwar investigations have revealed, however, that the effectiveness of the RPG-7s may well have been as important. The Egyptian and Syrian forces may have fired as many as 6,000 to 8,000 Soviet ATGMs, most of them Saggers, but the IDF could only confirm about 30 to 40 kills from ATGMs after the war out of losses of 840 and were able to survey the cause of all but about 200 kills. At most, Soviet missiles accounted for 8 to 25 percent of all kills and many of these missiles may have been RPG-7s. The ratio of RPGs to Saggers on the battlefield was approximately 5 to 1, and troops with the RPG-7 were scattered throughout the Egyptian and Syrian force structures while ATGMs were deployed only in selected forward elements.[28] Nevertheless, when the IDF out-maneuvered the more visible ATGM elements, it often ran into forces equipped with RPGs. It then tended to treat all hits as having inflicted more damage than really occurred, while the RPG-7 continued to be slighted.

It is only in examining the tank losses during the first three days of the war, however, that the Sagger seems to have achieved a relatively high number of kills. Even in this time period, the losses caused by the Saggers were almost equalled by the losses caused by the much more numerous RPG-7s.

On the first day of the war, according to Lt. General Shazly:

> Twice, groups of enemy tanks managed to break through our infantry lines to reach the water's edge and bombed our bridges and ferries, inflicting significant damage. But it was a hopeless struggle. With RPG-7 portable anti-tank missiles and RPG-43 anti-tank grenades, our

infantry fight back. Before sunrise, the few surviving tanks are in retreat.[29]

What Shazly apparently did not know or did not elaborate on was that the Israelis did not plan on these tactics. These poorly coordinated counterattacks resulted from Israel's confused C[3] situation. As is typical of most serious losses among armored maneuver units in the wars under study, a failure in C[3]I proved far more important than the technical performance characteristics of tanks and their supporting armor.

The Egyptians, in turn, had trouble dealing with targets in the area which were out of range of the RPG-7 but too close to be hit with a Sagger missile (which needs time to stabilize in flight). This stemmed in part from the weapons performance characteristics summarized in Table 2.11. After the war, General Shazly had a sharp exchange with Soviet General Lashnekov on the need to resolve this problem.[30] If the Egyptians had had a system similar to the U.S. Dragon (then in Israeli use), they would not have had this problem.

As for the Israelis, they did not acquire modern ATGMs until the U.S. delivered U.S. crew-served guided antitank weapon (TOW) systems toward the end of the war. They did have light antitank weapon (LAW) antitank rockets but found their range to be too limited. They seem to have fired less than 20, although some Israeli sources indicate a higher number. The LAW has only about half the speed and range of the RPG-7. Israel had purchased French SS-11s and Cobra ATGMs after 1967, but found the first generation guidance systems on these weapons required too high a training level to justify deployment in a mobilization-based force. The Egyptians, incidentally, experienced the same problems with Soviet ATGMs with first generation guidance, but opted for an extensive training program. They even deployed training simulators to the rear of the combat units sent across the Suez.

The IDF's experience with TOW was more confused than enlightening. Israel rushed the systems to the front shortly before the cease-fire but had to hastily improvise training and tactics. The IDF scored some 13 hits against 9 tanks out of 20 firings but experienced problems because the fire control on several systems was miswired. It also attempted to improvise night sights and improved long-range sights with mixed success. It seems likely that third-generation systems like TOW (which only require sighting on the target rather than tracking of both the missile and target) would have greatly improved Israel's initial defense, but there is no way to be certain. The IDF did, however, extensively deploy TOW after the war.

TABLE 2.12 Buildup in Arab and Israeli Antitank Guided Missile Launcher Strength: 1967–1974

	May 1967	Sept. 1973	Sept. 1974
Israel	UNK[a]	280[a]	280[d]
Egypt and Syria	UNK[b]	1,500[c]	1,500[c]
Egypt	UNK	1,000[c]	1,000[c]
Syria	UNK	500	500
Jordan	0	0	36

[a] SS-10 and S-11 French ATGM.
[b] Had some early marks of Soviet ATGM.
[c] SAGGER and SNAPPER; only SAGGER seems to have been used.
[d] Largely TOW.

SOURCES: IISS, *Military Balance*, various editions (London: International Institute for Strategic Studies), and *Born in Battle*, various editions.

Tube Artillery

Massed Arab artillery did provide large volumes of firepower on both the northern and southern fronts. In describing the initial use of area fire, Egyptian Lt. General Shazly stated: "We had massed more than 2,000 guns behind our lines. Now our high-trajectory pieces, the howitzers and heavy mortars, began to pour up and over into the Bar-Lev forts and minefields and barbed wire entanglements."[31]

Table 2.13 shows that the Israeli stress on armor, airpower, and mechanized infantry had left artillery as well as regular infantry as the weak link in the Israeli order of battle. This can be traced to events prior to 1973, when the Israelis made little effort to integrate artillery into their overall concept of maneuver warfare. While armor and mechanized infantry were expected to have the high mobility needed to engage in a war of maneuver, most of Israel's 300 artillery pieces were towed. This made it impossible for the artillery to support fast-moving armored and infantry units on a variety of occasions. This was a shortcoming which the Israelis would work rapidly to overcome and correct once the war ended.

The problems led to a situation where a great deal of ammunition was expended on poorly targeted harassment and interdiction (HI) fire. The diaries on both sides indicated this generally had little effect and confirm that even accurate fire had little impact after the first few rounds because of each side's ability to take cover. Counter-battery fire was generally ineffective unless maneuver brought enemy targets within line of sight, although the Arab forces suffered

TABLE 2.13 Artillery System Performance

| | Changes in Artillery Numbers | |
	1967	1973
Israel	200	570
Egypt and Syria	890	1,955
Egypt	570	1,280
Syria	315	675
Jordan	35	130

SOURCE: IISS, *Military Balance*, various editions (London: International Institute for Strategic Studies).

unnecessary losses from moving too slowly and infrequently, and the IDF suffered losses because the Egyptians captured maps showing presurveyed firing points, and the Israelis often had trouble moving and supplying off road.

The IDF also experienced problems because it only had 7 to 15 days of ammunition stacks and rapidly expended them in poorly planned fire. This led to desperate resupply requests to the U.S., which airlifted in the ammunition; later studies showed, however, that the IDF had much larger remaining stocks than it initially claimed and exaggerated its needs to obtain rapid resupply. The Arabs, by contrast, stockpiled massive amounts of artillery rounds and did not experience significant logistics problems.

As has been discussed earlier, the Arab forces relied heavily on artillery, but they normally only made use of mass fire, and lacked adequate C^3, battle management, and beyond-visual-range targeting systems. Like the IDF, they also lacked adequate numbers of forward observers in their maneuver units. While the IDF's mobilization problems contributed to this lack in Israeli forces, the branch-oriented command system in Arab forces kept maneuver unit commanders from getting proper control over, or responsiveness from, their fire support.

The artillery on both sides did, however, cause serious casualties throughout the fighting. It also caused armored and mechanized units to seal themselves inside their respective vehicles. This forced them to rely on sighting and observation devices within the vehicles. Such actions correspondingly reduced the fields of vision for the troops manning the vehicles.[32]

The vital importance of long-range artillery as a harassment weapon was also seen in 1973. Israeli troops in particular made use of American 175-mm guns to shell the Damascus Military Airport for ten straight days during the war.[33] Both Egypt and Syria also made good use of Soviet long-range 130-mm guns.

Surface-to-Surface Rockets and Missiles

The Arabs had a major advantage in surface-to-surface missiles, which is reflected in Table 2.14. The Egyptians employed FROG-7 rockets on the southern front in an attempt to destroy the Israeli bridge that had been used by Israeli troops to the west bank of the Suez Canal. They were far too inaccurate, however, to have much effect. The Israelis were also able to destroy some rockets with anti-aircraft fire.

On the northern front, the Syrian FROG-7 rockets fired and struck near Nazareth and the Kibbutz Geva but were again so inaccurate as to be little more than harassment weapons. Nazareth, for example, is an Arab town and represents a very unlikely target for the Syrians. While Kibbutz Geva was a more plausible target, there were far more useful targets at which such a weapon could be directed. This illustrates the severe targeting and accuracy problems in using the FROG-7 with either conventional or chemical warheads. This was later demonstrated in the Iran-Iraq War when the FROG-7s fired at the Iranians by the Iraqis exhibited similar accuracy and targeting problems.

On 22 October, the Egyptians fired a SCUD missile into the Sinai desert. This was the first time that SCUD systems were used in actual combat. The purpose of this firing was more political than military since the Egyptians then faced a badly deteriorating military situation. The 22 October firing of the missile was meant to suggest that Sadat would not allow the Egyptian army to be totally defeated without first using all of the weapons at his disposal. Since the range of this missile is 180 miles, Sadat may have been studying his effect on IDF behavior.

In general, such demonstration firings have acted more to unite the enemy than discourage it. Most uses of new weapons since World War I have had very temporary shock effect, if any.

Mines and Barriers

The terrain and barrier systems that helped shape the war have already been discussed. The Israelis—who were on the defensive for a large part of the war—made use of a variety of defensive systems, including mines. In the areas where the most intense combat took place, these mines were largely neutralized by Arab artillery which

TABLE 2.14 Trend in Arab and Israeli Surface-to-Surface Missile and Free Rocket Launchers: 1967–1973

	Surface-to-Surface Missile and Free Rocket Launchers	May 1967	Sept. 1973
Israel	Lance	0	0
	Pershing	0	0
	Total	0	0
Egypt and Syria	FROG-7	0	48
	SCUD B	0	30
	Total	0	78
Egypt	FROG-7	0	12
	SCUD B	0	18
	Total	0	30
Syria	FROG-7	0	16
	SCUD B	0	?
	Total	0	16
Jordan		0	0

SOURCE: IISS, *Military Balance*, various editions (London: International Institute for Strategic Studies).

saturated the ground where minefields were believed to exist. Land-mine warfare also did not represent any significant improvement over past technology. The IDF, as did Egypt and Syria, followed traditional doctrine and uses, following policies similar to those used by the U.S. in World War II.

The IDF did feel that the minefields they had placed along the 1967 cease-fire lines on the Golan Heights played a useful role when the Syrians attacked in October 1973, but ordinary tank ditches and earth barriers were far more important.

Israel never fully completed its plans to build major barrier defenses on the Golan or on the edge of the Suez Canal. The IDF defenses on the Suez have been described earlier. The defenses on the Golan may be summarized as follows:

- Defense built around mobilizing a division-equivalent force.
- Tank barrier with minefields on both sides of ditch and observed by strongpoints.
- Twelve strong points on "Vilote" line from Mt. Hermon to Jordanian border, plus three against Lebanon, manned by reservists.

- Each strongpoint built on hillocks with thick basalt walls and defended by dense surrounding minefields.
- Strongpoints normally supported by one regular infantry and one regular armor brigade.
- Antitank weapons limited to recoilless rifles, bazookas, and three tanks per strongpoint.

The IDF relied on a large tank ditch on the outer perimeter of the Golan and the fortification of a number of strategic hillocks, few of which were taken by Syrian forces. It did not, however, heavily arm these forts. The Bar-Lev Line in the south consisted largely of earth barriers and bunkers. Little use was made of emplaced heavy weapons or artillery, and a system to cover the canal with flaming oil seems to have been cancelled after several abortive experiments. Israel claims it was never intended to serve as a genuine barrier function.

The IDF did, however, attempt to use defensive and barrier minefield concepts, with mines being deployed by hand in the 1973 period. Accurate records were kept of each minefield's location and deployment pattern. Each field was surrounded with barbed wire. When used near main roads, the minefields were located on either side of the road, acting as a barrier defense, and a roadblock placed across the road between the minefields.

The IDF preference was for the U.S. M-15 AT mine, deployed with anti-handling devices, although these were estimated to be only 50 percent effective in the 1973 war.

The Israelis utilized mine warfare to a considerable extent along the Suez Canal, with as many as 750,000 mines reported to be deployed at one point in 1973.[34] For the IDF, as well as the Arab states, minefields served to channel combat and limit enemy approaches, rather than stop or kill threat forces.

Following the 1973 war, the IDF expressed continued interest in new minefield technologies, looking to scatterable mine systems being developed in the U.S., artillery-delivered area munitions (ADAM) in an AT version, and, to a lesser extent, helicopter-delivered dispensing systems and a towed mine dispenser. The object was to acquire systems which would dispense the mines quickly and provide crude marking systems that would allow friendly tanks and personnel to navigate quickly through the fields.

The IDF also expressed considerable interest in counterbarrier and countermine systems and tactics. Within the IDF Tactical Engineer Equipment Development Unit, in addition to demolition and decoy sections, there is a counterbarrier section whose primary role is to locate enemy ATGMs and minefields. Currently, the IDF locates mines by mine-roller, scout, or reconnaissance elements (mounted and on foot), and by remote control vehicles.

The Egyptians made use of mines during the first part of the October War despite their offensive orientation. Egyptian commandos in particular had the mission of disrupting Israeli attempts to support or reinforce the besieged strongholds of the Bar-Lev Line. This was to be done partly through the use of ambushes but also through the use of mines. In this regard, there are a number of marshes and other natural and man-made obstacles in the Sinai. By supplementing these natural obstacles with mines and ambushes, the Egyptian commandos did inflict some disruption and delay. Had it not been for the fact that the IAF shot down most of the helicopters loaded with commandos on their way to the Israeli rear area in the Sinai, this disruption could have been more severe.

The Egyptians made good use of barriers for offensive purposes. They built a high artificial ridge on their side of the Suez with sufficient height to allow artillery spotting over the Israeli defenses on the other side and to serve as antitank guided missile firing positions. They heavily fortified and sheltered their SAM, C^3, and artillery positions, which helped prevent SAM suppression until IDF ground forces rolled up the SAM positions from the rear following the canal crossing, and IAF fighters began to make use of newly supplied U.S. air-to-surface missiles.

In general, the Arabs had superior combat engineering compared to the IDF. This was particularly true of Egypt which developed special high-pressure hydraulic systems to wash away the Israeli earth barriers on the edge of the Suez and set up excellent assault bridges and follow-on bridging systems. These could be lowered under the surface of the canal during daytime and this, coupled to a heavy emphasis on SAM defenses and night movement, kept the IAF from knocking out the bridges. The IDF, in contrast, experienced major problems in deploying its specially designed assault bridges and in getting them to function. It was only the weak Egyptian C^3 system and slow Egyptian response that gave the IDF time to reinforce its bridgehead in spite of major problems in combat engineering.

It is interesting to note in this regard that passive barriers and good combat engineering played an important role in the Iran-Iraq War, but that static minefields have had only a limited delay effect in all of the conflicts under study. This tends to reinforce the conclusion of several U.S. studies which emphasize the potential value of using artificial or natural barriers—including urban or built-up areas—and which indicate that it may be far more effective to deliver mines and smart submunitions by multiple-rocket launchers (MRLs) than to use large fixed minefields.

All-Weather and Night Target Acquisition Systems

The ability to detect, identify, and position enemy targets in overcoming an imbalance of forces is essential to the accurate delivery of firepower. If such target acquisition capabilities are present, the relative effectiveness of conventional forces can be greatly increased, enabling these forces to take advantage of natural terrain features, man-made barriers, and other advantages of combined arms operations. If they are not, they collapse the range of combat and deprive artillery and airpower of much of their effectiveness.

The Middle East, as a conflict environment, does not have the same weather phenomena found in regions such as Europe or Korea. While occasional rain and snow occur in areas such as in the Golan Heights, the major problems for the Arab and Israeli forces remain heat, ducting effects in terms of radar, acute shadow contrast during many parts of the day, the need to track rapid small-unit movements in desert areas, sand and dust obscuration, and target acquisition at night and at effective ranges. The 1973 Arab-Israeli conflict did, however, mark the use of night observation devices in a wide spectrum of systems for the first time. While actual night combat was limited, even the threat of such Arab capabilities gave the Arabs a new tactical advantage over the IDF, which generally lacked such devices.

The Syrians used this advantage with special effectiveness on the Golan Heights. Part of the reason that the Israelis were initially unable to hold back the advance of the Syrians was because of the superior Syrian night fighting capabilities.[35] The Syrians might also have taken better advantage of this capability had it not been for the unexpected death of one of their officers. Syrian Brigadier General Omar Abrash had planned a division-sized attack against the Israeli Seventh Brigade for the night of 7 October. The general was killed, however, on that same night and the attack was postponed until daylight. This was a fortunate development for the Israelis who were then exhausted, outnumbered, and without comparable night combat equipment.

The Arabs experienced further problems in night warfare because of problems in their C^3 and maneuver warfare training and organization. They lacked the command and control (C^2) and tactical navigation and location technology to make proper use of their night-vision devices and low night-signature firepower. This problem also characterized the Soviet forces in Afghanistan. The Arab forces did, however, make excellent use of night troop and resupply movements.

The Soviet night-vision devices used during this period also proved less flare- or flash-blind sensitive than the U.S. equipment rushed to the IDF. Both sets of equipment, however, lacked the surveillance capability both sides needed to cope with infiltration. It is also interesting to note that these same problems in night surveillance, land navigation, and C^2 capabilities emerge in the other wars under study. It was the Afghan and Iranian popular forces—relying on infantry infiltration and knowledge of terrain—which made the most effective use of night warfare and not the high technology forces.

Anti-Aircraft Artillery

The coarsest measure of the effectiveness of an air defense system is the number of aircraft shot down. On the Egyptian front, the IAF lost 51 aircraft during the October war. The Israelis flew about 8,400 sorties against Egyptian targets, meaning that less than 0.6 to 0.75 percent of the total number of sorties ended with the loss of the aircraft. This is less than half the loss rate the IAF suffered in the 1967 war, during which the Israelis lost 46 aircraft altogether, the great majority on the Egyptian front. A breakdown of IAF losses by front is not available for the whole 1967 war. On the first day of the 1967 war, however, the Egyptians downed 15 Israeli aircraft. On the first two days of the 1973 war, the Egyptians downed 14 Israeli aircraft. Bear in mind that the Egyptians had nearly three times the anti-aircraft artillery (AAA) guns they had in 1967, more than six times the SAMs, and the advantage of prior warning and deployment

In the first four days of the war—through 9 October—the Egyptians shot down over 30 IAF aircraft for about 1,900 Israel sorties, a loss rate of about 1.7 percent. This loss rate was scarcely catastrophic but was high during these first days of the war because the IAF was preoccupied with trying to cut the Egyptian bridges across the canal. Since the Egyptians anticipated this reaction, they sited heavy air defense protection within range of the bridges. On 10 October the IAF gave up trying to hit the bridges, and its loss rate through the remainder of the war fell to a very low 0.3 percent.

In the first days of the war, the Israelis also made virtually no attempt to suppress the air defense system, concentrating instead on trying to halt the flow of Egyptian men and material across the canal. Yet even on the worst day, 7 October, the IAF loss rate was a little under 3 percent, considerably below the peak rate of the 1967 war, which was nearly 4 percent on the first day. The performance of the

Egyptian air defense system in October 1973 was dismal in terms of aircraft shot down. Despite its enormous increase in size, its advance warning, its increased sophistication, and the fact that the IAF did not attack it in force for the first several days, the Egyptian defenders were barely able to match the kill performance of their 1967 predecessors.

Yet the effectiveness of Arab air defenses in degrading Israeli sortie effectiveness and freedom of action was one of the major shocks of the war. It is difficult in retrospect, however, to understand just why the IAF was so badly prepared to deal with the Egyptian and Syrian air defenses shown in Tables 2.15, 2.16, and 2.17. Israeli intelligence tracked this buildup in near real time and acquired extensive experience with Soviet AA guns and SA-2 and SA-3 missiles in the Canal War or War of Attrition in 1970. It was fully briefed on most U.S. SAM-suppression and air defense technologies at this time and was aware that the ZSU-23-4, SA-6, and SA-7 had been deployed to Arab forces. It is also important to note that for all the reports about the importance of the ZSU-23-4, both Egyptian and Israeli sources confirm that Egypt had less than 50 ZSU-23-4s when the war began and Syria had only about 20. Given their short range and the massive number of other AA guns deployed in Arab forces, these systems were scarcely decisive.

The IAF seems to have focused on the weaknesses in Egyptian and Syrian organization, revealed in exercises and test firings, rather than on weapons numbers and technical capabilities. It made political and readiness judgments it paid dearly for once the 1973 war began.

The performance characteristics of the main AA weapons used in the war are summarized in Table 2.18. The ZSU-23-4 anti-aircraft system performed well in the 1973 conflict, along with a number of older non-radar guided antiaircraft artillery pieces. In all, around 40 percent of Israel's aircraft losses were attributed to AAA and most to unguided guns. The ZSU-23-4s were deployed only in limited numbers and were not the source of most of these kills.[36]

Surface-to-Air Missiles

Surface-to-air missiles were one of the most well publicized weapons systems used during the war. As Tables 2.19 through 2.22 show, the Arabs built up massive forces, and Israel had significant Hawk, Redeye, and Chaparral strength. They were not effective in isolation but only when supplemented by other systems which could deal with low-level threats. Furthermore, the missile and sensor resources which the Egyptians and Syrians had to devote in order to

TABLE 2.15 Prewar Inventories of Ground-Based Air-Defense Weapons

Ground-Based Air-Defense Weapons	Israel	Egypt	Syria	Arab:Israeli
Anti-Aircraft	820	11,600	695	3:1
Vulcan/ZSU-23-4	0	44	20	NA
Surface-to-Air Missile Launchers	0	370[a]	120[a]	485:0
Shoulder-Fired	0	370[a]	120[a]	485:0
HAWK (Israel), SA-6 (Arab)	72	40	60	1.5:1
Other Crew-Served	0	800[b]	90[b]	890:0

[a]These were Soviet SA-7 missile launchers.
[b]These were Soviet SA-2 and SA-3 missile launchers.

SOURCES: Trevor Dupuy, *Elusive Victory* (New York: Harper and Row, 1978), pp. 389–556; *Born in Battle: The Yom Kippur War* (Tel Aviv, 1978), pp. 36–38; *Born in Battle: Suez 1970* (March 1980); David Eshel, *The Israeli Air Force* (Tel Aviv: Eshel-Dramit, 1978), pp. 48–76.

TABLE 2.16 Changes in Arab and Israeli Air-Defense Artillery: 1967–1984

	Air-Defense Artillery	May 1967	Sept. 1973	Aug. 1974	Mid-1984
Israel	Radar Controlled	200	200	200	500
	Other	350	800	800	500
	Total	550	1,000	1,000	1,000
Egypt and Syria	Radar Controlled	1,000	1,700	1,750	2,500
	Other	1,100	3,000	3,350	2,500
	Total	2,100	4,700	5,100	5,000
Egypt	Radar Controlled	400	1,100	1,050	1,500
	Other	600	1,700	2,000	1,500
	Total	1,000	2,800	3,200	3,000
Syria	Radar Controlled	600	650	700	1,000
	Other	500	1,250	1,250	1,000
	Total	1,100	1,900	1,950	2,000
Jordan	Radar Controlled	0	5	0	50
	Other	100	300	300	300
	Total	100	305	300	350

It is estimated that total ZSU-23-4 deliveries during 1967–1973 were 44 to Egypt and 20 to Syria for a total of 64.

SOURCES: Adapted from various editions of the IISS, *Military Balance* (London: International Institute for Strategic Studies), and data provided by the Egyptian Ministry of Defense.

TABLE 2.17 Changes in Arab and Israeli Air-Defense Radar Strength: 1967–1974

	May 1967	*Sept. 1973*	*Sept. 1974*
A. Israel			
EW/AW/C^3	6	8	12
SAM Site	5	12	16
Total	11	20	28
B. Egypt and Syria			
EW/AW/C^3	60	271	288
SAM Site	30	174	194
Total	90	445	482
C. Egypt			
EW/AC/C^3	50	225	240
SAM Site	30	135	150
Total	80	360	390
D. Syria			
EW/AW/C^3	10	46	48
SAM Site	0	39	44
Total	10	85	92
E. Jordan			
EW/AW/C^3	1	5	7
SAM Site	0	0	0
Total	1	5	7

SOURCES: *Jane's Weapons Systems, 1981–1982* (London: Jane's); IISS, *Military Balance*, various editions (London: International Institute for Strategic Studies); and General Dynamics, *The World's Missile Systems*, various editions.

protect a limited amount of air space were quite phenomenal. The Egyptian air defense force of 1973 was, for example, substantially larger than the present U.S. air-defense force.

Israel had learned to suppress the Soviet SA-2 and SA-3 surface-to-air missiles during the Canal War of 1970 but was not properly prepared to use the ECM gear it had obtained and had no experience with the self-propelled SA-6 or man-portable SA-7. In a collaborative piece published almost immediately after the war, Walter Laqueur and Major General (Ret.) Mattityahu Peled stated:

> Any hope Israel may have had of rendering Arab antiaircraft missile defenses ineffective simply by relying on the excellence of her pilots had to be given up. The new weapons, particularly the relatively small SAM-6 and SAM-7, have been proved highly successful against the fighter-

TABLE 2.18 Comparative Performance of U.S. and Soviet Radar-Guided, Light AA Guns: June 1974

Characteristics	ZSU-23-4	M163 Vulcan (SP) 60
Armament	4–23 mm guns (liquid cooled)	6-barrel, 20-mm Gatling (air cooled)
Tactical Range (Meters)	2500 with optics, 3000 with radar (Estimated 1300 effective range)	1500
Cyclic Rate of Fire (Rds/min)	1050 (per barrel)	1000–3000 (selectable)
Muzzle Velocity (m/sec)	930–970	1039
Ammunition	API-T, HEI-T	HEI, HEIT-SD
Radar Range (mm)	20 (Search mode) 18 (Track mode)	5 (Range only)
Fire Control (m/sec)	Optical speed ring, Periscope sight, GUN DISH Radar & Computer	Range only Radar Gyro Lead computing sight Sight current generator

SOURCES: *Jane's Weapons Systems, 1981–1982* (London: Jane's); *U.S. Army Weapons Systems, 1985*; Richard O'Neill, *Guide to the Weapons of the U.S. Army* (New York: ARCO, 1984); and Ray Bonds, *Weapons of the Modern Soviet Ground Forces* (New York: ARCO, 1981).

bomber. While air-to-ground missiles such as the American Shrike may be effective against the larger targets presented by stationary SAM-2 and SAM-3 bases, it is doubtful whether they will be very effective or not against far larger numbers of small, mobile SAM-6s and SAM-7s dispersed all over the place. Neither is it certain that electronic countermeasures will solve the problem, because at least some of the recently introduced missiles can be guided optically or carry infrared homing devices that are immune to jamming.[37]

This instant analysis, however, was wrong in regard to both the overall conduct of the air battle and in regard to the SA-6 and SA-7. Later studies showed the SA-6 and SA-7 accounted for less than ten and four percent respectively of the Israeli planes that were shot down. The SA-6 was not small, given its associated radars and C³ links, although it was mobile and turned out to be deployed in small numbers.

TABLE 2.19   Changes in Arab and Israeli Surface-to-Air Missile Launcher Strength:
1967–1980

	May 1967	Sept. 1973	Aug. 1974	Estimated 1980
A. Israel				
HAWK	50	75	102	200
Improved HAWK/SAM-D	0	0	0	50
Chaparral	0	0	12	50
Total	50	75	120	300
B. Egypt and Syria				
SA-2	200	495	525	840
SA-3	0	170	290	320
SA-6	0	100	140	260
SA-7, -8, -9	0	765	1,195	1,505
Total	200	1,630	2,150	2,925
C. Egypt				
SA-2	200	420	450	600
SA-3	0	220	240	240
SA-6	0	40	60	160
SA-7,-8,-9	0	600	90	1,000
Total	200	1,280	1,550	2,000
D. Syria				
SA-2	0	75	75	240
SA-3	0	50	50	80
SA-6	0	60	80	100
SA-7, -8, -9	0	165	395	505
Total	0	350	600	925
E. Jordan				
HAWK	0	0	0	24
Improved HAWK/SAM-D	0	0	0	0
Chaparral	0	0	0	12
Total	0	0	0	36

SOURCES: *Jane's Weapons Systems, 1981–1982* (London: Jane's); IISS, *Military Balance*, various editions (London: International Institute for Strategic Studies); and General Dynamics, *The World's Missile Systems*, various editions.

As Israel proved in 1982, it could be suppressed by using proper tactics and preparation. The SA-7 damaged a number of Israeli aircraft but rarely to the point that they were unable to return to their home base successfully. Furthermore, as the war progressed, the Israelis became more and more adept at using flares to distract the infrared guidance system of the SA-7 Grail. The SA-7's most useful function then became to disrupt IAF attack runs rather than shoot them down.

TABLE 2.20 Performance Characteristics of U.S. and Soviet Surface-to-Air Missiles Used During the October War

Characteristics	SA-2	SA-3	SA-6	HAWK
Max. Effective Range (km)	22	28–41	32	50
Max. Effective Altitude (ft.)	90,000	60,000	35,000	45,000
Min. Effective Range (km)	7.4–9.3	3–5.5	3.7–5.6	2.5
Min. Effective Altitude (ft.)	500–1,000	300	100	Radar Level
Total Flight Time (sec.)	67	35–40	40–50	90
Max. Vel. (MACH)	4.2	3.4	2.5	2.5
Reaction Time (sec.)	10–25	10–25	10–30	30
Reload Time (min.)	3–7	5	10	10–15
Warhead (lbs.)	420	140 HE	124 HE	110
Rate of Fire (sec.)	2 Msls in SALVO. 6 sec. interval	2 Msls in SALVO. 5 sec. interval	2–3 Msls in SALVO. Separated by 4–6 sec.	Ripple fire 1 Msl every 5 sec. SALVO fire 2 msls every 5–6 sec.
Guidance and Control	Command (Lead Angle or 3 Point)	Command (3 Point and Lead Angle)	Semi-active homing	Semi-active homing
Simultaneous Engagement	1 engagement at a time with 3 missiles	1 engagement at a time with 2 missiles	1 engagement at a time with 2 or 3 missiles	2 engagements at a time

SOURCES: *Jane's Weapons Systems, 1981–1982* (London: Jane's); *U.S. Army Weapons Systems, 1985*; Richard O'Neill, *Guide to the Weapons of the U.S. Army* (New York: ARCO, 1984); and Ray Bonds, *Weapons of the Modern Soviet Ground Forces* (New York: ARCO, 1981).

TABLE 2.21 Performance Characteristics of the SA-7, Redeye, and Chaparral

Characteristics	SA-7	Redeye	Chaparral
Max. Effective Range (km)	3.7	4.1	6
Max. Effective Altitude (ft.)	9–10,000	8,838	9,843
Min. Effective Range (m)	15	500	800
Min. Effective Altitude (ft.)	0–50	0	49.2
Total Flight Time (sec.)	12.4	17[a]	24
Engagement Aspect	Tail Chase Only	Tail Chase Only	Tail Chase Only
Warhead (lbs.)	2.6 (0.78 HE)	2.5 (0.87 HE)	25 (6.5 HE)
Max Velocity (MACH)	1.4	1.7	2.22
Reaction Time (sec.)	4–5	10	9
Rate of Fire (sec.)	25	NA	9
Guidance and Control	Passive infra-red homing, using uncooled lead sulfide detection	Proportional navigation guidance and infrared heat-seeking and passive homing	Proportional navigation guidance and infrared heat-seeking and passive homing

[a]Missile self-destructs at 17 seconds.

SOURCES: *Jane's Weapons Systems, 1981–1982* (London: Jane's); *U.S. Army Weapons Systems, 1985*; Richard O'Neill, *Guide to the Weapons of the U.S. Army* (New York: ARCO, 1984); Ray Bonds, *Weapons of the Modern Soviet Ground Forces* (New York: ARCO, 1981); IISS, *Military Balance*, various editions (London: International Institute for Strategic Studies); and General Dynamics, *The World's Missile Systems*, various editions.

To summarize, surface-to-air missiles had the following impact on the fighting:

- Arab SAMs did sharply degrade the effectiveness of IAF attack sorties.
- It is now estimated that 2,000 to 3,000 SA-2/3/6s were fired, or 50 to 75 missiles per aircraft killed.
- There were only about 100 SA-6 launchers versus 480 SA-2/3 launchers.

TABLE 2.22 Summary of Strengths and Weaknesses of Hawk and SA-6 Systems

	HAWK	SA-6
Strengths	- Greater range by a factor of two. - Range is 32 km and altitude is 45,000 feet. - Believed to be less vulnerable to ECM. - Good low-altitude capability. - Ripple-fire capability. - Can engage two targets simultaneously.	- Greater mobility; faster reaction time. - Automatic data link. - Shorter emplacement/displacement time—10–15 min. - Good low-altitude capability. No visible missile contrail. Built-in CBR protection and warning. - No signal required from ground to missile. - High acceleration. - 10–30 second reaction time.
Weaknesses	- Less mobile. - Vulnerable to attack due to reliance on cables between units. - Acquisition radar of uncertain reliability. - Requires greater number of vehicles per fire unit. - Cannot track slow-speed helicopters. - Longer emplacement/displacement time—30 minutes. - Visible exhaust trail. - 30-second reaction time.	- Shorter range—15–28 km; ceiling is 35,000 feet. - Transporter and erector soft targets and easily put out of action. - Only one illuminating radar per battalion. Unit inoperative if put out of action. - Vulnerable to ECM. - Uncertain system reliability and effectiveness.
Comments	- Improved HAWK has better reaction time. Allows manual or fully automatic fire. - It has built-in test equipment, improved medium- and low-altitude radar and better ECM resistance. - Its certified round is much more reliable. - Range is improved to 40 km and altitude to 55,000 feet.	- Should not be compared to HAWK in Soviet forces. Soviet Army units use a mix of SA-6s and other missiles.
Improved Hawk	- Reaction time reduced from 30 to 11 seconds. - Can displace by echelon, one unit firing while others move. - Can track slow-speed helicopters.	

SOURCES: *Jane's Weapons Systems, 1981–1982* (London: Jane's); IISS, *Military Balance*, various editions (London: International Institute for Strategic Studies); and General Dynamics, *The World's Missile Systems*, various editions.

- Some 5,000 SA-7 shoulder-launched SAMs were fired but killed only 30 to 33 IAF aircraft. This is a probability of kill (P_K) of about 0.1 percent.
- HAWK achieved about one kill for every three HAWK missiles fired.
- HAWK produced 15 to 25 times more kills per round fired than the SA-2/3/6 systems.
- Even though kill rates were low, the Arabs were pleased at the way their Soviet SAMs kept the IAF at bay.

Air Suppression of Ground- or Sea-Based Air Defenses

Turning to the air war, both sides faced the following conditions:

- No real time reconnaissance was available to either side. This was a critical limitation.
- Israel had good air-defense air control but poor attack-mission control. The Arabs lacked effective control for either mission.
- Each side's aircraft were roughly equivalent in air-to-air maneuver capability. The Israeli aircraft had superior guns and avionics.
- Israel had advanced air-to-air missiles. The Arabs had only the low-performance Soviet Atoll.
- The F-4E and A-4 had superior attack-mission performance to that of any Soviet aircraft in Arab hands.
- The Israelis had superior attack ordnance but could not use ASMs in significant numbers or make effective use of cluster munitions.
- For a variety of reasons, the IAF did not make effective use of its ECM and defense-suppression aids.

It was the emergence of a massive, integrated SAM and AA gun air-defense network in Egypt and Syria, rather than the sudden deployment of the SA-6 and ZSU-23-4, that forced the Israeli air force to switch its first priority from counter-air to counter-SAM. In 1967, the IAF achieved immediate air superiority and could concentrate its subsequent attacks on ground forces. In 1973, however, the IAF was compelled to concentrate on SAM-suppression tasks after its initial efforts at close air support and interdiction were countered by forward air defenses. While Table 2.23 shows it achieved a high level of kills, the suppression effort took so long that much of the IAF's air superiority could not be brought to bear.

From 18 to 22 October, the IAF engaged in a systematic effort to

TABLE 2.23 Destruction of SAM Sites

| | IAF | | | Ground | | Total |
	Destroyed	Damaged	Total	Action	Total	Deployed
Egypt	32	11	43	11	54	150
Syria	3	5	8	1	9	65
Total	35	16	51	12	63	215

SOURCE: *Defence Update* (No. 42), p. 19, and data from the *Born in Battle* series (Tel Aviv: Eshel-Dramit).

eliminate the Syrian air-defense system. This initially was very effective against Israeli aircraft and had seriously disrupted their effectiveness in close air support missions. The IAF had some success, but many of the SAM sites on the Syrian front remained intact at considerable loss to Israeli aircraft.[38] In one case, six Phantoms were lost in one day against a battery of Soviet SAMs. This forced the IAF to avoid many of these sites.[39] Nevertheless, up to 50 percent of the Syrian SAM sites were still knocked out or were forced to relocate around Damascus, leaving armored units vulnerable to air attacks.[40]

The Israeli attack on the Syrian missile batteries was hurriedly organized after its close air support missions encountered stiff air defense protecting Syrian troops in the Golan Heights area. Israeli Skyhawks and Phantoms attacked the Syrian missile batteries with rocket bombs and cannon fire in a four-day battle with only limited planning and comparatively poor targeting and control battle management. Although the IAF had the U.S. ECM gear to counter the SA-2 and SA-3, its pilots were not really trained in its use because of security reasons.

The IAF attempted to use such gear to fly around the edges of Syrian and Egyptian SAM sites rather than directly overfly them at the proper altitude. The IAF also encountered serious problems because it could not locate many Syrian and Egyptian SA-6 missiles. Further, even when it did locate them, it lacked the central battle management to properly brief its pilots. Although the Soviet SA-2 and SA-3 eventually were countered by electronic countermeasures once the IAF properly adjusted its equipment and briefed its pilots, such tactics were not consistently successful. The IAF also had only moderate success in improving countermeasures for the SA-6, which imparted comparatively heavy casualties with its much greater speed (Mach 2.8) and accuracy. The Israeli efforts to destroy these SAM sites had to rely primarily on conventional bombing tactics and U.S. Shrike missiles.

The IAF used similar tactics on the Egyptian front. The IAF began by approaching targets in the north from the direction of the Mediterranean, attacking the air defense system in the Port Said complex. The IAF eventually destroyed 43 sites between 18 and 22 October 1973.

The IAF attacks against the SAM networks utilized conventional bombs and anti-radar weaponry and ECM. Even with considerable technical and operational improvements in the IAF's use of ECM and attack profiles, the IAF faced a massive challenge in trying to destroy 170 Egyptian missile, radar, and air-defense control centers. In general, the IAF attacks utilized tactics of mass simultaneous attack and low-level ingress tactics. They also increasingly used electronic countermeasures, conventional ASMs, and anti-radar missile capabilities. The full SAM-suppression effort was only successful, however, when the arrival of ground forces on the West Bank allowed IDF ground forces to capture or destroy many of the bases with tanks, artillery fire, or direct infantry assault.[41]

The attacks on Egyptian missiles were particularly difficult because they had to be conducted against well-prepared and hardened positions on ridges overlooking the canal area with some mobile facilities moving with the 2nd and 3rd Corps in the Sinai. These mobile batteries were vulnerable to electronic warfare attacks because they utilized radio links for communication instead of land lines. In addition, SA-6 site communication was open to intervention from high points captured by the IDF and from its ELINT bases in the Hashiba.

In order to improve aircraft protection against SAMs, the IAF attempted to rig chaff dispensers from the airbrake compartment of its fighters. This jerry-built tactic did not work effectively and symbolizes the poor level of readiness and high-technology capability in the IAF when the war began. The Israelis had ample warning of Egyptian SAM radar developments in the 1969–1970 War of Attrition, and an adequate chaff dispenser should have been developed in the interim. Nevertheless, the final attacks which smashed the Egyptian SAM sites were combined arms operations, with artillery often playing a key role in massing firepower and the aircraft locating, harassing, and ultimately destroying the sites with conventional bombs and rockets.

The IAF also made extensive attempts to counter the SAM missiles with aerial maneuvers. These efforts drew on experience from the Canal War and the Vietnam War, where the same basic F-4 aircraft confronted many of the same missile systems. The IAF used a modified high-G, split-S evasive dive-to-the-deck tactic but often had disappointing results. The pilots who survived the missiles were vulnerable to the anti-aircraft cannon, e.g., the ZSU-23-4, as they flattened out. This limited the effectiveness of counter-SAM strikes as well as other bombing operations.

This situation was eased, however, after the arrival of new supplies of weapons from the U.S. American air-to-surface missiles did not provide a true stand-off capability, but they greatly increased the survivability and lethality of a given sortie. One example of this was the use of television-guided bombs, such as the U.S.-supplied Walleye which proved to be about 80 to 90 percent accurate in hitting either a target or a nearby high contrast area.

It is important to stress, however, that the IAF vastly increased its problems through its failure to project the full implications of the Canal War of 1970 and to consider Arab capabilities rather than its estimate of Arab readiness and intentions. The IAF went into the 1973 fighting with excellent aircraft and squadrons, but it was a low-technology air force with poor C^3I capabilities in every area but air-to-air combat. It came out of the war committed to advanced technology, electronic warfare, and C^3I, all of which it applied in 1982. This serves as an important lesson in both the importance of SAM suppression and in the relative value of high-cost/advanced-technology air forces.

Air-to-Air Combat

Israel achieved consistent victories in air combat in the October War but experienced substantial difficulty in gaining air superiority. The IAF was forced to deal with other aspects of the air war first. The sheltering of Egyptian and Syrian airfields coupled to heavy SAM defenses also denied Israel many of the traditional benefits of air superiority.

The October War also involved a larger scale air-to-air combat than previous Arab-Israeli wars. Although reports on the number of air-to-air combat kills vary by source, there is no question regarding the superiority of Israeli aircraft and pilots in this war. The IAF carried out a large number of combat patrols aimed at involving enemy aircraft in air combat.

Israel flew about 4,000 air-defense sorties during the war, or roughly one-third of all the sorties it flew in combat. About 30 percent were flown by F-4Es; 65 percent were flown by Mirage IIIs or Vs; and a few were flown by A-4s or Super Mysteres which had to be committed in an emergency. This compares with a maximum of 10,000 Arab sorties in all types of missions—and as few as 3,800—although the Egyptians claimed to have flown some 6,815 operational sorties during the war. While the figures involved are uncertain, Israel seems to have flown about four times as many sorties per day per combat fighter as Egypt and six to eight times more sorties than Syria.[42]

In comparison to the Six Day War, where the number of air-to-air combats was reduced due to the destruction of the major part of the Arab air forces on the ground, the Yom Kippur War saw over 117 separate air engagements—with 65 over Syrian and 52 over Egyptian territory—involving over 450 aircraft. Ironically, Israel also achieved a higher kill ratio in 1973 than it did in 1967. While Israel's air-to-air kill ratio was 10:1 in the Six Day War, with complete air supremacy, its ratio grew to nearly 20:1 during the War of Attrition. In the Yom Kippur air battles, the IAF kill ratio reached 18.4:1. Israel downed 277 enemy aircraft while losing only six. The largest air battles took place on 8 and 19 October. On these days, the IAF lost only two pilots.[43]

Table 2.24 shows in part that Egyptian and Syrian air forces lacked the training of their IAF counterparts and maintained a low profile during the early stages of the war to preserve their strength. They initially only flew sporadic sorties in offensive roles, and these initially were coordinated with SAM units to avoid hitting friendly planes. Nevertheless, an incredibly high number of Egyptian planes were downed by Egyptian SAMs.

In general, air-to-air combat was characterized by traditional dogfight maneuvers with pilots using both air-to-air missiles and cannons. These aerial combat encounters were decided largely on the basis of superior pilot selection and training rather than fighter or missile technology, an area of decided Israeli superiority. The Israelis did, however, have superior avionics and air-to-air missiles, and this provided a substantial margin of difference. Most air-to-air kills were made with Sidewinder and Shafrir missiles, although the cannons also made a substantial contribution.[44]

Other estimates indicate that about 25 percent of all Israeli air-to-air kills were by Aim-9D and Aim-9G; about 40 percent were by Shafrir missiles; less than 5 percent were by AIM-7E radar-guided missiles; and about 30 percent were by guns and cannons. Estimates of kills per missile fired are very uncertain, but some Israeli sources claim about 50 percent kills per missile launched.

The primary Israeli fighter aircraft used in aerial combat were the French Mirage III and U.S. F-4. The Mirage III was re-engined with a General Electric J79 power plant, and Israel made its own version of the Mirage III, called the "Nester" fighter. These aircraft provided air cover and accounted for most of the Arab MiGs destroyed in aerial

TABLE 2.24 Comparison of Egyptian and Israeli Training Programs

	Egyptian		Israeli	
	Hours	*Length (wks.)*	*Hours*	*Length (wks.)*
Preflight	18	23	10	32
Primary	65	20	80	16
Basic	80	24	80	16
Totals	163	67	170	64
Advanced		12 to 16[a]	80	16
Annual	60 to 72[b]	52	200	52

[a]Does not include combat crew training.
[b]Programmed training is 150 to 180 hours per year, with 100 hours per year minimum; 60 to 72 hours per year is the actual time flown prior to the October 1973 war.

SOURCES: David Eshel, *The Israeli Air Force* (Tel Aviv: Eshel-Dramit, 1978); Trevor Dupuy, *Elusive Victory* (New York: Harper and Row, 1978), pp. 584–638.

combat. Although the F-4 also shared the air superiority role, it was used primarily as a strike aircraft against airfields and other interdiction targets. A comparison of the F-4 and MiG-21 is shown in Table 2.25.

The exact role of the Phantom and Mirage III in the 1973 war is not clear. Although the Israelis could be expected to exaggerate the use of their own aircraft, i.e., Israeli Aviation Industries developed versions of the Mirage III, it is unlikely that the Israelis identified that strongly with the Mirage of 1973.[45]

The IAF clearly benefited from superior air-to-air missile technology. The impact of aircraft avionics is uncertain. The IAF's French- and U.S.-designed fighters had far superior avionics to those of the Soviet-made fighters in Arab air forces. Nevertheless, the IDF was not a high technology air force. It trained and organized for close-in, air-to-air combat, using many of the close-formation techniques the U.S. had refined in Vietnam. As a result, the IAF again suffered from the same problems which surfaced in the Canal War, i.e., the War of Attrition. IAF pilots were not sufficiently familiar with their aircraft avionics to make optimal use of them. Although this was not necessarily critical in dogfighting, it had an important impact on air combat operations involving the use of ECM and the

TABLE 2.25 Summary Comparison of Major Advantages and Disadvantages of U.S. and Soviet Combat Aircraft

I. F4E vs. Fishbed J Export (MIG-21JI)

| F4E | | FISHBED J | |
ADVANTAGE	DISADVANTAGE	ADVANTAGE	DISADVANTAGE
1. Longer Range	1. Unreliable UHF Radio	1. Higher Sortie Rate	1. Poor Cockpit visibility
2. Greater Payload	2. Higher Maintenance man hours per flying hour	2. Small Size with with low visual or radar detectability	2. Poor close in missiles (ATOLL)
3. Air-to-Air Standoff (AIM 7)	3. Engine Smoke trail		3. No standoff missiles
4. Longer Range Radar			4. Short Range Radar
5. Air-Air Refueling			5. Very Dependent on GCI for Positioning
6. More Accurate Fire Control System			6. Unreliable ejector seat

A4 Versus Fitter B (SU 17)

ADVANTAGE	DISADVANTAGE	ADVANTAGE	DISADVANTAGE
1. Greater Payload	1. Slower	1. Speed	1. Poor cockpit visibility
2. Better Avionics and Fire Control			2. Acute vulnerability to Hits.
			3. Unreliable ejector seat

SOURCES: Chris Chant, *Military Aircraft of the World* (Novato, Calif.: Presidio, 1981), pp. 132–8, 147–60, and 194–6; Bill Sweetman, *Soviet Military Aircraft* (Novato, Calif.: Presidio, 1981), pp. 87–100 and 142–9; and Bill Gunston, *Israeli Air Force* (New York: ARCO, 1982), pp. 100–112, and *Modern Soviet Air Force* (New York: ARCO, 1982), pp. 62–70 and 92–6.

exploitation of the full range and performance characteristics of missile systems.

Another problem in air combat was that Israeli pilots were often forced to dodge surface-to-air missiles in the midst of aerial duels. Although Egyptian SAM units were supposedly turned off when the Egyptian air force was operating in the area, the IAF assumed that a few missiles would be unleashed by accident or for harassment purposes in the midst of an air duel. The validity of this threat was evidenced by the high numbers of EAF aircraft shot down by Egyptian SAMs.

The total pattern of air losses during the 1973 fighting is shown in Tables 2.26 and 2.27. The numbers in these figures show the basic asymmetry in the losses of each side. Israel lost 42 of 102 aircraft to surface-to-air missiles, or about 41 percent. Almost all were lost to crew-served missiles. Only 3 to 5 were lost to SA-7s. In contrast, Israel lost 3 aircraft in air-to-air combat—a ratio of 10 to 1 in favor of SAMs. If one includes all losses to ground weapons, the IAF lost 75 aircraft, of which 26 were definitely AA kills and 6 could have been SAMs or AA guns. This is a total ratio of ground versus air-to-air kills of 25 to 1.

In contrast, the Arab forces lost 22 aircraft to Hawk surface-to-air missiles and 78 to unguided Israeli AA guns. This is a total of 100 aircraft versus 261 in air-to-air combat, a ratio of 1 to 2.5, not counting 73 Arab aircraft forced into the ground, premature ejection, etc. This pattern illustrates the difficulties the IAF experienced in making use of its air-to-air superiority. It took not only a considerable amount of time for the IAF to win such superiority, but even after it was achieved, it did not give Israel freedom of action in attacking ground targets.

The data in Tables 2.26 and 2.27, however, are misleading in several ways. They do not provide any picture of the number of air-to-ground attack sorties degraded by Arab surface-to-air and air-to-air forces, although it is clear that these had a powerful effect in reducing the impact of the IAF on the land battle. The data also are strongly biased in favor of medium to heavy SAM kills from the SA-2, SA-3, and SA-6. After-action studies showedthat IAF pilots and officers tended to credit the heavier SAMs, and particularly the SA-6, whenever doubt arose over the source of a kill. Postwar damage studies indicated that the SA-7 and AA weapons accounted for a much higher proportion of total air losses.

This latter pattern is important for several reasons. The other wars under study also indicate that modern air forces tend to concentrate too much on the suppression of medium to heavy SAMs and underestimate the impact of SHORADS. As will be seen shortly, it also helps explain why fighters are far less effective and accurate in actual air-to-ground

TABLE 2.26 Air Losses in the October War, 1973

	Israel	Arab Total	Egypt	Syria	Iraq	Other Arabs
Fighter	103	390	222	117	21	30
Bomber		1	1			
Transport		1		1		
Helicopter	6	55	42	13		
Totals	109	447	265	131	21	30
Air-to-Air	21	287				
To SAM	40	17				
To AAA	31	19				
Misc. or Unknown	15	66				
Friendly Forces	2	58				
Totals	109	447				
Damaged	236	125				
Repaired in One Week	215	UNKNOWN				

SOURCE: Adapted from Trevor Dupuy, *Elusive Victory* (New York: Harper and Row, 1978), p. 609.

combat than their theoretical delivery accuracy, munitions lethality, and test-range performance would indicate.

Close Air Support

On the Israeli side, close air support was one of the most problematical areas of the war, and it has been the focus of on-going controversy in Israel since 1973. The general criticism of CAS was that it failed to achieve anything approaching a lethality or impact proportionate to the effort and resources involved; bombs did not fall close enough to their target; the coordination between attack aircraft and army units was poor to ineffective; and losses of personnel and aircraft to Arab anti-aircraft defenses and friendly forces made the costs to Israel intolerable for the advantage gained.

The IAF flew a massive strike and close air support effort. Israel flew some 7,300 attack/strike sorties out of a total of 11,200, or roughly 65 percent of all the sorties it flew during the 1973 fighting. Roughly 2,200 sorties, or 20 percent of all sorties flown, were by F-4Es. About 130 to 140, or one percent of all sorties, were by Mirages. About 600 to 640 sorties or about 6 percent were flown by Super Mysteres, and about 4,200 to 4,300 or 65 percent were flown by A-4s. Israel also achieved an outstandingly high sorties rate. Its F-4Es averaged 1.9 to 2.1 sorties per

TABLE 2.27 Aircraft Lost in Combat

| | 1967–1973 Losses | | | | | |
| | Air-to-Air | | Ground-to-Air | | Total | |
	'67–'73	'73	'67–'73	'73	'67–'73	'73
Israeli AF	2	15	15	77	27	107
Egyptian/Syrian AF	125	334	37[a]	97[b]	162	453

1973 Israeli Air Force Losses					
SA-2,3,6	SA-7	AAA	Air-to-Air	Unknown	Total
40	6	31	15	17	109

IAF Losses in the Bekaa Valley					
SA-2,3,6	SA-7	AAA	Air-to-Air	Unknown	Total
0	1	0	0	NA	1

[a]13 were lost to Hawk missiles.
[b]25 were lost to Hawk missiles.
SOURCES: James Peak, *Air Superiority and Airfield Attack: Lessons from History*, BDM Report (May 1982), prepared for the Defense Nuclear Agency, quoted in *Armed Forces Journal International* (March 1983), p. 80. The category "ground-to-air" was mistakenly published as "air-to-ground" in the article. The total figure of 107 includes 15 to 23 aircraft which were lost from unknown factors. The figures on losses from the Lebanon war are from work done by Lt. Col. Grey Swanson.

day; its Mirages flew 2.1 to 2.4 sorties; its Super Mysteres flew 2.2 to 2.6 sorties; and its A-4s flew 1.3 to 1.5 sorties. There is no doubt that IAF CAS operations were less effective in 1973 than in 1967 because the Egyptians and the Syrians chose to shield their initial offensive operations in areas protected by surface-to-air missiles. According to one source, 30 to 40 percent of the close air support sorties the IAF flew were lost to ground defenses in the first 72 hours of combat.[46] According to this report, 30 A-4s and several F-4s were lost in the first afternoon of battle. Eventually, Major General Peled, the Israeli Air Force Commander, ordered Israeli planes to keep 15 miles away from the Suez Canal in order to keep losses at a manageable level. The Israelis then turned their air force against ground targets in support of troops engaged in the Golan Heights.[47]

More was involved, however, than improved Arab air defenses. The IAF simply was not ready for the scale of the war that took place. The Israelis initially responded to a call for air support with sporadic air strikes on Egyptian forces about two hours after the war began on 6 October 1973 at 2:00 P.M. This response was essentially a token effort by a few alert aircraft in the Sinai. Israeli fighters were not prepared for emergency close air support missions of the type and scale necessary to destroy an invading army.

Israeli fighter aircraft were trained to be called in to deliver simple, short-range attack sorties at undefended ground-force targets. Instead they encountered massive Arab forces and heavy air-defense resistance from a barrage of missiles and guns. These included the SA-2, SA-3, the new SA-6, SA-7 Strellas, unguided AA guns, and the new radar-directed ZSU-23-4. At least half the attacking Israeli planes were shot down in this initial engagement and the more forceful attacks a few hours later.

The Israeli pilots and aircraft, mainly the A-4 Skyhawk and the F-4 Phantom, fought tenaciously in an extremely dangerous and confusing environment. "The IAF lost about 115 aircraft, almost all of them due to ground air defense, including 12 Dassault Brequet Mirage 3s, 35 F-4s, 55 A-4s, 6 Dassault Super Mysteres, and a half dozen helicopters."[48]

The IAF's night attacks against the Egyptian beachhead on 6 and 7 October were extremely risky and difficult, and it became clear that the Israelis were largely unprepared to use a new dimension in air warfare: the ground-launched PGM. Most of the attacks were poorly targeted, and many had little technical hope of success. The IAF had no central attack command to allocate sorties, analyze losses to air defenses, or manage the air battle. The emphasis remained in the west, from the initiation of the conflict until 8 October, with the IAF flying support missions for the beleaguered Israeli strongpoints along the Bar-Lev Line and other army units as well as interdiction missions against bridges and SAM sites along the Suez Canal.

On 8 and 9 October the IAF shifted to the close air support role against Syrian armored formations. Once again, however, attack sortie targeting and lethality were poor and the air-defense screen took heavy casualties in Israeli aircraft. Unfortunately for the IAF, however, there was no alternative to very risky, very costly operations. It is also clear from Arab sources that air support had more shock effect on the Syrian attacks, which were less well organized than the Egyptians, and played an important role in stopping the Syrian breakthrough. On the other hand, it is clear that the IAF had only limited success in killing Syrian armor.

Once the initial Syrian and Egyptian armored thrusts were halted by Israeli ground forces, the IAF's emphasis on close air support was shifted toward efforts to achieve air superiority, first by suppressing the SAM sites and finally by destroying the Arab air forces in air-to-air combat. By this time, however, the IAF's close air support effort was in near disarray in terms of cost effectiveness, tactical confusion, and personnel morale. Aircraft were getting hit at higher altitudes by SAM missiles, i.e., SA-2s, SA-3s, and SA-6s, and by cannons and Strellas at lower altitudes. The IAF's vulnerability at low altitudes was further increased by the use of dry passes prior to actual bombing runs to ensure against hitting Israeli troops and by the lack of targeting, training, and avionics to use in lower vulnerability attack profiles.

In contrast, the Arab air forces sought to maintain a low profile until the IAF was decimated by air defenses. The Egyptian air force did fly a number of initial air strikes and some follow-on support strikes and relied heavily on the use of protective hangar facilities to survive IAF interdiction efforts. These tactics provided good protection in the early phases of the war, but once Egyptian and Syrian forces advanced beyond their full ground-based air-defense network, the Arab air forces were forced into air-to-air combat with the IAF. On the Golan front, the air battle took on a ferocious intensity and a complex layering of mission roles.

> Syrian and Iraqi air forces were active over Golan with MiG-17s and Sukhov Su-7 and Su-20 fighter-bombers attacking Israeli ground forces with great determination and Syrian MiG-21 and Iraqi Hawker Hunters tangling with top-cover Israeli Mirages. More than 70 Arab aircraft were destroyed in air battles over the SAM sites during this period. At the peak of this battle, 27 MiGs were destroyed in one day.[49]

The Egyptian air force also emerged from its hangarettes after Egyptian ground forces left their air-defense shield in counterattacks designed to relieve the pressure on Syria and were fully committed to "last ditch" CAS missions once the Israelis crossed the Suez Canal. The Egyptians employed a heavy top cover of MiG-21s to try to protect strikes against Israeli tanks and troops by their Su-7s. This last ditch effort was doomed, however, because the MiG 21s flying top cover could not compete in air-to-air battles with the IAF in the Sinai and Egypt and because the EAF's Su-7s were very poorly flown and targeted. IDF war diaries show that most of the EAF and SAF attack sorties that did penetrate the IAF had remarkably little shock or damage effect. This was partly the result of the relatively primitive attack avionics and munitions on both the Su-7 and MiG-21, but the primary problem seems to have been poor attack training and the lack of any advanced recce, FAC, or other targeting system.[50]

As has been mentioned earlier, the cumulative impact of the Arab's heavy air defense not only reduced the number of Israeli aircraft in the attack mission but sharply limited the effectiveness of those that broke through the anti-aircraft screen. Both the disruption of mental concentration resulting from being shot at and the tactical maneuvering to avoid anti-aircraft rounds were debilitating to mission effectiveness. Pilots were pressed hard to survive, and it is not surprising that they did not perform up to training standards in such an environment. Nevertheless, the resulting ineffectiveness of the IAF's close air support role in the 1973 war became a major focus of the Agranat Commission inquiry on the war.

It also became clear after the war that the IAF's attack-mission efforts suffered from a number of defects which still provide important lessons:

- The IAF's sweeping victory in 1967 had led it to take its effectiveness for granted. It failed to properly examine its actual effectiveness in CAS missions after 1967 and failed to conduct realistic exercises.
- The IAF did not change its CAS methods and tactics sufficiently following the Canal War of 1970. It dealt with Egyptian SAMs as defensive systems and did not adapt its attack methods to reflect the overall growth of Egyptian and Syrian air defenses.
- The IAF training effort concentrated on air-to-air combat and gave far less priority to air-attack training. Performance on range-firing exercises was confused with operational capability.
- The IAF failed to create an effective C^3I system for attack missions to match its system for air combat. It relied on air superiority to give its attack aircraft freedom of action and on-ground commanders to call in attack sorties with only limited central control. It was forced to create an improvised command staff after the war began and to develop tactics for planning and allocating sorties to take account of Arab SAM and other air defenses in the midst of the fog of war.
- The IAF assumed that slowly processed photo and day visual reconnaissance and ground FACs would be adequate for targeting and damage assessment. None of these assumptions proved valid. Photo reconnaissance could not be processed in time for targeting anything other than SAMs or fired targets; Arab forces moved with virtual impunity at night; and the breakdown of the IDF's mobilization system and inadequate FAC training left IDF ground forces in a poor position to provide targeting. The IDF also repeated a chronic mistake in the use of airpower. It concentrated on targeting rather than independent damage assessment, although it is a virtually universal experience that combat pilots

do not provide realistic data on the effectiveness of attack sorties. As a result, the IAF could not recalibrate its attack operations on the basis of objective data.

• While the IAF made reasonably good use of U.S.-supplied air-to-ground missiles (AGMs) under emergency conditions, these factors further contributed to a gross exaggeration of the effectiveness of AGMs in the initial months after the war. It was only substantially later that it became plain that many PGM kills against armor were actually hits against tanks which were static and visible because they had already been killed by ground weapons. Similarly, a number of PGM hits were actually missile hits against the shadow of the target and had only limited effect.

These lessons were partly the result of the IDF's failure to properly assess its enemy, but they also represent a behavioral pattern that is typical of the failure of most of the air forces in later wars to realistically prepare for combined operations. Nevertheless, the IDF did learn from its 1973 and 1967 experiences (see Table 2.28), and this helped trigger a debate over close air support that led to major changes in the way the IAF approached the 1982 conflict. This debate is reflected in part in remarks that General David Elazar, chief of staff of the Israeli Defense Force during the 1973 war, made in 1975:

I see the Air Force's main role in the support of ground forces in interdiction—to achieve destruction of the enemy's military infrastructure, cause havoc among troop movements and, in one word, to paralyze the enemy forces. Even before 1973, I considered the subject of close air support the last priority task of the air force. I always believed that ground forces, secure from the enemy's air activity, should defeat enemy ground forces unaided. The October War reconfirmed my belief that close air support is costly in casualties, and that there is no positive ratio between relatively great losses and limited results.

However, both air and ground forces must be well prepared for cooperation in the execution of air-to-ground support. There are situations when, in spite of the above-mentioned limitations, close air support is necessary and even crucial. The massing of ground-to-air missiles, and the counter and evasive actions of the planes, greatly complicate cooperation—and the lesson drawn from the last war is that the old techniques must be changed.[51]

Major General Benjamin Peled, IAF Commander during the 1973 war, made the following points concerning the close air support role:

Close air support in our definition is that type of air-to-ground operation where a ground commander assesses his own situation, evaluates that

TABLE 2.28 Airbase Attacks by the IAF in 1967 and 1973

	1967	1973
IAF Sorties Against Airfields	490	468 (at least)
Arab Aircraft Destroyed on the Ground	370	22
IAF Losses in Airbase Attacks	19	7
IAF Kill-to-Loss Ratio	19:1	3:1

SOURCES: Otto von Pikua, *Armies of the Middle East* (New York: Mayflower, 1979), pp. 22–26 and 162–168; Chaim Herzog, *The Arab-Israeli Wars* (New York: Random House, 1982), pp. 153–189 and 241–305; Col. David Eshel, *Born in Battle: The Six Day War* (Jerusalem: Eshel-Dramit, 1979), pp. 16–30; Trevor Dupuy, *Elusive Victory* (New York: Harper and Row, 1978), pp. 245–248, 333, 337, 549–553, 608–611.

he needs an air weapon to solve his immediate problem, calls for it, and gives the Air Force all the relevant data in order to get to his address. The Air Force sends a number of aircraft, and tells the commander of those aircraft to contact the ground commander and become his subordinate for the duration of the operation.

The massive destruction of ground forces was never actually carried out through that system. We also reached the conclusion that the doctrine of air-to-ground cooperation, laid down in the North African campaigns in 1941–44 by Lord Tedder and the U.S. 5th Air Force, were right for those times, but were very wrong for all other wars.

These realistic assessments came after the fact, but they are far superior to the optimistic assessments that many defense journals made after the war:

The Israeli Skyhawks protected by their Mirage and Phantom top cover did a devastating job eliminating these pockets of enemy armor. The British 30mm Aden gun, which the Israelis had substituted for the normal U.S. 20mm cannon on the Skyhawk, proved extremely effective at punching out Soviet tanks and armored personnel carriers. It was the quick strike capability of the Israeli Air Force against Egyptian tanks that made possible the lightning double sweep north to Ismailia and south to cut off Suez Canal.[52]

The IAF's experience in 1973 clearly illustrated the limits to which the Israeli air force could aid ground units without a high technology approach to close air support and extensive training in close air support. It made clear the need for an increased reliance upon electronic warfare and the early neutralization of SAMs. It forced Israel to re-define its concepts for air-ground operations in order to deal with new air-defense weapons and Arab tactics. In the post-1973 period, IAF Commander, Major General Peled, initiated very intensive research efforts on how the Arabs used SAMs and AAA. This clearly reflected Israeli concern to ensure its air superiority against an increasingly sophisticated and self-confident adversary.

As for Arab forces, it is unclear that they really expected to be effective in CAS against the IAF or learned much from the fighting. Both Egypt and Syria publicly claimed far more CAS missions were flown with far more effectiveness than was the case. Both Egyptian and Syrian officers, however, privately admitted their failures after the war with near fatalism. They did not realistically analyze their C^3I, training, and targeting failures or improve the realism of their CAS training. They generically blamed Soviet technology without analyzing the specific weaknesses in Soviet aircraft, munitions, and sensors, or correcting for such weaknesses with the assets at hand. It is interesting to note that Iraq launched air attacks on Iran in 1980 which exhibited an astounding insensitivity to the lessons of the 1973 fighting while Syria seems to have virtually abdicated any serious hope of success in 1982.

Interdiction and Long-Range Air Attack

The Israeli air force traditionally has used interdiction bombing at the preliminary and initial stages of a conflict to achieve early air superiority in both 1967 and 1982. In the October War, because the Arab air forces simply attacked first, the IAF was not properly prepared for interdiction missions and faced many of the same problems with respect to close air support. Only when the IAF was able to attack Syrian rear-area civilian targets, or Egyptian SAM sites in the latter days of the war, did IAF interdiction bombing reflect the thoroughness of planning and operational proficiency previously characteristic of the IAF in past conflicts. Unfortunately for the IAF, the air-defense screen at Egyptian SAM sites was still formidable, but it was gradually reduced by repeated attacks, from the ground and air.

The IAF attacks on Egyptian air bases had little effect once the IAF could penetrate Egypt's SAM defenses. The Egyptians managed to save most of their aircraft with hardened hangarette shelters. This furnished a clear lesson that protective hardening of aircraft shelters can minimize conventional bomb damage to aircraft and air-base facilities. The Israeli interdiction effort against Syrian airfields was more successful with several Su-7s, Su-20s, and transports destroyed on the ground. However, there was to be no repeat of the brilliant destruction of an Arab air force which preceded the June 1967 War.

The Egyptian air force did introduce, in the early phases of the war, interdiction sorties by its Tu-16 Badgers which launched Kelt cruise missiles. These attacks, however, are of little value in estimating the probable impact of modern cruise missiles. The Kelt is a slow-flying, high-radar cross section system. Of the 25 Kelts launched, all but five were destroyed by Israeli fighters and flak. One Badger was lost in these raids. Two Israeli radar sites and a supply depot were hit by Kelts.[53]

The Syrian and Egyptian air forces also attacked IAF airfields and other targets at the outset of the conflict. This attack focused on IDF command and control centers in Sinai and Golan. The Egyptians flew over 250 sorties against targets such as Refidim, Bir Tinada, Ofra, and other tactical points, i.e., Hawk missile sites, radar, artillery, and logistical areas.[54] Although these attacks had little effect in terms of physical destructiveness, they helped force the IAF to devote resources to air defense at a critical time. Ironically, the Arab air forces made strenuous efforts to avoid strikes over strongpoints defended by Hawk missiles and were considerably better prepared for the SAM threat than the IAF.

Neither side had any real strategic bombing doctrine, although the IDF immediately began such planning after the war. Israel did hit at key Syrian targets like refineries in an effort to put pressure on Syria to halt and withdraw its forces, but this was largely an ad hoc effort. The IAF also had a distinct edge in striking at rear area targets and supplies and a vast (at least 12–15:1) lead in the number of sorties against its enemy's rear areas. Most kills, however, were against low value and highly redundant supply depots and logistics movements. Few Arab sources viewed the IAF interdiction strikes as having more than a nuisance value. Virtually all concentrate almost solely on the land battle. This was in distinct contrast to 1967 but is typical of the experience in many other conflicts. Even when a multi-million dollar plane can kill one or more trucks per sortie, the military impact is usually sufficiently insignificant so that the attacked side pays relatively little attention to the result—particularly if it has learned to disperse, move at night, or reduce its logistic and rear-area vulnerability through oversupply. This highlights the potential importance of modern advanced targeting systems like the joint surveillance and target attack radar system (JSTARS) and new "smart" wide-area munitions.

Air-to-Surface Missiles

A great many claims have been made regarding the value of air-to-ground guided weapons during the 1973 war, but there is little evidence to indicate that they had a decisive impact on the battle.

The IAF only used about 175 electro-optically guided, air-to-surface weapons during the war versus about 40,000 pounds of conventional bombs. It only used about 50 Mavericks and did not acquire large stocks of U.S. PGMs until the major battles had been fought.

Various IAF sources have claimed high kill ratios (about 40 percent for the Hobo, 60 percent for the Maverick, and up to 80 percent for the Walleye). There is no way to validate all these claims, but it is important to note that the IAF only used most of these weapons under optimal conditions in terms of visibility and launch aircraft vulnerability and has made claims regarding tank kills that neither U.S. nor Egyptian sources confirm.

The IAF originally claimed about 100 PGM hits against tanks. This would be more than half of the total number of guided weapons fired, but studies of tank kills after the war indicated only three clear tank kills, two of which were killed by Rockeye. This is fewer tank kills than in the 1967 war, when Israeli fighters scored five confirmed tank kills. It is also important to note that the poor performance by Israeli fighters in killing tanks in the 1973 fighting was a major factor that led to extensive changes in weaponry, tactics, and avionics between 1973 and 1982.

The IAF did use more anti-radiation missiles, and some Israeli sources have stated that they fired nearly 200 Shrike anti-radiation missiles. There are no clear data on confirmed hits, but the IAF, after the war, only claimed about 5 to 7 percent hits per missile fired. It stressed that the main value of the Shrike was in suppressing Arab surface-to-air missiles and not in killing radars. In contrast, the Arabs claim to have fired some 26 Kelt missiles, most of which are anti-radiation missiles. As has been discussed earlier, these scored a maximum of three hits, although the claims involved are uncertain.

Air Reconnaissance, C³I, IFF, and AC&W

As in the land war, there was a much more equal contest in air C³I between the Arabs and the Israelis than previous (or subsequent) conflicts. Both the Arabs and the Israelis were assimilating foreign C³I, IFF, and AC&W technology in an essentially ad hoc manner; their training was limited, narrow, and too unrealistic to provide the mental and physical internalization of the systems available to make proper use of their technical potential. On the Arab side, not only was the technology foreign, i.e., most of the aircraft, sensors, and C^3/AC&W links were of Soviet or European origin, the traditional command structure was far too rigid and compartmentalized to provide the integration, speed of reaction, flexibility, and objectivity required. On the Israeli side, tradition, bureaucratic inertia, and military *elan* weighed in favor of the conventional emphasis on the "jet jockey" approach to flying tactics in every respect but air control and warning for air defense. This was then relatively unsophisticated and relied on broad ground control vectoring using radars with medium- to high-altitude coverage.

As has been noted earlier, the Israeli air force had no real air attack operations center until one was improvised during the war. The IAF could not conduct effective night reconnaissance missions, although many Egyptian and Syrian movements occurred during this period. The IAF also failed to make adequate use of armed reconnaissance, track Arab SAM positions properly, and process day reconnaissance data. Many recce aircraft found high-value targets, but the IAF could not process and act on the data rapidly enough to be effective. Syria fought without an effective air C^3I system, had no real air recce capability and mission planning, had no real FAC capability, and committed its aircraft to combat using poorly controlled attack sorties and simple ground controlled intercept methods that virtually threw its fighters away in the face of a far better trained and organized Israeli fighter force.

Egypt could operate the equipment the USSR had installed when it deployed Soviet SAM and C^3I units during the 1969–1970 Canal War/War of Attrition, but lacked the discipline and organization to integrate it effectively, to properly operate many systems, or use many other key items of Soviet equipment. Once Egypt had to depart from its original plans to limit its attack to the area covered by its Soviet-installed C^3I facilities and SAM systems, it could not maintain an effective matrix of air and antitank defenses, radars and other sensors, and the command and control capabilities. Egypt, like Syria, also had only a limited number of effective or lethal land-based air defense systems and no fighters with modern avionics and radars.

Helicopters

Israeli and Arab use of heliborne troops in the 1973 war demonstrated the utility of helicopters as mobile troop transports for the insertion of commando troops in rugged geography. On the other hand, there is no evidence of any use of helicopters as an attack weapons system, i.e., using the aircraft's inherent mobility and versatility in tactical attack roles.

The helicopter displayed both its strengths and weaknesses during the 1973 war. The most important of these weaknesses was the vulnerability of these helicopters when employed in an environment where the opposing force maintains air superiority. The Egyptian loss of nearly 50 commando-filled helicopters to the IAF provided a dramatic illustration of this problem. These losses also occurred in spite of the limits in IAF sensor capability. If the IAF had an airborne or low-altitude warning system at that time, it is probable that the IAF could have destroyed enough helicopters to have eliminated the commandos as a significant factor in the combat.

The commandos that did penetrate the Israeli defenses were far more successful than their numbers would normally indicate. Individuals were able to ambush Israeli reinforcements, lay mines, destroy supply centers, and wipe out Israeli artillery. They were responsible for inflicting significant disruption and damage on the IDF. This strongly suggests the utility of such air-mobile operations under circumstances where the helicopters can be provided with some reasonable degree of protection.

In contrast, the IDF made only limited use of helicopters, primarily because key military personnel felt that they were too vulnerable to ground fire if they flew too low, but vulnerable to air defense networks if they flew too high or too slowly. As a consequence, the IDF used helicopters in a limited and unsystematic fashion, typically for the evacuation of wounded or the retrieval of downed pilots, rather than for tactical airlift or combat missions. The IDF helicopters were used for C^2 and reconnaissance but only in limited circumstances for resupply and troop delivery.[55]

Combined Operations

The most interesting aspect of Arab combined operations was the use of SAM systems to protect ground forces against air attack. The value of such defenses was illustrated when Egyptian forces moved out of the range of their missile umbrella. This enabled Israeli air and armored forces to conduct their most successful combined operations against those forces. On 10 October, for example, an Egyptian armored brigade was almost wiped out by joint efforts of the Israeli armored corps and air force.[56] Lt. General Shazly used this incident as a reason to oppose further moves out of the range of the air-defense missiles. According to Shazly: "Swift armored thrusts with close air support against unprepared men was the sort of war at which the Israelis excelled."[57]

Logistics and Support

Logistical and maintenance capability had a critical impact on the course of the war. In particular, the Israeli ability to repair damaged tanks and return them to combat played an important role in keeping the Israeli military functioning at a high level of proficiency. Repaired tanks represented an important element of combat strength in many cases and helped the Israelis to turn the tables on the Arabs. On the other hand, some Arab (and especially Syrian) tanks that were abandoned could have been quickly and effectively repaired in the rear area of the battlefield had the Arabs made a better effort in this regard.

The Israelis focused on getting U.S. resupply of key munitions and armaments. The delivery of some 73 to 76 new U.S. fighters during the war was critical to allowing the IAF to continue to press its attacks home in the face of considerable losses. In contrast, most U.S. deliveries of armor only arrived after the war, although the fact these deliveries were on the way again allowed Israel to commit its forces in spite of significant losses. The total U.S. deliveries of such armor eventually totaled around 175 tanks, 50 artillery pieces, and about 250 APCs.

The U.S. resupply effort also helped Israel in a number of other ways. A few tanks were delivered by air to provide Israeli forces with a major lift in morale. The U.S. helped with strategic reconnaissance and by rushing technical assistance in electronic warfare to help Israel deal with the new threat posed by Soviet surface-to-air missiles. The U.S. rushed in new types of air-to-ground missiles, including optically guided systems and TOW antitank guided missiles. Egyptian experts also charge that the U.S. rushed tanks by sea to El Arish on 10 and 11 October and provided U.S. air cover during the off-loading of these tanks. While such reports are uncertain, the fact that Egypt believed a major resupply effort took place during the war certainly affected its willingness to counterattack.

In contrast, the USSR demonstrated that it could rapidly assemble and move large amounts of both aircraft and armor to Egypt and Syria. Egypt and Syria got about 175 new fighters with about 50 going to Syria. They got nearly 500 tanks, with about 300 going to Egypt, and they got about 50 artillery pieces and 100 APCs. In fact, the USSR provided roughly three times the total number of tanks during the fighting that the U.S. eventually supplied to Israel after the fighting. It also supplied roughly twice the amount of fighter aircraft. Further, the USSR sent massive additional amounts of munitions, including surface-to-surface missiles. These latter shipments were important because the Egyptians and Syrians rapidly depleted their missile stocks during the early days of the fighting. This provides a powerful lesson regarding the advantages the USSR gains through its massive weapons stocks and large production base.

It is also important to note, however, that the Egyptians were far less happy with the Soviet resupply effort during the war than Western sources estimated at the time. The initial Soviet deliveries consisted largely of equipment that had been scheduled for delivery long before the war. Many of the initial shipments did nothing to help the Egyptians cope with their critical needs and shortfalls. As a result, the Egyptians were far more impressed with the limited deliveries of high-technology equipment provided by the U.S. during its airlift to Israel than with the high volume of Soviet shipments, few of which met their combat needs.

More generally, the IDF proved to have made a serious error in underestimating its munitions needs and rate of equipment losses, although Egypt and Syria made the same mistake. Both sides were forced to seek "crash" resupply efforts from the U.S. and USSR. The most critical of all these deliveries were the U.S. shipments of munitions. Israel had only 7 to 15 days of munitions supplies when the war began and had given its logistics units a low readiness and mobilization priority. Coupled to poor fire discipline, this rapidly led to ammunition shortages, supply bottlenecks, and desperate pleas for air resupply from the U.S. The prewar lack of logistics readiness also led to poor maintenance or supply of mobilizable combat equipment and imposed additional problems in the form of Israel's limited war reserves of equipment. This could have been crippling if the U.S. had not rapidly responded to the IDF's requests—which allowed them to take the risk of consuming their munitions long before U.S. resupply actually arrived—and if the IDF had not had the flexibility to improvise improved logistics management and use combat unit vehicles for self resupply.

As has been noted earlier, the Egyptians and Syrians had built up massive forward-supply depots. They also followed the Soviet model of using up combat units rather than sustaining and resupplying them. This greatly reduced their logistics management problems as well as their logistics vulnerability—a strength Iraq exhibited in the Iran-Iraq War. In contrast, Israel had let its mobilization and depot system decline and this gave the Arabs a significant advantage. Over 300 Israeli reserve tanks and nearly 100 tanks for Israel's regular forces were not combat loaded when the war began. It took nearly half a day to accomplish this combat load when the crews arrived and nearly 100 reserve tanks had to be issued to combat-ready units because of maintenance problems with their tanks. Many units were short nearly 10 percent of their combat supplies and nearly half of Israel's reserve tanks proved to have some form of maintenance failure. This cost Israel the availability of more than 5 percent of its tank force during the early days of the fighting. These failures occurred in many other areas of the IDF's equipment pool, and it was often forced to commandeer civil equipment when this could serve as a substitute. This provided a graphic lesson in the value of keeping all active and reserve combat equipment combat ready—a lesson that Israel reacted to by revamping its reserve and peacetime maintenance system after the war.

The emphasis on logistics oversupply in Soviet equipped forces has obvious advantages over the general pattern of understocking or undersupply common in most Western forces and seems preferable to the U.S. emphasis on complex centralized logistic management systems.

Naval Systems

The trend in naval forces on each side is shown in Table 2.29. The losses on each side are summarized in Table 2.30. The naval side of the 1973 war was fought largely between fast-attack craft, often referred to as guided-missile, fast-attack boats. Most naval operations consisted mostly of small-unit actions, coastal raids, and support for commando forces and intelligence gathering missions. The Egyptian navy did conduct a naval blockade that restricted neutral, commercial shipping in designated war zones, but this had little practical effect.[58]

The Egyptian navy was equipped by 1973 with a variety of surface ships, including: twelve submarines (6W and 6R class, ex-Soviet), five destroyers (four ex-Soviet S Rory class), three escorts (ex-British), and thirteen fast-patrol boats (eight Osa and F Komar class with Styx surface-to-surface missiles). The Syrian navy was composed of six fast-patrol boats, three Komar and three Osa class, with Styx surface-to-surface missiles. The Israeli navy had a force of two submarines and thirteen fast patrol boats, two Reshef-class missile boats and twelve Saar-class missile boats, armed with the Gabriel anti-ship missiles and two Dabur-type coastal patrol boats.

All three navies put a heavy emphasis on the role of the guided-missile gunboat. These vessels combined characteristics of speed, maneuverability, and firepower. They have the important advantages of being relatively inexpensive, reliable, and maneuverable than more ponderous naval vessels. On the other hand, because of their light, unarmored structure, they are highly vulnerable to air or missile-boat

TABLE 2.29 Arab and Israeli Naval Force Losses

A. Changes in Arab and Israeli Naval Force Strength: 1967–1974			
	May 1967	Sept. 1973	Aug. 1974
Israel			
Patrol Boat	2	24	18
Torpedo Boat	9	8	0
Destroyer	2	1	0
Submarine	4	3	1
Long Missile Boat	0	12	12
Missile Gun Boat	0	0	2
Egypt			
Torpedo Boat	48	46	47
Small Missile Boat	8	8	5
Large Missile Boat	10	11	12
Destroyer	6	5	5
Submarine	13	12	12
Landing Craft	5	15	14
Syria			
Torpedo Boat	17	11	12
Small Missile Boat	4	6	6
Large Missile Boat	—	—	2

B. Prewar Force Ratio of Boats and Ships			
	Israel	Egypt	Syria	Arab:Israeli
Missile Boats	14	17	9	1.9:1
Swift Boats	18	0	0	0:18
Small Craft	10	24	2	2.6:1
Torpedo Boats	0	34	13	47:0
Destroyers	0	5	0	5:0
Frigates	0	3	0	3:0
Submarines	2	12	0	12:1

SOURCES: IISS, *Military Balance* (London: International Institute for Strategic Studies); *Jane's*, various editions.

attack. Their primary assets are speed, evasiveness, and versatility. However, any boat has inherent restrictions of mission performance, range, cargo space, and vulnerability to small arms which accompany a small hull. In addition, they do not have the accommodation and deck space necessary for the elaborate radar, ECM, and other sophisticated and often cumbersome defensive gear required of a blue-water naval capability.

The Israeli emphasis on the fast-attack boat was rooted in the

TABLE 2.30 Naval Orders of Battle and Losses: Egypt and Syria

| | Egypt | | | | Syria | |
| | Mediterranean | | Red Sea | | | |
Type	Start of War	Sunk/ Damaged	Start of War	Sunk/ Damaged	Start of War	Sunk/ Damaged
Submarines	10	0	2	0	0	0
Destroyers	3	0	2	0	0	0
Frigates	2	0	1	0	0	0
Missile Boats						
OSA	12	2/2	0	0	3[a]	1/0
KOMAR	1	0	4	0/3	6	2/0
Torpedo Boats	28		6	0/0	13	
P-6		1/0				
P-4			1[b]			1/0
Small Craft						
LCT	11	0/1	3			
T-43 (MSF)	9	0	1	0	2	1/0
Other				2/0[c]		
Totals	76	3/3	19	3/3	24	5/0

[a]Since termination of hostilities, Syria has received four more OSAs.
[b]Captured by Israeli forces at Suez.
[c]NISR-class Coast Guard boats (similar to SWIFT boats)—one destroyed at Suez and the other destroyed at sea.

SOURCES: Trevor Dupuy, *Elusive Victory* (New York: Harper and Row, 1978), pp. 556–7 and 609; and Chaim Herzog, *The Arab-Israeli Wars* (New York: Random House, 1982), pp. 308–14.

sinking of the Israeli destroyer, *Eilat*, by three Egyptian KOMAR-class guided-missile boats using the Styx missile on 21 October 1967. According to Lt. General Saad el Shazly, the Egyptian Chief of Staff in 1973, the incident had the following impact:

> The world's navies had studied the event, none more than Israel's. The enemy had concluded that its main naval striking power should henceforth be fastattack boats equipped with SSMs and torpedoes. They bought 12 SAAR-class vessels from France, and started to build their own RESHEF-class in Haifa Shipyards at the rate of two per year. (The first was launched on February 19, 1973.) Simultaneously, they designed an even lighter class, the DABUR. . . . We reckoned the enemy had built two of the DABUR type before the October War.[59]

By 1973, the Israeli navy had countered with small modern SAAR-class gunboats for an offensive naval capability. These craft had a hull length of 147 feet and a displacement of 220 to 250 tons. Powered by three diesel engines, the SAAR could reach speeds of up to 40 knots. Its primary armament was the Gabriel anti-ship, surface-to-surface missile with a range of 22 kilometers. These missiles utilized inertial guidance at launch with terminal homing as the missile approaches the target. The 143-pound warhead was too small for autonomous homing. The Gabriel was generally far more accurate and easier to operate than its counterpart, the Styx SS-N-2, although the Gabriel's range was only about half that of the Styx used on the Osa-class craft. The Styx's semiactive system also required the launching ship to illuminate the target, limiting the rate at which missiles could be launched and exposing the ship to return fire.[60] According to Israeli reports, the Gabriel was used for the first time off Latakia, a Syrian port, sinking a T-43 minesweeper and three guided-missile boats.[61]

The Reshef-class missile boat was an improved and enlarged Israeli version of the Saar. It measures 190 feet in hull length by 25 feet in beam width and displaces 415 tons. The Reshef then carried eight Gabriel missiles in the ready-to-launch mode. The storage magazine served as the launch cannister, significantly reducing handling requirements and time-to-launch. In addition, the boat carried two fully automatic 76-mm and two automatic 20-mm anti-aircraft cannons. Current versions of the Reshef carry Gabriel Mark II and the anti-ship missile, Harpoon. The Reshef has longer range and better cruise characteristics than the smaller Saar craft.[62] The electronics in recent versions of the Reshef include one Thompson-CSF Neptune TH-D1040 radar, one Seleria Orion RTN-10X radar, one Elta MN-53ECM system, four chaff/decoy rockets, and one ELAC sonar.

Because of the variance in strategic objectives, weapons inventories, geography, and political and military leadership, Egypt and Israel fought different naval wars. Egyptian strategy emphasized a naval blockade outside the range of the IAF. The Egyptian planning for naval fire support for land operations and coastal defense was premised on the need to avoid naval operations vulnerable to air attack. In practice, Egypt only made sporadic excursions along the Sinai coast in hit-and-run coastal bombardment or commando missions. Most of the naval battles occurred as the result of attacks by Israeli missile boats on Egyptian naval facilities.[63] Similar clashes occurred between Israeli and Syrian missile boats at Minat al-Baydo, the Syrian naval command center, Latakia, Banias, and Yartas.

Israeli naval forces did not attempt to disrupt the Egyptian naval blockade because of a lack of effective air cover at long range. Israel's underlying strategic premise was that a blockade would have little or no effect in a short war. The tactic of the Israeli navy was to confront the Egyptian navy when it moved to conduct bombardments against targets in the Sinai.[64] As Table 2.30 shows, however, the Egyptian emphasis on its blockade and its reluctance to avoid unprotected confrontations denied either side the opportunity for a major naval victory.

The main naval lesson of the 1973 war was to confirm the threat that modern ship-to-ship missiles posed to surface vessels. The economic and military cost of a major naval surface vessel makes it an intolerable loss for most small navies. The war did not really test the capability of fast patrol boats and larger and better-armed ships, however, or the impact of modern sensor and fire-control systems. The importance of these craft was, of course, heightened by the fact that the best defense against them was with a counterpart fast-attack craft or by means of aerial attack.

For a profile of Israeli naval development before and after the 1973 war, see Table 2.29. Israel has since purchased new coastal submarines, landing craft, and a large number of missile boats, including a corvette of the new Aliya class, although its peace with Egypt has largely eliminated the threat in the Red Sea and funding constraints have limited Israeli purchases since the mid-1970s.

Chemical/Biological Weapons and Defensive Systems

No chemical or biological weapons were used in the October 1973 War, and no allegations of chemical- or biological-agent use were made. There is, however, some indication that the Egyptians were prepared to use CBW weapons as a possible response to an Israeli nuclear strike. In the years leading up to the October War, Sadat publicly indicated the availability of this option. This may have been true or it may have been simple bravado in the face of a militarily superior adversary. It may also have been an attempt to suggest that a deterrent was available to Egypt when none existed.

Nuclear Weapons

Nuclear weapons were not used during the 1973 Middle East War nor is it likely that either the U.S. or USSR would have released nuclear weapons to their regional allies. There were, however, reports in *Time* magazine that Israel had ordered its weapons made ready during the worst period of the Arab offensive and that the emissions associated with nuclear materials were detected as coming from a freighter in the Alexandria harbor.[65] This suggests the presence of nuclear warheads which could have been used in conjunction with weapons such as the already delivered SCUD missiles.

The presence of possible Soviet nuclear devices may have been used as a deterrent against the possibility that Israel would be pushed into utilizing nuclear weapons of its own. While Israel has never officially acknowledged the existence of these weapons, Israeli leaders do admit that they have the technology to build them.[66]

Changes in the Force Structure During 1973–1982: The Practical Lessons of the 1973 Fighting

Both Israel and Syria drew further lessons from the 1973 fighting during the period between 1973 and 1982. Syria in many ways adapted to the lessons of 1973 by seeking numerical and technological parity with Israel. It concentrated on a massive Soviet-supplied military buildup and developed forces similar in many ways to those Egypt possessed in 1973.

Syria did significantly improve many aspects of its military organization and training, but it achieved high standards only in terms of fighting from organized and well dug-in defenses and ambushes. Constant expansion and turbulence meant it acquired new equipment and technology far faster than it could absorb them. Involvement in Lebanon limited military training, and political controversy divided the army or gave it internal security objectives that did little to prepare it to fight Israel.

The scale of Syrian force expansion is illustrated by the fact that the Syrian army went from an active strength of 120,000 in 1973 to 179,000 in 1982. Syrian tank strength rose from 1,170 to 2,990, and Syrian armored fighting vehicle (AFV) and APC strength rose from 1,000 to 1,600. Syrian air force manpower rose from 10,000 to 30,000, and Syrian combat aircraft strength rose from 326 to 450.

The basic problems in this expansion are illustrated by the fact that Syrian tank and artillery strength nearly tripled, but active personnel increased by less than 50 percent, and Syria's reserve structure remained ineffective and poorly organized. More than ten billion dollars worth of Soviet arms were poured into a force structure that simply could not absorb them and which remained heavily politicized.[67]

In short, Syria became dependent on static and defensive mass without acquiring Egypt's ability to adopt the new tactics, technology, and C^3I system necessary to organize and master its new arms. It experienced constant force upheaval and turbulence, expanded and modernized far beyond the point where this expansion began to have negative effects, and kept its forces politicized at a time when they needed to become steadily more professional.[68]

In contrast, Israel reacted to the lessons of 1973 with far more effective changes. A commission headed by the chief of the supreme court, Shimon Agranat, found major faults in Israel's preparation for the war, its treatment of intelligence warning, and its conduct of the battle. Chief of Staff David Elazar was forced to resign. The military intelligence chief and southern front commander were also forced to resign. While Minister of Defense Moshe Dayan and Prime Minister Golda Meir were cleared on the grounds that they had received insufficient information from the general staff, the public and the Knesset were far more critical. Both Israeli leaders suffered a severe blow to their reputations.

Israel went on to make a number of important changes in its operational art. These changes may be summarized as follows:

- *Israel developed a much more advanced command and control system.* It developed organized corps level and regional defense forces. It gave its division-level organization real meaning and coherence. It organized its air force to provide both an effective central command for managing attack missions and a modern centralized air defense system. Fully mobile command systems were developed for the task force or *ugda* commands. Sophisticated data networks were set up for integrating combat formations, support units, and logistical units. Remotely piloted vehicles (RPVs) were provided at the task force level to provide real time intelligence.
- *Total active personnel in all services was increased to reduce vulnerability to surprise and to provide a larger cadre of highly trained technical personnel.* It rose from 75,000 in 1973 to 172,000 in 1982—an increase of 130 percent. Regular active army personnel more than doubled from 11,000 to 25,000, while changes in the conscription laws and the increased use of women increased the number of conscripts from 50,000 to 110,000. The standing army more than doubled.
- *This increase in active forces did not mean reduced operational dependence on the reserves.* Reserve personnel rose from 275,000 to 450,000, an increase of over 60 percent. At the same time, reserve training was radically restructured to improve its technical content and realism.
- *Israel went from a tank and fighter force to a combined arms force.* It bought large numbers of self-propelled artillery weapons, modern antitank weapons, and medium and heavy infantry weapons. Israel had no independent artillery brigades in 1973 and fifteen in 1982. The Artillery Corps became a major branch and acquired long-range systems like the 290-mm multiple rocket

launcher, which carried submunitions, RPVs, and computerized fire-control systems.

- *Israel became a balanced technology force.* Israel added high technology C³I and battle management technologies to its previous emphasis on modern armor and having the best possible fighter aircraft. It added modern fire-control systems and night-vision devices. It adapted U.S. electronic warfare systems and made several important advances in remotely piloted vehicles and sensor systems. It added the E-2C and Airborne Warning and Air Control System (AWACS) functions to its management of the air battle. It bought large numbers of smart munitions and developed advanced rocket launchers. It modified its APCs and bought or made a highly advanced mixture of combat engineering and support equipment.
- *Israel simultaneously doubled its armor.* It had about 1,225 tanks in 1973 and 3,800 in 1982. It had eleven armored brigades in 1973 and thirty-three in 1983. Israel also modified its tanks to use 60-mm mortar launchers on its tank turrets to help suppress antitank weapons by firing mortar rounds with smoke- and high-explosive warheads.
- *Israel made major increases in its infantry, fully mechanized its field forces, and added territorial defenses.* It had nine infantry and four paratroop brigades in 1973; by 1982, it had ten mechanized brigades, five paratroop brigades, and twelve territorial infantry brigades. Israel had fewer than 1,000 modern covered and tracked APCs in 1973. In 1982 it had around 4,000.
- *Mobile infantry which could move with tanks became essential to provide the fire support to suppress enemy infantry and antitank weapons.* The infantry was heavily mechanized to allow it to maneuver with tanks, and the M-3 half-track was largely replaced with modified M-113s. Israel created elite infantry units which were specially trained to fight in integrated combat actions with its main battle tanks. These were mounted on M-113 armored personnel carriers and integrated at the battalion level with M-113s carrying 81-mm mortars to provide close support. Combat engineers were mechanized, armored, and organized to move forward with armor and mechanized infantry.
- *Israel procured its first real attack helicopters.* Israel bought six U.S. AH-1G helicopters in 1975. These were only equipped for close support, with 7.62-mm machine guns, M-19 grenade launchers, and 1,000-pound rocket pods, but operational testing rapidly led Israel to upgrade them to the "Q" version which carried TOW antitank missiles. In 1978, it bought its

first true antitank helicopters, the AH-1S, and then the Hughes 500MD defender for scouting and close support. These were integrated into the IAF as a potential solution to the problem of providing highly mobile antitank kill capability that could take advantage of terrain masking and avoid most surface-to-air missile defenses in the forward edge of the battle area (FEBA).

- *Israel shifted to focus on defense of the Northern Front.* Two of Israel's three active divisions were committed to the Northern Command, with three in reserve. The Southern Command had one active division and two in reserve. (In 1982, Israel mobilized and deployed seven divisions on the Northern Front with three going into Lebanon and four acting as reserves and replacing active units on the Golan.) The IDF's active presence on the Golan, which was two armored brigades in 1973, was increased to well over a division, and the Golan was heavily fortified with artillery and antitank weapons in place.

- *Israel nearly doubled its munitions stocks.* They increased from around 14 days of supplies for intense combat at the beginning of the 1973 fighting to 28 days by mid-1975. It steadily built up its stocks in the years that followed.

- *Israel shifted from a system of supply on demand to one of over-supply at the front.* This system is backed by the use of helicopters, aircraft, and tracked vehicles to provide quick-reaction forward supply. This in many ways was a shift from the U.S. concept of unit pull to the Soviet concept of logistic push.

- *Israel radically improved medical services and protection gear.* Major medical and surgical teams were brought much closer to the front. (This change failed in practice in 1982 since most major casualties were evacuated to the rear.) Units made far heavier use of protective vests. Helmets became far more standard, although not without resistance. Tank crewmen were given fireproof suits, and new tank extinguisher systems became standard.[69]

These changes are the clearest possible indications of how Israel interpreted the operational lessons of the 1973 fighting. It is important to note, however, that Israel came more and more to stress the simultaneous speed of reaction of all elements of combined arms as a way of preserving maneuver in the face of the steadily growing technical sophistication of Syrian forces and as a means of countering the steady improvement in the armament and defensive fighting capabilities of Arab forces. It stressed speed of reaction and independent action, while it sought to create a C^{3}I system that could still provide central control and allocation of forces.

These concepts pushed the state of the art in tactical mobility and independent maneuver and pushed C^{3}I to its limits. They also created some serious uncertainties regarding Israel's ability to make its new concepts work even before they were tested in the 1982 fighting:

- The new force structure and concept of operations were extremely expensive—almost beyond the limits of what Israel could afford in terms of finances and manpower.
- Exercise after exercise revealed serious uncertainties regarding Israel's ability to achieve the speed of reaction and fusion of combined arms that it desired.
- Israel never came fully to grips with the development of a doctrine for urban or mountain warfare. It made some advances in these areas, but it planned more for action on the West Bank and Golan than offensive action in Syria, the East Bank, and Lebanon.
- Israel failed to fully address the technical and tactical risks of fighting in urban areas and the need for infantry that could play an assault role in mountain warfare. It never properly examined the vulnerability of the APC or the extent to which they could directly support tanks against well dug-in and well-positioned defenders in areas where armored forces could not find room to maneuver.
- While Israel restructured its forces for combined operations and as a balanced technology force, it left its helicopters under the command of the Air Force. The Air Force's natural focus on the fighter made helicopters something of a stepchild within Israel's force modernization efforts. As a result, Israel failed to fully examine the role that large-scale employment of helicopters could play in operations and bought relatively limited numbers.
- Israel improved its C^{3}I but failed to improve the strategic and political structure or its intelligence, or the ability to use its intelligence structure to influence the key cabinet-level decisions upon which operations had to be based. Military intelligence remained under the de facto control of the chief of staff and minister of defense and failed to provide independent reporting to the cabinet.

As part of the broad political divisions which emerged within Israel, the Likud came to dominate many aspects of Israel's intelligence community. While some branches of Israeli intelligence retained their quality, others became politicized or simply became passive. The public and political face of Israeli intelligence also acquired an increasingly anti-Arab character with strongly xenophobic and racist overtones.

Finally, and most important, Israel left its higher command structure virtually alone. It treated the near panic in the Ministry of Defense that occurred during the height of Arab success in 1973 as an aberration. It did not create effective land-force commands for central operational control of the war. It relied on a unified interservice command which was better suited for planning than for battle management. Israel also never came to grips with the proper form of ministerial control of the armed forces. Israeli forces remained under the control of the minister of defense rather than the prime minister or the cabinet as a whole.

Notes

1. President Sadat did achieve an extraordinary degree of security; only 20 senior officers seem to have known of his intention to attack during the year before the war. This group was selectively broadened about a month before the attack, but only about 20 percent of the officer corps in the attacking units knew an attack was imminent even a week before the attack, and the mass of the forces involved were told only days before the attack.

2. For the details of both warning and the War of Attrition see Trevor Dupuy, *Elusive Victory* (New York: Harper and Row, 1978), pp. 343–386; Chaim Herzog, *The Arab-Israeli Wars* (New York: Random House, 1982), pp. 193–224; Edward Luttwak and Dan Horowitz, *The Israeli Army* (New York: Harper & Row, 1975), pp. 299–336; Nadav Safran, *Israel: The Embattled Ally* (Cambridge: Belknap/Harvard, 1982), pp. 261–277; Alvin Z. Rubenstein, *Red Star over the Nile* (New Jersey: Princeton, 1977); Ze'ev Schiff, *A History of the Israeli Army* (New York: Macmillan, 1985), pp. 178–189; Ezer Weizman, *On Eagle's Wings* (New York: Macmillan, 1976), pp. 260–280; Lawrence L. Whetten, *The Canal War: Four Power Conflict in the Middle East* (Cambridge: MIT, 1974); Yaacov Bar-Siman-Tov, *The Israeli-Egyptian War of Attrition, 1969–1970* (New York: Columbia, 1980).

3. Moshe Dayan, *Story of My Life* (New York: Warner, 1976), p. 633.

4. Herzog, op. cit., pp. 118, 200. See also Dupuy, op. cit., p. 233.

5. Herzog, op. cit., p. 254.

6. Ibid., p. 252.

7. Ibid., p. 266.

8. Herzog, op. cit., pp. 253–254.

9. Dupuy, op. cit., p. 406.

10. Herzog, op. cit., pp. 270–271.

11. Ibid., p. 199. See also Dupuy, op. cit., p. 437.

12. Dupuy, op. cit., p. 585.

13. Dayan, op. cit., p. 568.

14. Lt. General Saad El Shazly, *The Crossing of the Suez* (San Francisco: American Mideast Research, 1980), p. 274.

15. Ibid., p. 252.

16. Avraham Adan, *On the Banks of the Suez* (San Francisco: Presidio Press, 1980), p. 141.

17. Richard A. Gabriel, *Operation Peace for Galilee* (New York: Hill and Wang, 1984), p. 202.

18. Anwar el-Sadat, *In Search of Identity* (New York: Harper and Row, 1978), p. 250.

19. Adan, op. cit., p. 82.

20. Shazly, op. cit., p. 240.

21. Dupuy, op. cit., p. 416, and Shazly, ibid., p. 225.

22. Adan, op. cit., p. 226.

23. Ibid., p. 222.

24. Dupuy, op. cit., p. 488.

25. R.G. Lee, *Introduction to Battlefield Weapons Systems and Technology* (New York: Brassey's Publishers Ltd., 1981), p. 19.

26. For a sample of the PGM debate, see James Digby, "Precision-Guided Weapons," *Adelphi Paper 118* (London: IISS, 1976), and John J. Mearsheimer, "Precision-Guided Munitions and Conventional Deterrence," *Survival*, Vol. XXI, No. 2 (March/April 1979). For a recent debate, see the series of articles by Richard Petrow, "The Smart Weapons Debate," *Electronic Engineering Times* (September 10, 1984), p. 1.

27. On the destruction of the 190th Brigade, see Colonel Edward B. Atkeson, "Is the Soviet Army Obsolete?" *Army*, Vol. 24, No. 5 (May 1974), pp. 10–16.

28. The Egyptians did make extensive use of the Saggers at long ranges, and Lt. General Shazly has commented that his forces had a higher demand for Saggers than anticipated but a lower demand for RPGs. See Shazly, op. cit., p. 275.

29. Ibid., p. 232.

30. Ibid., p. 276.

31. Ibid.

32. Dupuy, op. cit., p. 594.

33. Ibid.

34. When the 1973 disengagement between Egypt and Israel took place along the Suez Canal, the IDF was unable to recover all the deployed mines and was forced to furnish U.N. forces with maps of uncleared minefields.

35. Dupuy, op. cit., p. 449.

36. Uri Ra'anan, "The New Technologies and the Middle East: 'Lessons' of the Yom Kippur War and Anticipated Developments," *The Other Arms Race*, (Cambridge, Mass.: MIT Press, 1969), p. 84.

37. Walter Laqueur, *Confrontation: The Middle East and World Politics* (New York: Quadrangle Books, 1974), pp. 131–2. On the role of ECM in the air-SAM battle, see the early report by Barry Miller, "Israeli Losses May Spur ECM Restudy," *Aviation Week & Space Technology* (October 29, 1973), p. 16.

38. "Yom Kippur Special," *Defence Update* (No. 42), p. 21.

39. Dupuy, op. cit., p. 465.

40. Herbert J. Coleman, "Israeli Air Force Decisive in War," *Aviation Week and Space Technology* (December 3, 1973), p. 49.

41. *Defence Update*, op. cit., p. 21.

42. Dupuy, op. cit., pp. 549–552.

43. *Defence Update*, op. cit., p. 22.

44. Coleman, op. cit., p. 21. According to this author, the aerial cannon made only a few kills.

45. Bill Gunston, *An Illustrated Guide to the Israeli Air Force* (London: Eshel-Dramit, 1982), pp. 132–135.

46. Roy M. Braybrook, "Is It Goodbye to Ground Attack?" *Air International*, Vol. 10, No. 5 (May 1976), p. 245. Coleman, op. cit., p. 18.

47. Ra'anan, op. cit., p. 84.

48. Coleman, op. cit., p. 18. Dupuy, op. cit., pp. 419–421.

49. Coleman, op. cit., p. 19.

50. Ibid., p. 21.

51. Louis Williams, *Military Aspects of the Yom Kippur War* (Tel Aviv: Israeli Ministry of Defense, 1975), p. 249.

52. Coleman, op. cit., p. 21.

53. Ibid.

54. *Defence Update International*, No. 42 (Cologne, West Germany), p. 18.

55. Dupuy, op. cit., pp. 592–3.

56. Herzog, op. cit.

57. Shazly, op. cit., p. 262.

58. Dupuy, op. cit., p. 557.

59. Shazly, op. cit., pp. 23–24.

60. See Stan Morse (ed.), *Modern Military Powers: Israel* (New York: The Military Press, 1984), p. 150.

61. Dupuy, op. cit., p. 368.

62. Ibid.

63. Dupuy, op. cit.

64. Ibid., p. 561.

65. William Quandt, "Soviet Policy in the October Middle East War," *International Affairs* (October 1977), p. 97.

66. Galia Gielan, *Yom Kippur and After* (London: Cambridge University Press, 1977), p. 122.

67. These figures are based on estimates in IISS, *Military Balance*.

68. Based on the author's discussions in Jordan and Syria and with various U.S. government officials.

69. See the author's *Jordanian Arms and the Middle East Balance* (Washington, D.C.: Middle East Institute, 1983), pp. 27–181, and Trevor N. Dupuy and Paul Martell, *Flawed Victory* (Washington, D.C.: Hero Books, 1985), pp. 37–98; Gabriel, op. cit., pp. 3–29 and 191–213; Safran, op. cit., pp. 317–331; Ze'ev Schiff, *A History of the Israeli Army* (New York: Macmillan, 1985), pp. 230–238.

3

THE 1982 WAR IN LEBANON

The fighting during the 1982 conflict between Israel, the PLO, and Syria reflected many of the patterns established during the 1973 conflict and during earlier fighting between Israel and its Arab neighbors. At the same time, the strategic situation changed radically during the period between 1973 and 1982. Egypt and Israel reached a peace settlement which has since been steadily reinforced by Egypt's shift of resources from military to civil spending and Egypt's growing dependence on U.S. aid. Jordan gave priority to economic development and limited its military development largely to improved defensive capability. Iraq became bogged down in a bloody war with Iran, and lost much of its taste for adventures. As a result, the Arab-Israeli conflict narrowed down to a guerrilla war between Israel and the Palestinians and a military confrontation between Israel and Syria which was limited to Lebanon and the Golan Heights.

The Combatants

These changes in doctrine and force structure between 1973 and 1982 set the stage for Israel's 1982 invasion of Lebanon, but the 1982 conflict was as much a test of politics and irregular forces as a test of Syrian and Israeli military capabilities. As Table 3.1 shows, the 1982 conflict was a limited war, in which both Israel and Syria committed only part of their total forces. The Palestinian forces involved never fully deployed and never fought with any cohesion, and the key Palestinian forces affecting Israeli operations were largely militias and popular volunteers fighting under improvised command.[1]

The June–September 1982 War in Lebanon (which the Israelis call Operation Peace for Galilee) involved Israeli military operations in an attack on several hostile forces within Lebanon. These forces included the Syrian Army and Air Force, the military arm of the PLO, and various leftist Lebanese groups.

TABLE 3.1   Israeli and Arab Forces Engaged in the 1982 War

	Israel [1]	Syria [2]	PLO [3]
FORCES			
Troops	76,000	22,000	15,000 [4]
Tanks	800	352	300
APCs	1,500	300	150
Crew Served Anti-Tank Weapons		200	.
Large Anti-Tank weapons	-	-	200-300
Major artillery pieces	-	300	350+
Anti-Aircraft Guns	-	100	200+
Total Combat Aircraft	634	450	0
Total Aircraft Engaged	364	96	0
Attack Capable Aircraft	275	225	0
Armed Helicopters	42	16	0
Non-Organic Major SAM Launchers	-	125	-
LOSSES [5]	1,538	5,000	5,000
Killed	268	1,000?	1,200
Wounded	1,270	4,000?	3,700

Adapted from Trevor N. Dupuy and Paul N. Martell, Flawed Victory (Fairfax, VA: Hero Books, 1986), pp. 86-94, and 140-141, and Richard A. Gabriel, Operation Peace for Galilee (New York: Hill and Wang, 1982), pp. 232-236.

1. Total Israel forces engaged in operation. The active Israeli forces included Seven army task forces, plus dedicated Air Force and Naval units. Task force A for the coastal road had the 91st division (six reserve mechanized brigades) and the 211th armored brigade from the 162nd division. Amphibious Task Force B for the Awali River landing had elements of the 96th division and the 50th Paratroop Battalion. Tack Force C for the central axis had the 36th Division, less the 7th Armored Brigade. The Bekaa forces group had Task Force H, with the 252nd Division, less the 460th armored brigade; Task Force V with one armored and one mechanized brigade; and Task Force Z with the 90th division. Task Force D was the Northern Command Reserve and had the 162nd Division less the 211th Armored Brigade.

2. Syrian and allied forces in Lebanon. Syrian forces began the war with one tank division (lst), two tank brigades, and one mechanized brigade and independent elements, plus two infantry brigades and one tank regiment of the Syrian controlled Palestine Liberation Army. One of these infantry brigades was attached to the PLO.

3. The bulk of PLO equipment was not deployed, and some eight poorly coordinated and often hostile force elements were involved with at least 6,000 of the regulars deployed in Beirut. Fatah has 6,000 men and one tank and one artillery group. SAIQA had about 2,000 men in three infantry battalions, PFLP had 1,000 men in four infantry battalions, DFLP had 1,000 men in 10 infantry companies, PLP had 600 men, PLS had 300 men and ALG had 1,500 men in one tank group and two infantry battalions. About 6,000 regular PLO troops were in the South, with most in the coastal area or north of the Litani and about 2,100 in the center and southeast. One brigade of the Syrian trained Palestine Liberation Army was also released to PLO command.

4. Plus 18,000 militia.

5. Includes only losses in direct action through July, 1982. The Israelis, for example, lost 654 killed before Israel withdrew from Lebanon.

The Israelis expected significant military support from allies, or quasi-allies, among the Christian Lebanese and were surprised by their lack of response. This surprise was especially unpleasant since the Israelis had for years supplied money, training, and instructors to the Lebanese Right.[2] The lack of Maronite support may also have violated a secret agreement between the Lebanese forces of Beshir Gemayal, the Phalange, and the Israeli government.[3] Israeli Defense Minister Ariel Sharon was especially upset with the Phalange because he felt he had obtained agreement that far-reaching military coordination would occur once the IDF had reached Beirut. When this did not occur, Sharon attacked the Gemayal family with the same vehemence he had once praised them: "They're acting just like Arabs. I saw the fear in their eyes."[4]

As a result, the Israelis carried out the invasion of Lebanon alone, and, as will be discussed later, with very divided objectives at the political and high-command levels. They initiated a three-pronged invasion: One Israeli force swept along the Lebanese coast, a second force advanced in a central column to Beaufort Castle and then to the mouth of the Bekaa Valley, and a third force advanced into eastern Lebanon. The basic tactics the Israelis used throughout the campaign were to try to use combined arms and air support to carry the advance forward at a pace too rapid to allow enemy forces to retreat and consolidate and to surround and bypass well-defended urban areas. The Israeli forces involved in this action included about 60,000–76,000 troops organized into eight divisional groups.[5]

The PLO had approximately 15,000 fighters scattered throughout Lebanon to meet this invading force.[6] These troops were armed with weapons ranging from the modern to the obsolete. The PLO's small arms were largely current or near-current generation weapons, such as AKMs, AK-47s, RPG-7s and SA-7s.[7] Its heavier weapons, however, were often obsolete. The PLO's tanks, for example, consisted predominantly of World War II vintage T-34 tanks. Former Israeli Chief of Staff Rafael Eitan has stated that the PLO also had T-54/55 tanks which are newer than the T-34s, but these tanks date back to 1950, were never really employed, and were heavily worn and largely obsolete.[8] PLO training and organization were adequate for defensive, small-unit infantry combat in fixed prepared positions but were otherwise exceptionally poor. Organization and leadership above the squad level were simply terrible, and the major refugee camps improvised more effective forces under attack than the PLO created before the war.[9]

The PLO's regular forces had been organized into three infantry brigades by 1981. Each of these brigades (Karameh, Yarmuk, and

Castel) was supported by several artillery and support units, as well as a small tank unit which was expected to expand eventually to battalion strength. The PLO's primary maneuver units were organized into battalion- and brigade-size units, but the PLO still preferred to operate in small platoons and squad-sized groups. The larger PLO units often broke down into smaller groups under pressure. This usually made it easier for the Israelis to use their mobility to concentrate overwhelming force on PLO positions.

Part of the reason that the PLO was uncomfortable with brigade- and battalion-sized units was its lack of training for large-scale operations. Only once in its history had the PLO conducted a large-scale training exercise with its regular combat forces. This occurred in 1981 when four battalions of Fatah's Karameh brigade practiced the conquest of a mock-up Israeli settlement which they called "Begingrad."[10] This exercise, however was heavily politicized. The PLO had almost no real maneuver and combined arms training.

The PLO had some support from the Lebanese during the fighting, but this support was fairly limited. The Lebanese Shi'ites, who would later become the most bitter and effective enemies of the Israeli post-war occupation, were initially content to remain on the sidelines while Israeli and PLO forces fought. Mahmoud Ghadar, the commander of the southern military wing of the Amal (Shi'ite) forces, was so concerned that Amal troops stay out of the fighting that he issued orders that the Shi'ites were not to resist the Israeli advance and should turn their weapons over to the Israelis if this was requested. Ghadar's orders, and the general political attitude they reflected, severely limited the number of Shi'ite Lebanese who fought beside the PLO.[11]

The Druze (many of whom had been the PLO's allies during the 1975–1976 civil war) also chose to sit out the 1982 invasion. Like the Shi'ites, they saw no reason to sacrifice their own young men to help the PLO in a battle it could not win. The most significant Druze leader, Walid Jumblatt, ordered his troops not to fire upon the invading Israeli troops, nor even to lay mines on the narrow roads within the Shouf mountains. This decision was a double disappointment since the Druze could have inflicted real harm on Israeli troops advancing into the Shouf, and since Walid's father, Kamal, had been one of the most steadfast defenders of Palestinian interests in pre–civil war and civil war Lebanon. Walid Jumblatt had inherited the leadership of the Progressive Socialist Party, and much of the Druze community, when his father was assassinated in 1977.

The quality of individual PLO commanders and troop units at lower command levels varied widely. This was in part due to different training and levels of political commitment among fighters. In general, the troops and junior officers fought better than their commanders, and the more extreme factions fought better than the more moderate ones. The high-ranking leadership of many PLO units was taken by surprise in spite of months of warning from Arafat and many outside sources. Many bolted for Beirut and left their commands somewhat demoralized and disorganized as a result, although the leadership and local forces in several key refugee camps like those at Ain al-Hilweh and Rachidiye fought quite well.[12]

Another problem with regular PLO forces resulted from factionalization within the PLO. This led to a lack of cooperation within the PLO force structure at a time when these troops should have been preparing for joint resistance against the Israelis. One particularly telling form of disagreement between the factions involved artillery shells. On a variety of occasions, commanders of Al Fatah (the PLO's largest and most dominant organization) entered the positions of the smaller guerrilla organizations and confiscated their shells. In at least one case, this led to a gun battle with an unspecified number of casualties.[13] Similar disagreements affected other forms of supplies, and cooperation in command and control and cross reinforcement were equally poor.

The quality of PLO training was generally low. PLO training tended to be physically exhausting and psychologically unpleasant. The PLO adapted special forces and guerrilla techniques with little relevance to the large-scale mechanized infantry combat the PLO was organizing and equipping to fight. This training included such absurdities as killing rabbits and snakes and then eating their meat under simulated combat conditions. It stressed hardship, revolutionary rhetoric, and martyrdom. It failed to stress cooperation, leadership, use of heavy arms, C^3, and battle management. It often had great showmanship but rarely had military substance.

In fact, the best PLO fighters in the war were the relatively untrained home-guard militia troops who were defending their own homes within the refugee camps. These forces fought fiercely and tenaciously with limited regard for their own lives. Indeed, many of the PLO forces defending the camps fully expected that the best they could hope for was an honorable death. One leader of the defenders of Sidon (who was also a mullah) told his troops, "The Jews are killing everyone. Better to die in the camp, at home, bearing arms than on your knees in front of a firing squad."[14] The home-guard fighters were for the most part young men in their late teens and early twenties. According to one source, each camp had about one militiaman for every eight residents of the camp. Older men served as support personnel who were given little if any combat training. These individuals were known as "trade unionists."[15]

In addition to PLO forces, there were five brigade-sized elements of Syrian or Syrian-controlled Palestine Liberation Army (PLA) troops in Lebanon which had been stationed in that country since 1976. These troops included modern armored and infantry units, and 30 commando battalions. Some of the armored units were equipped with the current generation Soviet T-72 tanks. These units were of special concern to the Israelis because the Israelis were uncertain about their ability to kill them with standard NATO 105-mm tank guns.

The Syrian forces in Lebanon were reinforced during the course of the war by two armored divisions taken from the Damascus sector.[16] These divisions left the Golan Heights front without reserves and moved only after the IDF clearly proved it intended to attack Syrian forces, as well as the PLO, and would not halt at more limited territorial objectives. This has been widely interpreted as a signal of Syria's interest in avoiding any widening of the war.

There is no doubt that the Syrian Army was the toughest adversary the Israelis faced in Lebanon. The Syrian commandos continued to display courage and professionalism throughout the course of the war. Their morale was high, and they executed a series of planned retrograde operations that never degenerated into routs. The basic Syrian strategy was to establish an ambush, strike at Israeli units, and then engage in a retrograde and emplace a new ambush. These "aggressive delay" tactics were clearly meant to erode the combat power of the invading Israelis while blunting their ability to maneuver and outflank Syrian forces. They were often successful, and IDF commanders developed considerable respect for individual Syrian units and unit commanders.

It is significant that the Syrian and PLO troops made little effort to cooperate with each other in their initial conduct of operations against Israeli forces. Indeed, the Syrians' predominant interest seems to have been to insure that the Israelis did not place themselves in an advantageous position to attack Damascus.

The Terrain

Terrain had a key impact on the fighting in terms of tactics, strategy, and politics. The terrain in Lebanon is quite different from the open desert terrain that the Israelis had become expert in fighting during their previous campaigns against Egypt, although it is similar to the terrain of the West Bank and the Golan Heights. Lebanon is a small, well-populated, and heavily urbanized country, dominated by mountains, valleys, river, and its coastline on the Mediterranean.

The war was fought in three distinct main sectors: (1) the western sector; (2) the central sector; and (3) the eastern sector of Lebanon. The western or coastal sector included the narrow coastal plain, and the road along it, all the way north to Beirut. The coastal plain averages no more than 2 kilometers in width. Its landscape is marked by several indentations of a multitude of natural bays and harbors. The Lebanese mountain ranges rise above it and reach heights of 6,700 feet south of Beirut. Because of its geological structure, abundant springs erupt all along the mid-western slopes of this ridge. The mountainous terrain at the edge of the coastal plain is difficult for the transportation of troops, heavy equipment, and assault weapons and creates severe limitations on the mobility of armor and other tracked fighting vehicles. The coastal road is the only good north-south line of communication in Lebanon but can be blocked by flanking positions all along the western slopes of the mountains. These positions lie between a couple of kilometers and several hundred meters from the waterline. Towns and villages, such as Tyre, Sidon, and Damour, are also potential roadblocks, as are the refugee camps in the coastal area. The coastal zone is, however, open to amphibious landings and naval gunfire can easily hit any target in the zone.

The central sector includes the Arnoun Heights (the Nabatiye area) and commands the bend of the Litani River and the primary communication center between the southern tip of the Bekaa Valley and the seashore south of Sidon. The Nabatiye area is a good launch point to attack Beaufort Castle (the conquest of the Beaufort Castle area was a prerequisite for an orderly advance into the eastern sector). The central area is cut by several rivers and deep gorges and contains the ridge and upper western slopes of Lebanon's mountain range. It is trafficable, but the roads are poor, extremely narrow, and vulnerable to ambush.

The eastern sector includes the Bekaa Valley from the mountain slopes to the east and west. The many hill settlements, agricultural terraces, and orchards afford concealment and provide excellent defensive positions. Troops operating in this sector must move through the Bekaa Valley along the slopes of the Hermon (the Anti-Lebanon range). The eastern sector also includes the slopes of the Anti-Lebanon Mountains which reach 9,230 feet at Mt. Hermon. The Anti-Lebanon crests determine the borderline between Lebanon and Syria. The eastern slopes of the Anti-Lebanon are abrupt and create a solid barrier between the Bekaa and the coastal valleys. As a result of this barrier, military operations along the coast and east of the Lebanon range become difficult to coordinate. This is evidenced by the road network.

The Litani River in southern Lebanon provides an effective barrier to advances northward of the Tyre-Marjayoun line and farther across the Bekaa. Its crossing requires either bridges or river-crossing equipment. Numerous other gorges, cliffs, defiles, and sharp turns also create natural barriers or ambush points. In many cases, an advancing commander is immediately confronted with a choice between taking casualties or slowing his rate of advance to secure his flanks, protect a crossing, or scout out an ambush. This terrain-dominated trade-off between time and casualties proved to be a critical factor in shaping Israeli behavior, particularly given the uncertainty that developed regarding the IDF's ultimate goal.

At the same time, however, Lebanon's terrain offered any force with superior naval forces, heliborne and air mobility, and combat engineer forces a distinct advantage. Any relatively static force can be leap-frogged or bypassed, and even in the central sector, combat engineers could rapidly create or expand routes through mountain areas. This gave the IDF a massive advantage over the PLO and a significant advantage over Syria.

It is also important to distinguish between terrain-dominating territorial and political objectives. Israel could create territorial buffer zones by advancing to the key east-west river valleys through southern Lebanon. The most important of these rivers is the Litani, which turns west south of Beaufort Castle and flows into the coast of Tyre. This was the logical stopping point for a territorial buffer zone since it included the territory of various pro-Israeli factions in Lebanon, involved only one major city, and still meant pushing PLO forces outside the range of all but the northeastern tip of Israel.

The next logical line was the Zaharani River, which meant occupying more refugee camps, but driving the PLO out of Beaufort and securing Nabitya and Marjayoun. Each step farther north meant entering steadily more hostile areas and occupying more cities. The Awali River meant taking Sidon, and the Damour River meant holding a position within range of the main PLO concentrations in and around Beirut.

The impact of terrain is very different, however, if the political objective is to destroy the PLO or dominate Lebanon. Destroying the PLO meant occupying or dominating Beirut—the political and military center of PLO strength in Lebanon—and containing or conquering enough refugee camps in the south to prevent guerrilla warfare. Dominating Lebanon meant forcing Syria out of Lebanon by conquering the Bekaa Valley, seizing the Beirut-Damascus Road, and being able to pose a "second-front" threat to Syria by being able to attack eastward toward Damascus.

Each of these objectives involves a radically different set of trade-offs between how fast an attacker must move, the amount of planning and support required, and the willingness to trade casualties for speed. If the attacker plans only for a limited objective at the start, expanding the objective later means giving the enemy time to organize and improvise in exceedingly difficult terrain, only to eventually confront the need to beseige Beirut and deal with Syrian forces attempting to defend a vital national objective.

The practical impact of Lebanese terrain is, therefore, to demand careful prior planning and allocation of forces and a clear objective from the start. This was to prove critical throughout the war in shaping the IDF's failures and successes.

The History of the Conflict

While the complex internal politics of Lebanon almost inevitably led Syria and Israel to intervene in Lebanese affairs, the key forces that led up to the conflict were the Syrian-Israeli arms race and the steady rise of PLO power in Lebanon. The Syrian-Israeli arms race is summarized in Table 3.1 and Figures 3.1 through 3.7. After Camp David, Syria attempted to single-handedly reach parity with Israel. As Table 3.1 and Figures 3.1 through 3.7 show, Syria was often successful in meeting this objective in terms of sheer weapons numbers and arms imports. As is seen in Figures 3.8 and 3.9, Syria, however, did not have the military budget, mobilization system, leadership, or training to give it anything approaching the IDF's effectiveness and readiness.

The IDF, in turn, carried out the restructuring and force shifts discussed earlier. While many problems remained, the IDF in many ways succeeded in converting to a high technology force structure and placed far more emphasis on combined arms and combined operations than ever before. At the same time, the IDF did continue to debate whether or not it could ever use such techniques to restore the speed and freedom of maneuver it had exhibited in 1956 and 1967 and particularly in an attack on Syria or through the rough terrain in Lebanon.

The IDF planned and debated its 1982 attack on Lebanon from roughly the mid-1970s onward. The Israelis conducted a limited attack

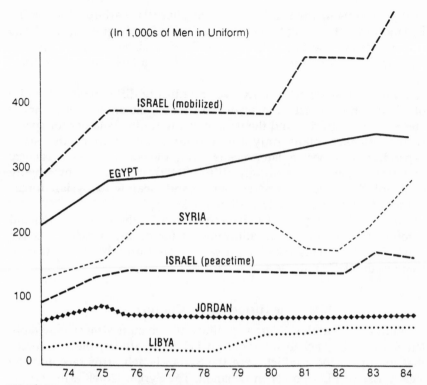

FIGURE 3.1 Comparative Trend in Army Manpower. Adapted from IISS, *Military Balance* (London: International Institute for Strategic Studies), all yearly editions from 1975 to 1985; Stan Morse, *Modern Military Powers: Israel* (New York: The Military Press, 1984); and U.S. ACDA, *World Military Exports and Arms Transfers* (Washington, D.C.: GPO), 1976 and 1981 editions.

on Lebanon in 1978 (under the name Operation Litani). This attack, which began on 14 March 1978, had most of the military ingredients Israel used in its subsequent invasion in 1982. According to Ezer Weizman, who was then Israel's minister of defense, Operation Litani was marked by mistakes in both planning and execution, and the IDF forces moved too slowly and without proper combined arms cooperation. The 1978 incursion into Lebanon did, however, allow the IDF to refine its operations against the PLO.[17] It allowed the IDF to learn from a "practice war" and to measure the response of the PLO, although Syria opted not to fight except in one limited instance.[18]

Regardless of problems encountered in Operation Litani, there also is little doubt that Israel learned much about the use of combined arms operations and that these lessons led to improved coordination in the 1982 fighting. The Israelis devoted a great deal of time to potential military operations in Lebanon during the years between Operation

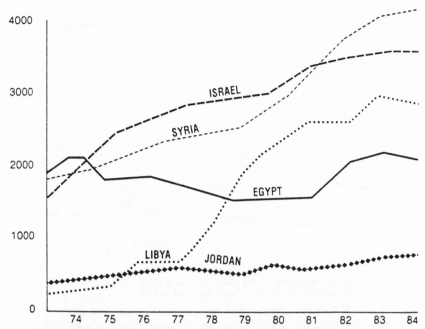

FIGURE 3.2 Comparative Trend in Medium Tank Strength. Adapted from IISS, *Military Balance* (London: International Institute for Strategic Studies), all yearly editions from 1975 to 1985; Stan Morse, *Modern Military Powers: Israel* (New York: The Military Press, 1984); and U.S. ACDA, *World Military Exports and Arms Transfers* (Washington, D.C.: GPO), 1976 and 1981 editions.

Litani and the 1982 invasion. In making these studies, the Israelis were able to build a substantial data base on major factors which were to relate to the upcoming conduct of operations in Lebanon.

Selected Chronology of the War in Lebanon

The chronology of the 1982 war is relatively straightforward at one level and extremely complex at another. The first three days of fighting were essentially the history of a brilliant Israeli offensive, with limited objectives, in which Israel rapidly achieved its announced objectives in invading Lebanon in spite of major terrain barriers and did so with negligible losses. While the performance of the Israeli Defense Force was scarcely perfect, it still represented an outstanding achievement in both combined arms and combined land-air-sea operations.

At another level, the Israelis had broader political and strategic objectives which led Israel to systematically expand its scope and which gradually transformed its character into a war against Syria and a war for control of Lebanon. In both cases, the IDF won the battle but lost the ultimate conflict. The war ended with Lebanon more

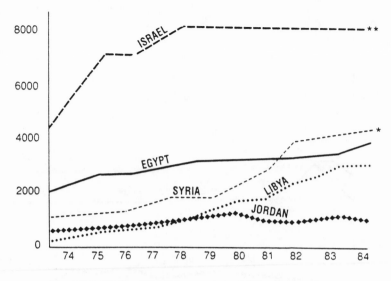

*No precise estimate available. Some are as low as 2,200.
**Some estimates count only AFUs and go as low as 4,000.

FIGURE 3.3   Comparative Trend in Other Armored Vehicle Strength. Adapted from IISS, *Military Balance* (London: International Institute for Strategic Studies), all yearly editions from 1975 to 1985; Stan Morse, *Modern Military Powers: Israel* (New York: The Military Press, 1984); and U.S. ACDA, *World Military Exports and Arms Transfers* (Washington, D.C.: GPO), 1976 and 1981 editions.

hostile to Israel than when it began, with Syrian influence in Lebanon substantially higher, with the PLO surviving as a threat, and with Israel's reputation severely damaged by its own political decisions and by the bloody consequences of internal Lebanese politics.

1970–1981. The 1982 fighting came as much because of the unresolved outcome of the 1967 and 1973 wars as from any specific cause affecting Lebanon. The fighting between the PLO and King Hussein for control of Jordan in 1969 and 1970 drove the PLO into Lebanon and laid the groundwork for a PLO mini-state that came to dominate much of West Beirut in Lebanon. This PLO presence helped trigger a civil war in Lebanon that inevitably led to both Israeli and Syrian intervention in Lebanese affairs and in which the various factions were sufficiently well balanced so that no clear end could be brought to the fighting.

The peace treaty between Egypt and Israel then transformed the Arab-Israel conflict into one between Israel and Syria and the PLO, as well as helped create a massive Syrian-Israeli arms race. It also made Lebanon the one area where the PLO could strike at Israel and made southern Lebanon an almost inevitable zone of contention between

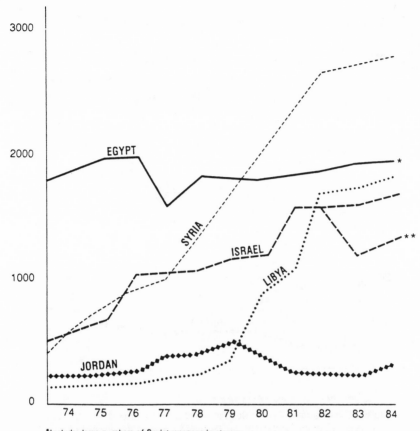

*Includes large numbers of Soviet weapons in storage.
**Precise estimate of active weapons not available.

FIGURE 3.4   Comparative Trend in Artillery and Multiple Rocket Launcher Strength. Adapted from IISS, *Military Balance* (London: International Institute for Strategic Studies), all yearly editions from 1975 to 1985; Stan Morse, *Modern Military Powers: Israel* (New York: The Military Press, 1984); and U.S. ACDA, *World Military Exports and Arms Transfers* (Washington, D.C.: GPO), 1976 and 1981 editions.

Israel and the PLO. From 1978 onward, this struggle escalated as increasing PLO border raids and rocket and artillery strikes on Israeli settlements led to steadily more severe Israeli reprisals, temporary cease-fires, and then a new conflict.

This led to a limited Israeli invasion in March 1978, called Operation Litani. This drove the PLO out of southern Lebanon, but U.S. and other external political pressure forced Israel to withdraw and, within a year, the PLO had reasserted itself in Lebanon. This led several Israel planners, including Israel's minister of defense, Ariel

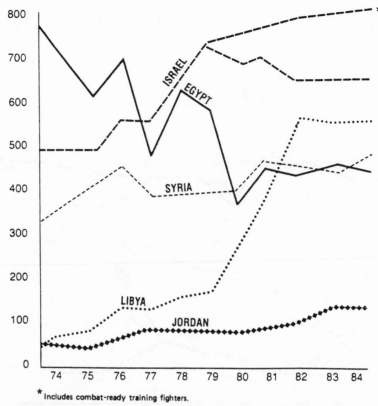

* Includes combat-ready training fighters.

FIGURE 3.5 Comparative Trend in Combat Aircraft Strength. Adapted from IISS, *Military Balance* (London: International Institute for Strategic Studies), all yearly editions from 1975 to 1985; Stan Morse, *Modern Military Powers: Israel* (New York: The Military Press, 1984); and U.S. ACDA, *World Military Exports and Arms Transfers* (Washington, D.C.: GPO), 1976 and 1981 editions.

Sharon, to conclude that only a full scale Israeli military operation to destroy PLO power in Lebanon could fully secure northern Israel. While it is not possible to date the formulation of the Israeli attack plan, Israel began serious planning for an invasion that could fully secure southern Lebanon not later than the spring of 1979, and this plan at least considered military action against Syria and the option of moving north to Beirut.

This Israeli planning effort was reinforced by the failure of the United Nations force in southern Lebanon (UNIFIL) to prevent a new series of PLO attacks in 1980 and 1981 and by Syria's ruthlessness in seizing control of Zahle, a largely Greek Orthodox city in the Bekaa Valley, in April 1981. This gave Syria control of the Beirut-Damascus

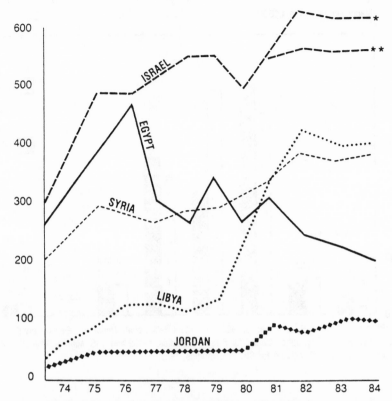

*Higher total includes Kfir trainers, but not TA-4 E H or Magister trainers.
**Does not include SU-7 or MiG-21 Soviet aircraft now in low state of readiness and repair.

FIGURE 3.6 Comparative Trend in High-Performance Jet Fighters. Note that Lebanon has no high-performance aircraft and is therefore not included. Adapted from IISS, *Military Balance* (London: International Institute for Strategic Studies), all yearly editions from 1975 to 1985; Stan Morse, *Modern Military Powers: Israel* (New York: The Military Press, 1984); and U.S. ACDA, *World Military Exports and Arms Transfers* (Washington, D.C.: GPO), 1976 and 1981 editions.

Road and raised growing questions in the minds of Israeli planners regarding its long-term ability to dominate Lebanon. From May to July 1981, the PLO launched some 1,200 rocket attacks on 26 towns in northern Israel. These incidents created the political and military climate that eventually led to the Israeli invasion in June 1982.

August 1981–June 1982. Israel massed four times near the Lebanese border in preparation for an attack. The attack was called off on each occasion due to international political pressure. The plan of attack called for a rapid advance to cut off the main PLO forces in southern Lebanon and to block their line of retreat to Damour and Beirut within

(Manpower Shown in 1,000s)

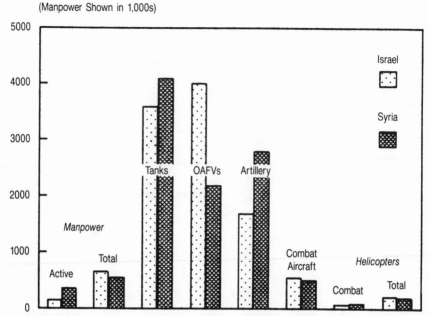

FIGURE 3.7   The Israeli-Syrian Balance: 1982. From Mark Heller, et al., *The Middle East Military Balance 1983* (Tel Aviv University, Jaffee Center for Strategic Studies, 1983), and IISS, *Military Balance, 1982–3* (London: International Institute for Strategic Studies, 1983).

72 hours. Contingency plans existed to engage Syria if it resisted. IDF forces were to advance rapidly and bypass the refugee camps and cities.

Disclosure of the details of these plans, largely because of Israeli briefings to U.S. officials and the press, led the PLO to adopt a strategy limiting the amount of forces and equipment it deployed forward and calling for rapid retreat after limited delaying actions. This strategy was never transformed from political doctrine into military plans and preparations.

24 July 1981. The U.S. arranged an informal cease-fire after Israel hit back with air and border raids.

July 1981–June 1982. In spite of the cease-fire, PLO forces carried out some 290 more attacks, killing 29 Israelis and wounding 271. Israel constantly retaliated with air raids, limited operations, and support to Hadad's "Christian" forces in southern Lebanon.

3 June 1982. Shlomo Argov, the Israeli Ambassador in London, was shot in the head by three terrorists. These later turned out to be connected with Syria, rather than the PLO, and one attacker was a Syrian intelligence official.

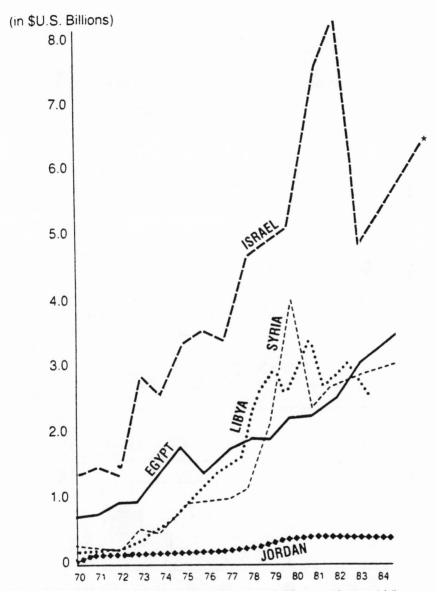

(in $U.S. Billions)

*IISS indicates range is $4 to $8 billion, given aid, war cost, and dollar conversion uncertainties.

FIGURE 3.8 Comparative Trend in Annual Defense Expenditures. Adapted from IISS, *Military Balance* (London: International Institute for Strategic Studies), all yearly editions from 1975 to 1985; Stan Morse, *Modern Military Powers: Israel* (New York: The Military Press, 1984); and U.S. ACDA, *World Military Exports and Arms Transfers* (Washington, D.C.: GPO), 1976 and 1981 editions.

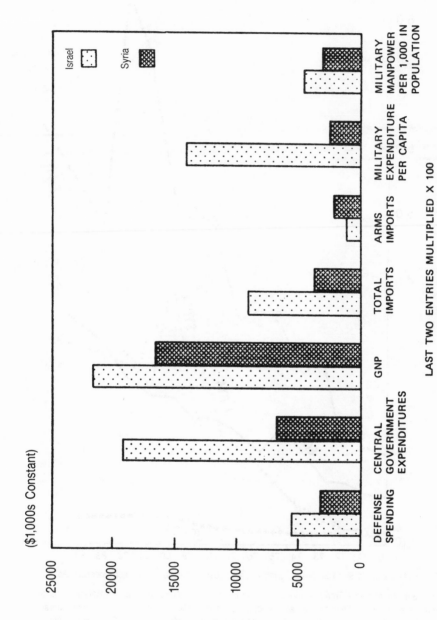

FIGURE 3.9 Israeli vs. Syrian Defense Effort: 1982. From Mark Heller, et al., *The Middle East Military Balance 1983* (Tel Aviv University, Jaffee Center for Strategic Studies, 1983), and IISS, *Military Balance, 1982–83* (London: International Institute for Strategic Studies, 1983).

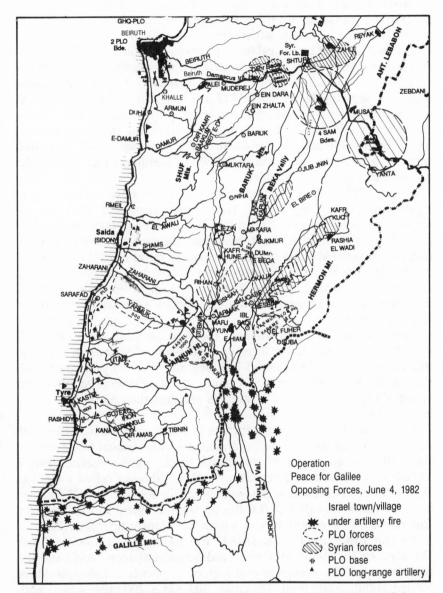

FIGURE 3.10 The Situation at the Start of the Israeli Invasion. Source: Israeli Ministry of Defense.

4 June 1982. The Israeli Air Force launched large-scale raids on PLO targets, including headquarters and military depots in Beirut. Arafat responded with a 24-hour artillery barrage against the villages supporting Hadad in southern Lebanon and northern Israel. Thirty strikes hit some 23 Israeli settlements.

5 June 1982. The Israeli cabinet approved a limited Israeli attack to create a security zone in southern Lebanon which was somewhat arbitrarily set 40 kilometers from the Israeli border. This zone was based on securing Israel from PLO artillery and rocket fire but was extremely vague in definition. It was eventually measured in two very conflicting ways. The first was from Rosh Hanikra, in central Galilee, which limited the zone to the Awali River. The second was measured from Israel's northern-most border town of Metulla, which limited the advance to a line south of Beirut.

6 June 1982. The IDF invaded southern Lebanon at 11:00 A.M. in Operation Peace for Galilee. The cabinet-approved goal was to achieve the security zone, and initial IDF planning was based on this goal. The Israeli minister of defense and chief of staff also, however, had two additional attack plans. One was to move north to Beirut and destroy the overall PLO military presence and political power base in Lebanon. The second, or "Big Plan," called for full-scale war against both the PLO and Syria and the creation of a Christian-dominated friendly Lebanon.[19]

The IDF attack was rushed forward without time for full mobilization of the IDF's three combat-ready divisions in order to minimize the risk of successful U.S. or other external pressure to halt the attack. At the same time, six hours of daylight were sacrificed for speed. Only half the combat reserves and less than 50 percent of the logistical units were activated.

Israel launched three main thrusts to cover each main north-south approach. There were seven separate *ugda* or divisional task forces in these thrusts, and three of these task forces were combined into a 35,000-man corps-sized force with roughly 800 tanks called the Bekaa Forces Group. The forces in the west eventually totaled some 22,000 men and 220 tanks. Roughly 76,000 troops were assigned to the Northern Command for the operation, along with 1,250 tanks and 1,500 APCs.

At the time the IDF attacked, the Syrians had the 1st Tank Division, an independent mechanized brigade, sixteen SAM batteries, and a number of commando and support elements in Lebanon. These totaled about 23,000 men, 320 tanks, 300 APCs, 200 crew-served anti-tank guns and missile launchers, 350 artillery weapons, and 80 anti-aircraft guns. One tank brigade and commando and support units were in the Anti-Lebanon Mountains; one tank brigade and commando and support units were near Beirut; one mechanized brigade, a PLA mechanized brigade and tank regiment, and Syrian commando and support units were in the Bekaa. Additional Syrian mechanized elements were north of the Beirut-Damascus Highway.

The PLO had eight different armed elements defending southern Lebanon, with a total of 9,000 men. The Castel Brigade, with 6,000 men, defended southern Lebanon from the coast to Mount Hermon. About 2,000 men were concentrated near Tyre. About 1,000 more men covered the coastal road between the Litani and Zahrani rivers, the greater Sidon area was defended by 1,500 men, and the Nabatiye region by about 1,500 more. The Yarmuk Brigade had a battalion in the Aishiye-Rihane area, and the Karame Brigade was deployed in Fatahland on the slopes of Mount Hermon. The Ain Jalud Brigade, with less than 1,000 men, defended the region between the Awali and Damour rivers. About 6,000 regular PLO forces defended Beirut. These forces had a total of about 300 T-34, T-54, and T-55 tanks, 150 APCs, 300 Sagger launchers and antitank guns, 200 AA guns, and 350 artillery weapons, but many were not deployed.[20]

The initial Israeli timetable called for a war of three days to overrun all PLO positions in southern Lebanon including Sidon, with the military defeat of the PLO by 8 June and consolidation of the IDF position by 9 June.

6–7 June 1982. In the west, the PLO began its retreat toward Tyre and the refugee camps after several hours of fighting. The IDF crossed the Litani and reached and bypassed Tyre in the west, although not without some delays because of a successful series of PLO ambushes. Organized PLO resistance then, however, started crumbling rapidly.

The first elements of a large IDF amphibious force landed at night north of Sidon at the mouth of the Alawi. They blocked the coastal road and began to move inland. Organized PLO resistance virtually halted in southern Lebanon by the morning of 7 June.

In the center, IDF forces attacked the Litani crossing areas at Beaufort Castle and the other bridges across the Litani. By nightfall on 6 June, all of the crossings except the one at Beaufort Castle were in Israeli hands. Beaufort Castle, which is several hundred meters above the Litani gorge, was attacked shortly after dusk and taken by the morning of 7 June. About 35 PLO killed and wounded were left behind, and the Israelis suffered 6 killed and 28 wounded. During the night, Nabatiye was encircled, and IDF units moved to link up with IDF forces in the west.

In the east, the Bekaa Forces Group immediately came under fire from forward Syrian and PLO elements. This resistance, however, was not serious. Syrian forces retreated in considerable disarray. In the case of the PLO, elements of the Castel Brigade put up scattered resistance. The Krama Brigade retreated east and north without a fight and left most of its equipment and ammunition behind.

Israel did not, however, push its advance in the Bekaa. Having achieved most of its security zone goals in the first day, it virtually halted until 9 June, although Syria had not organized its defense and was at its most vulnerable position in the war. It was not clear whether this delay in Israeli action was the result of efforts to keep Syria out of the war or Sharon's failure to pressure the Israeli cabinet to support a major attack on Syria.

The Israeli Air Force flew extensive attack sorties, virtually without opposition. An IAF Skyhawk was shot down by a PLO missile, the IAF's only combat loss of the main period of the war.

7–8 June 1982. IDF forces in the west advanced past Tyre and began mopping up operations in the border area. The refugee camp at Rachidiye outside Tyre was encircled. The commander of the PLO unit in Tyre, Azami Zarayer, abandoned his troops and fled north. Rachidiye, however, has massive ammunition and weapons stocks and PLO irregulars dug in and fought. Only half of the camp was taken by the night of the 7th. Other IDF forces moved rapidly north toward Sidon and linked up with elements of the IDF forces in the Central Sector at the mouth of the Zahrani River on the night of the 7th. The coastal refinery and its oil stocks fell intact into IDF hands. By the morning of the 8th, Sidon was encircled.

The commando elements of the IDF landing force at the Awali were steadily reinforced to brigade strength, and Israel used up to 14 landing craft with air, submarine, and missile-boat escorts. Elements reached north to within 7 kilometers of Damour and 20 kilometers of Beirut. Other elements secured the coastal plain in the land area while a third group went south and blocked the road north from Sidon.

In the central sector, IDF forces occupied Nabatiye, after limited resistance, and then the Arnoun-Nabitye plateau. The PLO ceased to operate as an organized force in this sector by the night of the 7th and became almost totally dependent on Syria. Elements of the central sector task forces linked up with the IDF forces in the west near Sidon. Other elements rapidly moved some 30 kilometers north along the heights above the Bekaa with only scattered and ineffectual Syrian resistance. By the night of the 7th, elements of the IDF were near the Besri River.

In the east, the IDF task force consolidated positions on the Hasbaiya-Kaoukaba line and moved east of Hasbiya (which was roughly parallel to the Zaharani River). Aside from some scattered shelling, the IDF won its objective in the Bekaa without serious opposition.

The IAF provided air support virtually at will. The only air combat resulted in the loss of one Syrian MiG-23, the first sign of Syrian air activity since the war began.

8–9 June 1982. In the west, the IDF mopped up final opposition near Tyre and at the Rachidiye refugee camp. The IDF then moved more than 60 kilometers through very rough terrain and over two major water barriers. The main problem in the south was sorting out civilian and PLO elements and dealing with scattered individual resistance. In 48 hours, the IDF had taken all major positions south of the Awali River, except Sidon and the el-Hilwe refugee camp. The IDF spent some six days, however, trying to negotiate a surrender and cease-fire of the remaining PLO forces in Sidon and of the el-Hilwe camp before taking it by force. The first three days of fighting and the major battle sites are summarized in Figures 3.11 and 3.12.

Other elements of the IDF crossed the Damour River, and the city was enveloped on the night of the 8th. Strong Popular Front for the Liberation of Palestine (PFLP) resistance was encountered by the IAF and Israeli Navy. They eventually pushed the PFLP out of Damour, but at this point, some 6,000 to 7,000 of the 9,000 PLO forces in southern Lebanon at the start of the fighting had either escaped to Beirut or into Syrian positions.

In the central sector, IAF forces had their first serious clash with Syrian forces near the Besri bridge (northeast of Sidon). This clash resulted in the first high command order to move as quickly as possible to the Beirut-Damascus Road. In spite of extremely difficult mountain roads, the IDF advanced nearly 50 kilometers in one day in the central sector and reached Beit ed Dine and the Safa River—the southeastern defenses of Beirut—and approached Ain Zhalta, about 10 kilometers from the Beirut-Damascus Road.

The IDF then decided to move north through Ain Zhalta to cut the Beirut-Damascus Road. This signaled a clear intention to attack a vital Syrian objective and triggered intensive fighting in Ain Zhalta with Syrian tank and commando forces. On the evening of the 8th, IDF elements were caught in an ambush in Ain Zhalta and took serious losses. The Syrians remained entrenched around Ain Zhalta.

In the east, the IDF objective was switched from seizing a defensive zone to an attack on Syrian forces. IDF forces assaulted and took Jezine after resistance by newly arrived and poorly positioned Syrian troops and the PLO Yarmuk Brigade. Other troops drove north of Mimes toward Rashaiya and drove through a Syrian ambush and defense position near Wadi Shebaa. Syrian resistance was still relatively

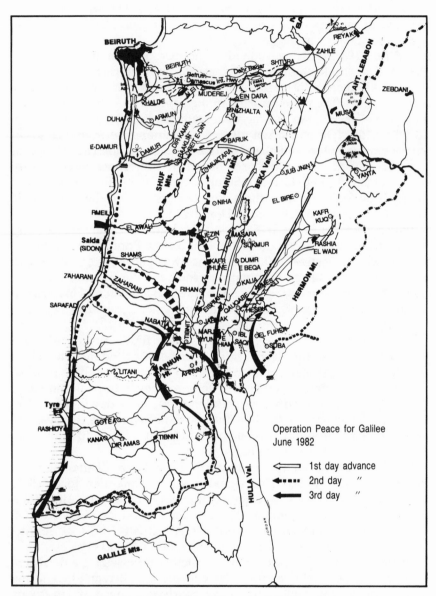

FIGURE 3.11 The First Three Days of Fighting. Source: Israeli Ministry of Defense.

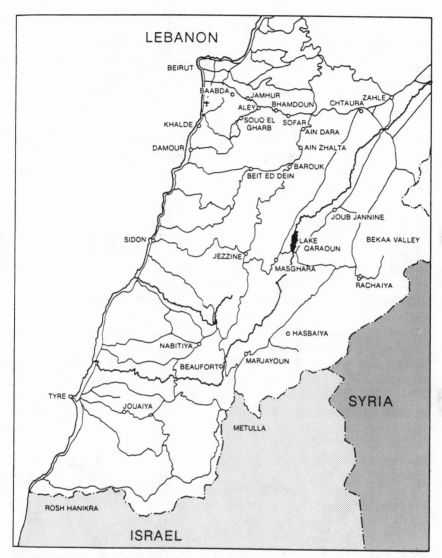

FIGURE 3.12 Major Battle Sites Throughout the War. Source: Israeli Ministry of Defense.

light and ineffective, but the IDF chose not to engage Syrian units in Wadi Shebaa.

Scattered air-to-air combat led to the loss of six Syrian MiG-23s over Beirut, Sidon, and Damour.

9–10 June 1982. In the west, the battle for Sidon continued but only for a limited number of PLO-held areas in the center. The attack on the el-Hilwe refugee camp was postponed. Other IDF elements moved north on Damour and began to meet stiffer PLO resistance and many ambushes as the fighting increasingly took on the character of urban warfare. The PFLP put up the best resistance of any PLO force. Damour was taken in a sunrise assault, however, on 10 June. Syria then realized that Beirut was under attack and rapidly established a defensive position near Khalde and Ain Aanoub with PLO backing.

In the center, the limited remains of the IDF force were bogged down in Ain Zhalta on the 9th but moved forward to reach Syrian positions by conducting a night march. By dawn on 10 June, IDF forces were ready to attack Syrian positions around Ain Zhalta.

In the east, the war then shifted character, and Syria became fully involved. Syria had already moved three more SAM batteries into Lebanon on 7 June and had begun to pull units out of the Golan. This seems to have been more a matter of posturing than serious military intent but created a situation where an IDF effort to surprise Syrian air defenses in the Bekaa became time-sensitive. At the same time, PLO forces fled north into Syrian-occupied territory, and exchanges between the IDF and Syria increased.

At 2:00 P.M. on 9 June, the IDF launched a massive attack on the nineteen major surface-to-air missile batteries that made up Syrian land-based air defenses in the Bekaa. The Syrian Air Force attempted to provide air cover for its missiles, and some 100 Israeli and 50 Syrian fighters engaged. Within hours, 17 Syrian SAM batteries and 29 Syrian MiGs were destroyed, along with many Syrian ZSU-23-4 and other AA guns.

IDF ground forces continued to advance, but against full-scale Syrian resistance. Syrian antitank helicopters were used in considerable numbers, and some Syrian close support sorties were flown. Hilwe was taken after brutal fighting, and the IDF was within one kilometer of Dhunaybah and took the village of Lavi. While Syria continued to fight, the Syrian main defense was breached with relatively limited IDF losses.[21]

10–11 June 1982. In the west, fighting continued in Sidon and resulted in heavy IDF use of artillery, air, and naval guns. The city hospital became the center of the PLO position and the fighting. El-Hilwe was left in PLO hands. The IDF advanced north, however, to the outskirts of Khalde, south of Beirut airport, making extensive use of air and naval gunfire support. The IDF decided to envelope PLO and Syrian forces southeast of Beirut and cut them off from the coastal road. IDF forces took control of the southern Shouf.

In the center, the IDF attacked Syrian positions near Ain Zhalta from the south and north, and the Syrians withdrew in confusion once they no longer had a fixed defensive line. IDF forces advanced but were held up at the next Syrian strongpoint at Ain Dara. After initial air and helicopter attacks and the successful use of antitank helicopters against Syrian tanks, the IDF commander decided not to try a frontal assault and took positions in the heights about three kilometers from the Beirut-Damascus Road.

The fighting was intense in the east. Early on the morning of 10 June, IDF forces engaged the 1st Syrian Tank Division—which had 300 tanks and 150 artillery pieces—in the area north of Lake Karaoun and south of Joub Janine and Rashiya. Sustained combined arms warfare took place, and the Syrian forces were driven north as the IDF moved toward Bekaa and Kfar Quoq in the eastern Bekaa, took Kafraiya, and drove north toward Kabb Elias and the Beirut-Damascus Road. The Syrians then deployed the 3rd Tank Division into Lebanon as the forces in the Bekaa began to lose unit cohesion.

On the night of the 10th, however, advancing IDF forces rushed into the defensive perimeter of 1st Tank Division forces near Sultan Yacoub. The Syrians had prepared an excellent ambush, and the result was brutal night fighting. IDF forces were halted south of the Beirut-Damascus Highway during the night of 10–11 June, as Syrian reinforcements entered Lebanon in strength. A Syrian tank brigade was caught in mid-movement by IAF forces, however, and lost 20 tanks and many of its vehicles to air attack.

By the morning of 11 June, Syria had moved extensive reinforcements into Lebanon around Zahle and the Beirut-Damascus Road, but many Syrian elements were cut off and without supplies. The IDF pushed forward, trying to reach the road before a 12:00 A.M. cease-fire with Syria was to go into effect. It was largely halted by elements of the Syrian 3rd Tank Division, although a number of Syrian T-72s were lost. The cease-fire deadline arrived with IDF forces north of Baka and Joub Jannine in the eastern Bekaa and in the Ain Dara/Ain Zhalta area in the western Bekaa.

The fighting in the air continued as Syria continued to commit its MiG-21 and MiG-23 to one-sided air combat against IAF fighters. The total Israeli kills reached 65 Syrian aircraft by the end of the 10th. Over 80 Syrian aircraft were lost in a three-day period.

11–12 June 1982. An Israeli-Syrian cease-fire took place in the Bekaa, but not in the west. IDF forces took all but a few positions in Sidon and moved steadily farther north. Khalde was taken with limited resistance. On the night of 11–12 June, many Syrian and PLO units withdrew to Beirut, while IDF forces increasingly encountered Syrian commandos.

IDF forces in the center moved steadily forward by infiltrating through mountain areas but did not reach the Beirut-Damascus Road before the cease-fire.

The Israelis declared a unilateral cease-fire with the PLO at 9:00 A.M. on 12 June. The PLO tacitly accepted.

The IAF shot down eighteen more Syrian MiGs shortly before the cease-fire.

13 June 1982. At 11:00 A.M., IDF paratroopers linked up with the Lebanese forces of the Maronites outside Beirut. Meanwhile, the cease-fire broke down, and heavy fighting broke out for control of the presidential palace at Baaba and for Khalde to the west of Beirut on the Beirut-Damascus Road. The fighting until the siege of Beirut is summarized in Figure 3.13.

14–17 June 1982. The Israelis gradually seized the area around Beirut. Baaba was taken on the 14th. The Israelis called for a Syrian withdrawal from the area around Beirut. Syria refused. Extensive fighting occurred along the Beirut-Damascus Road.

The el-Hilwe refugee camp was taken on the 14th–15th, after extensive surgical shelling, bombing, and hand-to-hand combat. By 17 June, the IDF losses included 214 killed, 1,176 wounded, 23 MIAs, and one POW. The Syrians had several hundred killed and thousands wounded. PLO losses were estimated at around 1,000 killed, 2,200 wounded, and 5,000 POWs.[22]

There was now little organized resistance in Beirut. Many experts later argued that the IDF could have taken Beirut at this point with negligible Syrian or PLO resistance.

20 June 1982. The IDF finally took full control of Beirut International Airport. Beirut could not be fully cut off, however, because the Syrians controlled access to the west and the Beirut-Damascus Road, and the PLO had positions in the west. The IDF decided to lay full siege to the city.

At this point, PLO, PLA, and Syrian resistance stiffened, and organized defenses existed in West Beirut.

22 June 1982. The cease-fire totally collapsed on the 22nd and 23rd as the IDF began its attack to seize control of Beirut. The IDF launched a full-scale attack to control the western portion of the Beirut-Damascus Road. Fighting broke out at Jamhur, Aley, Bhamdoun, Sofar, and

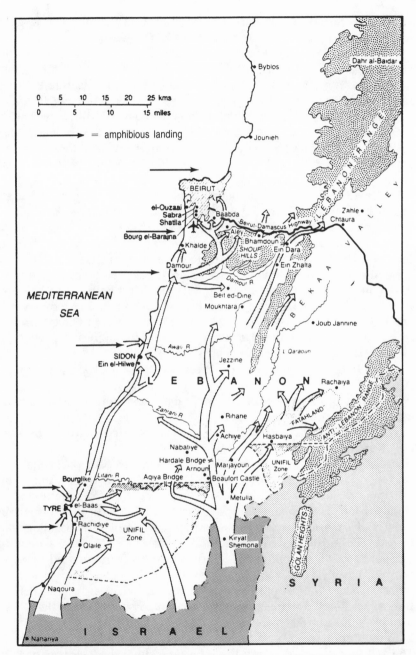

FIGURE 3.13 The Fighting Up to the Siege of Beirut. From John Laffin, *The War of Desperation* (London: Osprey Publishing Ltd., 1985), p. 60, and materials provided by the office of the spokesman of the Israeli Defense Forces.

Hammana. Syrian air-defense positions around Beirut were largely destroyed, and major artillery and air strikes began.

23–25 June 1982. Intense Syrian-Israeli fighting occurred for the control of access to Beirut and the Beirut-Damascus Road as far east as Hammana. The IDF took full control of the road from Baabda to Sofar by the morning of the 25th. A new cease-fire was agreed to at 6:00 P.M.

At this point, some 14,000 Arab troops were encircled in Beirut, with 10,000 from the PLO, 2,000 from a Syrian-supported PLO brigade, and 2,300 from a Syrian brigade. The main military problem was the presence of over 350,000 civilians in the PLO-controlled area of West Beirut.

1 July 1982. The Siege of Beirut was reported to begin, although efforts by American negotiator Philip Habib to persuade the PLO to evacuate did not really break down until 2 July.

3 July 1982. After an attempt to negotiate PLO withdrawal from Beirut broke down, the IDF decided to lay an organized siege to Beirut. It started an artillery duel designed to break the cease-fire, edged slowly to the "Green Line" dividing East and West Beirut, and forward into the PLO and Syrian positions with constant small-unit movements. The IAF kept up harassing attacks. Israel constantly, however, offered an escape route to civilians and expressed its willingness to negotiate the evacuation of Syrian and Lebanese troops.

4 July 1982. The IDF sealed off West Beirut. A blockade was now in effect.

5–12 July 1982. IDF artillery barraged West Beirut. Shortages of food and water became serious.

13–20 July 1982. Artillery attacks alternated with efforts at negotiation.

21 July 1982. The PLO infiltrated through Syrian positions and started attacks on IDF forces. The IDF replied to these attacks by starting a major series of air and artillery attacks on West Beirut.

23–26 July 1982. Israel launched major air raids on PLO targets in West Beirut after dropping warning leaflets. These escalated to include PLO-dominated residential areas after 27 July. Constant pressure was kept up on PLO areas and PLO-dominated refugee camps.

Israel hit at Syrian positions along the eastern part of the Beirut-Damascus Road. Syrian forces took serious losses although they were then built up to 60,000 men.

Syria deployed three SA-8 batteries into the Bekaa on the 23rd. The IAF destroyed all three the following day. The IAF began daily attacks on Syrian and PLO positions in West Beirut.

28 July–3 August 1982. The IDF systematically tightened the noose around Beirut with constant air attacks and artillery shelling of military targets and a slow advance in to the outskirts of West Beirut. IDF forces landed at Jounie, a Christian port north of Beirut.

4 August 1982. Israeli forces drove into Beirut after the latest round of talks with the PLO collapsed. They advanced across the Green Line and north from the airport toward Lailaki. The main thrust at the Museum Crossing on the Green Line was halted by stiff PLO resistance. Nineteen IDF soldiers were killed and 64 wounded, although all three major refugee camps were now outflanked. It was clear to the IDF that any frontal attack on West Beirut would involve costly urban warfare and house-to-house fighting. The U.S. criticized Israel for attacking in the midst of what it felt were successful negotiations.

6 August 1982. PLO reached agreement with Habib on all major points regarding evacuation.

9 August 1982. The Israeli government was formally presented with the Habib plan. IAF air strikes continued, but there was no major fighting.

10–11 August 1982. Israel launched a massive air and artillery bombardment of Beirut in spite of near agreement to PLO withdrawal. Sharon later claimed it was in retaliation for PLO artillery fire which killed two Israeli soldiers and wounded 77. The Israeli cabinet, however, disagreed and forbade further air attacks on Beirut unless authorized by the cabinet.

13 August 1982. PLO identified 9,500 troops to be evacuated.

18 August 1982. The Lebanese government agreed to PLO evacuation plan.

19 August 1982. The Israeli government agreed to the PLO evacuation plan.

21 August 1982. The first PLO forces withdrew.

25 August 1982. The first U.S. Marines for the Multi-National Force (MNF) to supervise the evacuation arrived.

27–30 August 1982. Land evacuation to Syria began. Arafat left Lebanon on 30 August.

31 August 1982. IAF shot down a MiG-25, raising the total number of Syrian losses in the war to 88 aircraft.

10 September 1982. U.S. Marines in the MNF left Lebanon.

14–15 September 1982. Bashir Gemayel was assassinated on 14th. Israel occupied West Beirut on the 15th and 16th.

16–18 September 1982. Phalangists conducted massacres at Shatila and Sabra refugee camps. Some 700 to 800 were killed.

20–21 September 1982. The Lebanese government asked for the return of the MNF. Amin Gemayel was elected president.

24–27 September 1982. The MNF returned to Beirut.

19 April 1983. A truck bomb hit the U.S. Embassy in Beirut. The blast killed 63, including 17 Americans.

28 August 1983. Amal seized control of West Beirut from the Lebanese Army. The Army recovered the area, but major civil fighting continued.

2–3 September 1983. The IDF was redeployed to southern Lebanon after 260 attacks were staged from that area, in which 200 Israeli soldiers were killed or wounded.

16 September–22 November 1983. Arafat returned to Tripoli. A long brutal battle began between the PLO and Syria.

23 October 1983. Truck bomb attacks on the MNF killed 241 and wounded 100 U.S. Marines and caused 150 casualties in the French force.

10 November–4 December 1983. The U.S. unsuccessfully sought to conduct reprisal attacks with naval gunfire and bombers.

4 February 1984. The Lebanese Army began its final collapse.

21–26 February 1984. U.S. Marines withdrew from Lebanon.

The Politics of Turning Defeat into Victory

The irony that shapes any historical analysis of the 1982 conflict is that Israel won its original military objectives with negligible losses and under favorable grand strategic conditions and did so within days of the beginning of its invasion. Israel attacked on 6 June and destroyed the limited organized Palestinian military presence in southern Lebanon. It succeeded in occupying the desired security zone within 40 kilometers of the border within a period of about three days. It did so without any major encounters with the Syrians and at a cost of only 25 dead, 96 wounded, and 7 missing in action.

If Israel had stopped at this point, when it had already won the war its cabinet and prime minister had authorized, it might well have created a climate where Lebanese Christians, Druze, and Shi'ites would have prevented the return of Palestinian forces. While Israel had fallen behind its own timetable in seizing the security zone it sought in southern Lebanon, this was unimportant in terms of the original operational objective. Israel slowed badly only in the area near the "red line" where Syrian forces were deployed. It otherwise conducted a brilliant three-pronged "all arms" attack through extremely difficult terrain and with minimal losses.

There were, after all, only about 6,000 Palestinian regulars in the field in the south, and only a handful of the total equipment shown in Table 3.1 was deployed. Further, the PLO regulars quickly retreated to Beirut in the face of the Israeli attack, a retreat that often turned into a rout when key Palestinian commanders deserted their men and ran.

Israel would only have faced the problem of dealing with the Palestinian militias and volunteers in the camps and cities in the south and in finding a way to force their surrender without having to take the losses and inflict the civilian casualties inevitable in such a form of urban warfare. The IDF showed it could do this when it took the Rachidiye Camp south of Tyre with negligible losses. Further, if Israel had stopped at the 40-kilometer mark that was its original objective, the IDF would not have had to take the El-Hilwe Camp south of Sidon, which involved some of the heaviest fighting with the Palestinians in the war.

After 9 June, however, Ariel Sharon's hidden agenda created chaos out of order and snatched defeat from the jaws of victory. Sharon systematically thrust Israeli forces into expanding, but undefined, strategic objectives which were never properly defined. Sharon's goals, although not those of the Israeli cabinet, included the creation of a Christian-dominated and friendly Lebanese state and the expulsion or destruction of all Palestinian military forces in Lebanon.[23]

Sharon forgot, or rejected, a basic strategic and operational principle that Israel had followed ever since 1948: He attempted to win an absolute victory over an Arab state, something that Israel simply lacks the political and military means to accomplish. His objectives were open-ended and might well have dragged Israel into a pointless all-out war with Syria that it was not prepared to fight and which would have had no predictable end. He ignored the political realities in Lebanon and attempted to restore a Christian dominance lost at least a decade earlier in the face of an Islamic resurgence that made a backlash inevitable.

Sharon also forgot the operational need to achieve results before the U.S. intervened. His need to conceal the true purpose of the war from the cabinet, and many of his commanders also deprived the IDF of its ability to plan and execute a quick and decisive pattern of operations. If the IDF had planned for these objectives at the outset and had driven directly to seize Beirut, had destroyed Palestinian forces before they could organize their defense, and had cut off Syrian forces from their major line of retreat through the Beirut-Damascus Road, it is likely that Israel would have at least have achieved its major military goals by 20 June.[24]

TABLE 3.2 Syrian and Israeli Forces and Losses in the Key Initial Battles of the 1982 War

FORCES	Israel [1]	Syria [2]
Force Ratios on 8-11 June 1982		
Troops	35,000	22,000
Tanks	800	300
APCs	1,500	352
Crew Served Anti-Tank Weapons	-	200
Major artillery pieces	-	300
Anti-Aircraft Guns	-	100
Close Support Aircraft	275	225
Non-Organic SAM Launchers	-	125 [1]
Force Ratios in Bekaa Valley Battle Phase One: Late 8 June 1982		
Troops	35,000	22,000
Tanks	800	300
Close Support Aircraft	275	225 [2]
Non-Organic SAM Launchers	-	120 [3]
Force Ratios in Bekaa Valley Battle Phase Two: 8-11 June 1982		
Troops	34,000	28,000
Tanks	750	400
Close Support Aircraft	250	130
Non-Organic SAM Launchers	-	12
ESTIMATED LOSSES		
Personnel		
Killed	195	800
Wounded	872	3,200
Missing and POWs	15	150
Total	1,082	4,150
Tanks [4]	30	400
Aircraft and helicopters	0	90
SAM Launchers	0	120
% Casualties Per Day	1.05	5.53

1. Seventy-six launch units. SA-2 units had 1 launcher, SA-3 units had 2, and SA-6 units had 3.
2. Reduced to 195 by mid-afternoon on 9 June.
3. Reduced to 8 launcher units with 12 launchers by mid-afternoon on 9 June.
4. Minor damage was inflicted on 100 more Israeli tanks.

Adapted from Trevor N. Dupuy and Paul N. Martell, *Flawed Victory* (Fairfax, VA: Hero Books, 1986), pp. 221, 222, and 225, and Richard A. Gabriel, *Operation Peace for Galilee* (New York: Hill and Wang, 1984), pp. 232–236.

As Table 3.2 shows, Israel achieved a very favorable initial force ratio in the Bekaa, which was reinforced by Israel's ability to achieve air supremacy and Syrian delays in reinforcing the Bekaa and deploying for battle. In practice, however, Israel's key thrusts against Syrian forces and Beirut could never be given the overt priority needed for success, and even the key commanders involved were often left in the dark as to their ultimate objective. The Israeli thrust against Syria came far too late and indecisively, and the IDF often confronted prepared and well dug-in Syrian forces.

While Syrian forces did not fight well in terms of fighting as an organized central force, the slow Israeli advance gave smaller Syrian elements time to deploy and dig in, and such elements generally fought well using a combination of tanks and antitank weapons supported by helicopters. Syrian commandos did particularly well and made excellent use of terrain to delay Israeli forces by retreating from one ambush position to another. As a result, Israeli troops suffered avoidable losses and delays in encounters with Syrian forces in several battles in the Bekaa like that at Sultan Yacoub, in the fighting for Zahle and Rayak to take the Beirut-Damascus Road before 12 June, and earlier at Ain Zhalta on the coastal road on 7 and 8 June.

Only Israel's brilliant performance in the air and in suppressing Syrian ground-based air defense and President Assad's deliberate decision to delay the reinforcement of his forces in Syria to avoid provoking an Israeli attack allowed Israel to avoid far more serious losses. Israel's politics had crippled both its ability to maneuver and its sense of operational direction and led it into meeting engagements against well-positioned forces, one of the operational problems Israel had sought to avoid throughout its history.

Similarly, the IDF advanced far more slowly in making the 90-kilometer advance to Beirut than it had to because it was never clear to its field commanders what the goal really was. When Israeli forces did link up with Maronite Phalange forces on 13 June, eight days after the war's start, the IDF paused on the edge of a Beirut it had never intended to reach and probably could have taken the city and disorganized PLO forces in a quick thrust.

Israel then laid a siege to Beirut which destroyed the willingness of the Muslim and Druze Lebanese to tolerate either an Israeli presence or a Christian regime, a disaster reinforced by its bombing and artillery assaults on Beirut and indirect participation in the Maronite massacres of Palestinians in the Sabra and Shatila refugee camps following the assassination of "President" Bashir Gemayel on 13 September 1982. Sharon succeeded in redefining Liddel Hart's concept of the "expanding torrent" in a new and singularly inept way. He kept pushing each element of Israeli forces a bridge or mountain too far.

This pattern of events also, however, makes it extremely difficult to judge the operational lessons of the 1982 fighting. A debate still is going on within the IDF and Israel as to how many of Israel's operational problems in 1982 were the result of problems in its operational art and how many were the legacy of Sharon.

Even relatively small actions like the battle for Beaufort Castle, which involved negligible Palestinian forces, can be viewed either as being the result of command decisions to bypass Palestinian forces and let them retreat—decisions which would have been wise given the limited objectives known to field commanders—or as the result of problems in command and control. The slow advance on Syrian forces and the Beirut-Damascus Road can be seen as the result of Sharon's need to expand the war in stages without informing his commanders or as the result of a lack of infantry trained for mountain warfare and the support of armor against dug-in Syrian forces and problems in the coordination of combined arms.

There is no way to distinguish true problems in the operational art from the consequences of a key strategic failure, and this has affected virtually every effort to analyze the history of the fighting. A flood of books has emerged since the war proving (a) Sharon was at fault, (b) the IDF had a deeply flawed force structure and major weaknesses in its art of war, and (c) Sharon was right and/or the IDF performed almost flawlessly. Unfortunately, Israel has classified much of the key information involved, and there often is no way to distinguish the operational art of war from the operational art of history.

Casualties and Losses

Estimates of the casualties that resulted from the 1982 fighting are shown in Table 3.2 and in Figures 3.14 to 3.15. It is important to note that many of the casualties in the fighting were Lebanese civilians, and no fully reliable estimates exist of Syrian or PLO losses. This makes any estimate highly speculative, and estimates of losses of Lebanese civilians have often been exaggerated as part of attacks on Israel.

CASUALTIES

| ISRAEL | Killed: 368
Wounded: 2,383
TOTAL: 2,751
POW: 7 | SYRIA | Killed: 1,000
Wounded: 3,000
TOTAL: 4,000 | PLO | Killed: 2,000 (?)
Wounded: 3,000 (?)
TOTAL: 7,000 (?)
POW: 250 |

EQUIPMENT LOSSES

| ISRAEL | Tanks: (up to) 150*　　APCs: (up to) 175
Aircraft: 2　　Helicopters: 3 |

| SYRIA | Tanks: 350-400　　MiG Aircraft: 92
SAM Sites: 29 |

| PLO | Trucks, APCs, & Tanks: 2,600 (captured by Israelis)
Artillery pieces: 1,700 (captured by Israelis)
Munitions: 6,000 tons (captured by Israelis) |

*But the Israelis claimed only 30-40 lost.

FIGURE 3.14 Lebanon War: Casualties and Losses. From Yezid Sayigh, "Israel's Military Performance in Lebanon, June 1982," *Journal of Palestine Studies*, Vol. 13, No. 1 (Fall 1983), and information provided by an IDF spokesman and the Embassy of Lebanon.

What is most striking, however, is just how limited Israel casualties were, particularly when it is remembered that Israel lost nearly 60 percent of its killed in small guerrilla actions after it had completed its encirclement of Beirut. It is clear that there is no correlation between the use of modern technology, large numbers of modern weapons, and high casualties.

Ironically, the first major Arab-Israeli war, fought largely by poorly armed infantry, was by far the most lethal in terms of military casualties. This lesson regarding the lack of correlation between modern technology, weapons numbers, and casualties is supported by the pattern of casualties in the other wars under study. High technology combat often produces far fewer casualties than regular infantry or guerrilla engagements.

154

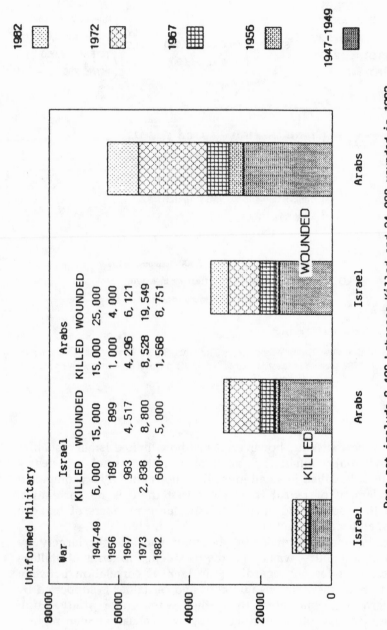

Uniformed Military

| War | Israel | | Arabs | |
	KILLED	WOUNDED	KILLED	WOUNDED
1947-49	6,000	15,000	15,000	25,000
1956	189	899	1,000	4,000
1967	983	4,517	4,296	6,121
1973	2,838	8,800	8,528	19,549
1982	600+	5,000	1,568	8,751

KILLED   WOUNDED

Israel   Arabs   Israel   Arabs

Does not include 8,400 Lebanese Killed and 34,000 wounded in 1982

1982

1972

1967

1956

1947-1949

FIGURE 3.15   Direct Military Casualties in the Arab-Israeli Wars: 1947–1984. From Richard Gabriel, *Operation Peace for Galilee* (New York: Hill and Wang, 1984); Yezid Sayigh, "Israel's Military Performance in Lebanon, June 1982," *Journal of Palestine Studies*, Vol. 13, No. 1 (Fall 1983); and various sources interviewed by the authors.

Threat Assessment Technologies

All of the forces involved in the 1982 war had an excellent understanding of the size and capabilities of opposing forces before the war began. Moreover, various versions of the Israeli attack plan were widely circulated before the war began. Although the PLO lacked any technical means of collecting intelligence, Arafat had obtained an attack plan remarkably close to the one Israel used in Operation Peace for Galilee. However, PLO commanders in many cases deserted their troops, leading to a subsequent unraveling of command structures. This was a major contributing reason for PLO fighters being pushed back to Beirut and amounted to a de facto reliance on Beirut as an urban barrier, and external intervention, to save the PLO from itself.

The practical problem the PLO faced was that it was more an occupation force, whose military elements were organized along political and ideological lines, than a force designed to fight against Israel. The warning was there, but C^3 structure, organization, and training were not. If the PLO had been organized and led half as well as Syria's commandos, they might have inflicted far more casualties and greater delay on Israel. Warning is useless without military capability, an understanding which Arafat displayed in an interview in *The Economist*. At least five months before the invasion, Arafat started issuing warnings to his commanders that the attack might reach as far as Beirut, and it is clear that he had a good picture of the briefing maps Sharon had used in Washington to explain his "contingency plan."[25]

The problem for the PLO in using this warning was twofold. First, the command system was so propagandized and political it could not distinguish real warnings from political gestures, particularly when the warnings were constantly repeated and there was no way to predict the precise time of the attack. The second problem was that the PLO's divided military elements could not really react to warning. The logical PLO strategy would have been defense in depth, holding a few strongpoints only to delay the IDF's advance, but constantly moving from one ambush point to another with full preparation in terms of scouting, weapons deployment, training of special units, etc. The refugee camps in the south should have been organized, trained, and equipped to force a prolonged siege. Guerrilla elements should have been trained to remain in place after the Israeli advances and then should have attacked them from the rear. In practice, the PLO continued to train for infiltration and artillery/rocket attacks on Israel, regular army operations, and generic combat training. No real defense plan emerged, and no pre-attack organization worthy of the name took place. Like the PLO, Syria almost certainly had access to Israel's plan of attack and clear warning that an attack was imminent. The problem faced was the classic one of distinguishing capabilities from intentions.

Syria also clearly sought to decouple itself from the PLO. Syria's chief of staff, Major General Hikmat Chehabi, downplayed PLO warnings of an attack at a meeting in Damascus with Abu Jihad and Brigadier Abu al-Walid of the PLO only a week before the attack. Syria pulled its radar-controlled 57-mm AA guns out of the Kaldeh area and stripped pro-Syrian PLO and PLA units of many of their SA-7s a week before the war began.[26] Syria made surprisingly little effort to hold the Shouf or secure the rear of any PLO position.

During the first few days of the war, Syria clearly acted on the belief that Israel's intentions were limited to an attack on the PLO, and Syria took only a limited defensive stance. Syria avoided reinforcing its position in Lebanon and the Bekaa because it feared that it would provoke Israel into broadening its attack. It seems to have acted on the assumption that it would secure its own strategic position and be able to dominate the unoccupied parts of Lebanon once the IDF defeated the PLO.

Israel's problems were more complex. Israel had excellent technical intelligence using PHOTINT, ELINT, and HUMINT. These assets provided excellent order-of-battle and targeting intelligence before the war, and Israel made effective use of reconnaissance aircraft, E-2Cs and specialized ELINT aircraft, RPVs, helicopters, and at least some illegally obtained U.S. intelligence data both before and after the conflict. Nevertheless, Israel made several critical mistakes in threat assessment:

- It never fully unified its intelligence structure. The regular army intelligence operation was paralleled by a separate operation under the minister of defense which operated on ideological lines and supported his broader ambitions in seeking the control of Lebanon and a strategic defeat of Syria.
- Israel failed at the highest echelons to understand the true political structure and motives of any major ethnic element in Lebanon. It grossly overestimated Maronite support and willingness to fight alongside Israel. It failed to understand the motives of the Druze and Shi'ites and rapidly turned them from friends to enemies. It overestimated Sunni strength and willingness to act in independence from Syria. As a result, Israel largely alienated formerly friendly or tolerant Lebanese factions in southern

Lebanon and the Shouf, worsened the Lebanese civil war, became associated with the massacre of Palestinian refugees, and created a power vacuum that Syria eventually filled.

- Israel failed to assess the risk of irregular Palestinian action. It focused too narrowly on the PLO and PLA and underestimated the risk from improvised guerrilla or popular forces, especially those in the Palestinian refugee camps to the south and along the coastal plain.

- While Israeli intelligence could operate effectively in the air-combat and air-defense suppression missions without regard to Israel's central strategic objective, it could not do so in the case of the land forces. The effective allocation of resources required all elements to know from the start whether or not the siege of Beirut and driving Syria out of Lebanon were key objectives. Without such information, tactical intelligence assets became focused on more limited objectives, and intelligence did not adequately track Syrian activities in the northern Bekaa or developments near Beirut and in the Shouf.

- Insufficient allowance was made for "wild card" operations by the enemy and low-level harassment. Small amphibious heli-borne operations were carried out which were of critical importance but whose timing and success were sharply affected by very small PLO elements fighting almost at random. Similarly, Israeli intelligence did not allow for constant low-level irregular military action and the resulting impact on the Israeli rate of advance. Israel had a virtual monopoly of sophisticated intelligence assets and operational intelligence reaching beyond the FEBA. It is important to note, however, that the value of Israeli technology has generally been exaggerated and that HUMINT was more critical to Israeli decisions than SIGINT, ELINT, and PHOTINT in shaping the strategic course of the war and the land battle. It is also important to emphasize that the IDF's greatest failure, largely at the insistence of the Israeli defense minister, was one of characterizing the Christians, Druze, and Shi'ites as friendly forces. The Christians failed to provide the support the IDF counted on, and IDF actions eventually turned the Druze and Shi'ites into far more dangerous enemies than the PLO.

In addition, it is clear that Israel's most serious problems occurred at the highest policy level. The key failures in strategic intelligence occurred before the war began. These failures not only made Israel's military victories meaningless but turned the Israeli campaign into a massive strategic defeat.

The key lessons that emerge from the intelligence failures on all sides are similar to those of the October War, Iran-Iraq War, and Falkland Islands War, and, possibly, of the Afghan war as well. First, no tactical intelligence can substitute for failures in strategic intelligence and net assessment. Second, no intelligence technology can overcome the disastrous cost of political preconceptions and blind ambition at the policy level.

SIGINT

SIGINT played a major role in the war, largely because of the PLO. During the war in Lebanon, Israel displayed a high awareness of the messages and orders that were being passed among PLO units and elements in the PLO chain of command. They were also aware of the messages that were not getting through to the PLO. Israeli Prime Minister Begin, for example, is reported to have been absolutely delighted by the news that the PLO commander in southern Lebanon was unable to inform Arafat of activities at the front during the first day of the invasion.[27] The PLO made little use of commercial secure-communications techniques and even of elementary communications-control procedures.

The IDF also seems to have been able to use SIGINT and ELINT against Syrian ground forces, although with far less success. Syria used land lines, secure communications, and communications discipline to reduce Israeli intercepts. The IDF was able to use ELINT with great effectiveness against the Syrian Air Force. The techniques involved are discussed later in this chapter.

The PLO lacked any SIGINT capability. Syria does seem to have used ELINT and direction-finding techniques against Israel with some success but had no ability to break into the IDF command net. It also seems to have had limited Soviet SIGINT and ELINT support, although this was not provided in high volume until after August 1982.

It is clear from postwar reports, however, that even transparent SIGINT access to enemy communications would often have had limited value. The complex political situation at the higher command levels of the PLO, IDF, and Syria led all three sides to communicate a great deal of misleading material and to reflect a great deal of confusion at the command level. This heavy politicization of communications traffic presented a major problem in all the wars under study and later presented serious problems for the U.S. peacekeeping forces in Lebanon. Even with good HUMINT support, which may often be lacking, access to SIGINT may have little value, even when secure communications are not present or effective.

PHOTINT

The IDF had a near monopoly of PHOTINT, and the Pollard case indicates it may have had access to U.S. satellite photos and electronic order-of-battle intelligence as well. Israeli reports indicate that the IDF had good recce aircraft and RPV coverage of every aspect of the battlefield, and some Israeli press reports indicate that the IDF had extensive photo support from the U.S.

It is interesting to note, however, that IDF use of photo and electro-optical techniques rarely allowed the IDF to characterize PLO and Syrian movement in rough terrain and built-up areas. While the IDF went to considerable lengths to exaggerate its real time intelligence capability after the war in order to enhance its deterrent mystique and Israeli military exports, it failed to get useful data on ambushes and troop movements to its commanders and lacked the area coverage, endurance, and near real time collection and processing resources to cover Syrian forces.

PLO movements presented another kind of problem. Photo and television coverage of urban and built-up areas often gave only vague and contradictory data on infantry and troop functions and the purpose of PLO facilities. The PLO had learned to shelter many activities and adopt confusing and covert movement patterns. Its internal problems added to this confusion as did the independence of action of many elements.

These problems were far less critical in the case of surface-to-air missiles and some anti-aircraft defenses. The IDF could combine ELINT and PHOTINT, and Syria moved its forces far too rarely, showed poor omission discipline, and adopted easily recognizable set-piece deployments. They did, however, lead to extensive mistargeting or mischaracterization of Syrian and PLO buildings and facilities. Interviews with IDF officers indicate that the IDF often misinterpreted the purpose of given buildings or facilities or could only make estimates after this function had changed. This led to significant mistargeting in Beirut or to a need to use area or multi-target strikes with severe damage to civilians and considerable political backlash.

The West is almost certain to encounter similar problems in the future and must operate under much sharper political and collateral damage constraints. It is unclear that any threat-assessment systems can eliminate most of these problems, but the obvious solutions are (a) effective near real time fusion of SIGINT-PHOTINT-HUMINT, (b) near real time processing and dissemination with heavy emphasis on targeting and damage assessment, (c) improved area coverage, (d) improved endurance, and (e) night- and poor-weather visibility coverage. It is unclear what even the most advanced theater system can do or how the obvious limitations of SAR, SLAR, MTI radar, EO systems, FLIR, etc., in dealing with complex movements in built-up areas can be overcome. It is clear, however, that the most advanced technology available needs to be applied to this task if Western forces are to operate effectively, and in a politically survivable mode, in Third World areas.

HUMINT

The Israeli interest in Lebanon also led to the implementation of a number of HUMINT operations within the country prior to, during, and after the war. The details of many of these operations have not been made public. They are, however, known to have been involved in all major elements of the Israeli intelligence community. This includes the Mossad (which is mandated to operate outside Israel), Shin Bet (which is basically an internal security organization but also had counterintelligence functions in Lebanon), and military intelligence.

The Israelis put considerable effort into analyzing the results of the intelligence that they had gathered. They did this with the belief that Lebanese operations of some sort were possible and had to be considered seriously. The elite Golani commandos, for instance, fully expected that they would eventually have to storm Beaufort Castle. Correspondingly:

> Its men studied the castle's fortified positions and connecting trenches, sat through films shot by intelligence drones, and practiced various assault tactics until they had them down pat. Thus, when the war came, it was only natural that the conquest of the fortress should be assigned to the unit that had been preparing for it for years.[28]

The PLO and particularly Yassir Arafat expected that a war in Lebanon was just a matter of time. Egyptian intelligence sent Arafat summaries of the Israeli preparations for a major ground operation, while friendly U.S. sources also passed useful information to the chairman.

Additionally, a variety of leaks and rumors emerged from Lebanese sources close to the Israelis. The most concrete sign of the impending invasion, however, was undoubtedly the December 1981 massing of troops on Israel's northern border. This led Arafat to the concrete conclusion that an invasion was coming and to political attempts to deter the invasion by halting PLO operations and even releasing detailed maps of the IDF invasion plan. The only question was when. As has been discussed earlier, however, the PLO lacked the organization, leadership, and military effectiveness to act on nearly perfect strategic warning. This again illustrates the potential political weakness of many Third World forces and the value of threat assessment that can identify these weaknesses before a war begins and allow the West to capitalize upon them.

Mossad is known to have had (and undoubtedly retains) significant links to the Lebanese Phalange.[29] These links appear to have grown out of 1976 meetings between then–Prime Minister Yitzhak Rabin and Sheik Pierre Gemayel and played a critical role in deluding Sharon and Begin into believing they could count on active Maronite political and military support of the Israeli invasion.

It was at this point in time that cooperative relations including arms transfers were arranged. These links continued to grow and expand as time progressed. The Maronites, and especially the Phalange, therefore, became an important source of intelligence for the Israelis. Most of this intelligence was of fairly low and questionable quality. This was especially the case with regard to the PLO's capabilities and intentions. Furthermore, any sensitive Israeli information that came into the possession of the Phalangists was generally leaked.

The Shin Bet seems to have been less optimistic about the Christians but made mistakes of its own. It is known to have mounted a number of postwar operations in that part of Lebanon that remained under Israeli control in 1982. These operations involved the rounding-up of suspected members of the PLO. Such actions did not, however, prevent the development of an effective resistance to the occupation since the Lebanese Shi'ite community and not the PLO soon became the dominant element of the resistance.

A further complication for Israeli counterintelligence arose when an explosion destroyed Israeli military headquarters in Tyre on 12 November 1982. This explosion was officially explained to be the result of a gas leak. It resulted in the deaths of 90 military persons and 12 Shin Bet agents.[30] It became clear in the months that followed, however, that Israeli HUMINT was focused far too narrowly on the PLO and that Israel lacked objective and detailed HUMINT on Lebanon's various factions. This concentration on the threat, as distinguished from friendly and neutral elements and political movements in a Third World country, proved equally disastrous to the U.S. in Vietnam and in its peacekeeping mission in Lebanon. It poses an obvious and crucial lesson for threat assessment in future Third World conflicts.

Effective and Secure C³I

The maintenance of an effective command and control structure was a problem for both the Israelis and the Syrians. The PLO failed almost totally to maintain any kind of centralized control over its forces on the battlefield.

The Israelis appeared to have made acceptable use of communications security (COMSEC) equipment during the 1982 war in Lebanon. This was a marked improvement over Israeli communications security in the 1973 war which was inferior to that of the Arab forces.[31] Israel did, however, have serious command and control problems which may have exacerbated technological C^3 problems during the war.

Many of these problems related to the Israeli tendency to switch units from one command to another to meet new threats or to reorganize by task in response to the changing nature of the terrain. Commanders were seldom well-briefed on their role in any overall strategy. Most believed that the IDF was only going to make a limited incursion into Lebanon. When the IDF was ordered to push beyond the original 40-kilometer limit, many commanders were caught unaware. This was in sharp contrast to the beliefs of the PLO, who assumed Beirut was the target of the Israeli invasion.

Another Israeli C^3 problem involved the shifts in command that occurred throughout the war. Task forces were assembled and disassembled at regular intervals with the chains of command correspondingly disrupted and rearranged. This type of disruption meant that by the time the problems in a chain of command were reduced through practice, a new chain of command was required. Therefore, as the Israelis neared Beirut, they found it progressively more difficult to maintain effective command and communications.

It is significant that there were a number of incidents where command and control broke down. On several occasions, Israeli armored units attacked each other as a result of the breakdown in communication. One of the most serious incidents involved two battalions of the same brigade which were approaching the crossroads of Ain Katina, near the town of Jazzine. These battalions were converging on the town from different directions. For some reason, each assumed that the other was a Syrian column and opened fire. This led to a three-hour battle in which casualties occurred in both units.

The IDF also suffered from (a) a radio net that often failed in mountain and built-up areas, (b) an inability to handle the volume of message traffic involved, (c) overcompartmentation that separated command, communications, and intelligence activity, (d) a lack of digital or automatic routing and verification, and (e) a lack of central leadership and cohesion because the defense minister attempted to set covert goals and objectives, which meant command intentions had to be kept out of the C^3I net.

As will be discussed later, the IDF C^3I net failed to provide tight links among forward combat commanders and between these commanders and air and artillery units. Its reaction times were too slow, and it depended heavily on preplanned attacks and overscheduled rates of advance and individual-unit actions. Several IDF commanders had warned of these problems after exercises during 1978 to 1981, and the IDF has since attempted to correct some of them. Israeli officers are deeply divided, however, over whether or not the technology and organization exist to solve them. Many feel that the operational capability of modern C^3I technology is grossly exaggerated and poorly exercised, simulated, and understood. They favor more emphasis on defense as a means of reducing the pressure on the C^3 net. Other officers show a keen interest in concepts like the new Soviet offensive maneuver tactics and the U.S. air-land battle. It is striking, however, that the IDF C^3I net often failed or was inadequate over a very narrow front, after a practice invasion, and in spite of extensive exercises. This lesson should be a general warning to the West and any force relying on complex modern C^3I technology.[32]

The PLO and Syria are reported to have made extensive use of commercial telephones throughout the urban areas of Lebanon. This provided instant communications for these forces, but it also enabled the Israeli military to identify PLO locations and to plan responses to the orders that they intercepted from the telephone system. The PLO in Beirut had poor communications with its combat commanders in various sectors of the city, although its command center rotated throughout West Beirut. This command center came under the central direction of the Joint Forces Command and at the PLO level was controlled by the Higher Military Council under Arafat and Kalil Wazzir (Abu Jihad).[33] Former Jordanian Colonel and Sandhurst graduate Said Musa (Abu Musa) is also reported to have played a major role in directing the Joint Forces in Beirut. Significantly, many of the Syrian troops that had been trapped in the city reportedly came under PLO command.

Syrian forces showed good C^3I discipline and organization and were able to function well as long as they operated defensively from well-established positions or could slowly retreat. Syria relied heavily on land lines and did not provide the transparent communications intelligence furnished by the PLO. Syria also did not provide the same high HUMINT profile as PLO forces and did a relatively good job of dispersing and digging-in its ground forces. This made it far more difficult to locate and target Syrian units as long as they fought from relatively static positions, although they were easier to locate in movement. This illustrates the steadily improving C^3 capabilities of many Third World countries when they fight defensively. It is also notable that their land C^{3}I nodes were far less easy to characterize and attack than their air or SAM nodes. This is likely to present a similar problem in future combat.

Both sides exhibited very different approaches to combined arms and began with different sources of technology and arms. As Table 3.3 and Figures 3.16 and 3.17 show, the PLO had only limited sources of arms. Syria depended largely on Soviet-bloc arms and had a nearly 2:1 lead over Israel. Israel, however, had developed a major arms industry of its own.

Israel also had developed one of the most sophisticated operations research and test and evaluation capabilities in the world, all of which could be calibrated against continuing low-level combat and tailored to the specific combat conditions of one relatively small area and limited range of opponents and fighting conditions.

Syria's highly politicized armed forces had been corrupted by efforts to exploit Syria's occupation of Lebanon and made little use of Syria's technical capabilities. Syria operated largely "by the book" on the basis of Soviet training and doctrine and made only marginal technical improvements in its weapons. It did not seek to apply technology or operations research to either combined arms or combined operations.

The PLO concentrated on fund raising and the political and economic administration of the territory it occupied in Lebanon. It conducted set-piece exercises and made no attempt to conduct effective tests or operations research. It politicized its exercises and training. It created shelters for many of its arms without regard to the need for an emergency distribution system.

This different behavior again illustrates the critical importance of accurate prewar HUMINT, which realistically examines the readiness and organization of Third World forces and of operations research before and after a conflict. Syria and the PLO failed to adopt realistic approaches to effectiveness, organization, and combined arms. Iraq and Iran began their war with similar problems and developed more realism and readiness only in the course of a prolonged war. The USSR experimented with different combat and organizational approaches but relatively slowly. In the Falklands, Britain benefited from the realism of its prewar training and good operations research before and during the war. Argentina's Air Force showed excellent prewar readiness and technical planning and good intrawar ability to adapt to unanticipated combat conditions. Its army's approach to combined arms was lethargic to the point of impotence.

In any case, the net result of each side's prewar approach to combined arms favored Israel.

TABLE 3.3   Weapons Transfers in the Lebanon War: 1978–1982

TRANSFERRED TO	TRANSFERRED FROM						
	USSR	EASTERN EUROPE	PRC	US	WESTERN EUROPE	OTHER	TOTAL
ISRAEL	0	0	0	4,400	10	5	4,415
PLO	150	75	5	0	5	25	260
SYRIA	8,200	530	20	0	820	270	9,800
LEBANON	0	0	0	170	70	10	170
TOTAL	8,350	605	25	4,570	905	310	14,645

SOURCE: Adapted from U.S. ACDA, *World Military Exports and Arms Transfers* (Washington, D.C.: GPO, 1983), and Mark Heller, et al., *The Middle East Military Balance 1983* (Tel Aviv University, Jaffee Center for Strategic Studies, 1983).

Combined Arms

The Israeli forces in Lebanon had far better combined-arms balance than in 1973 but continued to display the long-standing Israeli bias in favor of armor and against infantry. While many effective combined-arms operations did occur, the IDF often tried to use armor without proper support. These operations were almost always more costly in terms of lives and equipment than operations in which the Israelis adhered to combined-arms principles.

Opinions differ, however, as to how well Israel functioned in using its task forces to conduct effective combined-arms operations and in speeding its rate of advance. Some critics, including Israeli military officers, feel that Israel experienced a steady series of problems because it failed to meet its operational schedule and maintain the rate of advance called for in its war plans. Other critics feel Israel generally achieved outstanding results, based on the performance of other forces and realistic expectations, given the failures at the highest level of command. These latter critics seem to be correct. The Israeli attack plan set what often seem to be impossible goals based on insufficient initial force to achieve the objective and insufficient allowances for the "friction of war," for terrain, for inevitable limited

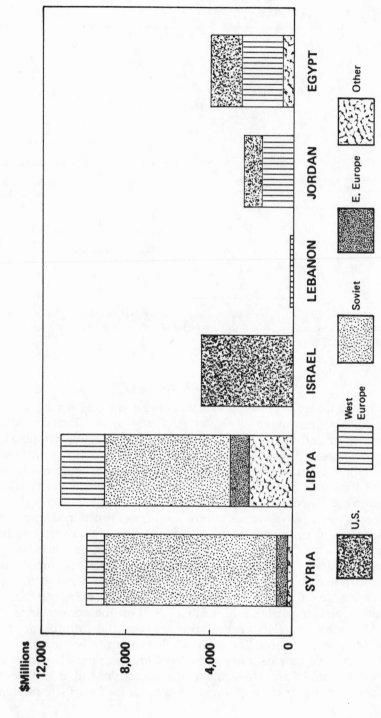

FIGURE 3.16 Arab-Israeli Arms Imports: 1978–1982 (by Importing Country and Supplier). Adapted from ACDA data.

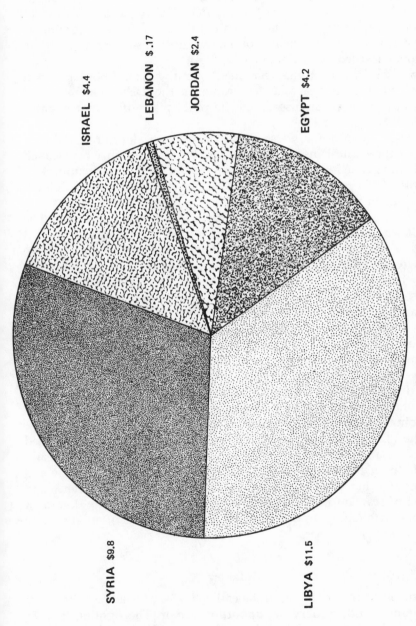

ISRAEL $4.4

LEBANON $ .17

JORDAN $2.4

EGYPT $4.2

SYRIA $9.8

LIBYA $11.5

FIGURE 3.17 Arab-Israeli Arms Imports: 1978–1982 (Share of Total by Importing Country, in Billions of Dollars). Adapted from U.S. ACDA, *World Military Exports and Arms Transfers* (Washington, D.C.: GPO, 1983), and from Mark Heller, et al., *The Middle East Military Balance 1983* (Tel Aviv University, Jaffee Center for Strategic Studies, 1983).

local losses, and for delay to deal with irregular forces. The primary fault seems to have been in plans and command decisions that confused the high command's desire for a quick decisive war with actual military capability. No army can conduct effective combined operations when impossible expectations are transformed into orders without consistent clarity of purpose.[34]

This does not mean that combined operations could not have been improved at the tactical and technical level. The IDF's problems in C^3I have already been discussed, and its problems in its armor-infantry mix will be discussed shortly.

A shortage of artillery also took place periodically during the war. One of the earliest instances of this occurred in Jezzin where Israeli tanks were called upon to perform an assault without any supporting infantry.[35] To compensate for this lack, the unit commander, Colonel Hagai, attempted to arrange for artillery support. Before he was able to do so, Major General Bar-Lev ordered an immediate attack. The result was a predictable problem with Syrian Saggers and RPGs that led to a number of IDF tanks being knocked out that would not have been lost with proper combined arms support.

Syrian troops displayed an interest in combined arms and attempted to use combined-arms teams in a variety of circumstances. Although Syrian operations were flawed, they nevertheless exhibited a clear awareness of the importance of using tanks, infantry, and artillery in coordinated efforts. In many defensive operations throughout the war, Syrian commando teams operated in close and effective cooperation with tanks. These combined-arms teams were often especially effective in inflicting damage on Israeli armored columns. Syrian armor and elite infantry units also appear to have operated very well when coordinating the defense of urban areas.

The PLO almost seems to have attempted to pioneer "uncombined arms" as a response to the IDF and consistently failed as a result. While the IDF had its weaknesses, it could react far more quickly and coherently than the PLO. While the lesson is obvious, coherence and speed of reaction in C^3I and combined operations are the dominant factors in shaping military effectiveness and are often far more important than numbers.

Infantry

One of the major lessons of the earlier 1973 war was the importance of infantry and artillery in supporting armor. The fighting in 1973 showed that IDF armor had difficulty in operating without enough supporting infantry to suppress hostile troops equipped with anti-armor PGMs and rocket launchers. Israel did expand its infantry arm after 1973 but not at the same rate that it continued to expand its tank forces. This priority reflected Israel's continuing interest in using tanks as "mobile artillery" to suppress hostile infantry rather than ground troops. This decision stemmed in part from a desire to maintain the shock effect and speed of heavy armor and to keep casualties low, but it was a decision that Israel may have come to regret in the course of the 1982 fighting.

The doctrinal question that has consistently plagued Israel is when and how much infantry should be used as a screen for tanks. By using the infantry this way, the Israelis make their infantry vulnerable to small arms fire, but if they fail to do so, they leave their tanks vulnerable to anti-tank weapons. The IDF tried to sidestep the issue after 1973 by rebuilding its previously neglected artillery arm. This did not work in Lebanese terrain, however, since they could not use artillery to suppress small pockets of hidden ambushers in the same way they could use artillery against organized infantry formations in more open terrain.

The continued Israeli stress on armor and use of armor-heavy combat teams was evident throughout the Lebanon war. In many instances, tanks proceeded with very little infantry support, and this occasionally led to serious Israeli problems. The mauling of an Israeli armored unit at a wadi near Ein Zehalta would probably have been avoided if infantrymen had preceded the armored units. The Syrians emplaced ambushes along the road into the wadi while using their own tanks on the wadi's far side as bait to attract the Israeli armor. The plan worked well, and the Israeli unit became vulnerable to intensive antitank fire by Syrian troops.[36]

A very different situation occurred near Kafr Mata where Palestinians belonging to an organization called "Force Bader" prepared an ambush along the road to this town. The members of Force Bader apparently expected that the Israelis would advance along the road in an armored column that could be ambushed and destroyed. To a certain extent the Palestinians were right, since Israeli tanks were advancing along the road in a column type of movement. In this case, however, Israeli tanks were supported by dismounted paratroopers advancing along the slopes of the road. These Israeli infantry surged forward once the PLO ambush had begun and quickly broke it up. Israeli troops then began hunting down the remnants of the force which had tried to fall back. By the time this action was over, around 50 Palestinians had been killed, with no Israelis dead and only three wounded.[37]

The price the IDF paid for inadequate infantry support might have been much higher if the PLO had been able to use its forces more effectively. The combat forces of the PLO were made up almost entirely of regular and irregular infantry forces. Artillery and armored forces existed, but they were small, poorly trained and organized, and were not well integrated into the PLO's fighting units. Furthermore, most of the PLO's tanks were obsolete T-34s, which were in extremely poor mechanical condition. Many of these "tanks" were incapable of independent movement and had to be towed by tractors from place to place to be used as stationary defenses. It was the small, relatively disorganized, "stay behind," bypassed, and improvised PLO forces that proved most effective.[38]

Syria made extensive use of commandos and mechanized infantry during the fighting in Lebanon. The commando battalions exhibited standards that were much higher than those found in the Syrian army as a whole. Their junior commanders provided good leadership for the troops, and the commando units cooperated successfully with tank formations.[39] The Syrian commando units are made up of the best Syrian troops available. Their discipline, training, and leadership are excellent, and their successes clearly show by contrast how little the Arab world has gained whenever it has traded mass for quality. The commandos are also considered very reliable by the regime, who placed them in Lebanon at a time when the occupation of that country was not universally popular with Syria's Sunni Moslem majority. What is most notable, however, is that the IDF came to respect them as being roughly equivalent to IDF forces on a one-to-one basis. This reflects a broad trend toward the emergence of highly effective elite units in Third World forces, and one the West must be prepared to react to in future low-level wars.

Personal Weapons

Israeli troops were equipped with American small arms as well as the domestically produced Galil assault rifle. Israeli infantry troops found this rifle to be particularly effective in close combat situations such as those that occurred at Beaufort Castle.

The Galil design borrows heavily from the Soviet AK-47 assault rifle. There are three models of the Galil. These are:

- an assault rifle with an eighteen-inch barrel;
- a light machine gun with a carrying handle and bipod; and
- a short assault rifle with a thirteen-inch barrel that is used by paratroopers.

A thirty-five round magazine is standard for the assault rifle versions of the Galil, while a fifty-round magazine is provided for the machine gun version. It is notable that many of the world's successful assault rifles draw on Soviet models but that no other nation has drawn heavily on recent U.S. designs.

Syria and, for the most part, PLO troops were equipped with modern Soviet small arms. The standard personal weapons of the Syrian Army were the 7.62-mm AK-47 assault rifle and the 7.62-mm AKM assault rifle. The PLO infantry tended to be equipped with the AK-47, although other weapons such as the German G-3 rifle also turned up in their hands on a few occasions.

Within Lebanon, both the Israeli and Soviet-made assault rifles were often particulary useful because of the short range at which many battles occurred. This type of close-quarter combat is an ideal situation for using light, high-firepower weapons such as the AK-47, AKM, or Galil.

Tanks and Armored Vehicles

The 1982 fighting did not involve mass battles between tanks of the kind that occurred in 1973, but it did involve the extensive use of armor in mountain and urban warfare. It also produced some important lessons regarding the relative capability of Soviet and Western tanks and the survivability of APCs in rough terrain.

Much of the Lebanese terrain favored ambush tactics. Narrow roads and mountain passes were particularly dangerous areas for advancing in armored or other military vehicles. This is an especially favorable environment for the use of antitank weapons by a defending force. RPGs were particularly useful against Israeli light-armored fighting vehicles and APCs in this terrain and were reported to have been used in quantity by PLO forces. Former Israeli Major General Chaim Herzog has claimed that the PLO used children aged 12 and upward to man some of these ambushes.[40]

The combination of terrain and widespread proliferation of anti-armor weapons helps explain why it proved much safer for Israeli troops to deploy in a tank rather than an APC. Reducing the Merkava's basic ammunition load to 40 rounds and leading infantrymen into the rear hatch compartment greatly reduced infantry vulnerability. While the Merkava has no firing ports for the troops to use while the tank is on the move, it is unclear that this presented any tactical problems; the M-113 also lacked such firing ports and provided much less operational crew visibility than the Merkava.

Tanks

All but one of the tanks committed to the invasion had been combat tested in previous conflicts. The Centurion, M-48, M-60, T-54, T-55, and T-62 had been employed in previous Arab-Israeli conflicts, and the T-72 had been used in the Iran-Iraq War. The exception was the Israeli-designed-and-produced Merkava. The IDF had over 3,000 MBTs when the war began. These consisted primarily of 1,100 Centurions, over 1,000 M-60s, 600 M-48s, and converted Soviet tanks. The IDF also, however, had over 200 Merkavas. The Merkava received its baptism of fire in Lebanon and had to contend with some of the latest Soviet armor and antitank weapons. The Merkava's performance against Arab antitank weapons is examined later in this work and provides some interesting insights into tank-to-tank combat.

The Merkava is slower than most tanks it was designed to fight and still uses the standardized NATO 105-mm gun. Nevertheless, it performed with considerable success in tank-to-tank combat within Lebanon. The tank's front-mounted engine and wide track give it excellent climbing and rough terrain capability, and its suspension and other parts are exceptionally easy to repair, even under combat conditions.

The spaced armor of the Merkava was reported as especially effective in providing for tank survivability in tank-to-tank combat. The hull structure and angle of the turret are also considered well designed for crew protection. Damage control systems within the tank worked well. In particular, the tank is equipped with an explosion suppression system that uses an inert agent (Freon 1301) to contain the explosion caused by hostile projectiles, and a detector known as the Spectronix, which can detect a fire in three milliseconds. This system helps account for a very low level of burn casualties among Merkava tank crewmen. This burn level was also in marked contrast to the problems encountered by IDF crewmen of the M-60 and Centurion tanks in 1973 and 1982, where a far higher rate of burn casualties took place. The significance of this situation was not lost upon conscript Israeli tank crewmen who have since made a special effort to be assigned to units containing only Merkavas.

The 105-mm gun on the Merkava is smaller than the main caliber gun on a number of Soviet-made tanks, including the Syrian-held T-62, T-64, and T-72 tanks. This smaller 105-mm gun was chosen because improved Western 120-mm designs were not available and because it provided standardization with other Israeli tanks. The IDF has since borrowed West German and U.S. 120-mm gun technology, including the full range of production technology, and may well upgrade the Merkava's guns in the future.

Nevertheless, the 105-mm gun on the Merkava worked well. The Merkava's basic combat load of ammunition is 83 rounds which is a larger number than those carried by any other tank presently in the Israeli inventory and gave it extensive sustained fire power. The Merkavas frequently used the Israeli Military Industries' (IMIs') Mill armor-piercing, fin-stabilized, discarding-sabot round. This round is the M-111 and is called the Hets or arrow. It is an armored piercing fin-stabilized discarding sabot-tungston (APFSDS-T) kinetic energy round and can kill at ranges over 5,500 meters. The Merkava has an excellent laser range-finder and fire computer and a barrel shroud nearly 30 percent more efficient than that on the M-60, which keeps deviation to only 3 mils. Under practical conditions, the Merkava can achieve kills against a T-72 tank at ranges of 1,500 to 2,000 meters. This round is known to have been able to penetrate the frontal armor of the T-72 during the Lebanon war. This penetration capability is important since the T-72 was designed in a way that maximizes armor at the expense of maneuverability, and some doubt existed before the war about the frontal kill capability of even the improved NATO 105-mm round. The effectiveness of the 105-caliber main gun may, however, be partially accounted for by the close range at which some of the tank battles were fought.

An additional unique advantage of the Merkava is a rear compartment that can carry up to ten infantrymen or 200 rounds of extra ammunition. This advantage is often utilized by having three of the four tanks in an armor platoon carry troops in the rear compartment while the fourth carries extra ammunition for the entire platoon. During the Lebanon war, the Merkava's rear compartment was also used to evacuate wounded troops. On one occasion, a Merkava drove an airborne unit into a PLO occupied house which was then stormed from the inside.

The Israelis claim that the Merkava did a good job of fighting in urban areas, although this is normally a difficult environment for armored combat. They attribute this success to the armored skirts of the Merkava, which they claim dramatically reduced the vulnerability of the tank in an urban setting and should be applied to other tanks. It should be noted, however, that the Merkava was not committed to heavy combat in Beirut or against urban forces armed with modern ATGMs or the latest Soviet rocket propelled grenades (RPGs).

The changes that the Israelis made in the Merkava after the war are indicative of the lessons of that war as perceived by Israeli armor experts. The new Merkava II has a higher horsepower engine which gives the tank even greater maneuverability and ability to travel over rough terrain without overheating.[41] They have given it improved spaced and reactive armor and will equip it with 120-mm guns.

The Syrians used a variety of Soviet-made tanks during the Lebanon war, including T-72s. Israeli General Rafael Eitan called the T-72 the world's second best tank, after the Merkava. The Israelis do, however, claim to have knocked out several T-72s of the Third Syrian Armored Division with Merkavas and hint that the total of T-72s destroyed by Merkavas may go as high as nine. Syrian sources seem to confirm these claims.[42] Eitan further stated that T-72 tanks burned just as rapidly as the other Soviet-made tanks. This may indicate that the armor of the T-72 may not be as formidable as previously believed, and it is interesting to note that neither the U.K. nor France have credited the T-72 and "T-80" with the same weight of armor as U.S analysts.[43]

Unfortunately, the 1982 fighting did not provide many insights into the comparative impact of advanced sights and fire control, tank guns, weight of armor, reactive armor, and advanced spaced armor. The combat was too limited and occurred under too specialized a set of conditions in terms of range, terrain, C^3, and tactical conditions to generalize about the future.

What is notable is that Syrian tanks fought much better defensively than in 1973, although largely in ambushes, well-established defensive positions in rough terrain, under conditions of tactical surprise, and when heavily supported by infantry. The 1982 fighting did not provide any sustained test of Syrian maneuver capability, and Syrian maintenance was poor. Syrian repair crews in the field could only perform elementary repairs, and Syria either had to abandon tanks or tow them back to Damascus. This leaves some major uncertainties regarding Syria's overall readiness. Interestingly enough, Syria reacted to the war by seeking to upgrade its Soviet-built tanks with West European fire-control equipment and sights and heavily pressed the USSR for the T-80. It also has attempted to sharply improve its armored maneuver training.

Armored Personnel Carriers

Armored personnel carriers were used throughout the Lebanon fighting by both Syrian and Israeli troops. These systems exhibited problems throughout the war and especially in rough or urban terrain.

One weapons system that emerged from the fighting with a particularly damaged reputation was the M-113 armored personnel carrier. The problems that emerged in the M-113 in Vietnam and in the 1973 war were even more apparent during the Lebanese conflict. This was partially the result of the fact the war was fought in less open terrain and increased opportunities for snipers using hand-held antitank weapons. The Israelis had hoped that adding firepower to the M-113 would give it enough suppression capability to make up for its vulnerability. This concept might have been more effective in the desert, but it was hopelessly ineffective in Lebanon. Israeli troops found the M-113 to be so vulnerable under these conditions that they often chose to travel to their objectives on foot rather than ride in what they considered to be a highly vulnerable vehicle.

In making the above decision, many Israelis might also have been influenced by the experiences of the 1978 invasion of Lebanon. During this action, RPG and PGM hits on M-113s had particularly devastating results. Another problem with the M-113 which was manifested in 1982 involved the fact that these systems were vulnerable to overhead artillery fire. Furthermore, the M-113s, once struck by a projectile, burned very rapidly.[44]

The M-113 did not prove to be well designed for self-defense. In addition to the problem of poor armor and a high silhouette, its weaponry is something of an afterthought. There are no firing ports for the troops to use to improve visibility, rapid exit is difficult and often impeded by combat damage. Machine guns must be mounted on top of the vehicle where the gunners are clearly visible and totally unprotected. While TOW and cannon turret versions of the M-113 are available, these were not deployed in any significant number, provide relatively poor combat visibility, and do not affect the M-113's basic vulnerability. Some M-113s did have partial protection by add-on reactive armor and composite armor. These do seem to have had better survivability.

The Israelis are reported to have used a converted Centurion tank as an infantry fighting vehicle in Lebanon. This vehicle was observed in Lebanon in 1984 but probably did not participate extensively in the 1982 war. The converted Centurion has had its turret removed and replaced with machine guns and other infantry attachments. It apparently was developed because of the continuing vulnerability of M-113s to ambushes in Lebanon. The new vehicle retains its original Centurion armor and is less vulnerable to such systems as RPGs, land mines, and remote-control bombs.

The Syrians used the BMP-1 and other Soviet-made APCs and infantry combat vehicles (ICVs) during the war in Lebanon.[45] Few data are available on the performance of Syrian APCs, but it does appear that the Syrians used their APCs largely for support and avoided any frontal combat with Israel. An Israeli tank battalion trapped near Sultan Yakoub was, however, severely mauled by Syrian missiles and RPGs. About 30 Syrian APCs are believed to have been involved in this attack.[46]

Since the war, the Syrians have emphasized tanks supported by dismounted infantry. The IDF has sought to find replacements for the M-113 but does not have the resources to replace it with Israeli-made weapons or the U.S.-made M-2s or M-3s. It also still has to rely on large numbers of lower quality RBYs, BDRM 1/2s, Shoets, OT-62s, and BTR-50Ps. As a result, the IDF has had to order large numbers of additional M-113s and rely on adding reactive armor kits and more firepower. Israel has, however, increased its use of the APC-like capabilities of its Merkava tanks, its use of helicopters, and its use of dismounted infantry. It has also further upgraded its M-113s, using modifications tested in the 1982 fighting. These modifications included add-on armor and added firepower, but it is unclear that they are an adequate response to the M-113's vulnerability.

Precision-Guided and Specialized Munitions

Anti-armor PGMs played a significant role in the combat operations of both sides of the conflict, although the Syrians and the Israelis relied on these weapons to a much greater extent than the PLO or Lebanese Left. The Israelis made less use of ATGMs than the Syrians because of the Israeli emphasis on offensive and armored warfare. PGMs are not good offensive weapons, unlike tanks, and cannot gain rapid ground. The Israelis stress ways by which tanks can overcome PGMs, and the thrust of their research and development (R&D) and tactical training clearly reflects this emphasis.

The most important antitank weapon in the Israeli inventory is the TOW long-range anti-armor system. This system was initially transferred to Israel in the U.S. arms lift that accompanied the 1973 war. It is wire-guided, has a range of 3,000 meters, and, when properly used, is very accurate. Unlike most Soviet systems transferred to the Third World, the TOW is a true third-generation system where the operator only has to keep the sight on the target, not track both the missile and target and manually guide the missile to the target.

As originally delivered, the IDF felt the TOW was vulnerable to hostile countermeasures, including radio frequency (RF) countermeasures, direct and indirect artillery, smoke, night fighting, laser range-finders, infrared (IR) jamming, searchlights, and widebeam amplitude modulated devices. Rather than develop its own system to replace the TOW, the IDF designed a set of upgrades and modifications for the TOW, meeting most of these problems. Later modifications ensured that Israel had corrected virtually all of their objections to the system by the time war broke out in 1982. The Israelis also had an opportunity to develop doctrine and plans for the use of the

TOW. This was significant since the TOW's third-generation guidance system greatly reduced the IDF's training burden, and the weapon could be distributed broadly within the IDF forces. The ground forces made TOW a key weapon, along with paratroop and other elite assault forces they felt were likely to encounter tanks and hard-point defenses.

One interesting way that the Israelis employed antitank PGMs in the Lebanon war was through the employment of a Special Maneuver force commanded by Brigadier General Yossi Peled. This unit was composed of Israeli paratroopers and infantry equipped with TOW missiles, helicopters, and a variety of anti-armor weapons. It had been organized specifically to kill tanks and was expected to be used to prevent Syrian armored reinforcement of units in the Bekaa Valley. In order to accomplish this, the unit was forced to climb into the Jabaal Barouk Mountains where it assumed control of the heights and later covered the advance of other Israeli forces moving toward Joub Jannine.[47] Syrian armored units attempted to reinforce the Bekaa Valley and encountered Peled's troops. In the fighting that ensued, nine Syrian tanks were struck by ATGMs.[48] The IDF also made effective use of helicopters firing TOWs, and these helicopters dominated IAF claims of 100 tank kills from the air during the 1973 fighting.[49]

The Israelis have tended to play down the effectiveness of the TOW in the Lebanon operation, possibly to increase the export potential of the Merkava tank. Additionally, the Israelis may be trying to avoid being placed in a position where the United States will deny requests for aid in terms of tanks in favor of PGMs. The IDF has, however, placed extensive orders for the improved TOW (ITOW) and ITOW conversions since the war.[50]

The Syrians are known to have used a variety of antitank weapons including Sagger, Spiggot, Milan, and HOT missiles, as well as RPGs. These were often effective, although it is not possible to distinguish between types. Syria did, however, score more kills against APCs than tanks. One additional weapon system that appears to have been highly effective in Syrian hands was the French-made Gazelle helicopter armed with HOT antitank missiles. The Syrians used these helicopters in pop-up tactics, and they were reported to have performed well in an antitank role. The HOT missile was particularly destructive, and it generally completely destroyed any armored vehicle it hit. It proved far more lethal in terms of total-vehicle and high-crew kills than Soviet ATGMs or the Milan. The Israelis have admitted to losing seven tanks to HOT missiles fired from Gazelles. Had the Israelis not enjoyed complete air superiority, it is possible that the Syrians could have done much more with the Gazelles to knock out Israeli armor. Approximately twelve Gazelles were shot down by the Israelis during the war in Lebanon.

The Syrians clearly did use AT-3 Saggers against Israel in the Bekaa Valley. The Sagger, like the TOW, has a maximum range of 3,000 meters. It is a wire-guided, second-generation system, however, and is much more difficult to guide to its target than HOT or TOW. The AT-3 does, however, seem to have been more effective than the Soviet missiles available in the 1973 war. The Sagger was used continually by Syrian commandos cooperating with tanks. Although each round had a relatively low P_k, large-scale use of the Sagger had considerable cumulative kill effect and a powerful deterrent effect in slowing IDF operations. It seems likely that in combination with Syrian tanks, the Sagger could have made a full-scale IDF invasion of Syria very costly.

The PLO also had about 30 to 50 Soviet AT-3 launchers but rarely brought them to bear against the Israelis.[51] Although PLO units are known to have used Sagger missiles, they normally used the unguided RPG-7 antitank rocket-propelled grenade, which has a far shorter range and much less explosive power. One of the many wild boasts that Yassir Arafat made during the course of the Lebanon war was that his troops could have destroyed 400 Israeli tanks if they only had the RPGs to do it. Given the number of RPGs the IDF captured in PLO depots, the boast exemplifies the PLO's inability to distinguish between military rhetoric and reality.

Many of the RPG-7 attacks that were successful were made at very short range and cost the life of the PLO operator. These included one-man units—often boys—who stayed in caves dug at ambush points or who were committed as "martyrs" in one-man attacks on IDF forces. The limited range of the RPG-7 kept the operator from surviving. The PLO, however, rarely deployed cross-reinforcing RPG-7s and Swaggers or enough ambush points to prevent flanking or piecemeal destruction of such points. Multiple ambushes often simply signaled IDF troops that they had entered a defended zone.

The RPG was much less effective against tanks than other Israeli armor and other vehicles. Israeli trucks and armored personnel carriers were especially vulnerable to RPG attacks. While some tanks were damaged, with crewmen killed or injured by such weapons, the frequency of such hits seems to have been very small. This seems largely a function of range rather than firing opportunities. An RPG has more range than most Western man-portable systems in large-scale use but still has to be fired from extremely close range to inflict significant harm on a tank.[52] According to the Israelis, their own Merkava tank did particularly well in Lebanon with regard to RPGs.[53]

One Israeli source also claims to have seen Syrian Sagger missiles and RPGs bounce off U.S. M-60 tanks which had been retrofitted with a new Israeli outside armor skirt that encircled the turret. The IDF provided this anti-armor skirt for some of its armor as a corrective action after the PLO began scoring hits against the flanks of Israeli tanks and against the space between the rear turret box and the tank hull. While such a system was not used on many APCs in the 1982 war, the Israelis are known to have developed a similar system for the M-113 APC. This system is, however, only half as heavy as the "special defense kit" developed for the Merkava tank and may still seriously retard the APC's maneuverability and movement.[54]

Nevertheless, the IDF preferred the Soviet RPG-7 to the U.S. light antitank weapon. It felt that the LAW had too short an effective range and that the RPG-7 was more lethal, rugged, reliable, and easier to carry. This Israeli attitude reflects an almost worldwide rejection of U.S. infantry weapons by those nations that do not receive them under the foreign military sales (FMS) program. It also reflects a broad lesson regarding the value of the emphasis the Soviets put on high-quality, direct-fire infantry weapons and technology.

Tube Artillery and Multiple Rocket Launchers

Tube artillery was used by all three major combatants involved in the war in Lebanon. The tube artillery in the possession of the Israeli army at the time of the conflict included 48 M-110 203-mm howitzers (self-propelled), 140 M-107 175-mm guns self-propelled (SP), 300 M-109 and 300 Soltam L-33, M-50, and M-70 self-propelled 155-mm howitzers (M-68/71 towed self-propelled howitzer, 100 D-30 122-mm towed guns), 130-mm guns and 105-mm howitzers. Weapons which were particularly useful throughout the war included the 203-mm M-110 SP howitzers and 155-mm M-109 SP howitzers.[55]

The Israelis used tube artillery for area bombardments during the war, as well as aerial bombardment. One of the most important uses involved the urban areas that Israel had surrounded and bypassed, including the cities of Tyre, Sidon, and Damour. The PLO and PFLP put up some of its most fierce resistance of the war in or near these cities. The Israelis engaged in a thorough and methodical bombardment of PLO defensive positions using both tube artillery and multiple rocket launchers before attacking these strongholds.

Tyre was the first well-defended urban area that the Israelis encountered on their advance. This was an area which the IDF had completely bypassed in its earlier 1978 operations in Lebanon. The Israelis chose to seize the town on this occasion, however, and appear to have done so by heavily exploiting their advantage in artillery. Israeli infantry moving into the city appear to have moved slowly and methodically, calling for artillery fire as they went. Once PLO troops revealed their positions, they were subjected to intense bombardment unless they were prohibitively close to Israeli troops. This artillery fire may have also been useful in setting off booby traps in the path of advancing Israeli troops.[56]

The next formidable and well-defended urban area that the Israelis encountered was the port city of Sidon. They appear to have used the same tactics as those used in Tyre. Again, extensive bombardment was utilized to support advancing Israeli troops. Furthermore, the Israelis also chose to launch a combined-arms amphibious and air-mobile attack against Sidon in order to outflank the PLO forces in that stronghold. This assault began on 6 June 1982 and received extensive support from naval gunfire. The assault on Sidon began from the sea with fast-moving columns advancing over land to join it within a day. Damour, by contrast, did not involve a sea-based assault, but the IDF made extensive use of naval bombardment.

The effectiveness of the Israeli attack on Sidon may also have been assisted by the behavior of Ismail al-Hajj, the PLO military commander of the Sidon district. He was reported to have fled the area as Israeli units approached. Many Palestinians believed that Ismail's behavior contributed to the speed of the Israeli advance, and his actions were reported to be the subject of a subsequent Fatah inquiry.[57]

Intensive bombardment by the Israelis was significantly less effective against the Syrian and PLO troops and targets in Beirut. This is because the PLO had done a great deal over the years to prepare for the possibility of receiving shelling (although not necessarily Israeli shelling). This preparation involved an elaborate network of shelters and tunnels within the PLO controlled portions of the city.[58] The Israelis tried to compensate partially for these PLO advantages by using large-caliber artillery pieces as direct fire weapons against urban PLO targets. They called this technique "sniping," and it often involved firing single shots at point-blank range. It rarely, however, had much effect.[59]

The heavy bombardment of West Beirut by Israeli land, air, and sea forces seems to have been conducted largely for its political shock-effect and to force the PLO to evacuate. It did, however, have some military significance on the PLO and Syria. A few stationary fortifications and some heavy weapons systems were destroyed. The PLO's freedom to maneuver was also hampered by the bombardment, and the PLO's ability to organize for combat was therefore impaired.

The PLO was, however, prepared for such a contingency by establishing those large, well-stocked, underground bunkers coupled to the supporting network of shelter tunnels under the city that were discussed earlier. This minimized actual casualties among the Syrian and PLO forces under attack and increased the ratio of civilians killed to the military killed.[60] This helps account for the fact that none of the PLO's high-ranking leaders in Beirut were killed or wounded in the Israeli bombardment of PLO targets.

Several particularly important targets that the Israelis consistently placed under heavy bombardment included the Palestinian-controlled Fakhani quarter and the sports stadium complex in West Beirut. Yet this was where the PLO had excavated its most secure bunkers and tunnels, and IDF intelligence on many of these targets was limited. The effects of these attacks were correspondingly limited. The encirclement of Beirut did little to deny the PLO weapons, since they had already accumulated and stored tremendous numbers of small arms. Upon the evacuation of the PLO fighters from Beirut, the Israelis seized many of the weapons and were amazed at the quantity the PLO had amassed.[61] Likewise, the PLO apparently had far larger quantities of food, water, gasoline, and medical supplies than the IDF expected—little of which was affected by either artillery fire or bombing.

Another weapon Israel used in the 1982 Operation Peace for Galilee campaign was the multiple rocket launcher. These weapons systems are just entering the U.S. inventory, but Israel first adopted MRLs in 1967. It used 122-mm, 160-mm, BM-24 240-mm, and MAR-290-mm multiple rocket launchers. These include both captured, Soviet-designed MRLs and domestically produced MRLs. The fact that the Israelis would allocate the resources to produce domestic versions of the MRL is a good indication of the value they ascribe to such systems.

The first of the MRLs to enter extensive IDF service was the 12-ramp or 24-launcher 240-mm Soviet-made BM-24. This system was captured in large numbers from the Arab armies in 1967. New ammunition for this system is currently being produced by Israeli Military Industries (IMI).[62] The 290-mm medium-artillery rocket system is a hybrid MRL which is in service with the Israeli ground forces. This system consists of a quadruple frame launcher mounted on a Sherman tank chassis. Another more recent system is the IMI-designed 160-mm MRL. All of the above systems are believed to have seen service in Lebanon. Finally, Israeli BM-21 122 MRLs were observed and photographed firing at hostile targets in Beirut. It is assumed that these MRLs may have been captured during the course of the war from either the Syrians or the PLO since they are relatively new Soviet systems. In spite of various rumors, there is no evidence the Israelis used MRLs with guided warhead or "smart" submunitions. They do seem to have had cluster warheads, and smart submunitions are under development.[63]

It is unclear how the IDF mixed its use of tube artillery and MRLs. It is clear, however, that the IDF used MRLs effectively to suppress area targets including SAM sites. It is also clear that the IDF used advanced targeting systems effectively, including RPVs and artillery radars. It used recce photos for area targeting and used targeting and fire control with artillery radars and to control its overall patterns of fire. This seems to have been highly effective against easily characterized targets, but the IDF C³I system did not function smoothly in providing rapid and precise fire support to forward unit commanders. As has been touched on earlier, the IDF also had severe problems in locating and characterizing targets in rough and mountain terrain, at night, and in built-up areas where it was difficult or impossible to separate military from civilian targets.

Syrian artillery also included both tube artillery and multiple rocket launchers. The MRLs in the Syrian Army at the time included 122-mm BM-21s, as well as 240-mm and 140-mm MRLs. The Syrians also had several different types of 152-mm and 122-mm guns and howitzers as well as the S-23 180-mm howitzers and the M-46 130-mm guns. These systems were used through the Bekaa Valley where artillery duels between Israel and Syria characterized much of the fighting. This type of combat was especially heavy between 16 June and 22 June 1982.[64]

Syria used artillery to support Syrian maneuver forces throughout the fighting, but this support was reported to be slipshod. One problem that characterized Syrian use of artillery during the war was a refusal or inability to rapidly provide fire support in response to the changing tactical situation. This also made Syrian artillery more vulnerable to counterfire.

The Syrians also lacked any advanced targeting aids and had to rely on line-of-sight and area fire. They attempted to substitute mass fire on occasion but lacked numbers, the time to assemble such fire, and adequate supply. The Syrians also found it difficult to coordinate fire from weapons located in different areas and to rapidly shift fires from one target to another. Syrian performance was also erratic. Some units performed far better than others.

Nevertheless, the commander of the Israeli artillery corps indicated after the war that the Arabs as a whole, and the Syrians in particular, were steadily improving their artillery branches. He stated that Syria had greatly improved its precision fire since 1973 and its ability to use self-propelled artillery.

Surface-to-Surface Rockets and Missiles

Surface-to-surface rockets and missiles were used to a limited extent during the Lebanon war. Although both Israel and Syria possess such systems, the IDF seems to have been the only side to use such weapons. Although the details are obscure, the IDF seems to have used Ze'ev rockets in long-distance strikes against SAM sites and other distant military targets. Both sides avoided any general use of surface-to-surface missiles (SSMs), probably because they wanted to keep the conflict at a lower level of intensity than the use of these weapons would imply. In this regard, the use of even a battlefield rocket or missile can be seen as a threat to escalate a conflict.

Mines and Barriers

Arab forces used anti-personnel and anti-armor mines throughout the war. The Israelis were fighting a war of offensive maneuver and appear to have made little if any use of mines. The Arabs, and particularly the PLO, did not, however, make efficient use of landmine warfare.[65] This may have resulted from a rapid Israeli advance in the southern part of Lebanon. Even when the IDF advance did bog down, however, the PLO and Syria rarely exploited the opportunities to lay more mines, which existed but were not utilized.

One plausible reason for the comparative lack of Arab mine warfare has been suggested by Ze'ev Schiff and Ehud Ya'ari. According to their analyses, the collapse of the PLO chain of command led the PLO fighters to oppose Israel in isolated and non-cooperative groups which did very little to integrate mines into their defensive strategy. Had a command remained centralized at a higher level, mines may have been used more often in the south. Advancing Israeli troops captured PLO weapons stores loaded with thousands of mines.[66] The only real exception to this situation involved PLO guerrillas operating behind Israeli lines who were known to plant mines, set booby traps, and make hit-and-run attacks on Israeli forces.[67]

The PLO did make extensive use of earth barricades within Beirut in order to block or channelize the routes of possible Israeli advance. These earth barriers had to be pushed down by bulldozers in many instances before the Israelis could advance. Bulldozers were also used throughout the conflict for such tasks as the widening of roads to accommodate tanks and the process of moving war wreckage, such as vehicle shells from highways.

All-Weather and Night Target Acquisition Systems

Israeli night-fighting equipment included a variety of passive and active night-observation devices, light-enhancement devices, and tank-mounted searchlights. The Israeli Matador, a computerized tank fire-control system used in conjunction with a variety of tanks, was also put into operation during the 1982 war. This system has a passive night-vision attachment which includes an image intensification tube and an adjustable image brightness. The effectiveness of this system may have contributed to the fact that Merkava tanks are known to have been driven all night along steep mountain slopes without the benefit of headlights.[68]

Arab capabilities have also advanced since 1973. Syrian and Egyptian manuals, based on Soviet texts, deal extensively with night combat in mountains, cities, and other environments likely to be encountered in the Middle East. Exercises conducted since 1973, as well as Syrian activities in Lebanon since 1975, indicate considerable improvement in this area. The equipment employed by Syrian forces for night fighting and target acquisition include:

- infrared night-sighting devices on armored vehicles;
- night enhancement devices (e.g., 57-mm towed AT gun with starlight scope mounted as gunsight);
- fire-control radars, such as the Soviet Flap Wheel (RPK-1A); and
- active infrared equipment.

Syrian forces tended to mirror-image Soviet night-fighting tactics and Soviet doctrine, which stresses this capability. They made better use of night-movement techniques, however, than night operations.

The battle for Beaufort Castle was an example of a night action, but it occurred at night despite an earlier timetable that called for a daylight assault. This was not a problem for Israel's Golani infantry. They had long prepared for a night assault. Night-vision devices may have been used during this assault, but it is also possible that such equipment was ignored since the attacking APCs used their headlights and illumination rounds were fired. Another explanation for this type of behavior is that it might have involved an attempt by the APCs to distract the PLO in Beaufort while troops assaulted the fortifications on foot.

The Israelis have always had a natural interest in early-warning radars, given the small size of their country. All early-warning radars come under the jurisdiction of the Air Force which operates an early-warning and air-control network. The IDF has routinely flown reconnaissance missions over Lebanon since the late 1960s. In contrast, Syria has flown few recce missions, and none of the Lebanese forces had advanced recce or intelligence technology.

The IDF has several large early-warning radars and operates a number of smaller, mobile ground surveillance radars (GSRs). These are the U.S.-built PPS-5s and PPS-15s. While these systems were undoubtedly used in the war, data on their performance are not known.

Israel also used ground surveillance radars such as the EL/M2121 built by Elta. The system provides long-range detection of ground and near-ground targets and may help account for the fact Israel was able to kill 14 Syrian Gazelle gunships, capture another intact, and provide additional all-weather real time intelligence data for its helicopters and land units. It is interesting to note, incidentally, that Israel claims an 80 percent kill rate in using its own attack helicopters and missiles against PLO and Syrian armor.

Anti-Aircraft Artillery

The Israeli air-defense-suppression effort was so efficient that neither Syria nor the PLO made much use of AA guns except in the curtain or area fire mode. Even then, they had little effect, although it is important to note that the PLO seems to have had no idea of how to use its AA guns effectively, and the IAF did not attack the well-positioned Syrian AA gun defenses in Syria.

The IAF did make effective use of AA guns. The Vulcan anti-aircraft gun seems to have performed well during the operations in Lebanon. This system is known to have been involved in both ground and air actions during the war. According to one Israeli air defense lieutenant colonel, "Our force [the Israeli Vulcans] participates in battle for the double purpose of hitting enemy targets on the ground and providing antiaircraft defense."[69]

Israeli Vulcans are known to have shot down an unspecified number of planes, including an Su-7 Fitter near Gezin.[70] They might have shot down more planes were it not for the fact that Israeli troops were shielded from the Syrian airforce by the IAF. The Vulcan was also quite effective in providing covering fire for the ground forces as they advanced. Furthermore, the Vulcan proved itself an extremely effective system for assault on urban areas.

Surface-to-Air Missiles

Israel had little reason to use surface-to-air missiles during the Lebanon conflict. Israel achieved total air superiority in the first few days of the conflict, and the IAF was capable of shielding the ground forces from hostile aircraft. The effectiveness of the Air Force and Israel's initial SAM suppression effort did, however, lead to some Israeli disregard of Syrian and PLO SAMs which created problems on several occasions. This was especially true when the Israelis came under attack by assault helicopters, making use of anti-armor missiles, for the first time in their history. Syrian Gazelle helicopters could fire their missiles from beyond the range of the machine guns mounted on IDF tanks or APCs.[71]

No Israeli aircraft were shot down by Syrian ground forces throughout the war, but Israel did lose several helicopters. The PLO appears to have made a major effort to fend off the attacks of the Israeli Air Force which supported the advance of the Israeli Army. This was done by the use of SA-7 shoulder-fired, anti-aircraft missiles as well as older anti-aircraft guns. The Israelis, however, were more than prepared for the SA-7 after the 1973 Arab-Israeli War.[72] In order to protect their aircraft against the heat-seeking projectile fired from the SA-7 launcher, Israeli warplanes launched flares and thermal balloons to attract the missiles. This appears to have been a relatively effective tactic since only one Israeli plane was shot down by PLO-fired SA-7s despite intensive use of dive-bombing tactics. The shot-down plane was an older A-4 Skyhawk.[73]

Unlike 1973, the IDF made SAM suppression one of its most critical objectives of the war. It was so successful in this area that it becomes difficult to discuss any aspect of performance by the Soviet SAM systems in Syrian and PLO hands. In the process, the IDF succeeded in achieving a new standard of C^3I performance.

This was the key link integrating all the parts into a total military effort. Although personnel selection, training, and realistic exercises are equally important, the new C^3 technology provides a whole new dimension of capabilities in command and control.[74]

Israel was fully conscious of the vulnerabilities of modern C^3I and sensor systems organized, equipped, and trained to defeat its opponent. Syria failed to take the problem seriously and did not obtain meaningful Soviet aid and support. Israel was also able to draw on its experience in the October War, the U.S. experience in Vietnam, and various encounters between 1974 and 1982. It made brilliant use of operational experience.

Israel enjoyed a near total monopoly in advanced technology and software. It got extensive support from the U.S. and developed its own technical and industrial base to keep its C³I and electronic warfare capabilities fully up-to-date, and its systems tailored to meet its requirements.[75]

Syria's SA-2 and SA-3 missiles and most of its radars and key electronics were obsolete by 1982. While the evidence is unclear, Syria's SA-6s do not seem to have been fully modernized or kept up-to-date with changes to Soviet-held systems. The USSR did not provide the software or operations research data to allow Syria to use its heavy SAMs or new SA-8s and SA-9s effectively, and Syria was relatively careless in netting and deploying its various air-defense systems in the Bekaa and other areas outside Syria.

Israel had aircraft with state-of-the-art sensors, electronic countermeasure, electronic counter-countermeasure (ECCM), avionics, radar, computer, air-to-surface and air-to-air weaponry. It actively planned to destroy the Syrian missiles in Lebanon since they were first deployed in April 1981 and had come within hours of striking the initial SA-6 sites on 30 April 1981 only to cancel the mission at the last moment. It had then systematically practiced strikes on simulated SA-6 sites in the Negev.[76]

Syria had no AWACS, ELINT or electronic support measures (ESM), or electronic warfare aircraft. Its first-line fighters, the MiG-23 and improved versions of the MiG-21, lacked modern avionics, computers, and software. They not only lacked "look down" capability, they could not effectively "look up." Syria had no effective modern air-to-surface munitions and poor avionics for delivering conventional munitions. It had no modern air-to-air missiles and was still reliant on AA-2 variants which were roughly equivalent to the now obsolete AIM-9B and AIM-9C.

Israel attacked Syria's air-defense and fighter system using a tightly integrated mix of sensor aircraft, piloted and unpiloted attack and ELINT systems, and artillery. In contrast, Syria organized its air force, heavy SAM forces, and short-range air defenses into highly compartmented command structures which were not trained to cooperate and, moreover, lacked the software and hardware for effective communication. Key individual elements of the Syrian air-defense systems in Lebanon could not communicate effectively even with similar neighboring systems. Israel also had secure communications that were extremely vulnerable to relatively simple electronic countermeasures.

In spite of constant warning from the day it first deployed its land-based air-defense weapons to Lebanon, Syria had no clear battle plan or tactics for using its various air defenses and no concept of operations.

Israel had brilliant planning and command as well as control and a clear concept of operations. Unlike the land fighting, where individual Syrian combat units could perform well because they did not require a high technology C³I system and could not be targeted easily, the air and air-defense war required high technology, competent organization, and training at all levels. Israel's lead in C³I was inherently more effective.

Israel also demonstrated the value of a near real time electronic battlefield capability in both aerial combat and attacks on surface-to-air missiles in the Bekaa Valley region. The IDF used several ingenious devices in these operations:

- Remotely piloted vehicles equipped with a zoom magnification capability for high-resolution imagery display at command centers and other RPVs specially designed to force Syria to use its radars.
- New Ze'ev (Wolf) surface-to-surface missile systems or terminally homing artillery shells under army management, designed to fire against air-defense radars.
- Early warning aircraft, modified Boeing 707s equipped with jamming devices. This resulted in Syrian aircraft operating without ground radar control or vectors to targets.
- E-2C Hawkeye aircraft were utilized for command-and-control relay missions in addition to their radar surveillance missions. Israel reportedly modified the E-2C aircraft to provide for simultaneous control over 155 targets.[77] While this report is almost certainly untrue, the E-2Cs did have improved ESSM and could provide overall battle data to the forward F-15 controllers as well as individual fighters.
- F-15 fighters operating in an autonomous search-and-control mode to vector attacking fighters on Syrian fighters, while using the general air warning data available from the E-2Cs.

The Israeli attack on the Syrian missile radar sites is particularly interesting because the mission involved intense coordination in the ground support roles.[78]

It is impossible to sort through Israel's mix of security and misinformation to reliably describe all the details of Israel's SAM suppression effort. Israel has deliberately emphasized claims that it used secret technologies, has given its RPVs a more prominent role than it deserved, has circulated rumors about "smart warheads" for its MRLs, and has done its best to limit Syrian ability to understand Israel's attack and develop suitable countermeasures.

Israel has been conspicuously silent about the precise role of its four E-2Cs, four 707s, its smaller Avra and Beech electronic warfare systems, its use of balloon-carried sensors, its use of U.S. "Wild Weasel" variants of the F-4E equipped with Shrike anti-radiation missiles, and the importance of the ECM pods on its fighters. It also has deliberately downplayed the fact that conventional artillery and iron bombs, and not anti-radiation or electro-optical missiles, were used to kill most Syrian air defenses. Further, Israel has been relatively silent about the fact that it used simple flares and mixes of specially cut lengths of chaff, not active countermeasures, to blind many Syrian sensors.

Most of the Western interviews after the war reveal a strong technology bias toward electronic warfare. There are few data on intelligence, planning, command, training, or communications, all areas where Israeli C^{3}I had to excel for its air-defense-suppression technology to have any meaning.

It is obvious, however, that Israel was successful because it had superb intelligence on every level. The IDF began with information provided by recce and ESSM aircraft by the remotely piloted vehicles and agents on the ground.

The Israelis also made exceptionally heavy use of RF-4E Phantoms to provide aerial surveillance and, hence, intelligence support for their own ground forces both during and prior to the invasion. Maps circulated in Israel after the war show the exact location, effective range, and sensor coverage of virtually every radar, SA-2, SA-3, SA-6, SA-8, and SA-9 unit in or affecting the Bekaa target area.[79] According to various sources, Israel had the equivalent of a high resolution photomosaic of the Bekaa when it attacked which showed the layout of every major individual Syrian air-defense site in which no element was more than 48 hours old.

According to some IDF officers, Israel also had the equivalent of an operations map for each site that showed its electromagnetic characteristics, the required active and passive counterforce options, the proper method of air attack, and precise artillery coordinates. According to some reports, both the precise target registrations and proper angle of air attack were confirmed by photo recce using aircraft and RPVs, ELINT data, Israel land reconnaissance, and friendly Arab HUMINT.

The command and control phase of the attack plan was detailed to the point where a specific choice of the best attack mix for each site could be updated on the day of the attack, with choices between conventional iron bombs, cluster munitions, electro-optical systems like Maverick, anti-radiation missiles like Shrike, the use of given numbers and types of tube artillery rounds, or the use of multiple rocket launchers.

Most accounts agree that the rear-area mission was accomplished by a combination of F-16s with conventional and cluster bombs and F-4s with Shrike and Standard ARM missiles.[80] Israel may also have integrated the use of a still developmental computer-guided cluster-bomb missile or glide weapon into some phases of the attack. This system evidently has a range of at least 20 kilometers, with a payload of 1,200 cluster bomblets, and may have been used with good effect against Syrian rear areas. Israel does not seem to have had any smart warheads for its regular multiple rocket launchers; reports that it used armed RPVs on more than an experimental basis seems inaccurate. Radar-homing Ze'ev Wolf missiles are also rumored to have been used to attack the SAM sites at close range, after RPVs triggered the air-defense radars.[81]

In any case, Israel's strike plans were backed by a general active and passive countermeasure plan, along with a full air-cover plan. Israel's use of aircraft and RPVs to confirm damage and help plan follow-up attacks was equally well planned, as was reserve or alternative attack capability.

This plan was backed with a solid and self-critical training and evaluation effort, perhaps the most important single element of the "control" in C^3I. Israel combined dry runs and mission mock-ups with practical experience over Lebanon and Syria and seems to have been particularly successful in using such training to reduce the vulnerability of its Kfirs and F-16s in attacking positions with heavy SHORAD defenses and to adopt uses of cluster bombs that made them properly effective, a performance training-and-evaluation effort that U.S. air power has never matched.

This training-and-evaluation effort was also the key to a C^3I sequence to allow the coordination of air and artillery strikes under air-defense-suppression conditions. Israel seems to have been brilliantly effective in using artillery to disrupt SAM and other sites, then following up immediately with fighters while simultaneously conducting passive and active ECM, using flares, and Israel's E-2Cs and F-15s to provide radar and electronic order-of-battle monitoring of Syrian SAM and fighter activity.

As for the detailed sequence of Israeli attack, various sources indicate that the attack followed something approaching the following pattern.

Israel fully deployed its four E-2C Hawkeye AWACS/ESM aircraft and four 707 ELINT aircraft. These used Elta and other Israeli-built ECM devices to jam effectively SAM radar units and Syria's search radars while they simultaneously checked emissions for departures from past ELINT data and obtained updated jamming data for its aircraft using a computer system developed by the Elbit Company of Haifa.

The E-2Cs acted as a battle manager which could track Israeli aircraft as well as observe Syrian aircraft as they took off from runways in Syria using its APS-125 radar. The Israeli version of the E-2C can scan up to 3 million cubic miles of airspace and detect fighters at ranges of up to 250 miles. It can aid (not control) up to 130 separate interceptions and monitor up to 200 aircraft. Israel used its F-15s to provide autonomous search and forward control in detail. Israel has modified the original U.S. advanced radar processing system, which provides automatic detection, target acquisition, and clutter suppression, to meet its needs. This means improved coverage of ground targets and special software to allow joint operation with other Israeli sensor and early warning (EW) aircraft in air-defense-suppression and air-defense operations.

The Israeli E-2Cs also evidently have modified ALR59 passive detection systems which are tailored to provide ELINT and ESM capabilities that match the electronic orders of battle of Syria, Jordan, Iraq, Egypt, and Saudi Arabia. This doubles some aspects of the E-2Cs detection range, as well as provides a function missing from any version of the E-3A. Similar modifications or add-ons seem to exist for the E-2C's Litton L-304 computer, although U.S. Air Force and Grumman experts are uncertain as to the value of some of the Israeli changes.

The Israeli 707 ECM aircraft is both an electronic warfare and a command post aircraft and is semi-palletized to allow specific configuration for a given mission. The 707 ECM aircraft had ECM capabilities that far outclassed the limited frequency agility of the SA-6 and could evidently use data from the Mastiff RPV and alter its jamming patterns against systems like the SA-6 in near real time. Israel has also been successful in equipping these aircraft with a relatively sophisticated microprocessor-controlled exciter manufactured by Elta. This is called the E1/K7012 and allows Israel to use selective rather than barrage or noise jamming with minimal out-of-phase noise or spurious emission. This gives Israel an immunity to self-jamming which is probably superior to that of any NATO country (see the section in this chapter on close air support for additional details on C^3 assets).

Israel deployed a mix of RPVs designed to both force the Syrian units to activate their radars and engage while sending other RPVs to observe critical targets and provide real time ELINT on key units such as the SA-6. Some of these RPVs seem to have been specially adapted to give the radar profile and speed of Israeli fighters and made it almost impossible for the Syrians to avoid firing at such targets. This helped pinpoint the missile radars to IAF anti-radiation missiles. Israel also seems to have used F-4 launched Samson drones which have a radar signature and speed closer to IAF fighters.

Israeli artillery batteries began to hit at Syrian radar, SAM, and air-defense sites while Israel's multiple rocket launchers and surface-to-surface cluster weapons were used against area targets and targets farther in the rear. The initial surge of fire was sustained by carefully planned harassment fire throughout the attack.

At the same time, IAF F-4 and F-16 fighters flew extensive chaff and flare missions virtually blanketing the area. Israeli fighters were equipped with active jamming pods using updated versions of the Wild Weasel technology the U.S. developed for the F-4G. These include several families of Israeli systems, including the Elta EL/M-2001B.

There are some reports that Israel used its less capable fighters to drop flares and specially modified A-4 Skyhawks to suppress and attack ZSU-23-4 radar-guided AA guns, but the validity of such reports is unclear. In any case, Israeli fighters may have been supported by Avra Stol 202 forward ECM aircraft. This is a light aircraft carrying a dedicated jammer. Israel's Beech aircraft may also have been used as forward ELINT collectors, as well as CH-53 helicopters with airborne jammers.

While Israel established its full active and passive ECM blanket, low-flying fighters popped up from the blind spot in the Syrian radar coverage behind the southwestern ridge/mountain line of the Bekaa and began to use Standard Arm, Shrike, and Israeli-made anti-radiation missiles and electro-optical missiles, like Maverick, against the larger Syrian missile sites such as the SA-6 sites. This allowed Israel to hit key sites in several different ways at once. The Standard is a heavy missile with considerable range; the Shrike is designed to attack a battery's radar antenna; and systems like Maverick can be used against any target with suitable land contrast.

Depending on the source, Israel also used developmental laser illuminators on some RPVs to illuminate the most difficult targets and eliminate the need for fighter guidance of electro-optical missiles after lock-on. This greatly improved missile accuracy and fighter survivability.

Israel used the extremely accurate bombing computers on its F-16s and Kfirs to send conventional iron and cluster bombs against the SA-8 and SA-9 units which it was tracking with RPVs. The F-16 was particularly effective because of its high speed and ability to escape the target area. The one reported case of an armed RPV kill against a SAM is of an SA-8 kill.

Israel monitored this activity in real time with its Scout and Mastiff RPVs and ELINT aircraft. It was able to manage their portion of the suppression from the E-2Cs and may have used computer vans to help coordinate the land portion.

The end result was that the IDF killed 17 of 19 SA-6 Syrian missile sites in the Bekaa and several SA-2 and SA-3 sites. It accomplished this in no more than 10 to 20 minutes of active combat.

The IAF also deserves credit for its ability to suppress the SA-7, SA-8, and SA-9. It made excellent use of visual detection, flares and other decoy techniques, reduced vulnerability attack profiles, threat location and avoidance, aircraft-to-aircraft warning, and evasive action. Its overall success is still surprising, however, given the number of systems in PLO and Syrian hands. This had led to unconfirmed speculation that the USSR is not exporting its more sophisticated IR seekers to Third World countries.

The Israelis did not use their own surface-to-air missiles extensively in 1982. It is important to note, however, that the Israelis made important modifications to their Hawk missiles and have upgraded their Chaparral missile systems.

The Israeli Hawks had radar and guidance software that allowed intercepts at up to 70,000 feet. An Israeli Hawk battery in Lebanon shot down a MiG-25 at an even higher altitude and flying at Mach 2.5 on 30 August 1982. They also added a $30,000 Super Eye electro-optical detector to the Hawks in the mid-1970s to provide detection at ranges up to 30–40 kilometers and help them deal with ECM and IFF problems. According to one report, there were two confirmed cases in 1982 where this system prevented Israeli units from firing on their own aircraft.

As for Chaparral, they added an Amarit electro-optical and threat designation communication system for identification and target observation. According to Israel this doubled the operational engagement range at which the system could safely acquire and identify a target.

Air-to-Air Combat

The air war between Israel and Syria involved the largest and most intensive single air-to-air combat engagement in the history of the Middle East. This war is an important watershed in the history of aerial warfare because the outcome was largely dependent on the use and mastery of new air-to-air missile and computerized C^3I technology.

According to the IISS *Military Balance, 1982-83*, Syria began the war with a total inventory of 448 combat aircraft; Israel had a total of 602 combat aircraft. The designated fighter inventories of each country were equally lopsided; the Syrian Air Force employed approximately 20 MiG-23 BM Flogger E and 200 MiG-21 PF IMF aircraft. Although Syria had about 23 MiG-25 Foxbat As, they were apparently not utilized extensively in the war. It is not clear how many aircraft were actually combat-ready on the Syrian side. Contesting the Syrian MiGs was an Israeli inventory of 40 F-15s, 138 F-4Es, 20 Mirage IIICJ, 1 BJ, 160 Kfir C1, IC2, 66 F-16As, and 8 F-16Bs. It is, of course, important to note that the numbers of operational aircraft may have been substantially smaller.[82]

The air war was fought in the sky over Lebanon and the Levantine coast. The new C^3 and EW technology, however, cut a wide swath which tended to widen the area of conflict. The E-2C's ARS-125 radar and the ELINT systems on the 707s reportedly were able to observe Syrian MiGs leaving the ground in Syria.[83] Once again, several factors were in Israel's favor: tactical initiative, numerical preponderance, superior aircraft and weapons, and good intelligence of the Syrian threat.[84]

Aircraft

Syria's primary fighter aircraft were the MiG-21 PF and the export version of the MiG-23BM, designated Flogger E by NATO. The MiG-23 was designed as a Soviet response to the Israeli F-4 Phantom and was the equal of the Phantom in several respects, i.e., avionics and range. It should be noted that the Syrian MiG-23s seem to be closer to the Soviet version than the Iraqi. The Soviets have not, however, released their version of the High Lark fire-control radar to either country.

The Syrians also operated some MiG-23B Flogger F, otherwise designated the MiG-27. This is also a single seat, tactical attack aircraft. Its maximum clean speed at low altitude is about Mach 1.2 and about 1,055 mph at high altitude. The Flogger F has the engine installation and gun of the MiG-23 with variable inlets and lacks the comprehensive MiG-27 avionics. This aircraft uses a 23-mm 6-barrel Gatling Gun, seven external pylons for ordnance, and the AS-7 Kerry missile for an ordnance total of 4,200 lbs. Its combat range is approximately 600 miles with bombs and other ordnance. Reports indicate that the MiG-23B supplied to Syria has had extensive reliability problems.[85] The Syrians did not bring these aircraft to bear against Israeli targets, although they have considerable air-to-air combat capability. The Sukhoi 7 and 20, by contrast, were clearly unsuitable for this mission.

The Syrians lacked modern air-to-air missiles. They had to rely on variants of the Soviet AA-2 Atoll, an aging missile limited to moderate-range tailchase attacks. The Soviets did not release the Apex missile it uses on its own MiG-23s to Syria. The Atoll also had poor maneuverability or dogfight capability. There are reports that Syria had the more modern AA-8 and French R-550 air-to-air missiles, but it is unclear such systems were operational.

The major Israeli aircraft in the June 1982 Lebanon conflict were the F-15 Eagle, the F-16 Fighting Falcon, the F-4 Phantom, the Israeli Kfir C-2, and the A-4 Skyhawk. In addition, the Israelis employed the E-2C Hawkeye and other aircraft in the threat assessment and EW roles.

The F-15 Eagle is an air superiority fighter designed to confront the MiG-23 Flogger and MiG-25 Foxbat and their successors. The Eagle has high performance in terms of turn rate, acceleration, and rate of climb. It was designed with the air superiority or dogfight role in mind. It is powered by twin Pratt & Whitney engines which provide a very substantial increase in thrust/weight ratio over any previous fighter. Each engine provides 23,800 pounds of thrust. The Eagle has a maximum speed at low altitude of 921 mph, with a Mach 2.5 speed at altitude. The service ceiling is 63,000 feet. The F-15 has a maximum rate of climb of 40,000 feet per minute. It employs a Hughes APG-63 pulsed-Doppler radar and a head-up display unit for easy instrument monitoring by the pilot. The F-15 Radar has a search range of 150 miles and can interface with the computer-radar on the E-2C aircraft.

Since it was first deployed in the late 1970s, the F-15 has proved to be the most effective fighter aircraft in the world. Its armament includes one 20-mm rotating barrel gun and eight air-to-air missiles, such as the Aim-7 Sparrow and the Aim-9L Sidewinder. These sub-systems have proved to be extremely effective in combination with the F-15 "platform."

The F-16 Fighting Falcon is a lightweight, tactical fighter with exceptional maneuverability. It employs state-of-the-art aero-dynamics, avionics, and fire-control systems. A "fly-by-wire" system of electrical controls is utilized instead of the conventional mechanical linkages. This enables the aircraft to respond more quickly and accurately, thereby simplifying maintenance needs. It is slightly slower than the F-15 in level flight, i.e., Mach 1.2 at sea level and Mach 2 at altitude. It is nevertheless a highly agile aircraft and is well-suited for dogfighting. Its combat radius is about 575 miles.

The F-16 avionics package consists of comprehensive communication and navigation/attack systems, including the Westinghouse pulse-doppler ranging and tracking radar, Dalmo Victor ALR-46 radar warning system, Sperry Flight Systems air data computer, and Singer Kearfott improved SKN-2400 inertial navigation system. The USAF version utilized a KIT2A/TSEC cryptographic system, Marconi-Elliott head-up display, and a Delco fire-control computer. The extent to which the Israelis utilized these systems is classified, as are any modifications to the same.

The F-16 utilizes both the Gatling Gun–type cannon, the M61A1 20-mm, infrared, and radar homing missiles, i.e., the Sidewinder Aim 9-L and the Aim-7 Sparrow. Both of these systems are far more advanced than the Soviet AA-2 available to Syria. They are described shortly in the context of their use in actual combat over Lebanon.

The Kfir is an Israeli-manufactured, delta-winged, single-seat aircraft designed for the fighter-bomber role. It has developed out of Israel's experience with the Mirage IIICJ which Israel developed from French plans after the French cut off further supplies to Israel in the wake of the June 1967 War. A later version, the Kfir C-2, incorporates sharply swept fixed forewings above the wing-root leading edge, dogtooth extensions to the outer wings, and small fences on each side of the nose. Powered by the J-79, this aircraft can achieve slightly above Mach 1 (1.12) at sea level and Mach 2 at altitude. Its armament package includes two 30 mm DEFA553 cannon, each with 150 rounds. Its external weapon load can total up to 8,550 pounds plus two Shafrir air-to-air missiles. The range on internal fuel is reportedly 750 miles. The C-2 version has improved take-off and landing and considerably enhanced flight maneuverability. It is being followed by an advanced C-7 variant.

Israel also uses the Python III air-to-air missile in addition to the Aim-7 and Aim-9L. The Python III is an all-aspect, short-range, dogfight missile. The Python is a development of the earlier Shafrir 2 AAM. Reportedly some combat experience was accumulated from the June 1982 war. The specifications released to date are as follows.[86]

Length	3 m
Diameter	0.16 m
Weight	120 kg
Guidance	IR
Sensor Angle	30
Max Acceleration	30 G
Range (minimum)	0.5 km
Range (maximum)	15 km

The Python can be carried by any modern Western fighter aircraft without any special adaptations. Two can be carried on Kfir underwing pylons, four on a Phantom (two on each internal wing pylon), and two on the F-15 and F-4. Maintenance is reportedly simple, and special simplified ground support has also been developed.[87] (See Figure 3.18 and Table 3.4.)

Air War Threat Assessments

Israel's most important threat assessment system used during the 1982 war was probably the E-2C Hawkeye surveillance aircraft. This aircraft provides surveillance within a three million cubic mile volume, with detection and threat assessment out to almost 300 miles (480 kilometers). The main radar is the General Electric APS-125 which includes the advanced radar processing subsystem (ARPS) to increase sensitivity and major electronic counter-countermeasures (ECCM).

The Course of Air-to-Air Combat

The details of Israel's astounding victory in the air are less impressive than those involved in its suppression of Syrian SAMs. Syria's mistakes in structuring its land-based air defenses were forgivable within the normal limits of military professionalism. Syria's irresponsible use of its fighter aircraft was noted by then–Chief of Staff Lt. General Rafael Eitan. He stated after the fighting:

> The day we destroyed the batteries, we shot down 23 MiGs. They were very irrational in their attack on our air forces, literally bashing their heads against a wall. The basic tactic of the Syrian air force (was) to take to the air . . . get outside the protective range of their home based missiles, . . . and run for cover.[88]

A high-ranking Israeli Air Force officer made the same point when he was asked for his impressions of the MiG-23:

> I can't compare it when a MiG-23 is flown in a tactic that I can't understand or in a situation that I would never get into. The problem is that their pilots didn't do things at the right time or in the right place . . . the pilots behaved as if they knew they were going to be shot down and then waited for it to happen and not how to prevent it or how to shoot us down. Which was very strange because in the 1973 War the Syrians fought aggressively. It wasn't the equipment at fault, but their tactics. They could have flown the best fighter in the world, but if they flew it the way they were flying we would have shot them down in exactly the same way. I don't mean they were sitting ducks, but in our view, they acted without tactical sense.[89]

These Israeli comments are not exaggerated or ethnocentric. Syria flew its best aircraft into the Israel SAM suppression environment that

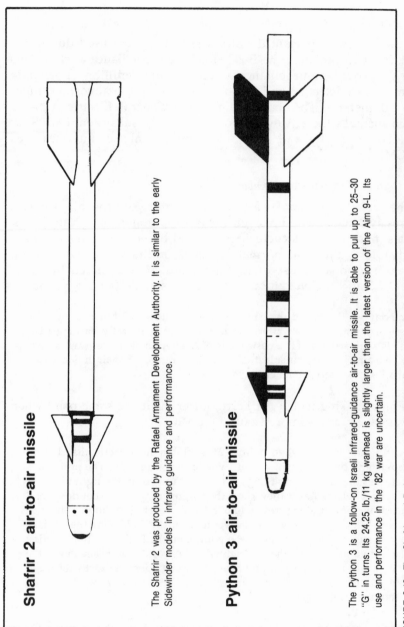

Shafrir 2 air-to-air missile

The Shafrir 2 was produced by the Rafael Armament Development Authority. It is similar to the early Sidewinder models in infrared guidance and performance.

Python 3 air-to-air missile

The Python 3 is a follow-on Israeli infrared-guidance air-to-air missile. It is able to pull up to 25–30 "G" in turns. Its 24.25 lb./11 kg warhead is slightly larger than the latest version of the Aim 9-L. Its use and performance in the '82 war are uncertain.

FIGURE 3.18 The Shafrir and Python III Israeli Air-to-Air Missiles. From information provided by an Israeli defense spokesman and from Stan Morse, *Modern Military Powers: Israel* (New York: 1984), p. 114.

TABLE 3.4 The Precision-Guided Munitions of the June 1982 Air War.

SYRIA[1]		ISRAEL[3]	
AIR TO AIR MISSILES	**AIR TO SURFACE MISSILES**	**AIR TO AIR MISSILES**	**AIR TO GROUND MISSILES**
IR GUIDANCE: AA-2 Atoll AA-8 R-550 Magic	*At-2 Swatter (Anti-tank)[2]*	*IR GUIDANCE:* Shafrir Python-3 MR-530 AIM - 9 Sidewinder AIM - 9L Sidewinder *RADAR GUIDANCE:* AIM - 7 Sparrow	*AGM-65A Maverick TV* *Walleye* *AS-11 Wireguided (helicopter launched)* *AGM-45 Shrike (anti-radiation)* *AGM-78 Standard Arm (anti-radiation)* *LUZ-1 - TV (existence is disputed)* *Harpoon (anti-ship)* *HOBOS TV-guided stand-off bombs* *GABRIE-(anti-ship)*

SOURCES: (1) Mark Heller, Don Tamari, and Ze'ev Eytan, *The Middle East Military Balance 1983* (Tel Aviv University, Jaffee Center for Strategic Studies, 1983), p. 227. The Magic missile may not have been available during the June 1982 war with Israel. (2) IISS, *Military Balance 1982–1983* (London: International Institute for Strategic Studies, 1983), p. 62. This item was not reported in the Heller volume noted above. The Swatter is a wire-guided missile launched from helicopters. (3) IISS, *Military Balance 1982–1983*, p. 199.

has been described. It did so although it knew Israeli E-2Cs could detect Syrian fighters the moment they left the runway and that Israeli fighters carried jam-resistant radios and were able to communicate through secure voice and data links despite Syrian jamming efforts.[90]

In practice, the Syrian fighters lost both communications and long-range radar coverage long before they came within combat range of Israeli fighters. Although they were critically dependent on ground controlled intercept tactics, they attempted mass air combat under conditions where they could not establish reliable communications with the ground and where Syrian ground sites could not provide useful radar coverage or vectoring. In addition, they flew into an area where Israel had already destroyed Syria's forward air sensors and was jamming the remnants.

The Syrians flew random search patterns after they lost communication with the ground. After they saw IAF fighters, they flew straight intercept profiles or simple jigs which made them extremely predictable. They seemed unable to fly complex small formation and routinely broke up into groups of one or two aircraft even when they were threatened with attack. These formation and C^{3}I problems were further compounded by the fact that the best Syrian fighter, the MiG-23, was forced to fly a peculiar high-low formation because the aircraft lacks both an effective look-up and look-down capability. The higher and lower formations are forced to act as each other's AWACS, a tactic that is hopeless the moment either group is engaged.

This was not only an ideal killing area for Israel's F-15s, F-16s, and other fighters, it also maximized the effectiveness of Israel's combination of F-15s, E-2Cs, and 707s in the C^3 role. Syrian intercept vectors were flown without terrain obscuration, and the E-2Cs and F-15s in the autonomous air-control role could vector F-16s and other F-15s to near-perfect engagement positions. Israel's active jamming of Syrian aircraft radars and communications was aided by prior use of chaff, a countermeasure that Syrian aircraft were unable to deal with but that Israeli aircraft could handle well.

Israel also made good use of new ground C^3 centers during this phase of the fighting. It had a new regional GCI center at Kafr Malik with both early warning and ESM/ELINT capabilities. At the same time, it had an effective central command and two other regional command centers. In practice, the regional center acted as the key battle management center for air-to-air, SAM, and SHORAD operations. While the exact configuration of such centers is secret, they have digital data links to Israel's E-2Cs and 707s and advanced computers and automatic displays. They may have a 657-11 system similar to the Cobalt Grande system in Spain. They definitely have air controllers with years of practical combat experience.

In short, Syrian aircraft entered into the air environment nearest Israel under conditions that gave Israel every possible edge. Israeli aircraft had effective individual countermeasures such as the EL/L-2000 series mentioned earlier. They operated as part of a fully integrated air control and warning system. They had secure and countermeasure-proof Tadiran radios. They had vastly superior pilot experience and training, and they had a concept of operations and clear tactics. They had superior radars and avionics.

The Israelis also had Aim-7, Aim-9L, Aim-9P3, and Shafrir missiles. This gave them operational radar-guided missiles and IR-guided missiles approaching a 360° launch aspect with far superior maneuverability to the obsolete AA-2 series of air-to-air missiles the USSR had provided Syria.

At longer ranges, Israel could use the Aim-7 to force Syrian formations to break up. The Aim-7E and F are Mach 3.5 missiles with ranges of 14 and 25 miles respectively and could bring Syrian aircraft under fire long before they could launch at Syrian missiles. This capability, coupled to Israel's vastly superior radars and EW capabilities, had already shown the Syrians their MiG-25s could not operate in Israeli-controlled air space, and the loss of two MiG-25 fighters and one MiG-25 recce aircraft was obviously a factor that led Syria to keep its MiG-25s out of the fighting.

Israel does, however, seem to have added a new twist during the fighting over the Bekaa. While the full details are not available, Israel evidently was able to use its F-15s in the air-control role to predict when a Syrian formation was flying a profile where its front and rear warning radars would allow Israeli F-15s and F-16s to launch missiles from an aspect where the Syrian radars provided only minimal warning. While the Aim-7 did not prove particularly effective as a killer, it served its tactical purpose—several Syrians ejected when they first received radar warning.

Israel also had a massive edge at visual ranges. Israel's IR missiles had maximum ranges of 6.2 to 11 miles and could be launched in head-on or side intercepts. At closer ranges, Israel's superior guns and avionics were aided by superior training and maneuverability. Israel's F-16s accounted for 44 kills during the fighting in June and July. The F-15s killed 40, and an F-4 killed one. The Aim-9L accounted for most kills. Cannon accounted for only about 7 percent of the Syrian kills.[91] About half of the 85 kills were MiG-21s and half were MiG-23s.

Israeli pilots also exploited the fact that the MiG-21 and MiG-23 have their best energy of maneuver at relatively high altitudes and are slower to maneuver at low altitudes. They exploited the fact that the avionics of all Soviet export fighters still provide poor support for air-to-air combat, a fact that Syrian pilots only fully learned from other Arab states after the war.

Even with these advantages, however, it is still striking that the Israeli C^{3}I system proved able to bring the elements of this superiority together at so many different levels. The importance of such C^{3}I capabilities is illustrated by the fact that Israel normally did not pursue combat across the Syrian border and usually had only one to two minutes in which to strike at Syrian fighters between the time they entered the Bekaa and then swept back into Syrian airspace. Nevertheless, Israeli sources claim 85 to 90 percent of air-to-air kills occurred in the Bekaa.

The overall result of both the air-defense-suppression and air-to-air combat efforts was that Israel killed 22 to 23 aircraft during this initial air-defense-suppression effort on 9 June 1982 and damaged seven as well as at least 17 to 19 major SAM complexes. The IAF killed 25 more aircraft and three helicopters on 10 June 1982, plus the two Syrian SAM reinforcement units discussed earlier. It shot down 18 more Syrian aircraft on 11 June, before a temporary cease-fire, bringing its total to 79 to 82 Syrian fighters shot down as against two Israeli fighters, one of which was a Skyhawk to an SA-8.[92] Israel's only other losses were an F-4 and several helicopters; it raised its total Syrian kills to 92 by the time the war was over. According to one source, the responsibility for air combat kills is 44 to the F-16, one by an F-4E, and the balance to the F-15.[93]

It is also interesting to note that the Syrians kept launching air sorties long after it became apparent they had no practical hope of breaking up the Israeli air-defense effort. While Syria briefly claimed that it had shot down 19 Israeli aircraft on 11 June 1982, Arab sources indicate that neither Assad nor the Syrian high command had any real illusions. Syria immediately appealed to Moscow for hope, an appeal that led Colonel General Yevgenyi S. Yurasov, a senior commander of the Soviet air defense forces, to rush to Damascus.[94] It is also clear that the claimed kills were not claimed by the surviving Syrian pilots and originated at the policy level within the Syrian government.

It is difficult to avoid the conclusion that most Syrian pilots knew they were being sent on suicide missions after the first day. This may explain the lack of aggressiveness criticized by senior Israeli officers. It is also clear that Syria's primary failures were not matters of C^{3}I tactics and technology, but rather the results of high-level decisions.

This raises the issue of command: What was the real intent of Assad and the senior Syrian officers in forcing the cream of their air force to fly under such conditions?

There are not reliable answers to this question. It seems doubtful that the Syrian high command intentionally would have lost so many aircraft, yet the losses were sustained over such a considerable length of time that commanders must have realized the outcome. The first day is explainable as the result of confusion, panic, and ignorance; the succeeding days are not.

Accordingly, it is impossible to reject the conclusion that Assad based his decision on the same kind of political and strategic factors that led him to expose his land-based air defenses in the Bekaa Valley. Assad may well have thrown away his air force deliberately to persuade the Arab world that he would indeed challenge Israel in order to improve his political influence and gain aid and to put pressure on the USSR and counter charges of indifference by the PLO. From this perspective, Syrian actions make some sort of strategic sense.

Close Air Support

Israel was far more effective in the close air support role in the 1982 fighting than in 1973. It was able to operate with comparative freedom from air attack during the first days of the war. The decisive destruction of the Syrian heavy surface-to-air missiles in the Bekaa and of Syrian fighters then gave it a high degree of freedom of action through Lebanon once Syria became fully committed to the war.

The IAF was able to respond quickly and effectively to support the ground forces throughout the IDF's advance north, and this support continued throughout the fighting for the Beirut-Damascus Road. As has been discussed in the chronology of the fighting, the IAF also caught a Syrian brigade in the open moving into Lebanon and was able to inflict significant casualties.

The IAF did, however, face a number of special conditions which affected its performance:

- The guerrilla nature of much of the conflict meant that Israeli strikes often had to be conducted against a furtive, mobile enemy offering only limited target opportunities;
- The urban location of major battles often provided Syria and the PLO with excellent cover and protection and meant the IAF had to limit its attacks to minimize civilian casualties;
- The complete air superiority the IAF achieved early in the war

meant that the main threat to its aircraft was SAM-7s, ZSU-23-4s, unguided AA guns, and small arms; and
- The use of a battle management aircraft and other C^3 assets, such as RPVs and EW aircraft in the air war, meant that once the IAF achieved air superiority and SAM suppression, these systems could be brought to bear in targeting on the close air support mission with exceptional effectiveness.

Israeli close air support started even before IDF ground troops advanced on 6 June 1982. Spearheading formations advanced under the umbrella of air support from A-4 Skyhawks, F-4E Phantom, and Kfir fighter bombers on both the coastal and central fronts.

The Israeli Air Force then systematically exploited every opportunity. Chaim Herzog has pointed out that close air support was especially important in dealing with Syria. On one occasion, a Syrian armored brigade, on its way to the front, was completely destroyed by Israeli air force interdiction.[95] On another occasion, the Syrians found themselves unable to consolidate a superior defensive position because of pounding by the Israeli Air Force.[96] Herzog also maintains that the greatest advantage that the Israeli forces had in this confrontation was that of complete air superiority. He also maintains that Israel's air victories were an important if not decisive factor in encouraging the Syrians to accept a cease-fire in Lebanon.[97]

The single Israeli aircraft casualty during the close air support effort Operation Peace for Galilee was an A-4 Skyhawk which was attacking targets in the Lebanese town of Nabatiyah. The plane was shot down by a PLO shoulder-fired SA-7 missile and the pilot, Captain Aharon Achiaz, was taken prisoner by the PLO.[98] This was an incredible performance given the hundreds of SA-7s fired during such attacks and the large numbers of AA guns in PLO and Syrian forces.

In general, air support was called on when ground forces could not bring tank or artillery guns to bear on enemy troops. The following account suggests both the tactics used and the intensity of the close air support battle.

> Where the tanks could not deploy to bear with their firepower, attack helicopters and heliported assault teams supported by artillery were moved in. In one of these clashes, an Israeli Cobra anti-tank helicopter was lost with its crew of two, probably knocked down by a Strellas SA-7. The Israeli Air Force also lost a Skyhawk, shot down by ground fire near Nabatiyah; its pilot, a reserve officer, was captured by the PLO.[99]

Unfortunately, not enough data are available to assess the performance of each of the major aircraft involved in the CAS mission, i.e., the A-4 Skyhawk and the Kfir C-2. Although some Israeli reports have expressed satisfaction with the Kfir, not enough data have been made public to confirm it as a success. It does seem clear that the Israelis benefitted from years of research, development, and training in the close support area. However, much of this improvement seems to have been as much the result of new C^3 assets, such as RPVs providing near real time damage reports, as improvements in pilot and aircraft weapons performance.

There is no doubt that the Israelis made substantial improvements in their operational effectiveness in the CAS role after 1973. At the same time, it is not clear how timely, accurate, and efficient many of their fighter-bomber strikes actually were. Some air strikes did hit friendly forces, and a number of IDF ground officers are severely critical of the accuracy of IDF strikes or complain about a lack of timely response to calls for CAS strikes. These delays occurred in an environment of absolute air superiority except for a few sporadic attacks by Su-7s and some attack helicopters.

Interdiction and Long-Range Attack

IAF attacks on fixed-site targets such as bridges and other hard-points were the only examples of true interdiction bombing in the Lebanon war. These attacks were consistently effective. The IAF attack on the SAM missile network in the Bekaa Valley on 9 June 1982 had many of the attributes associated with interdiction strikes, but this operation has already been analyzed in discussing SAM suppression.

The IAF was far less successful, however, in hitting urban targets. As has been discussed earlier, it lacked the targeting and intelligence to precisely identify and characterize targets in urban areas. While it tried to minimize collateral damage and civilian casualties, it did do severe damage in West Beirut with only limited military effect. The IAF also often lacked the ability to detect Syrian movements, particularly night reinforcements. It is unclear why this was the case, given its ability to use IR, SAR, and SLAR sensors.

The performance of IDF air-to-ground ordnance is also somewhat uncertain. It does seem to have had numerous misses with Maverick, and its improved cluster bombs seem to have had mixed success, partly because of the inability to target them precisely. IAF cluster bomb units (CBUs) also caused a substantial amount of the IDF's casualties from friendly fire as well as numerous post-strike civilian casualties, although at least some CBUs were highly effective against armor. It is unclear, however, from discussions with IDF officers whether the IDF had a clear air-attack doctrine for built-up and mountain areas or had subjected its weapons and munitions to full-scale test and evaluation for the kind of missions it flew in Lebanon. It is also unclear whether or not its major air strikes on Beirut in August 1982 were intended to have military or shock and political effect. The IAF may have bombed suspected PLO facilities for this reason, although reports of large-scale use of fuel air explosives for building busting do not seem to be correct.

Air Reconnaissance, C³I, IFF, and AC&W

The role of the IAF's C³I systems have already been discussed in broad terms, but several key systems are worth discussing in depth. The E-2C Hawkeye uses a digital moving target indication system.[100] The E-2C is a propeller-driven plane with a crew of five that can stay aloft for six hours. The Hawkeye can detect and track low-flying fighter aircraft at distances up to 220 miles; its radar is more effective for higher altitude targets.

A 24-foot, dish-shaped housing mounted on top of the fuselage carries rotating radar and IFF antennas. Sophisticated computer systems in the E-2C help discriminate between "background clutter" of radar reflection of low speed and stationary targets and low-altitude air aircraft.

The E-2C computer automatically correlates the coded signals of friendly aircraft with the computer-translated signal. The radar cannot, however, detect land targets. The E-2C data displayed on three consoles represent flight track information on hundreds of aircraft, separating friendly and hostile planes and giving range, bearing, altitude, speed, and other information on the aircraft. This data can be transmitted to friendly planes or to anti-aircraft ground missiles and cannons, either through ground stations or directly to other aircraft. The E-2C can handle about six to eight fully controlled intercepts and can provide significant data on 30 to 40 more and some location data on up to 150 aircraft.

The E-2C Hawkeye also has a "passive detection system" which can detect and precisely locate and track 300 emissions from airborne or surface transmitters at one time. The E-2C crew can detect when it is being "painted" by hostile radar, and they have the capability to pinpoint surface-to-air missile sites and other key radar installations.

It should be noted, however, that even Israel's modified version of the E-2C is scarcely state-of-the-art. It has far less ability to handle high density air data than the E-3A AWACS, far less low-altitude resolution and ground-clutter elimination, and less radar range for jam resistance. It also has limited data-link capability to friendly fighters. The IDF's successful use of the E-2C is, therefore, an indication that more advanced AWACS aircraft can be even more effective.

The IAF F-15 fighter has an internal, computer-assisted radar that is one of the most capable of any air superiority fighter in the world. It has a range of 200 miles and look-down ability similar to an AWACS. The radar on the IAF F-16 is similar but less advanced and comprehensive and has far less look-down capability.

The radar interface ability of E-2C and F-15 aircraft has proved to be of critical importance. The E-2C provides the role of battle management, integrating all of the relevant incoming data with computers capable of analyzing and automatically communicating with on-board systems in the F-15. The F-15 acts as an autonomous air controller. There is little doubt that this capability gives the IAF an important advantage over less sophisticated systems, where fighter-interceptor pilots are compelled to rely on ground-based radar personnel working off a static display board. It also provides an important lesson about the value of sophisticated radars, avionics, and data links in modern high-performance fighters.

The IAF Boeing E-707 functions as an electronic intelligence collector and as an EW platform. In the attacks on SAM sites in the Bekaa Valley, Boeing 707s provided stand-off jamming: distorting ground-based radar signals associated with the SA-6 missiles. Indeed, the 707's jamming mission is a direct response to the experience of the 1973 war with the SA-6. According to one report, over 300 SAMs were fired in the Lebanon war in spite of the SAM suppression effort and resulted in only two hits. Witnesses report that SAMs were frequently out of control immediately after launch as a result of jamming.[101] What is not clear is how this balance will shift in the future. The IAF has so far kept ahead of the improvements in Syria's SAMs and their related C^3 systems, but NATO forces are experiencing steadily greater problems in Europe. The importance of this electronic warfare duel is obvious; less obvious is judging the results of the outcome.

Three types of aircraft are currently used in addition to the 707s in the jamming role. These are the EV-1E Mohawk (see variation in designation in the above list), the Buch RV-21 and, since 1983, the R-12D. Because of the sensitive missions of these aircraft, operational details have not been made available. The IDF also used CH-53s with jammers. Although the general value of such systems is clear, it should be emphasized that they involve an uncertain high-technology duel.

Israel's success against Syrian MiGs in the war in Lebanon in 1982 made full use of this technology. Assessments of this success have tended to vary in terms of the weight attributed to the pilot and/or the aircraft. It is interesting to note that at least one IAF general felt that the romantic image of the jet fighter pilot is largely passe:

> Now it is really a pilot's knowledge of his electronics systems and his ability to read his computers quickly that allows him to "see" his opponent and launch his missiles. He may shoot down his opponent without even sighting him. . . .[102]

This view contrasts with the more traditional emphasis on the human factor expressed in former IAF Commander Ezer Weizmann's comment:

> The human factor will decide the fate of war, of all wars. Not the Mirage, nor any other plane, and not the screwdriver or the wrench or radar or missiles or all the newest technology and electronic innovations.[103]

Regardless of the emphasis subscribed to, it is increasingly clear that it is the total synergism of man and machine that now determines combat effectiveness. In terms of technology, the gap between the Israelis and the Arab adversaries was never wider.

Israel's effective use of RPVs is one of the most important lessons of the war.[104] Israel also used Samson and Delilah drones, but its two major types of RPVs were unquestionably of more military value. The Tadiran Mastiff is a low-cost system with a maximum airspeed of 100 knots, a mission duration range of up to seven hours, a nominal range of 100 kilometers, and a 20-step auto-pilot program. It has the ability to accept course correction from more than one up-link, a 30-kilogram payload, and simple field launch and recovery. The Mastiff operates up to 4,000 to 5,000 feet, although its operational altitude can be much lower; at least one Syrian SA-6 unit claims to have suddenly spotted one on the SA-6's TV sighting-device at a range under 100 meters.

The Mastiff uses a stabilized, gimballed TV camera for still photography. Maximum TV area coverage is 600 x 800 meters. The system weighs only 61 kilograms without fuel, and three trucks can carry as many as six systems, operators, and launch and recovery gear. Truck-mounted compressed air catapults allow launch without use of a cleared area.

Some versions of the IMI Scout have a similar TV capability, with the camera mounted on a gyro-stabilized platform and equipped with a 15:1 zoom capability. At 3,000 feet, it can cover about 50 square kilometers, and at maximum zoom (which it can achieve within about 4 seconds) it can provide a detailed view of an area 40 x 50 meters. Like the Mastiff, Scouts also have a panoramic still camera.

Many of the Scouts used in the June 1982 fighting, however, were ELINT collectors used to drop flares during missile suppression raids. These systems were operated over the Bekaa Valley for months before Israel's attack on Syrian land-based air defenses and were a key tool in providing ELINT for the development of Israeli electronic countermeasures.

The Scout and Mastiff are similar in many ways. Both are twin-boomed pusher aircraft with 18 to 22 HP engines and weighing about 250 to 260 pounds, although the Scout is shorter and has a smaller wingspan. Both have a small radar cross-section and engine exhaust systems designed to reduce their IR profile.

According to one fairly reliable source, Israel is still developing advanced payloads such as FLIR, imaging infrared capability, and active ECM. There are, however, reports that Israel used RPVs with laser designators in the fighting, although primarily to designate air defense targets for electro-optical air-to-surface missiles launched by Israel's fighters. Some use may have been made of RPVs with armed warheads, but on a very limited and experimental basis.

Neither type of Israeli RPV had secure or ECM-resistant up or down links at the time of the fighting, and plans to provide such links have not been as successful as Israel initially hoped. As will be discussed later, this may have serious implications since Syria has captured at least one Israeli Scout intact and has evidently developed jamming techniques that override the relatively primitive protective system that is intended to make Israeli RPVs automatically turn back toward Israel once their command link is interfered with.

According to one report, such RPVs were deployed down to the artillery CP level and linked to two Taiwanese copies of the Apple II computer. The Israelis in the forward CPs were able to use light pencils to designate targets picked up by the TV cameras on the Mastiff RPVs and get automatic artillery fire coordinate readouts which could then be transmitted in real time to fire units. The same procedures allow damage assessment and correction of fire.

Similar claims are made about the Israeli use of such RPVs in deploying armor, mechanized forces, and helicopters. Israel supported its C^3I system with intensive use of IMI Scout and Tadiran Mastiff RPVs as its forces closed around Beirut, and Israel was forced to shift to the extensive use of artillery. Ex-Israeli Defense Minister Ariel Sharon claims to have used an RPV to observe the members of the PLO during their evacuation from Beirut.

While Israel has stated that it flew over 70 RPV sorties per day during the fighting, it has not released a breakout by type of mission. It is clear, however, that Israel made use of both personal control stations (PCS) and a complex van-carried ground control station (GCS) to use its RPVs to provide data for artillery, maneuver unit, and air operations and to confirm the COMINT it received from the PLO. Israel's only confirmed RPV loss outside air-defense-suppression missions and recover errors occurred when an operator flew a Mastiff into a ridge.

Israel made extensive use of its RF-4Es in their usual mission role. While reports are conflicting, Israel only used comparatively limited numbers of its Bell AH-1s and Hughes Defender 500 MD helicopters in exposed attack or reconnaissance missions because of their vulnerability and was disappointed by the unexpected vulnerability of the AH-1. The RPVs, however, proved to be of consistent value in providing survivable information for land weapons and for fighter attack missions. The RPVs not only provided targeting data; they provided an independent source of information that allows Israeli fighters to clear the target area without waiting to observe the effect of their strokes and often allowed Israeli fighters to approach their targets from a less vulnerable angle.

Israel has been remarkably silent about its use of its Mohawk OV-1D high-performance observation aircraft. These have side looking airborne radar, advanced infrared sensors and excellent cameras, and had evidently been modified by Israel to carry specially tailored ELINT packages and surveillance radars. The Mohawk is a two-seat, multi-sensor observation aircraft powered by two 1400 shp Avco hycoming T53-L-701 turboprops. Its maximum speed is 289 mph in the SLAR mission, i.e., jamming, and 305 mph in the IR (infrared) mission. It seems to have been useful both in targeting Syrian SAMs and armor but the details are unclear. Israel also has been silent about its ability to jam or enter PLO Syrian land and air communication systems and to counter Arab jamming efforts.

Helicopters

Both Israel and Syria made extensive use of helicopters in the 1982 fighting, and both used attack helicopters against each other for the first time. In general, Syria entered the conflict with more experienced forces and a better concept of operations. Israel, however, had superior equipment, training, and command and control. It rapidly adapted its tactics and was able to use helicopters with great success,

Both Syria and Israel had been impressed by the U.S. experience with combat helicopters in Vietnam and the Soviet experience in Afghanistan. Both Syria and Israel had built up significant forces. Israel had 12 AH-1GS and 30 Hughes 500 MD attack helicopters and extensive lift and utility helicopters. These included 8 Super Felons, CH-53Ds, 2 S-65Cs, 29 Bell 206s, 24 Bell 212s, and 25 UH-1Ds. Syria had at least 16 attack helicopters, including 12 Mi-24s. It also has 10 Mi-2s, 75 Mi-8s, 4 Ka-25s, and 49 Gazelles for lift and utility missions. Many of the Gazelle and some Mi-8 helicopters were armed with machine guns and rockets. The armed Gazelles were sometimes used in the attack role.

Both sides used helicopters for critical lift and mobility missions. What was new was their attempt to use helicopters as substitutes for fighter aircraft. Like most of the world's forces at the time, they were experimenting with the use of helicopters in both close support and interdiction missions.

The Syrians had superior experience in using helicopters in combat missions in the rough terrain in Lebanon. They were experienced with the problems of dealing with mountain combat and had used their helicopters in this role during their intervention in the Lebanese civil war. They had worked out a concept of operations where helicopters usually flew independent interdiction missions in pairs or larger formations. The Israelis were operating more from theory. They attempted to work out a concept of using helicopters in close assault and to spearhead troop movements through mountain areas.

In practice, the Israelis found they were generally better off operating in the way that Syria has adopted. Helicopters were used successfully in some close support missions and were extremely valuable in the scout role to help Israeli forces rapidly locate the weak points in Syrian and PLO defenses, spot ambushes, and perform other real time reconnaissance missions.

In many cases, however, the Israelis had so much firepower in the forward area that they achieved near saturation. The helicopters also proved to create significant identification of friend-and-foe problems. Helicopters sometimes mistook Israeli forces for Syrian, and Israeli ground forces found it difficult to distinguish Israeli from Syrian helicopters. The IDF also found it difficult to give the helicopters under IAF command the kind of precise battle management and targeting data they needed.

As a result, the Israelis shifted many of their missions to the interdiction role and began to fly independent pairs in search-and-kill missions. These missions proved to be highly successful. Syrian ground forces were not particularly well trained to deal with the helicopter threat. They were slow to react, rarely seemed to hear or see the helicopters—particularly the relatively silent Hughes 500s—and lacked the kind of highly effective, light, forward air defenses that would have presented a major threat to the Israeli helicopters. In many cases, the closed-in conditions of the mountain areas seemed to aid helicopters in spite of altitude problems that affected power and agility. Land-force deployments were more predictable, and the helicopter provided even more useful visibility to the crew than in operations in smooth terrain.

Israel later made very high kill claims for its helicopters, some of which seem justified. Helicopters often could kill armored targets or assist in striking at mountain defenses that other firepower systems could not target or reach. The true kill scores for the helicopters on each side are impossible to determine, however, and some Israeli claims seem to be exaggerated.

As for heliborne assaults, Syria tended to use helicopters in a limited ferry role rather than in any major efforts as assaults or direct counterattacks. Israel, in contrast, often used helicopters to bypass obstacles and to restore the kind of deep thrust and freedom to maneuver it had often lost in the 1973 war. Heliborne troops landed successfully near Rachaya, Kafi Quoq, Baisour, and Yanta during the first part of the war and successfully enveloped and/or bypassed enemy troops. Israeli helicopters also landed troops to the east of Sidon and helped complete the encirclement of this strategic town.

Syria also occasionally made good use of helicopters. It had developed some good individual helicopter units that first proved themselves in the October War and then in the fighting in Lebanon from 1978 to 1980. It occasionally used antitank and armed helicopters effectively in 1982, but it never made large-scale use of its 95 Mi-8s or 30 Mi-24s. Syria also exhibited some of the same tactical and operational rigidities and training and command problems in using its overall helicopter force that affected its tank, other armor, and artillery performance.

Both sides produced somewhat contradictory reports on helicopter vulnerability. Syria both claimed high survivability using map-of-the-earth tactics and complained about the IAF's superior technical ability to locate and kill helicopters. The IDF claimed both high survivability and stated missions had to be cancelled or kept away from heavy concentrations of SA-7s and AA guns. IDF officers also indicate, however, that their helicopters were often exposed to fire because of inadequate C^3, and would have benefited greatly from a forward air-control system with the sophistication of the system developed for Israeli fighters.

The impact of the attack helicopter in shaping the Middle East balance was, therefore, still in its formative stages in 1982. It showed it had great potential to give skilled users added freedom of maneuver, however, and it may be able to play a critical role in gaining ground. It

TABLE 3.5   The Israeli-Syrian Helicopter Balance: 1982[1]

ISRAELI HELICOPTERS		SYRIAN HELICOPTERS	
TYPE	AMOUNT[2]	TYPE	AMOUNT[2]
Attack		Attack	
AH-1G/S Cobra	*12/12*	*SA-342 Gazelle*	*45/40*
<u>*UH-1D*</u>	<u>*25*</u>	*Mi-24 (Hind)*	*/12*
MD-500 Defender	*30/25/20*		
Heavy Transport			
CH-53	*35/33*		
SA-321 Super Frelon			
Medium Transport		Medium Transport	
AB-212	*60/24*	*Mi-8 (Hip)*	*95/72*
		Mi-2 (Hoplite)	*10/10*
		Mi-4 (Hound)	*10/8*
Light Transport			
AB-206 Jet Ranger	*30/29*		
		ASW	
		KA-25	*5/4*

[1]Data were obtained from three reference books: Mark Heller, et al., *The Middle East Military Balance 1983* (Tel Aviv University, Jaffee Center for Strategic Studies, 1983), pp. 119 and 227; IISS, *Military Balance, 1981–1982* (London: International Institute for Strategic Studies, 1982), pp. 52 and 57–58; and IISS, *Military Balance, 1982–1983* (London: International Institute for Strategic Studies, 1983), pp. 57 and 62.

[2]The different estimates are separated by slash marks. It is noteworthy that the Heller volume does not include the 25 UH attack helicopters (underlined). In addition, the only change between the 1982 and 1983 editions of *Military Balance* is a lower figure (by 5) for the Hughes MD-500 Defender for 1983, which may be a reflection of war loss.

is, after all, only 30 air miles from the West Bank heights to those on the East Bank. While tanks are limited to a few limited routes up the Golan, are blocked by the Yarmuk River gorge, and would be highly exposed in the Bekaa, helicopters can rapidly overcome such distances. No side, however, shows any sign of converting to large-scale helicopter forces.

Combined Operations

The Israelis used combined operations throughout the war. This primarily involved the Israeli Army and Air Force, although the Israeli Navy played an important role within the limits imposed by its size and capability. The Israelis made the interface between their army and air elements a centerpiece of their combat doctrine after 1967 and achieved considerable success.

They still, however, experienced some notable problems. The most serious of these problems was timing. The IDF set an extremely demanding, if not impossible, schedule for its offensive. At the same time, the Israeli defense minister expanded the scale of the operation on an ad hoc basis, particularly in regard to movements against Syria and Beirut. This compounded the combined operations problems discussed earlier, and meant that the air-land battle could not be conducted with anything approaching the careful planning used in air-defense suppression and air-to-air combat.

Those problems also led to a number of instances where air power had to be called in without proper mission briefing. It also led to a number of instances when close air support or interdiction bombing should have been used but was not. The IDF's limited amphibious operations were successful, but IDF ground forces failed to advance at the required rate, and much of their effect was lost.

The Israeli C^3 system could not handle the resulting confusion during key stages of the advance, and requests for air support came in too late or were misrouted. It is impossible to say, however, whether this was the result of the political turmoil at the high command level or the result of inherent problems in the IDF's combined arms organization.

The Israeli Air Force and Army experienced serious problems in executing combined operations in urban and built-up areas where there were large numbers of civilians. Throughout the war, Israeli pilots were called upon to attack small bands of PLO or Syrian troops who were fighting in close proximity to Israeli troops or Lebanese civilians. Accurate targeting and delivery were often impossible, and on at least one occasion, Israeli aircraft bombed an Israeli unit.[105] On other occasions, Israeli pilots either hit civilian targets or refused to drop their bombs because they had no way to distinguish the ground targets.[106]

Nevertheless, these problems should not be exaggerated. Once complete air superiority had been established, the Israelis were then in a position where their army could call for air strikes as they became bogged down on the ground. At Ain Dara, for example, air strikes and anti-armor helicopters were called on 10 June 1982 to help break up effective resistance by Syrian commandos. The IAF's ability to support the army when it became bogged down, or needed a hostile position "softened up," was important throughout the war. It was especially important in areas where Israeli ground forces met heavy, unexpected resistance; the el-Bas refugee camp near Tyre was one such area. Israeli troops attempted to penetrate the el-Bas camp on foot but failed to do so. At this point, air power was called upon to attack PLO positions within the camp.

The struggles for control of the various PLO camps were the most intense battles that the Israelis waged against the PLO. These battles also involved air-to-ground interface, although the previously noted problems with targeting were especially important in this kind of setting. When targeting became a significant problem for the actual delivery of ordnance, the air force was used for psychological warfare. In Tyre, for example, the Israelis announced through loudspeakers that they would use air power to neutralize any resistance to their troops entering the city. After making this announcement, low-flying Israeli planes engaged in mock bombing runs to underscore this threat. Similar operations occurred elsewhere throughout the war, including such actions as breaking the sound barrier and dropping propaganda leaflets.

This experience has broad importance for the West since it may well encounter similar problems in low-level wars. It will have to find ways to use air power while minimizing collateral damage and to conduct similar combined operations. The West, however, will generally have to use technology as a substitute for the IDF's ability to tailor its operations to one narrow area of the world.

Logistics and Support

The logistical requirements of the 1982 fighting were tactically demanding but did not impose a major burden on any of the forces engaged. Israel had several significant advantages, including the fact that it was fighting a one-front war, in close proximity to Israel itself. Additionally, the air superiority provided by the IAF throughout the conflict ensured that most resupply operations would not be interdicted by hostile aircraft.

Israel had converted its logistics to a Soviet-style "push" system as a result of its experience in 1973 and did not experience supply problems. Equipment maintenance did, however, turn out to be a problem for the Israelis. Part of this resulted from the lack of continuity in command and the rapid shift of forces between units. In some instances, tanks passed from unit to unit without being regularly serviced or maintained by any of the units they were attached to. This led to continuing mechanical problems with these tanks.[107]

The Syrians, for their part, set up massive stockpiles in the Bekaa but do not seem to have paid a great deal of attention to logistics. The poor pay of the Syrian occupation troops, as well as the residue of affluence remaining in Lebanon, generated a great deal of corruption. This corruption might have had some effect on the supply system, which reinforced other weaknesses. Whatever the reason, the Syrian logistical system displayed serious weaknesses. In Beirut, for example, Syrian troops had to depend upon the PLO for food and pay. No Syrian stockpiles existed for these troops to draw upon once Israel closed the Beirut-Damascus Highway.[108]

Naval Systems

The Israeli Navy was the only naval force to participate in the Lebanon war. Syrian naval forces remained out of the fighting. The Israeli forces used in the fighting included four Aliya (Saar 4.5) corvettes, with four Gabriel and four Harpoon surface-to-surface missiles; Reshef-guided missile patrol boats (Saar 4) with Gabriel and Harpoon missiles; and Saar 2 and 3 missile patrol boats with Gabriels. Israel also had a small amphibious force of three medium landing ships (LSM), six landing ship-tanks (LST), and three landing craft-utilities (LCU).

The Israeli Navy's most significant act during the war was to land a brigade-sized unit north of Sidon on 7 June 1982. This was the largest amphibious landing in the history of the Israeli navy. The unit that landed was composed of troops, tanks, and vehicles from the 96th Division, plus paratroops and naval commandos.

The Israeli Navy also imposed a naval blockade on the Lebanese coast and shelled a variety of shore-based targets. This blockade apparently was designed to prevent weapons from reaching the PLO by sea. Since Lebanon has a long sea coast and many of the PLO's strongholds were near the coast, this created an ideal environment for naval gunfire support.

It is interesting, however, that Israel was able to use a very small navy to conduct an amphibious operation and provide shore bombardment with 76-mm guns and Gabriel missiles and provide effective night operations as well. The IDF even used naval guns in cooperation with illumination flares dropped by Israeli aircraft.[109]

Chemical/Biological and Nuclear Weapons and Defense Systems

No chemical or biological weapons were used by either side in the 1982 war in Lebanon, although both Israel and Syria could have manufactured militarily significant amounts of such agents if they had so desired. The Israeli nuclear effort is described in the following chapter.

The Lessons the USSR Drew from the Fighting

The 1982 fighting was of obvious interest to both superpowers. Many U.S. sources published unclassified reports on the war, and this analysis has drawn heavily upon them. It is important to note, however, that official U.S. sources have never released any technical data on the lessons the Department of Defense drew from the war. The USSR has been equally reticent about releasing classified data, but it is interesting to note that unclassified Soviet sources gradually went from a defense of Soviet doctrine to far more flexible studies and analyses.

The Soviet treatment of air defense is of particular interest. The Soviets began by ignoring what had really happened. They made claims on 18 July 1982 that Syria killed 67 F-15s, F-16s, and various others fighters.[110] By October and November 1983, however, their thrust had changed. A Colonel V. Dubrov provided a far more realistic picture in *Aviatsiya i Kosmonavtika*.[111]

Dubrov stressed the importance of the E-2C and Israel's converted B-707 jammers in providing battle management and helping to blank Syrian radars. He stressed the value of free-ranging combat air patrol rather than GCI. He praised the use of RPVs as reconnaissance systems, methods of saturating air defenses, and methods of providing laser designation. He praised the ability of Western AIM-7 and AIM-9 missiles to work effectively in head-on and side-on intercepts, and he detailed the use of low-flying fighters with cluster bombs and PGMs, plus Israel's Wolf (Ze'ev) missile to suppress air defenses.[112]

Dubrov did conceal both the size of the Syrian defeat and the scale of Israeli tactical innovation, but it is obvious that the USSR realized the potential value of an AWACS as a forced multiplier and helped shape its own Moss and Mainstay aircraft designs as a result.

Other Soviet sources went on to describe the Israeli use of RPVs in great detail.[113] The same was true of the E-2C and Israel's tactics in using the F-15 and F-16. This latter analysis put great emphasis on the value of beyond-visual range combat by patrolling fighters. Still other articles provided detailed descriptions of U.S. jammers and anti-radar missiles. While it took until 1985 for Soviet sources to fully describe all of the Western technologies and tactics that Israel employed in the Bekaa, it was clear that the initial rigidities in Soviet studies virtually disappeared by the mid-1980s and that the Soviets learned a great deal from the fighting.

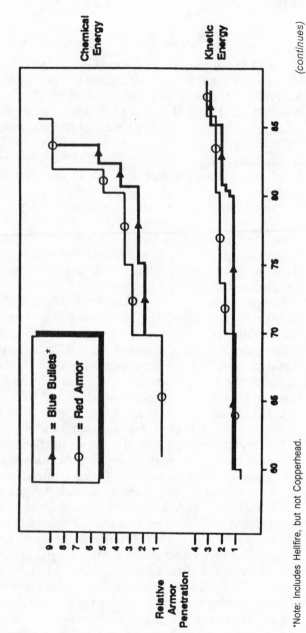

BLUE BULLETS VS RED ARMOR

*Note: Includes Hellfire, but not Copperhead.

(continues)

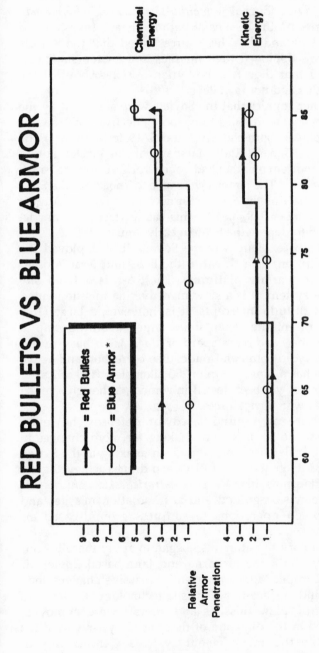

FIGURE 3.19 The U.S.-Soviet Duel in Tank and Antitank Weapons Technology: 1958–1988. From testimony by Gen. (ret.) Donn Starry, before the Senate Armed Services Committee, 13 April 1987.

This Soviet ability to learn from the 1982 fighting is equally striking in the case of surface-based air defenses. During December 1983 to July 1984, the Soviet journal *Vovenno-Istroricheskiv Zhurnal* published a long series on the lessons of both the Israeli invasion and the fighting in the Falklands.[114] This source hinted that the Soviets found that the Syrians deployed their missiles in a far too static and predictable way and that they felt the Syrian missiles should have been located on heights and not in valleys.

It is clear from other sources that the Soviets were surprised by the failure of some of their new missiles to be more effective than the SA-6. In 1982, they deployed both the SA-8 and SA-9 to Syria after the visit of Soviet Chief of General Staff Marshall Nikolai V. Ogarkov to Damascus for a post-mortem on what had gone wrong during the Israeli suppression of the SA-6.[115] The Israelis were able to knock out the SA-8 and SA-9 almost as easily as the SA-6 with new air strikes on August 10, and again on September 8, 9, and 13; this had at least some impact on the Soviet decision to deploy the SA-5 in early January 1983.

This experience helps explain why the Soviets then deployed the SA-5 (Gammon or Griffen) as a threat to the E-2C and Israel's other sensor and electronic warfare platforms. The SA-5 is a fixed site surface-to-air missile system. It is a slow maneuvering missile limited to medium- to high-altitude intercepts. It is, however, a large (16.5 meter/10,000 kilogram) missile. It can attack targets at altitudes up to 29,000 meters (95,000 feet) and has a speed of Mach 3.5. It has fire and track guidance, with radio-command midcourse correction and active radar homing. It also has a range of up to 250 kilometers (150 miles).[116] The SA-5 system has not yet been tested in combat, although a much improved version is now in Soviet forces.

The Soviet literature on ground-based air defenses, however, reflected the fact that the Soviets were making far more changes in their own surface-to-air defenses than they were making in the Syrian defenses. During 1983–1985, the use of RPVs and drones achieved great attention in Soviet journals like *Vovenno-Istroricheskiv Zhurnal.*[117] So did the use of television-guided and anti-radiation missiles and the ability of combined operations to suppress ground-based air defenses.

By 1983, Soviet military literature also began to apply these lessons to the weaknesses of both the airborne and land-based Soviet air defense system in Europe. More importantly, massive changes took place in Soviet air and surface-to-air missile technology, tactics, and command and control. New missiles and aircraft were deployed, Soviet tactics evolved in the direction of those used by Israel and the West, and new C³I/battle management systems were deployed.

Regardless of what the Syrians learned, the Soviets went on to rebuild their entire air defense system—a process that still goes on as of this writing.

At the same time, it is important to note that the West sometimes learned the wrong lessons from the 1982 fighting. Many Western experts tended to confuse the Arab use of export versions of Soviet weapons systems with the inherent weaknesses in Soviet use of the non-export version of such systems. They therefore assumed a Western superiority in many areas of tactical technology that did not exist.

While there are many aspects of conventional technology that illustrate this point, tank and antitank technologies and weapons may provide the best example. Armor is the area where the Warsaw Pact has the greatest advantage in numbers over NATO, and it is an area where the West has sought "force multipliers" for at least a quarter of a century. It is an area where the West has far more unclassified and classified programs than it can ever hope to fund to deployment and where the West estimated during 1974 to the mid-1980s that it had significant technical advantages in armor and firepower, largely as the result of the exploitation of captured export versions of Soviet weapons.

In fact, the U.S. learned in 1986 that the West had long fallen behind the tanks and antitank weapons the USSR had deployed in Eastern Europe in many key measures of advanced tank technology.[118] General Donn Starry provided striking testimony to this effect to the Senate Armed Service Committee in describing the findings of a recent Defense Science Board study:[119]

> Out of some thirty technology developments examined, the (Defense Science Board) Task Force found at least a dozen which had been funded at entry levels of development for twelve to fifteen years. This situation illustrates the fact that while we may be ahead of the Soviets technically, more and more the advantage is only on the laboratory bench. In fielded systems we display a notorious penchant for, "just a little more time and just a few more dollars and we can have so much more capability." Years and millions (or billions) later, we find ourselves with but a marginally better capability than we would have had had we fielded the technology sooner.

These comments are a warning about learning too much from captured technology. The lessons of the Third World regarding Soviet equipment may not apply to a war where NATO commanders have to meet a threat that may have the same weapons platforms but equip and operate them very differently.

Notes

1. For good detailed descriptions of the war, its combatants, and its political history, see Trevor N. Dupuy and Paul Martell, *Flawed Victory* (Washington, D.C.: Hero Books, 1985); David Eshel, *The Lebanon War 1982* (Jerusalem: Steimatsky's Agency, 1983); Richard A. Gabriel, *Operation Peace for Galilee* (New York: Hill and Wang, 1984); Rashid Khalidi, *Under Siege: PLO Decisionmaking During the 1982 War* (New York: Columbia University Press, 1986); John Laffin, *War of Desperation* (London: Osprey, 1985); and Ze'ev Schiff, *A History of the Israeli Army* (New York: Macmillan, 1985), pp. 239–262.

2. The Israelis were extremely bitter about the Lebanese Right's aloofness from the fighting and referred to these individuals as "chocolate soldiers." For a journalist's description of this bitterness, see Jonathan C. Randal, *Going All the Way: Christian Warlords, Israeli Adventurers and the War in Lebanon* (New York: Viking Press, 1983), pp. 6, 262. Also see "Lebanese Army Impotent Against Israel," *Los Angeles Times* (June 10, 1982), Part I, p. 8.

3. See Randal, op. cit.; Robert Friedman, "A Portrait of 'Free Lebanon,'" *Nation* (June 19, 1982); and Khalidi, op. cit., pp. 46, 137, 167–8, 176, 179.

4. Ze'ev Schiff and Ehud Ya'ari, *Israel's Lebanon War* (New York: Simon and Schuster, 1984), p. 190. Schiff and Ya'ari provide a detailed description of Sharon's negotiations with the Geymeyal family.

5. See Chaim Herzog, *The Arab-Israeli Wars* (New York: Random House, 1982).

6. For general background on PLO forces, see Walid Khalidi, *Conflict and Violence in Lebanon* (Cambridge: Harvard University, 1979), pp. 79–82 and 137–39; Dupuy and Martell, op. cit., pp. 25–27, 56–59, 87–89, 156, 159, 203; and Laffin, op. cit., pp. 7, 9, 16, 21–23, 92–98, 122–125, 200–206.

7. See James Feron, "Israel Puts Captured Arms on Display," *New York Times* (October 12, 1982), p. 6.

8. See Lt. Gen. Rafael Eitan, "We Learned Both Tactical and Technical Lessons in Lebanon," *Military Electronics/Countermeasures* (February 1983), p. 94.

9. See Khalidi, op. cit., pp. 57–72, 93–95, 101–106, 136, 141–144, 146–149, 159, 168, 178. Rabinovich is more favorable to the PLO in his *The War for Lebanon*, but Schiff is consistently critical as is Yezid Sayigh. See Sayigh, "Palestinian Military Performance in the 1982 War," *Journal of Palestine Studies* (Summer 1983), pp. 24–65.

10. Schiff and Ya'ari, *Israel's Lebanon War*, p. 83.

11. Ibid., p. 134.

12. Ibid., p. 136; Dupuy, op. cit., pp. 25–26 and 86–89; and Laffin, op. cit., pp. 17, 30, 124–125; Khalidi, op. cit., pp. 57–60.

13. Schiff and Ya'ari, *Israel's Lebanon War*, p. 86.

14. Ibid., p. 148; Khalidi, op. cit., pp. 51–62.

15. Gabriel, op. cit., p. 50.

16. Mark Heller, Aharon Levran, and Zeev Eytan, *The Middle East Military Balance 1983* (Tel Aviv University: Jaffee Center for Strategic Studies, 1983), p.

123.

17. Ezer Weizman, *The Battle for Peace* (New York: Bantam Books, 1981), pp. 274–279.

18. Many of the Syrian troops were deployed within a clear view of the invading Israelis, yet they took no part in the fighting beyond one minor and probably accidental encounter cited in Helena Cobban's, *The Palestinian Liberation Organization* (Cambridge University Press, 1984), p. 95.

19. Gabriel, op. cit., pp. 60–62.

20. Estimates based on Dupuy and Martell, op. cit., pp. 86–94. The IDF later listed the equipment it captured from the PLO as including 1,077 combat vehicles, including 80 Soviet T-34, T-55, and T-62 tanks; 202 mortars of 81-mm to 150-mm caliber; 56 Katyusha 122-mm and 130-mm rocket launchers; 70 heavy artillery weapons of 122 mm, 130 mm, and 155 mm; 158 light anti-aircraft weapons; 153 anti-aircraft guns of 20–100 mm; 1,352 antitank weapons, including 27 ATGM launchers, 1,099 RPGs, 138 recoilless rifles, and 88 major antitank guns; 28,304 small arms, 4,670 tons of ammunition, and 1,916 field communications pieces.

21. One must be very careful in the descriptions of intense battles in this fighting. For example, only four IDF soldiers were killed in defeating the Syrian tank brigade and PLO forces at Hilwe. The IDF has a fundamentally different view of casualties from those of other Western armies.

22. Dupuy and Martell, op. cit., pp. 136–7.

23. The best researched description of Sharon's actions can be found in Shai Feldman and Heda Rechnitz-Kijner, *Deception, Consensus and War; Israel in Lebanon*, Paper No. 27 (Tel Aviv University: Jaffee Center for Strategic Studies, 1984); Ze'ev Schiff and Ehud Ya'ari, *Israel's War in Lebanon* (New York: Viking Press, 1983). For good descriptions of the military problems and issues involved, see Dupuy and Martell, op. cit., pp. 98–146, and Schiff, *A History of the Israeli Army*, pp. 230–238.

24. Sharon is sufficiently controversial so that it is worth reviewing four of the many critiques of his performance in previous wars. See Avraham Adan, *On the Banks of the Suez* (San Francisco: Presidio Press, 1980), pp. 98–138, 168–177, 214–238, 247–281, 293–318, and 326–329; Edward Luttwak and Dan Horowitz, *The Israeli Army* (New York: Harper & Row, 1975), pp. 109–110, 112, 117, 233, 299, 355, 379–385; Herzog, op. cit., pp. 119–121, 123, 125–126, 134–138, 202–205, 220, 231, 250–255, 263, 267–279, 283, 338; and Trevor Dupuy, *Elusive Victory* (New York: Harper & Row, 1978), pp. 148, 150, 153–154, 161, 170–176, 182, 194–196, 243–244, 258–264, 270–271, 275–277, 359–369, 396, 422–435, 471–483, 486–490, 492–516, 527–529, 552, 585–586, 589, 597, and 601. Adan is an opponent of Sharon and should be treated as such. Luttwak, Horowitz, and Herzog are relatively neutral. Dupuy simply comments from the viewpoint of an American military officer and military historian.

25. See Khalidi, op. cit., pp. 57–58.

26. Ibid., pp. 78–81.

27. Schiff and Ya'ari, *Israel's Lebanon War*, p. 115.

28. Ibid., p. 124.

29. The Phalange is the militia of the Maronite, Christian *Katibe* Party.

30. Gabriel, op. cit., p. 118.

31. Gowri S. Sundaram, "Military Electronics in Israel: Second World Requirements But a Third World Economy," *International Defense Review* (January 1982).

32. See Khalidi, op. cit., pp. 67, 70–71, 73–98, 102–105, and 110–112; Dupuy and Martell, op. cit., pp. 25, 26, 56–62, 87, 89, 127; and Gabriel, op. cit., pp. 35–38, 47–53, 118–127.

33. The Joint Forces consisted of the PLO, the Lebanese National Movement, and the remnants of the breakaway "Lebanese Arab Army."

34. For a good contrast of views, see Dupuy and Martell, op. cit.; and Gabriel, op. cit.

35. Schiff and Ya'ari, *Israel's Lebanon War*, pp. 158–9.

36. Ibid., p. 162.

37. Ibid., p. 185.

38. Khalidi, op. cit., pp. 57–66; Schiff and Ya'ari, *Israel's Lebanon War*; and Ze'ev Schiff, "The Palestinian Surprise," *Armed Forces Journal*, February 1984.

39. Heller et al., op. cit., p. 261; Gabriel, op. cit., pp. 119–121; Khalidi, op. cit., pp. 55–57.

40. Herzog, op. cit., p. 402.

41. The Israelis have now raised the power level of the Merkava from 900 to 1,200 HP. This should help overcome the problems with power that were encountered during the Lebanon campaign. See Joshua Brilliant, "A Tank as Good as Any," *Jerusalem Post International Edition* (November 10, 1984), p. 23.

42. IDF units ambushed the Syrian 82nd Armored Brigade on 11 June 1986. This unit was equipped with the T-72, and nine are reported to have been burned.

43. Dupuy and Martell, op. cit., p. 128; Gabriel, op. cit., pp. 105, 198; Laffin, op. cit., p. 213.

44. Gabriel, op. cit., pp. 163 and 200; Laffin, op. cit., pp. 47, 49, 53, 55–58, 155.

45. Heller et al., op. cit.

46. Schiff and Ya'ari, *Israel's Lebanon War*, p. 178.

47. Gabriel, op. cit., p. 94.

48. Gabriel, op. cit., p. 100.

49. Dupuy and Martell, op. cit., p. 146.

50. Arab sources claim that the IDF had a laser-designated version of TOW and replaced the guidance wire with extra fuel to extend its range. These claims are not confirmed.

51. Laffin, op. cit., pp. 63–4, 77–8.

52. Richard Gabriel and John Moriarty, "Israel's Main Battle Tank Pounds Its Message Home," *Military Electronics Countermeasures* (January 1983), p. 131.

53. Ibid.

54. As quoted in "New Protective Measures for Tanks, Armored Cars," *Ha'aretz*, *JPRS (NE-SA)* (December 6, 1983), p. 44.

55. Gabriel, op. cit., p. 87.

56. Eric Pace, "In Sidon, 80 More Bodies for a Vast Bulldozed Pit," *New York*

Times (June 17, 1982), p. 1; Khalidi, op. cit., pp. 51–74; and Dupuy and Martell, op. cit., pp. 41, 56–60, 83–85, 105–109.

57. Cobban, *The Palestinian Liberation Organization*, p. 121; and Khalidi, op. cit., pp. 41, 56–61, 74, 83–5, and 105–109.

58. "Tunnel Network Laden with Arms, Linked Palestinians," *Washington Post* (October 7, 1982), p. 38.

59. Khalidi, op. cit., pp. 64–6 and 87–98.

60. Cited in "Israeli Jets Hit West Beirut; PLO Reports an Ambush," *New York Times* (July 26, 1982), p. 1; and especially "Tunnel Network Laden with Arms, Linked Palestinians," *Washington Post* (October 7, 1982), p. 38.

61. PLO troops did, however, run out of anti-aircraft ammunition. See "Pounding and Pondering," *The Economist* (July 31, 1982), p. 44.

62. See "Israeli Multiple Rocket Launchers," *International Defense Review* (August 1982).

63. Ibid.

64. Gabriel, op. cit., p. 108. Syria had over 2,000 artillery weapons in inventory. These included the M-1976 152-mm gun, M-38 and D-30 12-mm and 152-mm howitzers, and M-1943 and M-1973 122-mm and 152-mm self-propelled howitzers.

65. Sayigh, op. cit.

66. Schiff and Ya'ari, *Israel's Lebanon War*, p. 118.

67. Cited in "Israeli Jets Hit West Beirut; PLO Reports an Ambush," *New York Times* (July 26, 1982).

68. Schiff and Ya'ari, *Israel's Lebanon War*, p. 144.

69. *Born in Battle*, No. 27, p. 4.

70. Ibid.

71. Schiff and Ya'ari, *Israel's Lebanon War*, p. 160.

72. On the effectiveness of the SA-7 during the 1973 war, see Uri Ra'anan, "The New Technologies and the Middle East: 'Lessons' of the Yom Kippur War and Anticipated Development," in *The Other Arms Race*, edited by Geoffrey Kemp, Robert Pfaltzgraff, Jr., and Uri Ra'anan (Lexington: Lexington Books, 1975).

73. Michal C. Dunn, "The Air War in Lebanon," *Defense and Foreign Affairs Weekly* (July 1982), p. 32.

74. Reports about the war vary widely. For a comprehensive and detailed synthesis, see Benjamin S. Lambeth, *Moscow's Lessons from the 1982 Lebanon Air War* (Santa Monica, California: Rand Corporation, 1984), *passim.*

75. See Russell Warren Howe, "DoD Opts for Untested U.S. Drone," *Washington Times* (September 28, 1982), pp. 8–17.

76. See Martin Streatly, "The Israeli Experience: A Lesson in Electronic Air Combat," *Jane's Defence Weekly* (August 17, 1985), pp. 311–319; and Yossi Melman, "An Israeli Lesson in Electronic Warfare," *Jane's Defence Weekly* (October 5, 1986), p. 741.

77. Howe, op. cit., p. 17.

78. Ibid., p. 17; see also *International Defense Review*, Vol. 8 (1982), p. 1004, for the role of Teledyne RPVs in the attack on Syrian SAM sites. On the surveillance role of the RPV, see Phillip J. Klass, "Israel Demonstrates

Mini-RPV Utility," *Aviation Week and Space Technology* (October 4, 1982), pp. 59–63. This article describes the "Scout" mini-RPV built by Israel Aircraft Industries. It can be used for battlefield surveillance, using television optics and targeting artillery fire. See also Clarence A. Robinson, Jr., "Surveillance Integration Pivotal in Israeli Success," *Aviation Week and Space Technology* (July 5, 1982), p. 16, and Tamir Eshel, "The Eye in the Sky Mini RPV in the Modern Battlefield," *Defence Update*, No. 37 (Cologne, 1982), p. 2.

79. This area was 10 miles wide by 25 miles long. It was flanked on each side by mountain ridges rising to heights of over 6,000 feet.

80. Paul S. Cutter, "ELTA Plays a Decisive Role in the EOB Scenario," *Military Electronics and Countermeasures* (January 1983), pp. 135–137.

81. The role of the Ze'ev in this operation is obscure. There is some doubt about its functional type, i.e., whether it is an anti-radiation missile or a long-range artillery shell with terminally homing submunitions. See Lambeth, op. cit., p. 7.

82. *The Military Balance, 1982–1983*, op. cit., pp. 57, 62–63.

83. Robinson, op. cit., pp. 16–17.

84. See Lambeth, op. cit., p. 9.

85. Bill Gunston, *Soviet Air Power: An Illustrated Encyclopedia of the Warsaw Pact Air Forces Today* (London: Chartwell Books), p. 133.

86. Julian S. Lake, "Israeli Defense Industry: An Overview," *Defense Electronics* (September 1983), p. 103.

87. Hod Hasharon, "Israel," *Defence Update*, No. 37 (1983), p. 21. The exact role of this missile in the June 1982 conflict is not clear, but it was probably limited.

88. General Rafael Eitan in an interview with Paul S. Cutter, *Military Electronics and Countermeasures* (February 1983), pp. 94–102.

89. "Bekaa Valley Combat," *Flight International* (October 16, 1983), pp. 1108–1111. See also the interview with General Eitan, *Military Electronics and Countermeasures* (February 1983), p. 101.

90. John V. Cignatta, "A U.S. Pilot Looks at the Order of Battle, Bekaa Valley Operations," *Military Electronics and Countermeasures* (February 1983), pp. 107–108.

91. *Aerospace Daily* (August 5, 1982), pp. 193–194; *Wall Street Journal* (August 5, 1982).

92. Some sources indicate an SA-7.

93. Stan Morse, *Modern Military Powers: Israel* (New York: The Military Press, 1984), p. 125.

94. Most public reporting indicated Yurasov as first deputy commander. It is unclear that this is his true rank and position.

95. Herzog, , op. cit., pp. 377–394.

96. Ibid.

97. "Israel Strikes at the PLO," *Time* (June 21, 1982), p. 17.

98. "Bombs and Brinkmanship," *Newsweek* (August 2, 1982), p. 36.

99. *Born in Battle*, No. 27 (Cologne, 1982), p. 28.

100. Robinson, op. cit., pp. 16–17.

101. Morse, op. cit., p. 138.

102. See Jack Foisie, "Israel Pilots Flying U.S.-Made Planes: A Winning Team in Lebanese Air Battles," *Los Angeles Times* (June 29, 1982), p. 12.

103. *On Eagle's Wings* (New York: Macmillan Publishing Company, 1976), p. 178. Quoted in Lambeth, op. cit., p. 31.

104. The exact role in harassing and activating the SA-6s is not clear. Some assert that the Israelis used Samson and Delilah drones (from F-4s and ground launched, respectively); others suggest that the Scout and Mastiff RPVs functioned in this capacity. See Drew Middleton, "Soviet Arms Come in Second in Lebanon," *New York Times* (September 19, 1982). See the discussion in Lambeth, op. cit., p. 6.

105. This attack resulted in one tank being knocked off the road to Tyre, but no deaths. Schiff and Ya'ari, *Israel's Lebanon War*, p. 120.

106. Gabriel, op. cit., p. 162.

107. Schiff and Ya'ari, *Israel's Lebanon War*, p. 126.

108. Anthony Cordesman, *Jordanian Arms and the Middle East Balance* (Washington, D.C.: The Middle East Institute, 1983).

109. Gabriel, op. cit., pp. 142, 148.

110. *Krasnaya Zevzda.*

111. Col. V. Dubrov, "Aviation in the Lebanon Conflict," *Aviatsiya i Kosmonavtika*, No. 9 (September, 1983), pp. 46–47, and No. 10 (October, 1983), pp. 46–47.

112. See Marshall Less Miller, "The Soviet Air Force View of the Bekaa Valley Debacle," *Armed Forces Journal International* (June, 1987), pp. 54–56, and Lambeth, op. cit., pp. 35–36.

113. The Syrians had captured some of the Israeli RPVs in early 1982. They seem to have given them to the USSR for exploitation.

114. This analysis draws heavily upon a working paper by Helena Cobban called "The Lessons the Soviets Learned from Israel's June 1982 Strikes Against Syrian Ground-Based Air Defenses in Lebanon," 1986.

115. He is reported to have visited Damascus on July 19, 1982.

116. The system was first seen in 1963 and had its initial operation in combat (IOC) in 1967. It uses the Square Pair guidance radar, Back Net Surveillance radar, and Side Net Height Finding radar.

117. Cobban cites a long list of sources. The most important include G. Dolnikov, "The Development of Air Tactics in Local Wars," *Vovenno-Istroricheskiv Zhurnal (VIZ)*, No. 9 (September, 1985), pp. 34–43, as translated in Joint Publications Research Service; A. Kozhevnikov and T. Miktenko, "On Certain Trends in the Development of Air Defense in Local Wars, *VIZ*, No. 2 (February, 1984), pp. 59–64; G.U. Dolnikov, "Fighters in the Struggle for Air Supremacy," *VIZ*, No. 9 (September, 1985), pp. 62–71; V. Larionov, "Certain Questions of Military Art from the Experience of Local Wars," *VIZ*, No. 4 (April, 1984), pp. 46–52; M. Fesenko, "Fire Damage to Ground Air Defense Weapons," *VIZ*, No. 5 (May, 1984), pp. 66–73; R. Loskutov and V. Morozov, "Certain Technical Questions of the Armed Conflict in Lebanon in 1982," *VIZ*, No. 7 (July, 1984), pp. 75–80; I. Moronov, "The Israeli Pilotless Aircraft," *Zarubeznove Vovnnove Obozreniye (ZVO)*, No. 11 (November, 1982), pp. 46–

49; L. Semenov, "Electronic Equipment of the Hawkeye Airplane," *ZVO*, No. 9 (September, 1983), pp. 53–56.

118. Israel developed reactive armor as a result of the lessons of the 1973 fighting but kept it largely secret until after 1982. The West began to suspect that the Soviets had advanced armor in 1978 but were misled by the fact that Israel killed 122 T-72s in 1982 using 105-mm ammunition. A U.S. team inspected a Soviet T-72 in Afghanistan in mid-1983 but only found a space in the turret front that might have had advanced armor. Major Arthur Nicholson led a U.S. effort that found indications of space armor and brackets for reactive armor while leading a U.S. intelligence effort. He was shot and killed attempting to gather further data. The U.S. reached the firm conclusion that the Soviets had advanced armor in the summer of 1985; see John Barry, "A Failure of Intelligence," *Newsweek* (May 16, 1988), pp. 21–22.

119. General Donn Starry, "The Armor Anti-Armor Competition: U.S. vs. USSR," testimony before the Senate Armed Services Committee, April 13, 1988, pp. 2–3.

4

FORCE SHIFTS AND CONTINUING STRUGGLE: 1982–1989

The Impact of the 1982 Fighting
on the Continuing Arab-Israeli Struggle

No major conflict has occurred between Israel and its Arab neighbors since 1982. Nevertheless, the shifts in the Arab-Israeli military balance, and in the forces of Israel and its Arab neighbors, reflect both the lessons of the 1982 war and the broader lessons each nation has drawn from the regional and global arms race. Each country has dealt with these lessons in different ways, and the changes in the force posture of Egypt, Israel, Jordan, Lebanon, and Syria provide important insights into the lessons of modern war.

The overall shifts in the military balance in the region between 1982 and 1989 are shown in Table 4.1. These shifts provide an important preface to the lessons that can be learned from examining the actions of individual countries. They show that Israel and its neighbors have continued their arms race in terms of both force quality and force quantity. They also show that this arms race has been a dominating factor in shaping the economy of each of the nations involved.

At the same time, each nation has pursued a different approach to modernizing and expanding its forces. Israel has not increased its forces at anything like their past rate of expansion. It has increasingly emphasized technology over force numbers. Syria has attempted to both achieve "parity" in numbers with Israel and improve its force quality. Egypt has accepted its commitment to peace with Israel and has sought to restructure its forces around U.S. equipment. Jordan has sought to develop sufficient defensive capability to deter any military action by both Syria and Israel. Ironically, Palestinian forces have returned to Lebanon and a new Lebanese threat to Israel has developed in the form of Shi'ite factions in Lebanon, which owe their birth largely to the impact of the Israeli invasion.

TABLE 4.1 The Evolution of Arab and Israeli Forces: 1982–1989

Category	Israel		Syria		Jordan		Egypt	
	1982	1989	1982	1989	1982	1989	1982	1989
Total								
Defense Spending								
($billions)	6.1	5.1	2.4	2-4.0	0.4	0.8	2.1	4.6
Manpower (1,000s)								
Active	174.0	141.0	222.5	404.0	72.8	82.5	452.0	445.0
Conscript	120.3	110.0	120.0	180.0	-	-	255.0	250.0
Mobilizable	500.0	645.0	345.0	476.5	107.8	117.5	787.0	1,050.0
Army								
Manpower (1,000s)								
Active	135.0	104.0	170.0	300.0	65.0	74.0	320.0	320.0
Conscript	110.0	88.0	120.0	180.0	-	-	180.0	180.0
Mobilizable	450.0	598.0	270.0	570.0	-	-	620.0	820.0
Main Battle Tanks	3,600	3,850	3,990	4,050	569	979	2,100	2,425
OAFVs	8,000	11,100	1,600	4,150	1,022	1,374	3,030	3,590
Artillery/MRLs	960	1,450	2,100	2,800	274	247	2,000	1,700
Air Force and Air-Defense Forces								
Manpower (1,000s)								
Active	30.0	28.0	50.0	100.0	7.5	11.0	113.0	105.0
Conscript	7.0	19.0	-	-	-	-	60.0	60.0
Mobilizable	35.0	37.0	-	-	-	-	133.0	90.0
Total Combat								
Aircraft	634	577	450	448	94	114	429	441
Bombers	0	0	0	0	0	0	14	9
Attack/Int.	432	403	0	0	0	0	0	102
Attack	174	121	205	146	29	59	218	83
Interceptor	28	0	244	302	45	35	152	161
Recce/EW	28	24	0	6	0	0	45	24
OCU	0	0	0	0	20	20	0	0

continues

Israeli Force Developments Since 1982

One of the key operational lessons that Israel drew from the 1982 fighting was that it could often benefit more from improving the quality of its existing force strength and its ability to use its weapons more effectively, than from continuing to build up its weapons numbers.

Estimates of Israel's military spending after 1982 are difficult to arrive at because Israel's official defense expenditure data do not reflect all the costs of its force posture and because of the difficulty in adding the proper amount of U.S. aid into the Israeli total. The Israeli Ministry of Defense reported in early 1989 that defense spending in the national budget reached $3.2 billion in 1982, $3.2 billion in 1983, $2.7 billion in 1984, $2.6 billion in 1985, $2.5 billion in 1986, and $2.5 billion

TABLE 4.1 *(continued)*

Category	Israel 1982	Israel 1989	Syria 1982	Syria 1989	Jordan 1982	Jordan 1989	Egypt 1982	Egypt 1989
Armed Helicopter	42	80	16	148	0	24	24	75
Major SAM Bns/								
Bty/Sites	15	15	75	95	5	23	151	125
Navy								
Manpower (1,000s)								
Active	9.0	9.0	2.5	4.0	0.3	0.3	20.0	20.0
Conscripts	3.3	3.3	-	-	-	-	15.0	10.0
Mobilizable	10.0	10.0	5.0	6.5	-	-	35.0	34.0
Submarines	3	3	0	3	0	0	12	12
Guided Missile	27	24	18	12	0	0	19	23
Destroyer/Escort/								
Frigate/Corvette	2	4	2	2	0	0	8	6
Small Combat	44	31	12	15	9	6	56	36
Amphibious & Support	7	10	?	3	0	0	20	10

SOURCES: Adapted from various editions of IISS, *Military Balance* (London: International Institute for Strategic Studies), and the JCSS *Middle East Military Balance* (Tel Aviv: Jaffee Center for Strategic Studies, Tel Aviv University). Note that these figures do not show equipment in storage, and they use estimates which often do not reflect actual readiness of manpower and equipment. They also use dated material. For example, the IISS data for Israel reflect virtually no updating between 1982 and 1986 and grossly exaggerate the size of Egypt's operational forces and equipment holdings in both 1982 and 1989. In fact, virtually no Soviet-supplied equipment in Egyptian forces is fully combat-operational, and the effective strength of Egyptian forces is less than one-third the totals shown. These figures are deliberately presented as a contrast to the trend curves shown earlier which reflect more substantial adjustments by the author. The IISS data for aircraft also sometimes are not comparable from year to year, and the data for 1989 seem to have been adjusted to delete equipment in storage. This leads to a lack of comparability with the data for 1982.

in 1987. Military imports were reported to be $1.4 billion in 1984, $1.8 billion in 1985, $1.2 billion in 1986, and $2.4 billion in 1987. Total defense spending as a percentage of GNP was estimated to be 21 percent in 1984, 22 percent in 1985, 20 percent in 1986, and 17 percent in 1987.[1]

Arms Control and Disarmament Agency (ACDA) estimates that the total cost of defense to Israel in terms of domestic spending, loans, and foreign aid was $4.9 billion in current dollars in 1982, $5.6 billion in 1983, and $6.4 billion in 1984. This would put Israeli military spending at well over 20 percent of the GNP and over 25 percent of central government expenditures.

The IISS estimates Israeli defense spending at $5.6 billion in 1986, $5.1 billion in 1987, and $5.71 billion in 1988. The CIA estimates that Israel was spending roughly $4.6 billion on defense in the year ending

March 1987, less U.S. grant aid. According to the CIA, military spending was about 24 percent of the central government budget.

Israeli government estimates in early 1989 put direct annual domestic defense spending at $3.2 billion in FY1982–83 and FY1983–84, $2.7 billion in FY1984–85, $2.6 billion in FY1985–86, and $2.5 billion in FY1986–87 and FY1987–88. These estimates indicated that direct domestic defense spending was about 10 percent of the GNP in FY1988–89 versus 14 percent in the 1970s. The true total domestic cost of defense is difficult to estimate because of the problems in deciding how to allocate Israel's past military debts. For example, the U.S. Embassy in Tel Aviv estimates the total cost of Israeli domestic defense spending as being about 30–35 percent of the national budget in recent years, of which 12.5–15.7 percent was interest payments.[2] Senior Israeli officials, however, put the cost of all past war debts plus military aid and loans at 50 percent of the annual budget. Total defense spending—including U.S. aid—was equivalent to 18 percent of the gross national product (GNP). U.S. aid is estimated to have contributed an additional $1.2 billion in FY1981, $1.4 billion in FY1982, $1.7 billion in FY1983 and FY1984, $1.4 billion in FY1985, $1.723 billion in FY1986, and $1.8 billion in FY1987 and FY1988.[3]

One thing is clear: Israel faces continuing structural problems in its economy. These problems have been partly the result of Israel's defense burden, and they have been compounded by the cost of dealing with the Palestinian uprising. The Israeli economy recovered very slowly from the direct and indirect costs of the 1982 fighting, in spite of massive U.S. grant aid. During 1982 to 1985, Israel's gross domestic product (GDP) actually dropped from $23.2 to $22.0 billion, total debt rose from $18.3 to $23.9 billion, and the debt-service ratio rose from 26 percent to 33 percent. The resulting economic crisis unquestionably slowed the modernization of Israeli forces, forced serious cuts in Israeli manpower and readiness, and meant Israel has had to draw on war reserves for routine training and operations. Israeli immigration dropped 41 percent between 1984 and 1985 and reached its lowest level since 1948 during 1986–1988. These problems created major difficulties for the Israeli Defense Forces (IDF). In FY1987, for example, the IDF was forced to take a $700 million defense budget cut, at least $200–300 million of which had to come in the form of further cuts in readiness and training, and to reduce its domestic defense expenditures from a planned level of $3.2 billion to $2.53 billion.[4]

Israel no longer faces the kind of all-out economic crisis it faced in 1984 and 1985, when inflation was 445 percent and 185 percent, respectively. Israel's external debt dropped from $36.7 billion in 1984 to around $30 billion in 1988. Nevertheless, inflation has remained well over the double-digit level. The combined economic impact of Israel's economic problems and the uprising is difficult to cost, but Israeli government sources indicate that the uprising raised Israel's security costs by $221.5 million (400 million shekels) in the last operating year (April 1988–March 1989), helped cut income from tourism by 20 percent, and cut trade from the West Bank by $750 million.[5] The overall mix of economic pressures has forced Israel to cut back on domestic economic development as well as defense spending. There was little GNP growth in 1988, versus 5.2 percent in 1987 and 2.0 percent in 1986. Real wages continued to outstrip productivity gains in 1988, and exports remained constant after growing 11 percent in 1987. The current account balance remained in serious deficit in both 1987 and 1988, versus a surplus of $1.4 billion in 1986. Even with the cuts in Israeli government spending, the budget deficit is likely to reach $1 billion in 1988–1989, versus $750 million in 1987–1988 and a near balance in 1986–1987.[6]

These problems have grown worse since the beginning of 1989. Israel was forced to devalue the shekel by 13 percent in January 1989. Israel also had to cut its 1990/1991 defense budget significantly in January 1989 as part of cuts in its national budget which totaled $550 million in direct expenditures and $220 million in government price subsidies. These cuts in defense spending seem to have reached at least $165 million—the equivalent in Israel of 3,000 to 4,000 jobs.[7]

While U.S. aid to Israel reached $3.0 billion in annual grant aid in FY1986–FY1989, Israel faced the problem that it had some $10.5 billion in past foreign military sales (FMS) loans, which had been financed at comparatively high rates of interest. Total debt service costs on the FMS debt were $1.1 billion in FY1987, $1.1 billion in FY1988, $1.2 billion in FY1989, and were then projected to average $1.2 billion between FY1990 and FY1996. This left only about $1.8 billion annually in net aid.[8]

These financial problems also helped lead to some cuts in Israeli forces. Israel had an total active military strength of about 141,000 in late 1988 versus 173,000 in 1982. About 110,000 out of the total of 141,000 were male and female conscripts. About 41,000 males and 39,000 females fit for military service reach the age of 18 each year. Officers serve for 48 months, other ranks for 36 months, and women for 24 months. The key source of this manpower is the Jewish part of the population, although some Druze and Christian Arabs volunteer.

One thing did not change after 1982. The key to Israel's military strength still lay in its ability to rapidly draw upon combat-ready reserves and devote its military budget to equipment while allowing its labor force to remain at work except during times of crisis. Israel has a total population of about 4.2 million, excluding the Arab population of the West Bank, Gaza, and East Jerusalem. About 83 percent of these are Jews, with 17 percent non-Jewish (mostly Arab). All conscripts and volunteer males serve in the reserves until age 54, and women serve to 34 or marriage.

Israel also still had to cope with serious constraints in terms of total population. The CIA estimated that the total Israeli labor force was 1,400,000 in 1988. It estimated that there were 2,015,000 people in the age group from 15 to 49, and that out of 1,014,000 males, 839,000 are fit for military service, and that out of 1,002,000 females, 826,000 were fit for military service. The IISS estimated that there were a total of about 457,800 males and 435,000 women in the age group from 18 to 30 years and about 408,800 males and 414,000 women in the age group from 31 to 45 years.

Organized reserves had about 504,000 men and women in late 1988, with 494,000 in the Army, 1,000 in the Navy, and 9,000 in the Air Force. Reservists served in both the regular military and as Home Guards, and there were roughly 370,000 reservists in the force Israel might call up to man its regular forces. The Nahal (Pioneer Fighting Youth) had a heavy reserve element. Regardless of what population data one uses, this is an incredibly large mobilization pool given the size of Israel's total population and unquestionably produces the largest military forces in the world relative to population size.[9]

There is no doubt that financial and demographic pressures have helped shape Israel's forces since 1982. Some of the most important changes in Israeli forces since 1982, however, are based on the lessons Israel has learned in the art of operations and strategy. Israel has relearned its basic operational lessons about the need to seek quick and decisive limited results, to avoid impossible goals like occupying and changing the government of an Arab state, and the need to avoid guerrilla combat or wars of attrition. These may be the most obvious lessons of the 1982 war, but they also are probably the most important.

At the same time, Israel has learned other, more tangible, lessons. Israel has been driven to stress the following aspects of its organization, force structure, operational capabilities, and technology:[10]

CHANGES IN ORGANIZATION AND RESERVE STRUCTURE

- *Tailoring of Forces to Mission Requirements*: Israel continues to improve the tailoring of its forces by region. They are taught to use improved fixed-defense points; specially trained forces are organized and equipped to deal with such key defense tasks as an assault on the Golan or an attack on the West Bank; and reserves are dedicated to specific defense missions. The forces assigned to given areas are tailored to perform two operational functions as well as possible: first, to guard against surprise attack with the defense in place at a minimum cost in power and active presence; second, to secure key defense lines by using well-established defensive positions so that other Israeli forces can counterattack or go on to the offensive.[11]

• *Mobilization and Reserve Capabilities:* Israel still relies on its mobilization capabilities and reserve forces, but it is continuing to make them more effective. Roughly 80 percent of the 370,000 reservists that would be called up to existing reserve assignments would go to reserve divisions which are commanded and staffed at the headquarters level by full-time, active-duty officers. Reservists serve up to 60 days a year in active duty. Each unit normally receives three weeks of field training, with officers and NCOs receiving an extra week of training. Roughly 60 percent of all combined-arms training is conducted at night. Most specialists receive up to 12 additional days of individual skill training. Assembly areas provide all equipment and have stocks already loaded. Israel uses full-time maintenance and support personnel to keep these centers and their equipment ready and claims that more than 95 percent of IDF equipment is ready for use. Controlled dry storage is now used for most equipment and stocks.

Call-up is by code name over the radio, and mobilization can be accomplished by a public or concealed call. Each reservist is part of a neighborhood group with 10 to 15 members, with a leader and two assistants who are responsible for notifying the rest of the group. There are nine regional centers for mobilization. These centers have depots where reservists draw their prepacked personal gear, weapons, and some ammunition. They are then transported to an emergency store unit, with one unit per brigade and three per division, where they link up with their heavy equipment. Mobilization plans are exercised twice a year—once in an announced exercise and once in an unannounced exercise.[12]

• *Strategy, Tactics, and Battle Management:* More generally, Israel continues to examine how it can use land and air offensives to quickly destroy the Syrian and Jordanian armies in offensive action before the U.S. and/or Soviet Union can intervene at a political level. It also, however, is studying ways to use a combination of air and naval power to launch a crippling sequence of blows to (a) suppress Syrian air defenses and (b) use conventional munitions to so cripple the advanced elements of Syria's economy and infrastructure as to deprive Syria of recovery capability for several years. This latter capability is deliberately a "stand-alone" capability which would allow Israel's land forces to stand still at its defensive positions and launch a rapidly escalating series of air, naval, and missile attacks to force Syria or Jordan out of a war while minimizing any casualties.

- Israel is steadily improving its reconnaissance, targeting, C³I/battle management (BM), and damage assessment technology for both ground and air forces to allow tighter coordination between combined arms and the air and ground forces. The concept is one of operating in near real time so that the ground combat leader is given continuous information from the rear and can draw on immediate air and artillery support without delay or fear of "friendly" fire.

The key objective of Israeli battle management is to preserve freedom of action while maintaining a clear understanding at each echelon of what is going on. Another objective is to preserve "fluidity": to be able to rapidly mix and recombine force elements to meet a tactical situation without regard to rigid unit integrity and to be able to rapidly commit helicopter, reserve, or combat engineer forces to bypass enemy positions, find alternative approaches to maintaining offensive momentum, and aid units when they face superior numbers or an ambush.

- Israel is developing its own intelligence satellite and reconnaissance program. On 19 September 1987, it launched its first Offeq 1 satellite from the Palmachim launch site, south of Tel Aviv, using the Shavit booster from its Jericho II missile. Israel's initial satellite seems to have been designed solely for scientific purposes, but it is clear that Israel wants PHOTINT and SIGINT capabilities and the ability to use satellites for both warning and targeting purposes. Senior Israeli officers have sharply criticized the amount of satellite intelligence they received from the U.S. in the 1973 and 1982 wars, and Israel feels it can no longer count on flying reconnaissance aircraft in deep penetration missions over Arab territory. It is likely that Israel will soon deploy several intelligence satellites to cover the Arab world, although the level of coverage of communications and electronic emissions is difficult to predict, as is the level of imaging capability.[13]

CHANGES IN LAND FORCE CAPABILITIES

- *Command and Control:* Israel has made some important improvements in its land forces command structure since the 1982 war. It formed a new Field Forces Command (FFC) in 1984. This command has the mission of building fully integrated combined-arms forces. The Armored Corps, which dominated IDF ground forces for two decades, has now become a subordinated command.[14] According to some reports, Israel also created a Ground Force Command in 1983 in order to coordinate its Northern, Central, and Southern Commands.

These three regional commands remain the key operational commands in the IDF and are being strengthened to give Israel the equivalent of cohesive regional corps level or army group commands. The Northern Command has obvious priority because it is the command that would face Syria, but Israel has not rejected the concept of a thrust through Lebanon or even northern Jordan. It has continued to strengthen the fixed defenses in the Golan, and this both allows Israel to free forces to counterattack from the Golan and improves the ability of its territorial reserves to hold positions on the Golan while Israel's armored and helicopter forces strike across other lines of attack.

The active Israeli combat unit in the Golan, the Golani Brigade, is the unit which now faces an almost constant problem in southern Lebanon because of the return of PLO combat units and the buildup of anti-Israeli Amal and Hezbollah Shi'ite forces. The rise in tension forced the Golani Brigade to form a 100-man long-range patrol unit for operations in the Bekaa in late 1988, as part of the brigade's reconnaissance battalion. Israel has learned that no barrier defense or defensive line is a substitute for active patrol action.

- *Order of Battle:* According to recent reports, the three Israeli commands—or corps—now have the following order of battle: There are twelve armored divisions. There also are 17 independent mechanized and infantry brigades and five independent airborne brigades. This gives a total of 12 divisions and 22 brigades.[15]
- Three armored divisions are active armored divisions, with two armored and one artillery brigade each. They gain one armored brigade and one mechanized brigade on mobilization. There are five active mechanized infantry brigades, three of which have a special organization—one is paratroop trained, one is based on the NCO school, and one is based on the Nahal. The nine mobilized armored divisions normally have two or three tank brigades, one mechanized bridage, and one artillery brigade. The reserve forces also include one air mobile mechanized infantry division with three reserve paratroop brigades, 10 reserve

independent regional infantry brigades assigned to specific sectors of the border, and four reserve artillery brigades—each with five battalions of three batteries.

- Combat and service support forces include one Lance surface-to-surface battalion with 12 launchers and three active 203-mm self-propelled howitzer battalions.[16] According to some estimates, this provides a total maneuver unit strength of 110 tank battalions, 40 mechanized infantry battalions, 15 paratroop battalions, 30 infantry battalions, and 125 artillery battalions. This is an incredibly large mix of combined-arms elements for a country the size of Israel, even allowing for the fact it can rapidly mobilize around 20 percent of its roughly 4.2 million Jews and Druze.[17]

- *Main Battle Tanks:* Israel now has roughly 3,850 active main battle tanks, including some 1,080 upgraded Centurions, 561 M-48A5s, 1,300 M-60A1 and A3s, 250 T-54s and T-55s, 115 T-62s, and its Merkavas. This total compares with 3,600 main battle tanks in 1982.

- Israel has sought to build up its Merkava tank force as much as possible, but this buildup has been sharply delayed by a lack of funds, particularly during the time Israel was attempting to implement the Lavi project. Israel did, however, have at least 550 Merkava I/II tanks at the end of 1987 versus 200 in 1982. Israel's confidence in the Merkava was reinforced by studies showing it proved virtually immune to frontal fire during 1982, had higher crew survivability rates, and was much more agile over rough ground than the M-60. Israel did, however, conclude that superior tank firepower and fire control were vital and steadily upgraded the fire control on the Merkava. Interestingly, Israel found that a massive tank like the Merkava can be of great advantage in mountain and urban warfare and in ambush conditions.

The latest version of the Merkava is the Merkava III, which began production in 1989.[18] Virtually every component has been changed or modified since the Merkava II, except the transmission system. The Merkava III has a 120-mm smoothbore gun and storage capacity for 50 rounds; the electric-hydraulic drive system in the turret and for gun elevation has been replaced by an all-electric system.[19] It has a 360-degree threat warning system to detect enemy laser designators and possibly millimetric radars from advanced antitank guided-missile systems. New modular special armor covers the front and sides of the turret and sponsons and can be rapidly upgraded. Like previous Merkavas, the engine and transmission are in front. The Merkava III weighs roughly 61 tons combat loaded and is powered by a 1200 hp Teledyne Continental AVDS-1790-9AR engine. This gives the Merkava III a much better power-to-weight ratio than the 750 and 980 hp engines used in previous versions. It also has a greatly improved independent coil suspension system, with up to 600 mm of vertical road clearance and hydraulic rotary dampers on four of the six road wheels on each side for greater mobility. Costs are reported to be $2.3 million per unit versus $1.8 million for the Merkava II.[20] The Merkava does not have the agility, acceleration, and jump start capability of the U.S. M-1 but rivals it in virtually every other respect, carries more ammunition, and can carry some infantry in the rear.

- Fiscal pressures still limit Israel's procurement of the Merkava to roughly 25 percent of its tank force and production to around 100 per year. The IDF cannot keep its Centurions and M-48s in service beyond the year 2000 but has compensated by upgrading its Chieftains with improved fire control and add-on reactive armor, and by upgrading its M-60s to extend their useful life to 2010. This upgrading is called the MAGACH-7 program and includes a new engine, the same improved tracks used on the Merkava, improved fire control, and passive armor. The new engine is an improved Model 6A version of the U.S. Teledyne Continental AVDS-1790 diesel used in the existing M-60A and retrofitted to Israel's Centurions and M-48s. This improved version delivers 600 horsepower.

The improved fire control is evidently only fitted to the earlier M-60 and M-60A1 tanks and is the same computerized Matador system used on the Merkava. It was developed by Elbit and ELOP and has a laser range finder and a digital ballistic computer; it uses a meteorological mast on the rear of the turret to sense wind speed and direction, air pressure, and outside temperature.

The improvements to the armor include a new commander's cupola with two roof-mounted 7.62-mm machine guns, armored skirts with lateral protection, and passive armor fitted over the forward part of the roof, turret, nose, glacis, and sides. Unlike the reactive armor used on Soviet tanks, the Israeli armor provides protection against tank rounds and antitank weapons with kinetic, as well as chemical, energy kill capability. Israel also has third-generation 105-mm APFSDS rounds, and some sources believe Israel has deployed both 105-mm and 120-mm depleted uranium penetrator rounds.[21]

- Israel is also steadily increasing its number of tank transporters. It has found them to be an important way of both increasing the speed of armored movements and of ensuring that the maximum number of armored vehicles reach the front in fully operational condition.
- *Other Armored Vehicles:* Israel has found that regular APCs cannot survive combat against well-positioned infantry and defending forces. It has found the Merkava's ability to carry a small infantry squad in the rear of the tank to be vital in carrying men into close combat and in providing armor with infantry support. Israel cannot afford to modernize its force with anything approaching the number of new armored fighting vehicles it wants, but it is doing everything possible to modify the M-113 to reduce its vulnerability and its kill effects when it is hit, and to improve its firepower. The reductions in vulnerability include add-on armor, including composite and possibly reactive armor.
- Israel now has about 400 armored fighting vehicles, including Ramta RBY M-2 and M-3s and modernized captured Soviet BDRMs. It has Re'em armored fighting vehicles on order. Israel also has about 5,900 M-113 armored personnel carriers, most of which have been improved in armor and firepower, some BTR-50Ps, and some 4,400 M-2 and M-3 half-tracks, many of which are in storage or inoperable. Israel's total operational other armored vehicle (OAV) strength is probably around 8,000.
- *Infantry and Antitank Weapons:* Israel is trying to retrain and reequip its infantry to free them from over-dependence on armored vehicles. It also wants to give them more lethal light-infantry weaponry for urban and mountain warfare and is examining new rifle and submachine gun sights, like the "red dot" system, that aid in instinctive shooting.[22] It also is steadily improving their anti-armored warfare capability by giving them more BGM-71 TOW antitank guided weapons and by either modifying these systems or procuring more advanced versions from the U.S. Israel also continues to use the M-47 Dragon antitank guided missile and B-300 82-mm and 250 106-mm anti-armor rocket launchers. It has found the Dragon to be exceedingly difficult to operate and unreliable, however, and does not feel U.S. rocket launchers are light enough and effective enough. It relies far more on captured Soviet RPGs as a light antitank weapon.
- Israel is reported to have deployed its own Pickett and Togger ATGMs. It has recently started to produce the MAPATS laser-guided antitank weapons system. The MAPATS has an effective range of 4.5 kilometers, and its warhead is said to penetrate 800

mm of 300 Brinnel armor. The MAPATS is visually identical to the TOW and is aimed by keeping the crosshairs of a sight linked to laser on the target. The missile tracks the laser beam through sensors in the rear of the missile. Israel feels that this guidance method corrects problems it experienced in 1982 with firing wire-guided missiles like the TOW over water and through brush.[23]

- *Artillery and Multiple Rocket Launchers:* Israel is trying to improve the mobility and lethality of its artillery rather than increase its numbers of weapons. It is increasing its ability to provide supply for off-road surge fire and is keeping its stocks at a relatively high 30 days (one and one-half wars worth of munitions reserves). In spite of budget problems, Israel is putting heavy emphasis on improved C^3I/BM and on rocket launchers with smart or guided warheads which can extend range and improve cross reinforcement of fire, reaction time, accuracy, lethality, and volume of fire.

- Israel now has 110 M-46 130-mm guns and 140 M-107 self-propelled 175-mm guns. It is seeking more M-107s because it has found these long-range guns to be highly effective against targets in the rear of Arab forces. It has 70 M-101 105-mm howitzers; 100 D-30 122-mm howitzers, 300 Soltam M-68 and M-71, M-839P and M-845P, and L-33 155-mm howitzers; and 75 M-50 and 530 M-109A1 and M-109A2 self-propelled 155-mm howitzers. Israel also now has extensive stocks of high-technology improved conventional munitions (ICM), some of which are ten times more lethal per round than ordinary munitions.

  Israel has adopted the Soviet and Arab custom of placing heavy reliance on mass surge fire from multiple rocket launchers and has captured BM-21 122-mm and BM-24 240-mm multiple rocket launchers in service. It also has developed its own long-range LAR-160 160-mm and MAR-290-mm MRLs and MAR-350 90-kilometer range rockets to replace its Ze'ev or Wolf rockets. Israel claims that its own systems are considerably more accurate and easy to target than Soviet-designed systems. Finally, Israel has some 1,100 81-mm mortars and 120-mm and 160-mm mortars, some of which are self-propelled.

- Israel has widely deployed Hughes TPQ-37 weapon-locating radar systems and its own ELTA EL/M 2320 artillery radar system. It used both of these systems in the 1982 fighting. The ELTA system is a mobile, long-range fire-adjustment radar which is mounted on a tracked vehicle. It is designed for use with all of Israel's artillery and has day/night and over-the-horizon targeting capability. Israel claims that target-locating radars can improve the effectiveness per round by 100–200 percent and greatly reduce the time necessary for target acquisition. This claim tracks with similar test experience of other armies, which have found that artillery radars are critical in targeting today's highly mobilized artillery units and in allowing the rapid independent operation of artillery weapons.[24]

- *Surface-to-Surface Missiles:* Israel has steadily improved its ability to deliver surface-to-surface missiles. It has acquired Lance MGM-52 missiles with advanced conventional warheads from the U.S. It has Jericho II missiles, which are believed to be nuclear capable and which have been reported to have ranges varying from 450 to 800 kilometers.[25] (Note that there is no formal Israeli nomenclature for the "Jericho" missiles. The authors have used the terms Jericho I, II, and III.) It also has the Jericho III missile under development with intermediate range ballistic missile (IRBM) range. This missile has been tested at least twice (May 1987 and November 1988) at ranges in excess of 500 miles. It is believed to have a planned maximum range of around 940 miles. This would allow it to hit every major Arab capital, including Baghdad, and parts of the USSR.[26]
- The development of such a long-range missile follows a broad pattern throughout the region. Egypt, Iran, Iraq, Libya, Saudi Arabia, and Syria have all bought or sought long-range missiles. In Israel's case, however, such a missile could provide a near-term long-range nuclear strike capability. Unlike its Arab neighbors, Israel also now has the capability to launch its own satellites and develop effective surveillance and targeting systems. If Israel succeeds in deploying the Jericho III, it would provide a powerful regional time-urgent strike capability to which its Arab opponents could reply only with chemical or biological weapons—if that. It is obvious that Israel's policy of maintaining an ultimate deterrent to any military threat to its very survival is being given very high priority and is seen as an essential part of its strategy.
- It also is at least possible that one of the lessons Israel has drawn from the 1973 and 1982 wars is that it must develop some degree of deterrence against Soviet intervention in support of its Arab clients. The Jericho III may be able to reach Soviet targets in Odessa, Baku, and Tiblisi, and Israel now has the capability to develop missiles with much longer ranges.[27]
- *Air-Defense Weapons:* Israel still relies heavily on its fighters for air defense, and it has not modernized its land-based air defenses as much as the other elements of its land forces. This

may be because most of its anti-aircraft guns and all of its surface-to-air missiles are operated by the Israeli Air Force. The IAF does, however, have several thousand 20-mm air-defense cannons. It also has two active air-defense brigades with Vulcan and Chaparral and 30 M-163 Vulcan and M-48 Chaparral gun missile systems. It also has 50 rebuilt ZSU-23-4 self-propelled, radar-guided, Soviet-made AA guns and ZU-23-2 towed guns. It has 37-mm and 40-mm L-70 AA guns and now obsolescent MIM-42A Redeye man-portable surface-to-air missiles.

- Israel has improved the D-7 search-and-fire radar system it modified from the Fledermaus system, which it first deployed to assist its 40-mm L-70 guns in 1964. The new Eagle-Eye, or Kapuz, radar system allows six AA weapons to be linked to a common guidance system to produce a guided equivalent of "curtain fire." It also has an electro-optical system with a laser range finder. Israel found this to be essential in 1982 in order to allow the visual identification of friendly and hostile aircraft and to give battery commanders a visual image of their target.[28]

- *Combat Engineering and Support Forces:* The value of combat engineering in direct support of urban and mountain battles was clearly demonstrated in 1982. Israel has since built these forces up as a key combat arm for penetrating rapidly through mountain routes, repairing or replacing bridges, crossing barriers, and dealing with urban defense points. It is buying CUCV 4X 4s to replace its jeeps and large numbers of Subaru and Suzuki tenders to improve light logistic support in base areas.[29]

CHANGES IN AIR FORCE CAPABILITIES

- The Israeli Air Force now has an active strength of roughly 28,000 men and women versus 30,000 in 1982. It has roughly 19,000 conscripts, most of which are in air defense. It has some 577 combat aircraft, with up to 100 more in storage, as well as the 80 combat helicopters discussed earlier. This compares with about 634 combat aircraft in 1982, up to 270 of which were in storage.

- *Modernization, Readiness, and Cost:* The Israeli Air Force continues to emphasize training and has one of the most advanced combat training systems in the world. It also takes advantage of U.S. training centers. In addition to extremely selective assignments during active duty, Israel has developed a reserve system that requires exceptional performance from its air force reservists. There are no reserve squadrons in the IAF, and all squadrons can operate without mobilization. However, about one-third of the aircrew in each squadron are reservists. Reserve aircrew train 55–60 days a year and fly operational missions with the squadron to which they are assigned. In the event of a call-up, the reserve aircrews and operations support personnel report first and then support personnel for sustained operations. About 60 percent of the IAF reserves are in air- and ground-defense units.

- The IAF has, however, experienced severe financial pressures, in part because of the massive costs of the now cancelled Lavi fighter program. This led to reductions in other procurement and supply actions, the mothballing of some units, cuts in training levels and flight hours, a loss of operational tempo, and early grounding for a number of qualified pilots. Like many nations in the West, Israel has been unable to strike an efficient balance between defense industry, modernization, and operational readiness.

  These problems are also likely to continue. Although Israel has decided to order the F-16C instead of the Lavi and to avoid using the Lavi's avionics on the F-16C, it has still found the F-16C to be an extremely expensive airplane. It is unlikely that the IAF will be able to modernize its F-4s to anything like the level it once planned, and Israel is also developing another potential "budget breaker" in the form of a tactical anti-ballistic missile called the Arrow. The IAF may be able to cope with the lessons of war, but it is unclear that it can cope with the lessons of peace.

- *Command, Control, and Force Structure:* The IAF is now organized into 16 dual-capable attack/air defense squadrons, four attack squadrons, a reconnaissance force, an airborne early warning (AEW) unit, an ECM unit, a transport wing, a liaison wing, training units, seven helicopter squadrons, and fifteen surface-to-air Improved Hawk battalions with MIM-23B Improved Hawk missiles.

- In spite of the Lavi, the post-1982 changes in the IAF reflect the high priority it has given to maintaining its technical superiority or "edge" over Arab forces. The 16 attack-interceptor squadrons in the IAF now have 2/50 F-15s versus 40 in 1982. There are 4/113 F-4Es versus 138 F-4Es in 1982, 4/95 Kfir C1/C2/C7s versus 160 Kfir C1/C2s, and 3/70 F-16A/Bs and 75 F-16C/Ds versus 72 F-16A/Bs in 1982.

- Israel's F-15s and F-4Es have already been upgraded, and its F-15s have many of the features of the USAF MSIP I and II (multistage improvement program I and II) version of the aircraft. The F-16A/Bs will also be upgraded to match the improving capability of USAF aircraft, as will Israel's F-4s. Israel cannot afford to up-engine its F-4s, however, or to give them all the modern avionics it once hoped to buy. The IAF once hoped to deploy a "Super Phantom" but lacks the funds to do so.[30] The most Israel can afford for its F-4s is an $8 million per plane "Phantom 2000" upgrade. This will improve the IAF's 140 aircraft inventory at a rate of 10–12 aircraft each year. It will give the F-4E a modern avionics architecture, with 1553B data buses, higher power digital computers, a heads-up display, multifunction displays, an improved electronic warfare suite, and reinforcement and modification of the air frame.

- Israel's four fighter ground attack (FGA) squadrons have a total of 121 obsolescent A-4H/N Skyhawks versus 174 A-4s in 1982. The training units are dual capable in combat missions. They include 16 F-4Es, 10 Kfirs (which will soon be expanded to 70), 27 TA-4H/J Skyhawks, and 94 CM-170 Magisters/Tzugits.
- *Changes in Air Mission Emphasis:* As a result of its problems in developing the Lavi, Israel has recently modified its concept of combat aircraft improvement. In the period between 1982 and 1987, Israel stressed giving its aircraft the features most desired by its pilots. The resulting cost, however, led to studies that revealed that many pilot suggestions were tailoring the aircraft to provide features that demanded more and more specialized pilot skills and which were of only marginal benefit in terms of mission capability. Israel is now much more careful to analyze mission benefits and is designing its avionics to emphasize operability for all its pilots, not only the top-ranking ones.[31]
- Israel continues to give high priority to destroying and suppressing the enemy's air- and land-based air-defense capability during the initial stages of the battle. The sheer scale of Israel's success in suppressing Syrian air defenses is indicated by the fact that Israel only lost one A-4 during well over 1,000 combat sorties during the peak of the 1982 fighting, including the sorties delivered against Syrian ground-based air defenses in the Bekaa. Israel also was able to devote an extraordinary percentage of its total sorties to the attack mission, although it should be noted that even in the 1973 war, some 75 percent of all IAF sorties were attack sorties.[32]
- Israel is steadily improving its ability to use smart air munitions and ground-launched rockets and missiles against aircraft, SAM sites, and air bases. It now has AIM-9L, AIM-7E/F, R-530, Shafrir, and Python III air-to-air missiles in inventory. It also has Luz, AGM-65 Maverick, AGM-45 Shrike, AGM-62A Walleye, AGM-12 Bullpup, and Gabriel III air-to-surface weapons. Israel also has developed a large rocket-boosted glide bomb called

"Popeye" which the U.S. is evaluating for use on the B-52. It is a TV-guided missile, but the details are classified.[33]

- *Air-to-Ground Strike Capability:* Israel has continued to make improvements in its ability to use aircraft to support ground forces. It is steadily improving its air-to-ground munitions lethality and range, with an emphasis on high volumes of accurate delivery of dumb but more lethal munitions in low-vulnerability attack profiles. It has rejected reliance on the "smart munitions" and "point kill" for broad use in close-support and interdiction missions, although it is improving its ability to use such systems for shock and critical time-sensitive kill missions. It has instead purchased extensive stocks of fuel-air explosive and cluster bombs. These weapons are lethal over a wide area. The cluster bombs include 300-, 500-, and 1,000-pound versions of the APAT (anti-personnel, anti-tank) bomb.

- *Strategic Bombing:* Israel is steadily refining its strategic bombing capability and ability to strike at Syria and other Arab targets without striking at population centers. Israel has already demonstrated good performance in this area. In spite of press reports that Israeli attacks killed some 18,000 Lebanese and Palestinians and wounded some 30,000 more, the IAF and IDF generally went to great lengths to avoid killing civilians. While its strategic bombing plans remain highly classified, it is clear that Israel has steadily refined plans to launch a crippling air and missile strike at Syrian and Jordanian economic and military objectives that would minimize civilian casualties and have the goal of seriously reducing either nation's postwar recovery capability for several years to come.

- *Reconnaissance, C³I, and EW Capabilities:* IAF reconnaissance, EW, and C³I units have continued to be strengthened as a result of the lessons of the 1982 conflict and other recent conflicts. The IAF now has 14 RF-4Es and 5 RC-12s—roughly the same strength as in 1982 but with major improvements in their equipment. Its AEW units have four updated and Israeli-modified E-2Cs. The ECM units include a number of specially modified aircraft and RPVs, including six B-707s versus four in 1982. Some of the modified B-707 aircraft have airborne command functions. Israel also has a new AWACS-like version of its B-707 modifications under development called the Falcon. This aircraft will combine airborne warning, command and control, and intelligence functions. It will have a high degree of sensor fusion and up to 11 operator consoles, with the option of adding 6 more. It will have active radar array panels on each side, backed by an advanced monopule IFF. It will also have advanced electronic support measures, electronic intelligence, and communications intelligence. Its scan rate will be up to 10 times faster than the existing aircraft, with far more sophisticated target identification and tracking capability. The effective range of the radar will be 375–400 kilometers, and the aircraft will be able to stay on station at an altitude of 36,000 feet for more than 12 hours without refueling.

- There are 20 Bell 206 and Bell 212 ECM and SAR helicopters. Israel is designing a new variant of its B-707s called the Falcon which combines Israeli-designed early-warning and command-and-control equipment. They will have radars, IFF equipment, ELINT equipment, electronic warfare systems, and a variety of display systems.[34]

- *Electronic Warfare:* Israel has sought to improve, and has probably succeeded in improving, its edge over Syria in every aspect of electronic warfare. Israel has increased the capability of its smaller special-purpose electronic warfare aircraft in this mission and of its larger rockets and has greatly increased the sophistication of its ground-based forward electronic warfare and targeting efforts, although the details remain classified.

   The IAF's F-15s will, however, be upgraded with the electronic warfare package that the Israeli firm Elisra originally designed for the Lavi. This was rejected for Israel's F-16s because it was too expensive, but the advantages inherent in superior electronic warfare capability are another of the lessons Israel learned from the 1982 war, and this will be provided for Israel's first-line air-defense fighter.[35]

- *Night Attack or "24 Hour" Capability:* Israel has 60 more F-16Cs on order, although financial pressures have meant that only 13 can be equipped with Lantirn for night attack missions, and even these have Lantirn only for night targeting rather than for night navigation capability. Israel regards developing a 24 hour or night attack capability as a major priority and a key lesson from the 1973 and 1982 wars, where many interdiction targets only moved and were vulnerable at night.

- *Anti-Radar Attack Capability:* Israel also has 24 "Wild Weasel" F-4Es which are specially equipped to carry the U.S. AGM-78B Standard anti-radiation missile. These aircraft were used extensively in the Bekaa Valley operations in 1982 and reflect the fact that one of the key lessons that Israel drew from the 1973 fighting was the need for effective anti-radar missiles as a key air-defense-suppression weapon.

- The Wild Weasel F-4Es can carry four AGM-78Bs each. They have special J79-17B engines, AN/APQ-120(V)4 radars, and TISEO (target identification system—electro-optical) long-range optical-visual identification systems. There are special displays and provision for the launch of AGM-65 missiles. The aircraft do not have emitter location equipment separate from the missile, and Israel put its own improved Purple Heart seeker on the AGM-78Bs as a result of the lessons it learned in 1982. Israel is believed to be modifying other aircraft to use this anti-radiation missile system.[36]
- Israel also has a remotely piloted vehicle or drone called the Harpee. This would be able to loiter for extended periods over the battlefield and then home-in immediately on any radar that started to operate in the area, even if it only emitted for very short periods of time.[37] The Harpee is similar in concept to the U.S. Seek Spinner and Tactical Rainbow missiles. While the details of the Harpee's performance are classified, it is known that the system can loiter over the area near radars for several hours and then home-in on such radars and kill them with its warhead when they emit a signal. The Harpee has been tested in simulated missions where it did home-in and hit military radars. An even more advanced follow-on to the Harpee may be in service. Such systems, which seem to be called Samson and Delilah, would give Israel a greatly improved capability to destroy Arab air-defense systems without exposing high-cost aircraft and would confront an Arab force with the fact that it could never predict when its air-defense systems would be attacked.[38]
- *Remotely Piloted Vehicles:* Israel continues to expand its use of RPVs as a result of the 1982 war. Its current RPVs include the Mastiff, Scout, Teledyne Ryan 124R, MQM-74C, Chukar II, and Delilah. These RPVs perform a wide range of targeting and intelligence functions and use photo, IR, ELINT, and possibly small radar sensors. By 1987, Israel's Mastiffs and Scouts had logged some 10,000 flight hours and over 1,000 sorties, including the several hundred sorties they flew in 1982.
- Israel has also completed development of a third-generation RPV called the Pioneer, partly as a reaction to some of the lessons it learned in 1982. The Pioneer has a payload of 45 kilograms versus 38 for the Scout and an endurance of 8 to 9 hours versus 4 to 6 hours for Israel's older RPVs. Its speed is increased from 60 to 70 nautical miles per hour (NMH), and its airframe is made from composite materials rather than metal to reduce its radar signature. Like previous Israeli RPVs, the Pioneer is very quiet

and normally is hard to see. It has a ceiling of 15,000 feet and a video transmission range of up to 200 kilometers. The equipment on the Pioneer includes a TV camera, a thermal imager, electronic warfare equipment, and a laser range finder or designator. It will be deployed in field units with four Pioneers each and can be launched with a pneumatic catapult and rocket booster or on any 250-meter-long stretch of road. It can land in 70 meters with a net. The Pioneer will also have a greatly improved down link and display system and can be turned over to remote forward-deployed control stations. The normal range of the down link is 30 to 40 kilometers.[39] This gives Israel an even greater advantage in tactical reconnaissance and surveillance capability than it had in 1982 and allows the IDF to carry out such missions without exposing personnel.[40]

- *Surface-to-Air Missiles:* The Israeli Air Force continues to use a heavily modified form of the Improved Hawk, and Israel has 15 battalions of these surface-to-air missiles. The Israelis did not use their own surface-to-air missiles extensively in 1982. It is important to note, however, that the Israelis had already made important modifications to their Hawk missiles and had upgraded their Chaparral missile systems. The Israeli Hawks have radar and guidance software that allowed intercepts at up to 70,000 feet. An Israeli Hawk battery in Lebanon shot down a MiG-25 that was at an even higher altitude and was flying at Mach 2.5 on 30 August 1982.

  The Israelis added a $30,000 Super Eye electro-optical detector to the Hawks in the mid-1970s to provide detection at ranges of up to 30–40 kilometers and to help them deal with ECM and IFF problems. According to one report, there were two confirmed cases in 1982 in which this system prevented Israeli units from firing on their own aircraft. As for Chaparral, they added an Amarit electro-optical and threat designation communication system for identification and target observation. According to Israel, this doubled the operational engagement range at which the system could safely acquire and identify a target.

- Israel is examining two major future options to improve its surface-to-air defenses. The first is the lease of U.S. Patriot surface-to-air missiles. The second is the development of the Arrow anti-tactical ballistic missile with the capability to intercept short-range ballistic missiles with ranges up to 330 miles. The U.S. has agreed to pay for 80 percent of the development cost of the Arrow as part of its Strategic Defense Initiative.[41]

- *Helicopters:* Israel found in 1982 that its initial operational concept for using helicopters was wrong. The IAF had planned to use helicopters to fly close support. In practice, it found it had achieved firepower saturation in the forward area with its ground-based systems, had major IFF problems in not firing on its own helicopters, and could not spare the time to try to vector helicopters in against known targets. The IAF's attack helicopters rapidly changed behavior and began to fly search-and-kill missions behind the lines in an interdiction role. In spite of worries about power and survivability in mountain terrain, the IAF rapidly found that the helicopter could achieve surprise and considerable survivability by picking the right points of attack. It also found that ground forces had more serious problems in detecting helicopters in mountain terrain than on the plains. Army units moving in mountain areas proved to have more problems in hearing helicopters and to have problems adjusting to the closed-in terrain and spotting helicopters visually. Syrian army units also proved to have more predictable movements.
- The Israeli Air Force has continued to improve its attack and assault helicopter numbers as a result of these lessons, although some senior IDF officers feel these helicopters should not remain in the air force and that the IDF should get more helicopters at the expense of cuts in the numbers of attack fighters in the IAF. The IAF now has three squadrons with about 40 AH-1S/Q Cobra and 40 Hughes MD-500 attack helicopters versus 42 armed helicopters in 1982. It also has 33 heavy CH-53A/D transport helicopters, 17 UH-1D and 9 SA-321 medium transport helicopters, and 64 Bell 206A and 40 Bell 212 light transport helicopters.
- Israel found during the 1982 fighting that even light-attack helicopters like the Hughes 500D could survive and be effective against soft targets with rockets if they took advantage of their high agility, low sound levels, and terrain masking. The 500Ds repeatedly engaged enemy columns in interdiction missions. The IAF has successfully modified some 500Ds to carry four TOW anti-tank guided missiles in low drag launchers by removing the two rear seats.
- The IAF has converted most of its AH-1 Cobras to the S-3 type used by the U.S., and these can carry significant firepower: up to eight TOW ATGMs, a three-barreled 20-mm gun, two rocket pods of 19 rockets and/or bombs, illumination rockets and smoke rockets, and many have been modified to improve their survivability and add firepower. Israel ordered 25 more Cobras from the United States in a complex deal that leased the helicopters from

them. The cost of this lease was paid for out of the money the United States owes Israel for leasing 25 Kfir fighters which the U.S. Navy uses in simulating Soviet fighter attacks on U.S. aircraft.[42] According to some reports, Israel also has 12 AS-365 Dauphin helicopters it bought from the U.S. Navy.[43]

- Israel has acted on the lessons it learned in 1982 to take advantage of such advanced U.S. technology as helmet sights and rangefinder readout, which are aligned to the TOW sight and a separate laser rangefinder. These extend the operational range at which helicopters can hit targets with guns and ATGMs. Israel is also using U.S. systems to suppress helicopter IR emissions and U.S. radar-warning receivers.
- The IAF has equipped its helicopter crews with night vision devices and regularly trains for night combat missions. It is experimenting with its own laser-designated version of the TOW, called the Togger, and is seeking to develop a helicopter ATGM that can be fired for final target designation by an IDF soldier on the ground.[44]
- Israeli efforts to modernize its helicopter force will be slowed by money and skilled manpower shortages and by continuing debates over helicopter survivability. Israel has concluded that only the most advanced attack helicopters can provide effective close air support in the future against threats like a fully mobilized and deployed Syrian army and that such systems may be necessary in low-intensity combat missions once more advanced versions of light surface-to-air missiles like the Stinger C and SA-14III are available to forces like those of the PLO and Amal. Israel would like to have a squadron of 30 AH-64s in addition to its AH-1s. In practice, however, it has no surplus funds. As a result, it is seeking to lease at least 12-15 AH-64s from the U.S., plus UH-60A Blackhawk transporter helicopters. Israel now plans to modernize its Hughes 500Ds and AH-1s and deploy them in a mix with the AH-64. It will phase them out over 10 to 15 years, rather than 5 to 10 years, as it originally planned.

   Israel also plans to retain its Bell 212s and CH-53s longer than it originally planned and will phase them out over 15 years. It should be noted, however, that Israel has to fly relatively short distances and makes extensive use of Israeli-made short takeoff and landing (STOL) aircraft to perform support missions that are performed by helicopters in other forces.[45]

- *Air Transport:* The IAF's transport wing has not changed greatly since 1982. It includes 7 B-707s (five modified to be tankers), 21 C-130E/H, 18 C-47s, and 2 KC-130H tankers. The liaison forces have one BN-2 Islander, 5 Dornier Do-27 and 11 Do-28D, 20 Cessnas, 12 Queen Air 80s, two Westwinds, and 30 Super Cubs.

CHANGES IN NAVAL CAPABILITIES

- Israel is slowly modernizing its small 9,000-man navy. It is based at Haifa, Ashdod, and Eilat. The navy had about 3,300 conscripts in early 1989 and plans to grow to a strength of about 11,250 upon mobilization. All naval combat vessels are kept ready for immediate action.

- *Mobilization and Reserves:* Naval reserves represent about 25 percent of the fully mobilized navy. An annual plan is followed to augment ship crews with reservists on a daily basis. Any given crew billet may be filled throughout the year by a continuous flow of reservists, and training is conducted on the job. There are a few specialized naval reserve units, such as an emergency diving unit, and a crew for one of the navy's LCTs.

- *Naval Missions and Modernization:* Israel has given its navy relatively low priority because of funding problems, but it still feels that the 1982 war has shown that Israel must respond to the increases in Syrian long-range naval strike capability. One basic problem that motivates Israel's need to modernize its navy is its dependence on resupply: Some 95 percent of U.S. resupply in 1973 came by sea, but Israel has also had to react to Syrian orders for improved submarines and long-range anti-ship missiles from the USSR.[46] The end result has been a compromise modernization plan which calls for two modern submarines and three modern "deep water" surface ships. This plan was agreed to in 1985, but Israel has been slow to actually fund it.[47]

- *Submarines:* While submarines have never played a role in an Arab-Israeli conflict, they have become both regional status symbols and a potential means of interdicting commercial shipping and the movement of small navies, like that of Syria, in and out of port.

  In 1988, Israel decided to use U.S. FMS funds to replace its three Vickers-made Gal-class diesel coastal submarines made by Vickers with West German–made Type-206 submarines. This decision was taken after a wait of nearly five years, and Israel will only be able to fund two Type-206s, rather than three. The submarines will be called the Dolphin class and will be constructed in the FRG by a consortium of German firms under the administration of a U.S. contractor named Ingalls. The U.S. has agreed that Israel may apply $180 million out of U.S. FMS funds to the total program cost of $360 million. Israel has bought

Harpoon missiles for its submarines and Westinghouse NT37E torpedoes to replace its obsolete Northrop Mark 37s.[48]

- *Major Surface Vessels:* Israel's major surface forces now consist of four corvettes. Two are the Aliya-class corvettes (Sa'ar 5) it had in 1982, with four Gabriel II and four Harpoon ship-to-ship missiles and one Bell 206 Kiowa ASW helicopter. The two others are Romat-class vessels with eight Harpoon and eight Gabriel missile launchers. Israel now has 24 guided-missile patrol boats, versus 27 in 1982. These include eight Reshef (Sa'ar 4) with four to six Gabriel III and two Harpoon ship-to-ship missile launchers. It also has 12 Mivtach/Sa'ar missile patrol boats with two Harpoon and three to five Gabriel III missile launchers. It has a new guided-missile patrol boat, the Dorva, in prototype status. Israel has Phalanx close-in 20-mm defense systems on order in an effort to improve its anti-ship missile defenses.
- Israel would like to buy a total of four 1,200-ton Sa'ar Five corvettes but can only afford three. These ships have far more range, multi-mission capability, and advanced electronic warfare, missile protection, and sensor gear than Israel's existing corvettes. The hulls will be built at the Ingalls Shipyard in Pascagoula, Mississippi, at a cost of around $300 million and be fitted in Israel. Each Sa'ar Five will have two Dauphin helicopters, Barak vertical-launch anti-missile missiles, torpedo tubes, and over-the-horizon attack capabilities, possibly including a modification of the Pioneer RPV. The total cost of the three fully fitted ships will be around $750 million.[49]

    One of the lessons that Israel has drawn from the fighting in the Falklands is that it needs much better electronic and missile protection, and if it cannot afford four ships, it may operate its Sa'ar Fives in task groups with its older ships. This would provide some protection for the older vessels.[50]
- *Guided-Missile Weapons:* Israel has long been able to use anti-ship missiles as a means of winning naval superiority. Israel now has 24 guided-missile patrol boats versus 27 in 1982. These include eight Reshef (Sa'ar 4) with four to six Gabriel III and two Harpoon ship-to-ship missile launchers. These ships are to be modernized with Gabriel IV missiles and Barak close-in defenses. Israel also has 12 Mivtach/Sa'ar missile patrol boats with two Harpoon and three to five Gabriel III missile launchers. These ships date back to the 1960s and 1970s, however, and are now nearing obsolescence. The first models of a new 48-ton, 40-knot patrol boat, the Dorva, have completed construction but the boats currently are not planned to carry missiles.

Israel has also brought its new Gabriel IV anti-ship missile to the point where it is now operational. This missile has a maximum range of 200 kilometers and a 100–200 pound warhead. It represents Israel's conclusion that it must be able to significantly increase the strike range of its navy and its ability to stand off Israel's coast line and operate deeper into the Mediterranean.[51]

- *Close-in Defense:* Like other navies, Israel has learned the importance of close-in defense against aircraft and missiles. Israel has Phalanx close-in 20-mm defense systems on order in an effort to improve its anti-ship missile defenses. It has experienced problems with this system because it has been deployed too close to the water and has suffered from salt spray. It plans to develop its own close-in defense system called the Barak, but there have been major delays in its development, and it will not be ready before 1992.

- *Amphibious Forces:* Israel saw the benefits of amphibious assault during 1982, when it was able to bypass PLO defenses in south Lebanon. It has been examining the use of high-speed naval assault ships like hydrofoils for missions like rapid amphibious landings since the period before the 1982 war. It has two Shimrit (U.S. Flagstaff 2-class) hydrofoils, with two Gabriel and four Harpoon missiles. It also has a small naval commando of about 300 men with Firefish III attack craft. It has improved its "forced entry" capability to combine the use of 19 landing craft and 31 Dabur inshore patrol craft with its larger missile-equipped patrol boats.

The Challenges Israel Now Faces

Israel is far from eliminating its military problems as a result of the shifts and changes in its forces since 1982. It only has about 60–70 percent of the funds it feels it needs. There are deep and increasing divisions within Israel over its priorities for force improvement and over how its defense resources and U.S. aid should be spent. Israel faces continuing problems in dealing with Lebanon and the new challenge of a Palestinian uprising on the West Bank and in Gaza. Finally, Israel must come to grips with the growing proliferation of weapons of mass destruction throughout the area and redefine its need for a nuclear deterrent and for defenses against nuclear, chemical, and biological weapons.

Force Improvement Priorities and Defense Economics. Israel's problems with its domestic military budget have already been discussed. These problems have been offset in part by U.S. aid. Israel received some $7.9 billion in U.S. military financing between FY1950 and FY1978. It received $3.5 billion in FMS grant aid and loans in FY1979 as compensation for the loss of its bases and facilities in the Sinai. It received $1.0 billion in FMS in FY1980, $1.4 billion in FY1981, $1.4 billion in FY1982, $1.7 billion in FY1983, and $1.7 billion in FY1984. U.S. FMS assistance began on an all-grant basis in FY1985 when Israel received $1.4 billion worth of aid. It received $1.723 billion in FY1986 and received $1.8 billion annually in FY1987 through FY1989.[52]

In spite of this aid, Israel faced severe economic problems long before 1987. Israeli immigration dropped 41 percent between 1984 and 1985, and during 1986–1988, it reached its lowest level since 1948. The Israeli economy recovered very slowly from the direct and indirect costs of the 1982 fighting, in spite of massive U.S. grant aid. During 1982 to 1985, Israel's GDP actually dropped from $23.2 to $22.0 billion, total debt rose from $18.3 to $23.9 billion, and the debt service ratio rose from 26 percent to 33 percent.

The resulting economic crisis slowed the modernization of Israeli forces, forced serious cuts in Israeli manpower and readiness, and meant Israel has had to draw on war reserves for routine training and operations. In FY1987, for example, the IDF was forced to take a $700 million defense budget cut, at least $200 to 300 million of which had to come in the form of further cuts in readiness and training and to reduce its domestic defense expenditures from a planned level of $3.2 billion to $2.53 billion.[53]

Even with $1.8 billion annually in U.S. grant military aid during FY1987 to FY1989, Israel could only afford a total defense budget of $5.14 billion in 1987 and of $5.71 billion in 1988. To put these figures in perspective, Israeli expenditures in constant 1986 dollars totaled over $7 billion without any U.S. aid in 1983 and were about $6 billion in 1981, the period before the 1982 fighting.[54]

Total U.S. military aid to Israel is now well in excess of $24 billion, and almost all is currently being given in grant form. Nevertheless, Israel must service the debt on some $12.2 billion in past loans and pay roughly $1.2 billion a year in principal and interest. This means that the net value of U.S. military aid is considerably smaller than the annual grants imply. Israel also still operates in a climate of considerable economic strain.[55] Its economic reform or stabilization plan of July 1985 reduced inflation from triple digit rates to about 16 percent in 1986. The government has been slow to make the structural reforms necessary for continued growth, however, and military expenditures still run about 18 percent of the GNP, even though U.S. FMS grants make up about half of Israel's defense budget. External debt service adds up to 37 percent of all exports of goods and services and continues to put heavy pressure on the Israeli economy.

The Debates Over Military Industries and Technology Versus Force Improvement Priorities. It is not surprising, therefore, that there have been bitter arguments over how Israel allocates its resources. The most serious of these debates have so far been over Israel's investment in combat aircraft production and in its military industries. Israel spent 60–70 percent of its investment funds in its air force and military electronics during 1984–1986 and did so even though its economic problems forced it to put 90 of its 684 combat aircraft in storage, to cut its active ground force strength by over 10 percent, to delay the production of Merkava tanks and other modern armor, and to cut its naval modernization to the bone.[56]

Many in Israel, like Israel's Defense Minister Moshe Arens, felt that Israel could create a cost-effective approach to defense only by concentrating on advanced weapons and the growth of high-technology industry. They pointed out that Israel's arms industry had built up to a peak of nearly 80,000 workers and had become the sixth largest arms exporter in the world. According to some estimates, the arms industry impacted directly and indirectly on some 20–25 percent of the population and that Israel's military exports rose from $850 million in 1983 to about $1.3 billion in 1986, becoming Israel's largest category of exports.

Others felt that Israel could not finance all the improvements in its forces necessary to respond to the operational lessons of the 1982 fighting unless it abandoned the search to use military industry as a high-technology base upon which to build both civilian development and a major export industry. They felt that senior officials, like Arens, were putting far too much of Israel's money in the wrong place.

Israel's new fighter, the Lavi, became the most visible symbol of this debate and one that ended in disaster. The Lavi started out in 1980 as a low-cost replacement for the IAF's aging A-4s and Kfirs. By 1982, however, the decision was taken to power it with the advanced Pratt and Whitney PW1120 engine and turn it into a multi-role fighter that was supposed to outperform the F-16C/D. This decision was taken in part because the IAF concluded that an A-4/Kfir replacement as a ground-attack aircraft would not be a cost-effective investment. It felt such an aircraft would be too expensive to deploy for its mission benefits and that the IAF would be far better off in investing in a smaller number of high-performance dual-capability aircraft.

Driven by the leadership of Moshe Keret, the president of Israel Aircraft Industries (IAI), and Moshe Arens, who was then defense minister (and an ex–vice president of Engineering at IAI), the aircraft came to be regarded as Israel's hope for emerging as a major world exporter of advanced arms. The Lavi design also came to include the features necessary to survive in an extremely hostile environment, including very high speed, maneuverability, advanced electronic warfare capabilities, a low radar cross-section airframe, and very advanced avionics.

Israel, however, had little practical experience with large-scale systems integration or with the development and production of an aircraft that had to lead the world in many aspects of fighter performance. It constantly modified the aircraft design to use new advanced technology features without realistically estimating the costs. It ran into both design and manufacturing problems, and Israel had to turn to the U.S. for permission to obtain large amounts of advanced U.S. technology at little or no R&D cost and for the right to use a large part of its FMS aid on the Lavi project.

In spite of the fact that this U.S. aid was forthcoming, it became apparent that neither IAI or the Israel Ministry of Defense had the skills to manage the project. The design features of the Lavi were still allowed to grow to reflect the desires of Israel's pilots with little real regard to the marginal cost benefit of their desires or the actual benefits in mission performance. As a result, the aircraft became less desirable in real-world military terms and more of a technologists' and fighter pilots' toy.

The cost estimates of the Lavi project also became more and more politicized and less and less real. As a result, Israel and the U.S. became involved in a major debate over aircraft cost. U.S. defense experts estimated that the Lavi's development cost would be at least $300 million more than Israel budgeted and that peak production costs might be equal to 5 percent of Israel's GNP. They also estimated that its individual unit cost was escalating to a cost of $22 million per plane, including nonconcurrent spares, or about 45–65 percent higher than the advocates of the Lavi in Israel were willing to admit. The U.S. was particularly concerned because by the time these cost estimates were made, Israel was getting 90 percent of the funding for the Lavi project from U.S. military aid and only 40 percent of the development cost was going back to U.S. manufacturers.[57]

While the seriousness of these problems was widely understood by the top ranks of the Israeli military and by the Israeli cabinet, the Lavi project survived because it was perceived as a Likud project and Israel's cabinet faced the problem of a potential crisis within the Labor-Likud coalition. As a result, Israel attempted to deal with these issues by putting a cap of $550 million per year on spending on the Lavi.

This cap rapidly proved to be impractical. The project cost of the Lavi rose to $9.99 billion, or a flyaway cost of $17.36 million each, at production runs of 300 aircraft, a figure which involved the export of more than two-thirds of the total production run of 300 aircraft, although Israel had no foreign customer for the plane. This program cost compared with a program cost of $4.67 billion if Israel bought the same number of F-16C/Ds from the U.S. or $5.84 billion if it bought the F-16C/D with Israel's Peace Marble 2 design features. Israel also found it could not cost-effectively produce a combat aircraft as complex and sophisticated as the Lavi. Instead of being an Israeli-manufactured plane, the changes in design reached the point where they required Israel to import 60 percent of the parts and equipment from the U.S.

This steady rise in cost of the Lavi also gradually drove the total buy of the Lavi that Israel could afford for its own forces down from 400 aircraft to 300, to 150, and then to less than 100. These problems finally forced Israel to cancel the Lavi project on 31 August 1987.[58] The Israeli government took this decision by a 12–11 vote of the cabinet, in spite of the opposition of Prime Minister Shamir and most of the Likud members of the government. The Labor ministers uniformly supported the cancellation of the project, and one member of the Likud switched his vote. As a result, Arens resigned as defense minister on 4 September 1987 and left the cabinet, although he returned as foreign minister after the 1988 elections.

An additional factor that led to the cancellation of the Lavi was that the project now faced virtually uniform opposition by the senior officers of the IDF and had only limited support among the senior officers of the IAF. Israel's current chief of staff, Dan Shomron; deputy chief of staff, Major General Ehud Barak; and the current commander of the Air Force, Major General Avihu Ben-Nun, all opposed the project as being far too expensive and a misguided exercise in economic development that did not meet Israel's military needs. In fact, all three did their best in the spring of 1988 to kill the effort to go on with the Lavi's B-3 avionics because they felt they were far too expensive and were being continued only to avoid the political costs of further cuts in IAI. They failed largely because Israel's new defense minister, Yitzak Rabin, felt that he could not afford the political cost of such an action.[59]

The cancellation finally came at a point when the U.S. and Israel had already invested over $1.5 billion in the fighter, and Israel still faced additional costs of $1.2 to $1.4 billion, with $200 to $300 million for the avionics alone. The investment in the Lavi program had seriously undercut the modernization of every other aspect of Israel's forces. The terms of the cancellation agreement with the U.S. did make some $476 million available for either wind-up costs or new projects. Israel, however, was forced to use almost $400 million of the money for project cancellation and wind-up costs.

Even so, Israel's defense industries had to lay off large numbers of workers at a time when a general fall in world arms sales was hurting Israel's export markets, and it was suffering further from ending its arms sales to South Africa. Between 1985 and 1987, Israel cut the employees in its defense industries from roughly 80,000 to 60,000 personnel. It was only able to ease this situation by expanding its sale of advanced technology systems to the People's Republic of China (PRC) and turning to the U.S. for additional help in selling arms to the U.S. Israel announced plans to lay off another 1,500 to 2,000 defense workers in 1989, when the defense labor force will drop to around 45,000.[60]

The cancellation of the Lavi did, however, lead to some significant improvements in Israeli military capability. The IDF Ground Forces Corps was able to allocate some 47 percent of its budget to modernization in 1987 and 40 percent to training. Training programs increased by 30 percent in comparison with the "Lavi years." The ground forces were also able to sharply increase their budget for tanks, other combined-arms equipment, night combat devices, and field intelligence equipment. The changes also had a major impact in improving the quality of the intake of Israeli regular officers and NCOs. The drop out rate for officers was reduced from 40 percent to 34 percent and from 21 percent to 16 percent for other ranks. These improvements in the regular forces seem to be continuing, although the Palestinian uprising has had a serious disruptive effect on the reserves.[61]

In February 1988, Israel replaced the Lavi with an order for 60 more F-16C/Ds with associate support equipment, IIR target pods, IIR GBU-15 weapons systems, technical assistance, spare parts, training, and co-production equipment. The total cost of this package was roughly $2 billion, with $1.4 billion going to the combat aircraft and major defense equipment. The deal involved an $800 million offset in U.S. purchases from Israel.

The cancellation of the Lavi has scarcely ended the debate over the amount of technology that Israel can afford. Israel still faces problems in funding both its remaining high-technology weapons systems and its force modernization. It has embarked on an ambitious anti-tactical ballistic defense program called the Arrow. This system is designed to counter missiles with ranges up to 330 miles, and the U.S. has agreed to pay 80 percent of the cost of development.[62] That may also lead to a major cost escalation. Israel never succeeded in developing a high-volume capability to produce the Merkava tank until the Lavi project was cancelled, and it still has major problems in funding the armor and attack helicopters the IDF wants as high priorities.

Naval developments have also faced serious financial problems. As has been discussed earlier, Israel has long wanted to build its own new diesel submarines to match the Soviet delivery of Romeo class submarines to Syria and Libya. It has settled for purchasing the West German Type 209, but three submarines would cost at least $600 million. This means that Israel has had to settle for two West German Type 209 submarines. Similarly, Israel cannot afford to build the four new Sa'ar 5 missile corvettes it wants to modernize its navy. These would already cost $700 to 800 million.[63]

These weapons issues are only the tip of the iceberg. A growing number of Israeli critics feel that the combination of trying to build full-scale military industries and high-technology strike forces is still seriously undercutting IDF readiness and war-fighting capability. These critics point out the slow rate of modernization in the IDF's armor, serious cutbacks in exercise activity, a serious loss in the readiness of reserve forces, and the failure to improve the helicopter force. They cite a host of other financial compromises and trade-offs that they feel mean Israel is losing its operational skills at the price of technology. The practical question for Israel is the long-term force structure and modernization it can actually afford, given its economic problems, the continuing challenge posed by hostile elements in Lebanon and the Palestinians, and the proliferation of weapons of mass destruction in the Arab world.

The Continuing Problem of Lebanon. Israel still suffers to some degree from the impact of its "Vietnam"—its 1982 invasion of Lebanon. Unlike the U.S., Israel has not been able to withdraw from the scene of its problems. It has been able to sharply reduce the cost of its presence in southern Lebanon and the war's impact on the IDF's morale, but it still faces roughly the same level of security problems it faced before its invasion of Lebanon and the new problem of the Palestine uprising in the West Bank and Gaza.

The seriousness of the problems the Lebanon war created for Israeli morale immediately after the end of 1982 fighting are illustrated by the fact that the IDF lost over twenty times as many men *after* it had fully won its 40-kilometer security zone in Lebanon as it did in winning it. The problems are also illustrated by the fact that the IDF lost some 200 men between January and August 1983 and found itself caught up in trying to deal with some 260 attacks, all of which forced the IDF into new patterns of arrest and hostile actions against Lebanese civilians.

Sharon's broadening of the war had a serious impact on public confidence in the armed forces. In 1983 and 1984, Israeli opinion polls showed that less than 20 percent of Israeli professional officers felt the Israeli public held the Israeli armed forces in high regard, and many of Israel's best officers and NCOs left the military services far sooner than in past years.

The IDF has largely recovered from these problems, but it is clear that the war to secure Israel's border with Lebanon is far from over. Various factions of Palestinian guerrillas have slowly reestablished a presence in West Beirut and near Sidon and Tyre, and by March 1989 the PLO again had the most powerful military forces in southern Lebanon. The Israeli invasion also awakened and alienated Lebanon's Shi'ites—its largest single ethnic group. In the past, many Shi'ites had tacitly supported Israel and had fought in Hadad's "Christian" forces in southern Lebanon. After 1982, many joined Shi'ite militias that called for Israel's destruction.

By 1987, the net military threat to Israel in Lebanon had become at least as serious as it was before the 1982 invasion. Israel increasingly had to contend with hostile elements of the Amal, Iranian-backed Shi'ites in the Hezbollah or Party of God. The Amal was initially hostile to the Palestinians and showed little interest in attacking Israel, as distinguished from controlling southern Lebanon. In 1988, however, it formed a coalition with the PLO against the Hezbollah, its main rival for control of the Shi'ite movements in Lebanon. This led to at least a temporary agreement by the Amal to allow the PLO to strengthen its presence in southern Lebanon. The Hezbollah has formed a tentative alliance with more radical Palestinian groups and has always had the declared objective of destroying Israel.

This rebirth of Palestinian activity and the creation of strong hostile Shi'ite elements forced Israel to deal with a rising number of border clashes. A total of 30 squads attempted to cross the border in 1987, and IDF forces killed well over 20 Hezbollah and Palestinians in border incidents.

Israel met this challenge by creating a new 10–16 kilometer-wide security zone. This zone is covered in the north by a large network of Lebanese informers and agents of the security service. These cover most of the villages in the area, although Israeli experts estimate that Iran invested up to $100 million in the Shi'ite villages north of the zone in an effort to undermine Israeli influence in the period between 1981 and early 1988. The actual security zone is defended by a 2,500-man South Lebanon Army led by General Antonine Lahd. This force is heavily backed by the IDF and is Christian-led, although the Shi'ites have a majority in the zone.

Israel defends its own soil with cordons of razor wire and anti-personnel mines. It has an electronically monitored taut wire fence, and any intrusion can be located within 500 meters. A road runs behind it which is patrolled by commander cars and new armored personnel carriers based on the hull of the Centurion tank. Each has four Israeli soldiers equipped with MAG machine guns, mortars, and rocket launchers. The area between the road and the fence is regularly ploughed to show any movement and is monitored on foot by trained trackers.[64]

A line of strong points is a few hundred meters from the border. Two out of three of these strong points normally have 12-man squads, and the third has a company-strength force. These fortresses are surrounded by entrenchments. They are spaced at intervals of several kilometers and have lookout posts equipped with night vision devices and binoculars, backed by acoustic sensors and electronic surveillance equipment such as radars. Some of the older radars are being replaced by remotely monitored EL/M-2410 surveillance systems. There are larger compounds in the rear, equipped with helicopters and light fixed-wing aircraft for both search and attack missions. These now have tank units in support.[65]

The combination of pressure from Palestinian and Shi'ite forces has also led to a steady increase in Israeli patrol activities in southern Lebanon along virtually all of the 50-mile border and to an increasing number of Israeli air strikes against Palestinian and Shi'ite targets. Some sources estimate that Israel has to keep up to 1,500 men in Lebanon or near the border to deal with defense and internal security issues in southern Lebanon. Israel, in turn, charges that Syria is actively training and equipping both Palestinian and Shi'ite guerrillas to attack Israel.[66]

While Israel has responded by trying to create a tacit *modus vivendi* with the Amal and by focusing on attacking the Palestinians and the Party of God, it faces the nearly certain prospect of a continuing low-level conflict in southern Lebanon. If anything, the hostile Shi'ite factions it created as a result of its 1982 invasion of Lebanon are likely to be a more long-term threat than the PLO. The problems involved became all too clear in December 1988. Israel was forced to return to deep raids into Lebanon and launched an amphibious raid against radical Palestinian forces in the Popular Front for the Liberation of Palestine (PFLP) at a camp near Al Naameh, about midway between Sidon and Beirut.[67]

The end result is that Israel is stuck with at least one hand on the Lebanese tar baby. While Israel cannot disengage from Lebanon, it now has no practical hope of either dominating it or ever creating a friendly regime. In fact, Israel's 1982 invasion of Lebanon is likely to be its last attempt at political wars involving major land invasions of the Arab world.[68]

The Palestinian Uprising. Equally significantly, a major Palestinian uprising began on the West Bank and Gaza in late 1987. This uprising began on 8 December 1987 when an Israeli truck hit two Palestinian cars at a checkpoint in the Gaza Strip and killed four Arabs. This led to rumors that the Israeli driver had deliberately killed the Arabs and set off first a demonstration and then a rock-throwing riot. This riot triggered the pent-up pressures of years of frustration. Within days, riots spread to all parts of the Gaza strip, West Bank, and Arab areas of Israel. The riots also did not halt with time. They became part of a major nationalist movement.

The Palestinian uprising, or *intifada*, has now fundamentally changed the character of the internal security threat in Israel. It began on 9 December 1987 as sporadic demonstrations among Palestinian youth. By mid-December, it reached massive proportions. After nearly 21 years of virtual quiet, the Israeli government suddenly had to confront a mass popular uprising and to try to find means to suppress this uprising and to expand a government presence in the occupied territories to protect Jewish settlements and their lines of communication. This, in turn, meant that Israel had to commit much of its police force to dealing with the riots. Israeli defense forces had to rapidly shift from a focus on combined arms to being equipped with riot-control gear like rubber bullets, tear gas dispensers and grenades, helmets, and clubs.

Beginning in early January 1988, the IDF had to deploy three times its normal force in Gaza and twice its force in the West Bank. This led to much quicker and stricter reprisals and to the partial reorganization of the security effort. Israeli Defense Minister Yitzhak Rabin and IDF Chief of Staff Dan Shomron worked out a new plan for policing the territories. IDF training was changed to include riot-control training, large forces were used to quell the riots as soon as they began, and much more extensive use was made of detentions, arrests, curfews, and deportations.

Police duties in the area were transferred to the Border Police, an elite unit with military training, and a policy of graduated response was adopted, involving escalation from a warning through the use of tear gas, rubber bullets, water cannons, plastic bullets, and, finally, live ammunition aimed at the feet of demonstrators. Israel has also deployed new systems of its own, including stone-throwing machines (*hztatzit*), helicopters that can drop rocks, and long-range rubber bullets rather than rubber bullets with a normal range of fifty meters.[69]

These measures limited the Palestinian effort through early 1989 but did nothing to end it. Incidents continued through the course of 1988 and early 1989 and had a steadily greater impact on the morale and discipline of Israeli forces. The number of Palestinians killed in clashes with Israeli security forces rose from 8 in 1985 to 22 in 1986 and 54 in 1987. By late 1988, the number was well over 200.[70] On several occasions discipline broke down, and IDF troops abused or hurt Palestinians unnecessarily. Palestinians also steadily resorted to higher levels of violence.

In June 1988, Israeli sources estimated the costs of these measures as being $237 million and requested a budget supplement of $156 million to meet the costs.[71] By late 1988, estimates of the cost in terms of added mobilization, military spending, and diversion of effort from the civil sector ranged from $500 to $1,000 a year. The uprising also cost Israel 244,000 additional "reservist days" in the second half of 1988, often forcing reservists to serve 60 days per year. In February 1989, the uprising had lasted 408 days, led to more than 6,000 arrests, and cost 361 deaths and thousands of injuries.

During the month ending 9 January 1989, Israeli troops had had 2,790 clashes with Palestinians, 60 percent more than during the previous month. Twenty-six Palestinians had been killed, as many as during the first violent month of the uprising. Although Israel had decided to use more lethal plastic and steel bullets rather than rubber bullets to try to intimidate the Palestinians, the net result was an increase in military activity. Defense Minister Rabin also stated that the same was true of the deportation of troublemakers and the demolition of homes.[72]

The uprising also divided Israeli opinion between advocates of hard-line measures and those who advocated some form of peace effort. It helped King Hussein of Jordan decide to end Jordan's efforts to maintain a proxy civil service and government on the West Bank and has both revitalized and challenged the PLO. It also gave the PLO new credibility, although large elements of the uprising remained independent, and many were advocates of Islamic Fundamentalism and of a much more direct form of armed struggle than that recommended by the PLO.[73]

There is no way to predict how much more the Palestinian uprisings will escalate or what Israel's long-term response will be. It is clear, however, that Israel has not found any way to effectively suppress the uprising. The need to greatly increase patrol and internal security activity has kept many of the reserve forces in the Israeli Army from getting their normal training. It has forced the IDF to use its resources on missions that have no benefit in terms of experience in regular combat, and it has thrust the IDF constantly into grim confrontations with Palestinian demonstrators.[74]

The uprising has also led troops to make extensive use of rubber, plastic, and steel bullets; beatings; tear gas; and other internal security measures that hurt military discipline and morale. This, in turn, has created growing hostility within the armed forces toward performing these internal security missions, even among the elite airborne forces. The Israeli Army chief of staff put this well in a statement to a committee of the Knesset, "There is no such thing as eradicating the uprising because, in its essence, it expresses the struggle of nationalism."[75] There also is no question that this new form of "war" poses a major, long-term challenge to Israel.

The Problem of Weapons of Mass Destruction. Israel also faces the long-term uncertainty of what to do about chemical and nuclear warfare. Israel has long had its own nuclear effort. It began its nuclear research back in the early 1950s and signed a scientific and personnel-exchange agreement with France in 1953, when France was in the midst of its own struggles with the Arab world. Israel joined the Eisenhower administration's Atoms for Peace program and purchased a small reactor from the U.S. in 1955, which became operational at Nahal Soreq in 1960. As part of this agreement, Israel obtained some 6,500 Atomic Energy Commission reports from the U.S. and started exchange agreements which trained 56 Israeli scientists in the U.S.

Israel made its own decision to create a nuclear weapons capability in October 1957 when the inner circle of the Israeli cabinet decided to build a secret nuclear reactor at Dimona. Ben Gurion, Moshe Dayan, and Shimon Peres were some of the strongest supporters of this decision. They were motivated in part by their fear of the Arab arms buildup and of Egypt's decision to build both nuclear and chemical weapons following the Suez War of 1956. At the same time, Dayan and Peres seem to have felt that nuclear weapons would be the ultimate deterrent to any Arab threat to destroy Israel.[76]

The inner circle of the Israeli cabinet took this decision knowing that it could obtain covert French support to build a version of the Machon-2 reactor capable of producing roughly two to three plutonium weapons a year out of the reactor's spent fuel. Their decision did not meet with full support within the Israeli government, and six of the seven members of the Israeli Atomic Energy Commission quietly resigned. Nevertheless, the project was kept secret from the Israeli public and much of the cabinet. The Dimona site was under military control and was kept completely secure. It was publicly described as a textile factory.

The Israeli design of the reactor at Dimona was evidently

somewhat similar to the Savannah River reactor in South Carolina, which the U.S. uses to produce plutonium. France collaborated closely both in the design and in building the reactor, the above-ground reactor building, and an eight-story underground production facility during 1957–1959.[77] Cooperation ceased in 1959 only because De Gaulle felt that cooperation on weapons was too dangerous. Nevertheless, France continued to supply key equipment to complete the project. Further, Norway provided 20 tons of heavy water to Israel under the condition that the material would be used only for peaceful purposes and that Norway would be able to inspect its use. The heavy water was used at Dimona, and Norway was never allowed to inspect its use.[78]

A U.S. reconnaissance aircraft detected the characteristic shape of the above-ground reactor during an overflight of the area in 1960. When the U.S. requested an explanation, Ben Gurion claimed that the reactor was strictly for peaceful purposes, including industrial and medical research, and that the reactor had been kept secret to prevent Arab attacks. There are also some indications that gas and biological warfare research was underway at Dimona and the Weizman Institute at this time, but it is unclear what level of effort took place, if any, and whether it was defensive or focused on weapons production.[79]

A debate did occur within Israel over the creation of the Dimona reactor once U.S. questions exposed its existence. This led to the creation of a small anti-bomb movement, called the Committee for the Denuclearization of the Arab-Israeli Conflict. It also may have led to divisions within the Israeli government. Levi Eshkol replaced Ben Gurion as prime minister in 1963, and some sources indicate that he refused to fund the reactor out of government funds. As a result, Ben Gurion had to turn to Israeli industrialists and his supporters outside Israel. This may have been a reason that Israel began to build up a chain of foreign supporters in the U.S., France, Britain, and South Africa that later became critical to Israel's efforts to acquire fissile material and nuclear weapons technology.[80]

The work on the bomb project proceeded more slowly between 1963 and 1967, but the Dimona reactor went on-line in 1964. This was kept strictly secret. The Israeli government had made a quiet deal with the U.S. that it would not proceed to deploy nuclear weapons, and the U.S. agreed to sell Israel advanced conventional weapons like the A-4 Skyhawk and U.S. main battle tanks.[81] Nevertheless, Israel seems to have sent the spent fuel from its Dimona reactor to France for processing into weapons-grade plutonium.

Sources disagree over how much material was sent to France and reprocessed. Estimates of Israel's weapons production during the 1960s range anywhere from 1–2 to 15–20 weapons. While it is clear that

Israel built its own plutonium-reprocessing plant at some point in the 1970s, it is not clear exactly when this facility become operational. It seems likely that it was operational in the mid-1970s.[82]

Israel also aggressively sought out the material it needed to make large numbers of weapons from a number of new sources. At some point between 1964 and 1965, it seems to have acquired some 200 pounds of highly enriched uranium (9 to 22 bombs worth) from the Nuclear Materials and Equipment Corporation (NUMEC) in Apollo, Pennsylvania.

NUMEC also may have provided extensive access to the classified information stored at the plant. NUMEC was then headed by Zalman Shapiro, a former chemist on the staff of the Manhattan Project, a strong supporter of Israel, and co-owner of a food-processing plant in Israel. This firm was supposed to be examining the use of radiation to preserve foods. Shapiro co-owned the plant with the Israeli government and may have used it as a cover for exporting the material. NUMEC definitely gave a number of Israelis access to the plant. These included Raphael Eitan, a Mossad officer, Baruch Cinai, a metallurgist, and Ephraim Lahav, the scientific attache in Washington.

In 1967, Israel obtained additional material from Antwerp. The Mossad set up a dummy corporation in Italy and obtained the permits to import 200 tons of processed uranium ore, or "yellowcake." This material, which was enough to produce 40 to 50 bombs, was then diverted to Israel. Israel also seems to have obtained material from South Africa and Argentina, but the details are unclear. Israel only began its own yellowcake production from phosphate rock in the Negev in 1981.

Between 1967 and 1973, Israel adopted a strategy of undeclared nuclear capability. It made vague statements that implied it had nuclear weapons but had not assembled them, but it avoided any formal declaration. Israel conspicuously avoided singing the Non-Proliferation Treaty, however, and seems to have equipped its F-4s to deliver nuclear weapons after the U.S. agreed to sell the F-4s to Israel in 1968.

It is unclear how many weapons Israel had at the time of the 1973 war.[83] *Time* reported in April 1976 that Israel had hastily assembled its 13 nuclear bombs during the night of 8–9 October 1973 and sent them to nuclear arsenals.[84] This was one of the periods of greatest Arab success in the 1973 war, and such a report is credible. Some analysts have even speculated that it was Israeli warnings that it had assembled the weapons that led Henry Kissinger to agree to start the U.S. resupply airlift to Israel.[85] It is important to note, however, that this report has never been substantiated.

Other reports indicate that Israel had the improved Jericho II surface-to-surface missile in production as early as 1971, with a range of up to 300 miles and a 1,000–1,500 pound warhead. Israel did obtain the details of the Dassault MD620 and MD660 missiles and does seem to have started work on its own Jericho II adaptation of these designs as early as 1963, but these deployment reports seem premature. Other reports only put Jericho II production at 60 to 80 missiles by the mid-1970s. What is more likely is that Israel began to slowly deploy nuclear-armed Jericho IIs at some point in the late 1970s or early 1980s.[86]

Israel also faced at least the potential threat of Egyptian or Syrian use of chemical weapons in 1973. Egypt had used poison gas in the Yemens in the 1960s. Egypt continued its gas warfare research during the period between 1967 and 1973, and the USSR transferred at least some gas warfare technology to Egypt during 1972–1973.

These indicators were highly uncertain, however, and Israel did not take this threat seriously.[87] The IDF had little chemical weapons training when the 1973 war began. During the 1973 war, however, the Israelis captured large stocks of Egyptian and Syrian chemical defense gear, including the antidotes for nerve gas. While there are some indications that the Arab forces may simply have deployed standard-unit equipment sets provided by the USSR, the IDF felt that the threat was far more serious. Chemical warfare became a compulsory part of Israeli training, and IDF forces started training for chemical warfare at the brigade, divisional, and air-base level.

The state of Israeli nuclear testing has always been unclear. Sub-fission tests can confirm many of the performance details of a nuclear weapons design, and these tests are not detectable. There are reports that Israel and South Africa began cooperation on the development of both missiles and nuclear weapons in 1976, prepared for surface testing in the Kalahari Desert in 1977, and called the tests off after Britain, France, the Soviet Union, and the U.S. objected. These reports are unconfirmed, as are reports that Israel and South Africa detonated a small device in the southern Atlantic in September 1979. South African metallurgists, technicians, and scientists may also have worked at Dimona.

The exact methods with which Israel continued its nuclear weapons production in the late 1970s and 1980s are also unclear, although Israel seems to have adopted high-technology methods of enrichment like the use of laser isotope separation. By 1980, Israel seems to have had at least 100 nuclear weapons. By the mid-1980s, it seems to have had more than 200. This stockpile seems to have included some enhanced radiation weapons and some with variable yields of up to 100 kilotons or more.

As for delivery means, Israel had F-4 and F-16 fighters, and there are strong indications that Israel had now deployed up to 100 Jericho II missiles by the late 1970s to early 1980s and that some were deployed in sheltered sites in the Negev and Golan. The Jericho II is reported to have a range of at least 290 miles (480–560 kilometers). No one can confirm such reports of missile forces, but few experts doubt that Israel was producing up to ten nuclear weapons a year at its nuclear facility in Dimona throughout most of the 1980s.[88]

Beginning in 1983, however, Israel began to lose its monopoly on weapons of mass destruction. The Soviet Union, which had previously sold Syria FROG-7 and Scud B rockets, delivered longer range and far more accurate SS-21 missiles. It also became apparent that Syria was actively involved in the production of nerve gas and other chemical weapons and had at least started a serious biological weapons effort. For the first time, Israel faced the threat not only that the USSR might come to the aid of an Arab state but that an Arab state might acquire a significant first-strike or retaliatory capability.

While the USSR delivered only a relatively limited number of SS-21s to Syria, by the mid-1980s Israel faced the problem that Syria had well over 100 FROG, Scud, and SS-21 missiles. By 1987, it had 18 Scud launchers, 23 FROG-7 launchers, 12 SS-21 launchers, and over 200 missiles.[89]

Israel was particularly vulnerable to Syrian use of these systems because it was dependent on the ability to make free use of its air bases and, on fixed assembly centers, its reserves. This made Israel's military strength vulnerable to missiles carrying nerve gas warheads, and Israel's small population was heavily concentrated in Tel Aviv and a few other urban areas.

This growing vulnerability may have helped lead to the next development in Israel's nuclear effort, which was the testing of a much longer-range missile called the Jericho III which outside experts sometimes call the J3. This missile was said to use strap-down inertial guidance and was first tested in a firing into the Mediterranean at a range of 288 miles (460 kilometers). In May 1987, it was tested at a range of some 510 miles (820 kilometers). It seems to have been designed for ranges of 900–940 miles (1,450 kilometers), which would allow it to cover virtually all of the Arab world and even the southern USSR. These tests provoked strong Soviet protests but had little impact at a time when there were growing rumors that the USSR might sell Syria much longer range SS-23 missiles and long-range Su-24 strike aircraft.[90]

The threat to Israel grew steadily worse. In late 1987, Iran and Iraq began a "missile war" as part of their broader conflict; this demonstrated in brutal terms that long-range surface-to-surface missile warfare had become a permanent part of the regional balance. Iraq had already made extensive use of chemical weapons, beginning in 1984, but in early 1988, it made the massive use of such weapons a key feature of its successful offensives against Iran. Iran demonstrated its own ability to use long-range Silkworm surface-to-ship missiles.

It then became apparent that Saudi Arabia had bought CSS-2 IRBMs from China, although these seemed to have conventional warheads. Further, reports surfaced that Syria had reacted to the Soviet Union's agreement to destroy its longer-range theater missiles under the INF Treaty by buying Chinese M-9 missiles. This later purchase had a certain note of irony since Israel had been selling the PRC advanced military technology since 1984 and had signed a major new technical agreement in 1987.[91]

The prospects of the widespread proliferation of weapons of mass destruction became all too real. It was clear that Iran, Iraq, and Syria all had large-scale chemical warfare facilities in active production and new ones coming on-line, and Libya was just completing a major chemical warfare plant of its own. Egypt was caught attempting to smuggle long-range missile components out of the U.S. and the feedstock for chemical weapons from Canada. Both Iran and Iraq revived their nuclear weapons development efforts, and virtually every major power in the region began to seek long-range surface-to-surface missiles.

Israeli initial reaction was to continue development of the Jericho III missile program. It fired the missile again in November 1988 at ranges in excess of 500 miles. It is also possible that Israel now has the capability to develop missiles with much longer ranges which could cover much of the USSR. Livermore Laboratories calculated that the Shavit or Comet booster used to launch the Offeq 1 (Horizon satellite) was capable of delivering a warhead to ranges of 3,000 miles. Separate work by the Department of Defense indicated that the maximum range would be as much as 4,500 miles. There is no fundamental difference between a satellite launch vehicle and an intercontinental ballistic missile (ICBM) booster. U.S. officials note, however, that there are no current indications that Israel is developing the Shavit booster as an ICBM.[92]

It may be years before Israel's full reaction to these developments takes shape, and the situation may not be stable enough to permit Israel to do more than constantly change its plans to react to changes in the Arab threat. It is clear, however, that Israel is already stepping up both its retaliatory and defensive capabilities. The Jericho follow-ons are one symbol of these retaliatory capabilities. Israel also revitalized its own chemical warfare facilities south of Dimona in the mid-1980s, after Syria's deployment of chemical weapons and Iraq's use of these weapons in the Iran-Iraq War. Israel may now have production facilities for at least two types of chemical weapons and may have have stepped up its studies of biological weapons as well as chemical ones.

Israel's search for defense capabilities is going on at two levels: passive and active. In terms of passive defense, Israel is steadily improving the chemical defense capabilities of its armed forces and the overall capabilities of its civil defense. The IDF is now getting some of the most intensive nuclear-biological-chemical (NBC) warfare training outside the Warsaw Pact. The *IDF Journal* has steadily increased its emphasis on chemical defense since 1986. The IDF has produced and deployed advanced warning and sensor devices, greatly improved its quantity and quality of decontamination gear, increased training, and provided better protection gear for both manpower and equipment. The IDF Engineering Corps has chemical defense as a major mission and supports the IDF in extensive field exercises. NBC defense is now a compulsory part of every IDF exercise, and some critical land and air equipment and facilities have emergency protection against sudden chemical attack.[93]

Israeli Defense Minister Yitzak Rabin announced in 1987 that Israel had revitalized its civil defense effort and now had some four million gas masks in underground storage. Israel issued 37,000 gas masks and protection gear on a test basis in 1988 to two towns—one near Lebanon and one near Tel Aviv. This was a first step toward a national distribution program. It also began examining a national shelter program.[94]

In regard to active defense, Israel has changed its air-strike and air-defense plans to improve the IAF's capability to reduce air penetrations that might deliver chemical weapons, including the use of the large high-altitude cruise missiles the USSR has provided to some Arab forces. There are reports that Israel can now deliver retaliatory strikes with both chemical and enhanced radiation or low-yield nuclear weapons. While Israel has never said it would use such weapons, it is interesting to note Lt. General Dan Shomron's comments on how Israel would deal with the Saudi deployment of the CSS-2 and the threat of Arab missile attacks.[95]

> We have three answers. One is our ability to handle these missiles offensively and defensively. The second is the ability to retaliate. The third is civil defense. . . . Because of their inferiority in the air, the Arab countries wanted to find a way to bring terror. . . . That is what the missiles can achieve, they cannot win wars. . . . We can hit them much harder than they can hit us . . . there is a natural tendency to develop chemical warfare . . . and at a later stage, nuclear weapons . . . what is of concern is

the direction of the development . . . towards a more effective, threatening warhead.

Israel has undertaken two major high-technology developments related to the threat of weapons of mass destruction. One is the development of its own satellite program discussed earlier. Satellites are useful not only for warning and tactical purposes, but they also provide a way of monitoring Arab developments in producing weapons of mass destruction and the Arab deployment of missiles. They also allow Israel to greatly improve its long-range targeting capability and to strike at small military targets rather than large area targets like cities.

Israel is also developing its own missile defense concept. It is called the Theater Ballistic Missile Test Bed. This program is currently costed at $35 million, with the U.S. paying for 72 percent and Israel paying for 28 percent.[96] It is examining a system that includes an early warning and detection system, a layered intercept-kill system, and a battlefield management/command, control, communications, and intelligence (BM/C³I) system. Early warning would be provided by a mix of balloon-carried sensors, ground-based radars, RPVs overflying critical launch sites, and satellite coverage.

The layered defense system would include the Arrow anti-tactical ballistic missile (ATBM) for medium- to high-altitude intercepts. The Arrow is reported to be able to reach altitudes (or slant ranges) of up to 40 kilometers and speeds of up to Mach 9. The Mach 4.5 close-in defense missile would be the Rafale AB-10 and would be able to reach ranges of 10–20 kilometers. It would be deployed to defend key military and population targets. The Israeli firm of Tadiran is developing the BM/C³I concept.[97] The SDIO in the U.S. is paying for roughly $128 million of the estimated $160-million cost of developing the Arrow.[98]

Most U.S. experts feel the Israeli design is conceptually sound, and the U.S. has agreed to help fund the Arrow.[99] Israel, however, may run into many of the same problems as with the Lavi. While Israeli experts put the development cost of the Arrow at $140 million a year for two to three years, U.S. experts put the cost at $200 million annually. Even though Israel will only have to pay 20 percent of the development costs of the system, it is far from clear that Israel can fund the deployment of a layered, or even Arrow-based, system. While IDF planners generally feel that the Arrow is far more suited to their emphasis on deterrence, defense, and retaliatory capabilities than the Lavi, there is no question that the Arrow competes with other force-improvement priorities and is cutting into Israel's ability to maintain and modernize its conventional forces.[100]

As for Israel's nuclear strategy, the details of Israel's overall strike options, tactics, targeting plans, and modernization programs remain highly classified. It is also impossible to predict how Israel will decide if it is forced to choose between maintaining its conventional superiority and depending on weapons of mass destruction. At least some Israeli defense officials, including Shimon Peres, have long raised the possibility that Israel should shift from reliance on conventional forces for deterrence of major conflicts to reliance on nuclear forces. This issue has so far been resolved by maintaining the policy of reliance on strong conventional forces and an undeclared nuclear capability. Thus, Israel tacitly gets all the benefits of nuclear capability without the political costs of an openly declared deterrent. It is far from clear that the issue can be resolved this way in the 1990s.

The combination of the deployment of chemical weapons in Syria and the cost and manpower pressures on the IDF may force Israel into a more overt declaration of nuclear capability. This could have considerable importance given the size of Israel's present nuclear forces. There is virtually no doubt that Israel has at least 200 nuclear weapons that can be rapidly assembled and that, even if all the reports about missile forces are wrong, Israel can deliver these at ranges over 1,500 kilometers using refueled fighter-bombers.[101]

The end result is that Israel will confront the problems of constantly having to redefine its role in nuclear, chemical, and biological warfare and of establishing new levels of deterrence. This may even extend to deterring the Soviet threat of using nuclear weapons to support Syria in some future conflict, although reports that the Jericho III will have effective coverage of the southern USSR are far from confirmed. At the same time, the proliferation of weapons of mass destruction may well push Israel toward more reliance on a defensive posture on the land rather than an offensive posture. Israel's 1982 invasion of Lebanon may well be its last attempt at political wars involving major land invasions of the Arab world. The growing stockpiles of weapons of mass destruction on both sides make it harder and harder to avoid wars which focus on civilian and economic targets.[102]

Debates Over Force Restructuring and High-Command Issues

Given these pressures on Israel's forces and use of defense resources, it is not surprising that Israel has faced a number of serious debates within its high command. In addition to the Lavi dispute, various military critics within Israel have charged that Israel has given political stability higher precedence than command capability. They have cited the promotion of Lt. General Moshe Levy to chief of staff, following the forced resignation of Raphael Eitan, as a key example of a staff officer who they claimed lacked combat experience and who was promoted to a key position over such combat commanders as General Avigdor Ben-Gal and General Daniel Shomron. They also charged that Levy was a key example of a commander who added needless layers to Israel's command structure.

One example of such criticism came from Colonel Emmanuel Wald, the former head of long-range planning of the Israeli general staff. Wald issued a 700-page, four-volume criticism of these trends. He charged that Israel was losing its offensive capability and had politicized its promotion and command structure. He was particularly critical of the steady loss of high-quality mid-level officers and charged that efforts to create an effective central command structure have simply resulted in creating a bloated and ineffective bureaucracy.[103]

The seriousness of this debate is reflected in the fact that when Dan Shomron was eventually appointed chief of staff in April 1987, he promised a major shake-up of the IDF. He stated that greater emphasis was needed on the ground forces and less on the air force and that more emphasis was needed on quality than quantity. Shomron did help kill the Lavi and issued plans to reduce the number of brigadier generals in the IDF by nearly 25 percent, but the combination of the Lavi affair and the Arab uprising in the occupied territories that began in December 1987 seem to have delayed his reforms.[104]

The Israeli election of 1988 also exhibited a considerable polarization between Left and Right among retired military, with some favoring the trade of territory for peace and others favoring a strong hard line against the Palestinians. Israelis began to talk about "generals of the right" and "generals of the left," as exemplified by the Officers and Academics for Peace and Security to the Right (3 generals, 20 brigadiers, and 115 reserve officers) and the Council for Peace and Security to the Left (34 generals, 86 brigadiers, and 115 colonels).[105]

These groups revived all of the long-standing debates over the need for strategic depth versus the need for security and the legitimacy of annexation of all the occupied territories versus the threat that Israel would end up as a state in which Arabs were the dominant part of the population. The Israeli officers serving in the high command of the IDF seemed to favor the search for a peace settlement slightly more than the hard-line approach, but the real message of the comments of active and retired military officers on the issues in the campaign was that Israel's military and strategic planners faced as many serious debates about the future as they had ever had to face in the past.

Syrian Force Developments Since 1982

Like Israel, Syria has faced serious financial constraints on its ability to react to the lessons of the 1982 conflict and to its other desires to change and modernize its forces. Like Israel, Syria has sought to use modern technology to modernize its forces and has drawn some of the same lessons from the 1982 conflict and previous wars. Syria, however, has tended to emphasize numerical parity with Israel over force quality and the ability to use technology effectively. Unlike Israel, Syria has lacked an external partner capable of giving it the level of technology transfer it needs. As a result, Syria has tended to mirror many of the force developments in the USSR, but with a much lower level of technology and military effectiveness.

The easiest part of Syria's search for parity has been its effort to make increases in military manpower. Total active Syrian military manpower rose from 222,500 in 1982 to 404,000 in 1989. To put these numbers in perspective, the CIA puts the total Syrian labor force at 2,400,000. It estimates that there are 2,398,000 males in the age group from 15 to 49 and that out of 1,341,000 males, 839,000 are fit for military service. It estimates that 132,000 males reach military age (19) annually.[106] The IISS estimates that there are a total of about 542,000 males in the age group from 18 to 22 years and about 706,000 males in the age group from 23 to 32 years.[107]

The main resource limitation Syria has faced in developing its forces is a lack of financing. It has had to spend roughly 50 percent of its budget on military forces, and it has not been able to sustain increases in military spending through economic growth. Quite to the contrary, military spending has been a powerful force limiting Syria's ability to expand its civil economy.

Estimates of Syria's military spending after 1982 vary according to source, but the U.S. estimates that Syrian spending rose from $2.4 billion in 1981 to $2.8 billion in 1982, $4.2 billion in 1983, $4.3 billion in 1984, and $4.5 billion in 1985. This meant that military spending increased from 15–16 percent of the GNP to 23 percent, and from 35 percent of Central Government Expenditures to roughly 42 percent.[108] More recent estimates by the IISS indicate that Syrian military spending was at $3.68 billion in 1986 and $3.95 billion in 1987. This estimate seems to reflect a legitimate drop in spending after 1985. Syria simply could not continue to fund military spending of over $4 billion a year.[109]

In recent years, Syria's defense efforts have strained its economy and society to the breaking point. By 1985–1986, there were growing signs that President Assad was losing his former tight authority over the military and his intelligence branches, and new bombing incidents have occurred in the capital. Food and key consumer goods are in short supply. Meat and drugs are rising sharply in price.

The Gulf states have cut back sharply on their aid to Syria because of the cuts in their oil revenues, their objections to Syria's support of Iran in the Iran-Iraq War, and their objections to Syria's actions in Lebanon. Syria's annual growth in GDP fell from nearly 10 percent in 1981 to a steady decline of 1–2 percent after 1982. Syria's balance of trade deteriorated steadily, and its foreign exchange reserves dropped about $100 million. This is a poor climate in which to try to fund both modernization and high levels of active manpower and readiness, and Syria was unable to match its quantity with quality.[110]

The only reason Syria was able to compete at all with Israel was Soviet arms sales and military assistance, most of which were financed by Kuwait and Saudi Arabia. Syria imported $2.6 billion worth of arms in 1981, $2.6 billion worth in 1982, $3.5 billion worth in 1983, $2.1 billion worth in 1984, $1.5 billion worth in 1985, and $1.1 billion worth in 1986.[111] Virtually all of these arms came from the Soviet Union. These imports raised Syria's total arms contracts with the USSR to over $19 billion.[112] In fact, Syria has received between two and three times more arms imports than Israel since 1982. Roughly $9.6 billion out of a total of $10.83 billion worth of Syrian arms imports during 1982–1986 came from the USSR.[113]

In recent years, however, the Soviet Union has denied Syria further military credits and has put the supply of spare parts and ammunition on a cash payment basis. Syria has been unable to pay Yugoslavia for 200 T-72s it purchased from that country. It is now denied credit by most European and Third World arms suppliers. This has helped lead the USSR to refuse to supply modern attack and strike aircraft like the Su-25 and Su-24 and to limit the sale of MiG-29s to only 24 aircraft. The USSR may, however, also have denied Syria such systems—as well as long-range surface-to-surface missiles like the SS-23—because of disagreements over Syrian policy toward Iraq and Lebanon and an increasing Soviet interest in reaching an Arab-Israeli peace settlement.

The Soviet Union has provided other forms of help. Syria had over 4,000 Soviet military technicians in the country during the period immediately after its 1982 war with Israel, including many operating its SA-5 surface-to-air missiles and C^3I/BM sites. Some 1,000 Soviet advisors have departed since 1984, however, and some SA-5 sites now seem to be largely Syrian operated.[114] Even so, there were still roughly 3,000 Soviet bloc military technicians in Syria in 1988.[115] Syria has also been one of the few remaining countries receiving significant

Soviet economic aid. It had over 4,700 Soviet bloc economic aid technicians in country in 1988. It had received over $1 billion in economic aid since 1983, although it did not receive any such aid during 1986–1987. Syria also received substantial East European aid, although this virtually ceased in 1986.[116]

The Soviet connection, however, has not been an easy one. Syrian and Soviet relations have been strained by serious differences over Syria's intervention in Lebanon, and the USSR seems to be much more concerned with Syria's defense than its search for parity in offensive capabilities. The Soviet Union has conspicuously concentrated on strengthening Syria's defense capabilities within its own boundaries, and this has been even more true in recent years.

In March and April 1988, the USSR sent three high-level military delegations to Syria. These included delegations headed by Lt. General K.I. Kobets, the commander of Signal Corps and deputy chief of staff; Marshall Alexandr Efimov, the commander of the Soviet Air Force; and Colonel General Vladimir Pikalov, commander of the chemical warfare forces. The thrust of all these missions seems to have been that the USSR would help Syria consolidate its military modernization but not reach parity in offensive capabilities or support Syria's efforts to acquire weapons of mass destruction.[117]

The USSR has not been willing to give Syria many of the first-line weapons that Syria has asked for and often has restricted it to inferior export versions of the Soviet systems it has provided. For example, Syria is getting only two squadrons of MiG-29s, is getting them after Iraq and India, and is getting them two years later than it first expected to. Syria sought the SS-23 missile very actively, but the only tangible sign of such Soviet deliveries is a chrome-plated model of the SS-23 that once sat on Syrian Defense Minister Mustafa Tlas's desk.

Syria has also faced problems because of the growing cost of Soviet equipment. Kuwaiti aid has ceased, and Saudi aid has declined sharply from its peak of $540 million to $600 million a year. Iran no longer provides substantial oil aid. The Soviet Union generally insists on cash, and Syria has had severe problems in paying for the equipment it wants.[118]

Developments in Syrian Land Forces

In spite of Syria's funding problems, Syrian active army manpower strength increased from 170,000 in 1982 to 250,000 in 1989, with 130,000 conscripts. Army reserves increased from 100,000 to 270,000, and Syria established a special reserve of 50,000 men for rapid call up.

Syria has steadily expanded its order of battle. It built up its total strength in division equivalents from six divisions in 1982 to nine in

1986. Syria's divisional order of battle in late 1984 included the guards, 1st and 3rd armored divisions (largely T-72M tanks), 10th and 11th armored divisions (T-62M/K tanks), 5th and 7th mechanized infantry divisions (largely T-55 tanks), and 9th Mechanized Infantry Division (largely T-54/55 tanks). Syria raised its number of armored divisions from four to five in 1986. It also increased its mechanized divisions from two to three and created a full special-forces division. Many of Syria's older T-55s and T-54s were phased out for T-72s.[119]

In 1989, the Syrian order of battle included one Presidential Guard armored division, four regular armored divisions (3 armored, 1 mechanized, and 1 artillery brigade each), two mechanized divisions (2 armored, 2 mechanized, and 1 artillery brigade each). Each of these active divisions had 1 brigade at cadre strength. Syria clearly learned something about mobilization from the Israeli example.

Syria also had seven independent special forces regiments and a special forces division with five para-commando regiments. Its major independent support units included two artillery brigades, three surface-to-surface missile brigades, and nine surface-to-air missile battalions (27 batteries) with SA-6. The army also had two coastal defense brigades with SSC-1B Sepal and SSC-3 surface-to-ship missiles and long-range artillery.

Like Israel, Syria also improved the tailoring of its forces to deal with its primary threat. Syria significantly increased its deployments on the Golan during the early and mid-1980s.[120] Two of the new armored divisions—the 10th and 11th—were formed in 1983–1984 out of reserve and independent active brigades. Syria then built up a strength of three divisions in the Golan area, two of which were mechanized, although these were left in garrison and were not combat deployed. The new units gave Syria a new reserve in the Golan while freeing its 1st and 3rd armored divisions for independent action. Roughly 2,000 of Syria's main battle tanks were deployed within an 8 to 12 hour striking distance of Israel in early 1987, although Syria stood down some of its forces in 1988.[121]

Syria also strengthened its barrier defenses as a result of the 1982 war. Right after the fighting in 1982, Syria began to build a new defense line 10 kilometers from the Golan. It dug in and fortified large amounts of new artillery and created major new antitank obstacles. There are large earthworks with firing positions and obstacles to create kill zones and very large and complex minefields. These efforts now provide three major defense lines between the Golan and Damascus, and all are now covered by a belt of overlapping air-defense systems.[122]

This Syrian search for mass has been accompanied by improved maneuver training, improved training of both tank forces, and improved training of the antitank units and other defense forces that performed well in the Bekaa in 1982. Syria has not, however, been able to sustain past training levels as it has increased its manpower. Overall training standards began to decline in 1985–1986 and continued to remain at inadequate levels though early 1989.[123] Training quality and activity levels now seem likely to remain inadequate through at least 1990. Syrian combined-arms and combined-operations capabilities remain poor by Israeli, Western, and even Iraqi standards.

Syria greatly strengthened its commando forces as a result of the lessons it has learned from recent wars. It has built up its strength from about six battalions in 1973 (the 1st Commando Group with five battalions plus the 82nd Parachute Battalion) to at least 10 battalions at the time of the 1982 fighting.[124] It since has more than doubled these formations. Each of these units or *Fughs* has three infantry platoons with a large variety of weapons, including antitank guided weapons, special purpose machine guns, and rocket launchers. A debate exists over how many men are in these forces; some estimates indicate that each battalion has 250–350 men and that total manning may be as low as 9,000 and as high as 14,000. About 2,500–3,000 of these seem to be heliborne.[125]

As for equipment, Soviet arms sales allowed Syria to reach the point where it had more tank and combat air strength than Israel.[126] It acquired at least 500 new T-72/T-72M tanks after the end of the war and had about 950 T-72/T-72Ms in late 1988, out of a total main battle tank force of nearly 4,000.[127] It also has 2,100 T-54s/T-55s and 1,000 T-62 M/Ks. Some Israeli experts feel that some of Syria's T-72s have the advanced reactive armor and improved guns and fire-control systems present on Soviet T-72 tanks, but U.S. experts disagree.[128]

Syria has learned from past wars that it must give priority to equipping its most effective units. The T-72s go to its first-line armored units and Republican Guards. Its T-62s go to its second-rate armored units, and its T-55s go to its mechanized division. Syria could not, however, absorb all of these tanks into its active forces. About 1,100 of these are in static positions or in storage. Like most advanced equipment in Syrian forces, overall maintenance standards are poor.

Syria built up a much more modern force of other armored vehicles, following somewhat in Israel's footsteps. In 1989, it had 500 BRDM-2 reconnaissance and antitank vehicles, 2,350 BMP-1 mechanized infantry vehicles, and 1,300 BTR-40, 50, 60, and 152 and OT-64 armored personnel carriers. This is more than twice Syria's total of other armored vehicle forces in 1982, which then totalled roughly 1,600 vehicles. It gives Syrian infantry far more mobility and firepower. In

TABLE 4.2 Syrian Tank Strength: 1967–1988

Type	1967	1973	1979	1982	1988
PT-76	—	100	100	—	—
T-34	200	230	200	—	—
T-54/T-55	150	900	1,500	2,200	2,100
T-62	—	—	900	1,000	1,000
T-72	—	—	—	790	950
JS-3	—	30	—	—	—
Non-Soviet	50	—	—	—	—
Total	400	1,260	2,700	3,990	4,050

SOURCE: Adapted from various editions of IISS, *Military Balance* (London: International Institute for Strategic Studies), and Yohanan Ramati, "Moscow and Damascus," *Global Affairs* (Spring 1989), pp. 97–108.

many ways, Syria has evolved toward the Israeli concept of infantry mechanization, at least in terms of equipment, although it has not acquired the overall level of armor that Israel acquired for its infantry and rear-services elements.

Syria made only limited increases in its artillery strength after the 1982 war, in spite of the expansion of its combat unit strength. It went from roughly 2,600 artillery weapons to 2,800 in 1989. Syria did, however, make significant increases in its number of self-propelled weapons. In early 1989, it had 36 122-mm D-30 guns on T-34 tank chassis, 72 Soviet M-1974 (2S1) 122-mm guns, some ISU-152-mm guns, and 42 M-1972 (2S3) 152-mm howitzers. Syria put some of its older towed guns into storage and made serious efforts to acquire modern fire control and artillery radar systems. Syria also improved the training and target-acquisition capabilities of its multiple rocket launcher forces and deployed more of its 120-mm mortar forces in direct support. These changes were not radical, but they involved changes that made Syrian artillery organization closer to Israel's emphasis on the rapid movement of artillery and gave Syrian forces the capability to provide more immediate support to maneuver units.

Syria sought to improve its tank and antitank warfare capabilities in a number of other ways. It unsuccessfully sought to upgrade its Soviet-made tanks with British and other Western fire-control systems and cited its experiences in 1973 and 1982 as a reason for seeking such improvements. It also sought to buy British and French antitank guided weapons systems.

In practice, however, the only Western antitank weapons Syria has been able to acquire are a limited number of French Milan man-portable systems. It remains dependent on Soviet-made T-12 100-mm antitank guns and some 1,300 AT-3 Saggers and an unknown number of AT-4 Spiggots and AT-5s.[129] While a number of Syria's BDRM-2s are equipped with AT-3s, Syrian sources cite the lack of modern Western ATGMs with easy-to-operate third-generation guidance systems as a major problem in equipping Syrian forces. (Soviet systems still require the operator to simultaneously track both the missile and target and guide the missile with minimal help in stabilizing the system.)

Syria has also continued to expand its anti-aircraft gun strength, partly as a response to Israel's ability to locate and kill its surface-to-air missiles during 1982. Syria now has approximately 1,700 air defense guns, including ZU-23-2 towed guns, ZSU-23-4 radar-guided guns, M-1939 37-mm towed guns, S-60 57-mm towed guns, ZSU-57-3 57-mm guns, M-1939 and M-1944 85-mm towed guns, and KS-19 100-mm guns. It has consistently found the proliferation of light 23-mm guns to be far more effective than using limited numbers of higher caliber weapons.

Syrian Weapons of Mass Destruction

Syria reorganized its surface-to-surface missile brigades after 1982. It had more than 36 SS-21, 24 FROG-7, and 18 Scud B surface-to-surface missile fire units and Sepal SS-1B and SSC-3 coastal-defense missile fire units by late 1988.

Syria's surface-to-surface missile forces were organized into three surface-to-surface missile brigades, with another brigade completing its formation. The oldest unit is the 69th Rocket Brigade, which was first created in 1972 and was equipped with Syria's first FROG-7s. This unit had 18 transport-erector-launchers (TELs) and reloaders in 1988. Another brigade had SS-1c Scud-B missiles, with three battalions and 18 launchers. A third brigade had four battalions, with a total of 36 SS-21 Scarab missiles with a range of 120 kilometers, and a fourth brigade, with SSC-1B Sepal medium-range (300-kilometer) missiles, was completing formation at Latakia and Tartus. There were reports in 1987 that Syria might also be building a fifth brigade using the SS-23 Spider missiles deployed outside Damascus, but these reports seem to have been false.[130]

These changes involved far more than simple increases in strength. Syria came to see surface-to-surface missiles as a potential means of overcoming Israel's advantage in the air and also as a means of delivering weapons of mass destruction. This allowed such forces to both counter Israel's nuclear weapons and furnish a means of attacking Israel's air bases and mobilization centers.

Syrian troops steadily increased their NBC training after 1982. U.S. sources indicated as early as 1984 that Syria has actively been manufacturing and deploying nerve and other gases since the 1982 war. Syria seems to have modified a variant of the Soviet ZAB series incendiary bomb to use chemical agents and may have modified the PTAB-500 cluster bomb to carry chemical bomblets. It has chemical artillery shells and chemical rounds for its artillery. Syrian FROG and possibly Scud missiles seem to be acquiring chemical warheads.

By 1988, it was clear that Syria was seeking to produce biological as well as chemical weapons. While only chemical weapons were being produced in any quantity, Israeli experts felt these weapons included persistent nerve agents. These Syrian developments also seem to have aroused Soviet concern. Colonel General Vladimir Pikalov, the commander of the Soviet Army's chemical warfare forces, led a delegation to Syria in March 1988 whose main purpose seems to have been to warn Syria of the dangers of chemical warfare and possibly to warn Syria that the USSR would not support it if it used such weapons.[131]

The SS-21s in Syrian hands do not have chemical warheads, and Syria would find it extremely difficult to develop such a capability without Soviet support. The problems of developing and testing an advanced missile warhead are far beyond current Syrian capabilities. Given the accuracy of the SS-21, there is at least some long-term risk that Syria could eventually fire nerve agents successfully at Israeli air bases, C^3I sites, Dimona, and mobilization centers and seriously degrade Israeli conventional and nuclear capabilities.[132] At least some Syrian SS-21 surface-to-surface missile units seem to be kept in concrete shelters in the mountains near Damascus and in the Palmyra region, although they deploy forward in an emergency.[133]

Syria has also actively sought longer-range missiles that will give it the range to attack any target in Israel and which have the accuracy to attack Israel's air bases in the south and the nuclear facility at Dimona.[134] From 1984 onward, Syria unsuccessfully sought more SS-21s and the SS-12 or SS-23 missile from the USSR. It was particularly interested in the SS-23, which has a 500-kilometer range and which could have hit targets throughout Israel and Jordan and much of Iraq. It is clear that both President Assad and the Syrian defense minister actively sought such missiles and asked for SS-25 ICBMs once it was clear that the USSR would agree to the INF treaty.

Although various press reports appeared that Syria had established an SS-23 site, had a brigade of SS-23s, and had even deployed the SS-25, none of these reports has been confirmed. The USSR seems to have consistently refused to strengthen Syrian missile forces and to have shown considerable constraint in giving Syria advanced strike fighters. This helps explain why Syria sought M-9 missiles, with a range of 175 to 375 miles, from the PRC. According to some U.S. intelligence sources, Syria ordered these missiles in 1988, and they will be delivered during 1990 to 1991, although the PRC has denied this. Syria clearly feels it needs such missiles as a means of countering Israel's air supremacy. Syria not only is stockpiling nerve gas and other chemical agents, it is actively attempting to develop biological weapons.[135]

Syria's Search for More Effective Air Power

Syria has reacted to its defeat in 1982 by seeking more effective air power that can cope with Israel's technical superiority. It raised its total air force manpower from 50,000 men, including the Air Defense Command, in 1982, to 40,000 men in the Air Force alone in 1988.[136] It raised its combat air strength from 450 aircraft and 16 armed helicopters in 1982 to 448 combat aircraft and 110 armed helicopters in 1988. Syria not only replaced all the fighters it lost in 1982, it raised its Flogger F MiG-23BN strength from 50 to 60 aircraft and added 50 more Flogger E/G MiG-23s to its air-defense force. According to some reports, it converted the 25 MiG-25As in its air-defense force to 35 MiG-25E/Us. Syria bought 15 MiG-29s and sought Su-24s, Su-27s, and MiG-31s.

In early 1990, Syria will have a total of eight fighter ground-attack squadrons, with five squadrons of 3/33 Su-22s and 2/60 MiG-23BNs, and 14 interceptor squadrons, with five modern squadrons of 1/35 MiG-25s, 3/80 MiG-23MFs, and 1/15 MiG-29s. Syria also had 2/39 MiG-17s (in a dual role as trainers) and 1/15 Su-7s in its fighter attack forces, and 9/172 MiG-21s in its air-defense forces. It had 6 MiG-25R reconnaissance aircraft.[137]

It is notable, however, that the MiG-23s delivered to Syria after 1982 were virtually antiques by the standards of the late 1980s. They had none of the advanced attack-mission capabilities of attack fighters like the MiG-27 or air-defense capabilities of the MiG-29. They still had serious limitations in their radar and computer capabilities, even in medium- and high-altitude combat, and they had limited immunity to Israeli electronic warfare capabilities.[138]

The 24 MiG-29s were the only fighters in Syrian inventory with a real look-down/shoot-down capability.[139] These modern fighters do not have the fly-by-wire capabilities of U.S. fighters or all the advanced features of the new MiG-35. They do, however, have roughly the maneuverability of the F-16A, F-18, and Mirage 2000. They can outperform Western fighters in areas like knife-edge passes and tail slides, a maneuver used to break the track of Doppler radars in air-to-air combat. They had good short-take-off capability to use damaged or

TABLE 4.3 Syrian Combat Aircraft Strength: 1967–1988

Type	1967	1973	1979	1982	1988
MiG-17	20	80	50	85	38
MiG-21	5	200	215	200	172
MiG-23	—	—	64	82	140
MiG-25	—	—	—	24	35
MiG-27	—	—	—	—	30
MiG-29	—	—	—	—	24
Su-7	—	30	60	18	15
Su-20/22	—	—	—	40	33
Il-28	—	16	—	—	—
Non-Soviet	—	—	—	—	—
Total	25	326	389	449	492

SOURCE: Adapted from various editions of IISS, *Military Balance* (London: International Institute for Strategic Studies), and Yohanan Ramati, "Moscow and Damascus," *Global Affairs* (Spring 1989), pp. 97–108.

unimproved runways, although their high landing speed may present problems.

The version of the MiG-29 deployed with Soviet forces is armed with a single-barrel 30-mm gun linked to a laser rangefinder. It has provision for six underwing pylons and can carry six radar-guided AA-10 Alamo A air-to-air missiles or short-range AA-11 Archer air-to-air missiles. The MiG-29 can also carry bombs and rockets and be used as an attack aircraft. It has a coherent pulse-Doppler radar with a look-down/shoot-down capability and can detect fighter-sized targets to ranges of 100 nautical miles. This radar is backed up by an infrared search-and-track system and rangefinder, which is linked to a helmet-mounted sight which the pilot can use to track IR air-to-air missiles instead of the limited visual coverage provided by a conventional heads-up display. The aircraft has the Odd Rods IFF system and at least three electronic warfare antennas. It does, however, have a relatively large radar cross-section.[140]

The MiG-29s sent to Syria lack all the avionics and countermeasure capabilities of the Soviet version of the fighter. Further, they have far inferior electronic warfare capabilities, avionics, computers, and combat displays compared to Israel's F-15s and F-16s. No Syrian attack aircraft had avionics capable of the accuracy and night and all-weather performance of even Israel's F-4s, and Syria had very limited reconnaissance assets. Syria has not received any Su-24s, Su-27s, or MiG-31s, although there were indications in late 1988 that it might receive one or two squadrons of Su-24s as "compensation" for not receiving Soviet long-range surface-to-surface missiles and to balance Saudi and Jordanian acquisition of long-range strike fighters like the Tornado.

Syria did improve its flight-safety and basic-training procedures after 1982. Syrian Air Force maintenance and training standards did not improve strikingly after 1982, partly because of the lack of spare parts and underfunding. Western observers noted a number of major maintenance problems in Syrian units and a lack of realism in air-to-air and air-to-ground training in 1988 and 1989.

Syria has recognized that it must improve its battle management. Since 1984, it has received Soviet remotely piloted RPVs, including the UR-1, SD-3, and a new Soviet type.[141] It has improved its air and missile C^3I system, added improved low-altitude acquisition and EW/GCI radars, and is attempting to fully automate its Vector 2 air-control and warning system.[142] While it has not made major advances relative to Israel in targeting, electronic warfare capability, or air battle management, it has aggressively sought to improve all of its assets. Its major problem has been the unavailability of the most advanced Soviet weapons and technology or similar systems from the West.

Syria clearly felt that its attack helicopters served it well in 1982. Some sources indicate that Syria now has as many as 220 attack and assault helicopters, although it seems likely that it has only about 150. Syria felt its Gazelles equipped with HOT missiles performed particularly well in 1982. These were used in roving pairs against IDF tanks and armored fighting vehicles rather than as close-support weapons. Although Syria took nearly 25 percent losses (7 shot down and 2 captured) it found its helicopters had a freedom of action and survivability it could not achieve with fixed-wing aircraft. In 1989, Syria had built up to 50 French SA-342L Gazelles and had increased its Mi-24 attack helicopter strength from 12 to 50.[143] It also had 25 armed Mi-8s and 60 Mi-8 transport helicopters with light armament. It also had 30 Mi-17s with light armament and 10 Mi-2 Hoplites.[144]

In contrast, Syria has made only marginal improvements in its fixed-wing airlift. It now has two squadrons with 4 An-24s, 4 An-26s, 4 IL-76s, 6 Tu-134s, and 3 Mystere-Falcon 20Fs. Its only other major air formations are training units with 90 L-39s, 70 L-29s, and 20 MB-233s.

Syrian Air Defenses and the Syrian Air-Defense Command

Syria has tried to act on the lessons it learned in 1982 about the vulnerability of its land-based air-defense systems. It has increased its independent Air Defense Command to a total strength of 60,000 men. It has some 20 air-defense brigades with 95 surface-to-air missile batteries versus 50 batteries in 1982. Syria raised its medium and heavy surface-to-air missile unit strength from 23 units in 1976 to over 63 in 1986. Syria now has an estimated 200–240 SA-6 launchers and 320–392 SA-2 and SA-3 launchers. Syria has moved its air-defense net forward, including SA-6, SA-8, and SA-13 launchers. It also has improved its surface-to-air missile strength to a point where such air defenses virtually saturate its border areas, as well as cover all major military facilities and cities.

Syria has also acquired two SA-5 long-range surface-to-air missile regiments (each with two battalions of two batteries each) and as many as 48 improved SA-5 missile launchers. The SA-5s are relatively slow flying missiles but are useful in disrupting the operations of Israel's electronic warfare, command, and air-control and warning aircraft. Syria feels that the disruption or destruction of these aircraft is one of the critical lessons of the 1982 fighting.

The Soviets furnished the SA-5 to Syria in late 1982 and early 1985. They provided four battalions with 24 launchers. Two battalions were deployed at Dumayr, some 40 kilometers east of Damascus, and two at Shansar in northern Syria, southeast of Homs. The USSR agreed to provide similar systems to Libya in November 1984.

It is unclear, however, what variant of the SA-5 has been deployed to Syria. Relatively small changes in model are important because the SA-5 has had a troubled development history, and the more recent versions incorporate important improvements in electronics and terminal maneuvering capabilities which are critical to successful attacks on aircraft with electronic countermeasure capability. Syria may well have older versions of the SA-5. This would allow it to harass the IDF's slow-flying electronic warfare and command aircraft, but the SA-5s would probably be suppressed long before they achieved any kills.[145]

The SA-5 Gammon, or SA-200, dates back to 1963. It is a very large missile that is 10.6 meters long and 0.86 meters in diameter and has a top speed in excess of Mach 4. It has a minimal range of 60–80 kilometers, a nominal slant range of 250 kilometers, and a maximum ceiling of 30 kilometers. It uses the PRV-11 Side Net height-finding radar and Bar Lock or Back Net early-warning and acquisition radars. It also uses the Square Pair H-band fire-control radar.

The SA-5 was developed to kill U.S. bombers and reconnaissance aircraft at medium to high altitudes. The first version, the SA-5a, was obsolete before it was deployed and lacked the maneuverability, electronic warfare capability, and lethality to successfully attack U.S. bombers. The SA-5b was deployed around 1970 with a nuclear warhead but still lacked effective maneuverability and electronic warfare capability. The SA-5c was deployed around 1975, with improved capability in every area and both conventional and nuclear warheads. It has been steadily upgraded ever since, and a version with an anti-radiation seeker was deployed in 1983, but it is still a slow-maneuvering missile with sluggish controls and has never successfully caught up with Western developments in electronic warfare.[146]

Syria also has increased the number of shorter range SA-8, SA-11, and SA-14 missiles in its Army that it can use to shield its ground forces. The SA-13 Gopher is gradually replacing Syria's 27 batteries of SA-9s and gives Syria considerably better short-range ability to defend its ground forces, although the SA-13 does not have a truly advanced IR guidance system, and its theoretical 10-kilometer range is actually limited to line-of-sight defense. In total, these light surface-to-air missile units give Syria the equivalent strength of 150 anti-aircraft missile batteries. Further, Syria has some 305 SA-7 platoons scattered throughout its forces.[147]

Syria has steadily improved the integration or "netting" of its air-defense forces, its radars, and its electronic-warfare capabilities. It now has three fully computerized air-defense centers which can control both its missile units and its vector air-defense fighters. These computer links extend to its SA-6 and SA-8 missiles, and Syria is expanding its defenses to the northeast to cover an attack by Iraq or an end run by Israel. The Syrian system lacks many of the capabilities of current Soviet air-defense control-and-sensor systems and is probably still highly vulnerable to Israeli attack or electronic warfare.

Developments in Syrian Naval Forces

Syria recognizes its vulnerability at sea and to amphibious operations but concentrates instead on improving its land and air forces. It also tends to rely heavily on the threat of Soviet protection. Syria has, however, realized that it is becoming steadily more vulnerable to an attack on its ports or on shipping to and from Syria. Its main ports at Tartus and Latakia are also essential to Soviet resupply in a war. This has led Syria to expand its capability for submarine, surface, and amphibious warfare.

Syria's Navy has built up from 2,500 men in 1982 to 4,000 men in 1989. It has acquired three Romeo class submarines, built its missile-craft strength up to 22 ships, and acquired Polnochny-class LCTs. The end result, however, is somewhat unimpressive. Although the Romeo-class submarines Syria received in June 1985 and December 1986 give Syria a capability it lacked for nearly 20 years, the Romeo-class ships are obsolescent, if not obsolete.

Syria has actively sought to replace its Romeo-class ships with three Soviet Kilo-class submarines to replace its aging Romeo-class ships but lacks the money to do so and possibly Soviet willingness to sell.[148] The Kilos would make a difference. They are relatively silent and effective ships, with mines and 18 torpedos, two reloads and two spares. They have also been delivered to Algeria and India. These submarines now have limited operational capability.

Syria's major surface vessels consist of two obsolescent Soviet-made Petya-class frigates and 24 patrol boats. Only the 12 Osa-II patrol boats are relatively modern, and they are equipped with aging SS-N-2A ship-to-ship missiles and lack advanced radars and electronic warfare capability. Syria has had to virtually retire six Osa-I and six Komar boats. Syria has sought four Nanuchka-class missile boats from the USSR but has not received them.[149]

Syria's other ships include six Zhuk coastal patrol craft, one Natya-class ocean-going mine vessel, two coastal mine vessels, and six small inshore mine vessels. Syria has, however, acquired three modern Polnocny medium landing ships and 12 Mi-14 and 5 Ka-25 ASW helicopters. Its most recent deliveries were the third Polnocny-class landing ship in 1985 and a fourth Yevgenya-class inshore mine vessel in early 1986. Some Air Force helicopters are also assigned to the Navy.

Syria also seems to have reacted to the lessons of past conflicts by seeking a Soviet naval presence that could help deter an Israeli attack on its ports and possibly counter Israeli naval superiority and the tacit threat of U.S. naval action. Syria has improved its bases at Tartus, Latakia, and Minet el-Baida. Syria has also allowed the USSR to use Tartus as a support facility.

The impact of this shift must, however, be kept in perspective. Tartus has long been used to repair and maintain some of the Soviet ships in the Mediterranean. The Soviet Navy began to use Tartus regularly in 1969 and dramatically increased use of its facilities in 1976, when President Sadat expelled the Soviet military from Egypt. The only difference seems to be that there are now some piers and docking facilities where the Syrians are allowed only limited access. It is interesting to note, however, that these facilities have been developed under the direction of Admiral Sidorov, who supervised the expansion of the Soviet facility at Cam Rahn Bay. Admiral of the Fleet V.N. Chernavin, and his deputy, Admiral Grishin, both visited the base in 1987, and the Syrian facilities now seem capable of arming and supporting relatively large ships. Tartus is also the primary facility to maintain and replenish Soviet submarines in the Mediterranean, and a yard oiler, water tender, and submarine tender are now permanently deployed at the port. Soviet Naval Aviation has

has expanded its deployment of reconnaissance and surface warfare aircraft, and port calls have increased in frequency.[150]

Syrian Paramilitary Forces

Syria's paramilitary forces are largely oriented toward internal security. There are five separate intelligence services in Syria, many of which spy upon the armed forces and each other. There is a Republican Guard brigade for protection of the president, with T-72 tanks and artillery. There is also an 1,800-man desert guard for the frontier, and there are Saraya as-sira, or Struggle Companies, for special operations. The Ministry of the Interior has 8,000 men in the gendarmerie, and the Ba'ath Party has its own separate militia or "People's Army."

Syria trains and equips two to three Palestinian brigades with Syrian officers and advisors. They have roughly 4,500 men; 90 T-54/55 tanks; 105-mm, 122-mm, and 152-mm artillery weapons; multiple rocket launchers; AT-3 anti-tank guided missiles; and SA-7 light surface-to-air missiles. Part of these Palestinian units are in Lebanon.

Syria has also been one of the main causes of state-sponsored terrorism, although this activity has been kept under tighter control since 1986. Both Syrian intelligence and the Syrian Air Force run extensive networks of contacts with various radical factions in Lebanon and with other terrorist groups. Syria obtained the assistance of Bulgaria in setting up a special training camp near Damascus in 1983 and used this camp to train various factions in the use of car bombs and explosives. It has trained and equipped some Palestinian and Lebanese Shi'ite factions to act as kidnap and assassination squads, although their targets have been restricted to Arab targets in the Arab world and Europe.

While Syria cannot be blamed directly for the bombing of the U.S. marines and Embassy in Lebanon, Syrian officers worked with the Iranian-backed Shi'ite factions that carried out the April 1983 suicide bombing of the U.S. Embassy that killed 63 people. Similarly, the two trucks used by Shi'ite factions in the 23 October 1983 bombing that killed 241 marines seem to have been armed in the Bekaa by Syrian-trained personnel and moved along a route guarded by Syrian backed militias.[151]

The Remaining Problems in Syrian Forces

Syria has not been able to correct a number of basic problems it encountered in 1982. One of these problems is its lack of flexibility and speed of reaction in its high command and the high degree of politicization that limited the effectiveness of its military operations in both 1973 and 1982. Power is still over-concentrated in the hands of President Hafiz al-Assad, officers loyal to him, members of his family, and Alawite officers.

Complex dual chains of command exist to prevent a coup attempt, and Assad exerts direct control over the Syrian Air Force Defense Companies (Saraya al-Difa), the Struggle Companies (Saraya al-Sira), and the Republican Guard (Haras al-Jumhuriyya). While the defense companies were drastically reduced in strength after their commander—Assad's brother, Rifat al-Assad—made a grab for power during the president's illness, Syria still maintains three competing military elements simply to secure the regime.

Syria's six area commands—Damascus, Northern, Coastal, Central, Eastern, and Southern—do not command combat forces but layer another level of internal security forces over the Syrian command structure. The Special Forces Headquarters is also highly autonomous. While Syria does have a central operational command and operational commands for both the Golan and Lebanon, control of operations is still highly centralized in the rear, and the Syrian Army is still organized along relatively obsolete branch lines that give its individual branches for signals, training, logistics, etc., too much authority over both the creation of effective regional military capabilities in peacetime and the support of any sustained operations in wartime.

Problems in Manpower Quality

Syria still has major problems in training and manpower quality. Its training has improved in quality at almost every level, but its ability to make proper use of this training is often uncertain. Manpower management, and the proper matching of assignments to skills, is poor. There is constant turbulence and rotation in the officer corps, conscripts receive far too little training, and NCOs are poorly trained and paid.

Syria has deployed some 12,000 to 40,000 men in Lebanon at different periods since 1982. This has disrupted training and discipline, and widespread corruption exists within the armed forces, which often have taken the lead in smuggling and bypassing Syria's strict customs regulations. Maneuver and air combat training are still relatively static and slow moving. Advanced technical training and command exercise training have improved, but they are still mediocre by Israeli standards.

Syria also underfunds manpower quality. In spite of major increases in defense spending, Syria is spending one-third as much per man in uniform as Israel and is still underfunding its training activity, its pay and allowances for officer and NCO cadres, and its readiness and combat and service-support capability. Nearly 1,000 of its tanks do not have properly trained crews, and it has substantially less than one trained pilot per combat aircraft.

Problems in Syrian Intelligence

Syrian military intelligence is highly compartmented, with relatively poor information flow to operational commanders, and is organized as part of a Special Staff that combines internal security and covert operations. Syrian intelligence seems biased toward peacetime political problems rather than toward the support of combat operations. The transfer of technical intelligence to operational units remains poor, although Syria has steadily improved its COMINT and SIGINT capabilities, and Syria now pays considerably more attention to the need for secure communications and careful control of its electronic emissions.

Syrian Air Force intelligence and at least three other intelligence branches also act as an internal security force which permeates the military command structure. The Air Force commander, Major General Mohammed al-Khouli, devotes a considerable amount of his time to this role and directs many of Syria's activities in terrorism and covert operations. At least some of the Soviet and East European military advisors to Syria act as an additional form of internal security protection.[152]

Problems in Technology and Weapons Quality

Syria also has not received the modern land and air technology it needs from the USSR to give its growing force numbers real effectiveness against Israel. Syria is still largely limited to tanks without modern fire-control systems, and it lacks adequate night warfare aids. It has insufficient numbers of other armored fighting vehicles and many are not sufficiently effective for their mission. Despite Syria's 2,800 artillery weapons, it badly needs more self-propelled artillery and modern all-terrain logistic vehicles.

Syria still has to rely on comparatively low-grade export versions of Soviet fighters and air-to-air missiles. Even its improved ground-based air defenses remain vulnerable to the kind of countermeasures the United States used in its raid over Libya and lack the C^3I/BM technology to properly engage Israeli forces.

There are still some indications, however, that Syria may receive major new arms deliveries from the USSR, although many such reports may confuse Syrian desire with Soviet willingness to provide actual deliveries. Reports indicate that Syria may have ordered $2 billion more of arms from the USSR in 1986 and 1987, in spite of its debt problems and differences with the USSR over Lebanon. These sources indicate that Syria will get 60–65 MiG-29 Fulcrum and Su-24 fighters, more SA-8 surface-to-air missiles on armored vehicles, and more SA-11s, SA-13s, and SA-14s, as well as more SS-21s. Syria may also be getting improved radars and netting electronics for its air-defense system. Such reports are uncertain, and even if such deliveries take place, they will not cost Israel its technical edge. Nevertheless, it is far too soon to describe Syria's search for parity as a failure.[153]

Syrian Tensions with Israel and the West

It is also important to point out that Syria could well continue to be a major barrier to peace in the region. Unlike the PLO, Syria may find it impossible to compromise with Israel. One key issue is the Golan. While Israel has returned much of the Syrian territory it captured in 1973, it annexed 720 square miles of territory in 1981. This territory includes the Golan Heights west of Quneitra. It also includes positions that are absolutely critical to the defense of Israel.

While Israel might well be able to secure much of the West Bank against any foreseeable Palestinian entity, it is difficult to see how it could secure northern Israel if Syria occupied the Golan Heights and the slopes down to Lake Galilee. The 1,800-foot rise from the plains of Galilee would give Syria an immense value in launching armor attacks, in artillery and missile fire, and in sensor and surface-to-air missile coverage of Israel.

The reasons for Syria's insistence on recovering the Golan are equally easy to understand. They consist of national pride, the fact that Israel is occupying what was once Syrian territory, and the fact that Israeli occupation of the Golan brings the IDF within forty miles of Damascus and offers Israel offensive as well as defensive advantages. There is no easy way that Syria can now compromise with Israel over anything approaching a lease or a meaningful demilitarized zone as a solution to the problem.

Syria also has done little to build any basis for compromise or trust. The ruthless actions of the Syrian forces in suppressing the uprising in Hama and in dealing with the Maronites in Lebanon scarcely encourage Israeli flexibility. Neither has Syria's dealings with Iran or its continuing support of terrorist extremist elements of the Palestinian movement, such as the Popular Front for the Liberation of Palestine—General Command, increased mutual trust. While Syria has expelled the terrorists led by Abu Nidal, the end result has simply been a move to Libya. Syria also seems to be the sponsor of many of the recent "Palestinian" attacks on Israel across the Lebanese and Jordanian borders, as well as attacks on Palestinians who support Arafat's more flexible posture toward Israel.

The net result may well be that any peace between Israel and the Palestinians can come only at the expense of Syria. A continuing Israeli occupation of the Golan would make it far easier to arrive at a settlement that compromised Israel's existing military security on the West Bank. But Syrian opposition to such a peace may be so strong that any signs of compromise by Assad could well be little more than ploys to undercut a given negotiation. The end result may well be either that Syria succeeds in blocking a peace or that any peace can come only at the cost of hostility between Syria, any new Palestinian entity, and Jordan. Such tensions would, in turn, make any settlement of the Lebanese issue—and Syrian and Israeli withdrawal—even more difficult. This does not mean Syria is an impossible barrier to peace, but Syria's position certainly makes peace difficult to achieve.

The Slow Rebirth of Palestinian Capabilities

It is far too early to be certain about the size of the rebirth of the military capabilities of the PLO and other Palestinian factions, or what this rebirth means. The PLO is theoretically committed to seeking peace with Israel and some form of trade of territory for peace. At the same time, however, it has begun to rebuild military capabilities, which seem to go beyond the protection of the Palestinian population in that country and which are hard to justify if the PLO has really abandoned armed struggle. The question of whether the PLO is offering an olive branch or a gun is still far from easy to resolve.

Rebuilding the PLO's armed forces has not come easily. The PLO evacuated a total of 14,300 "fighters" by its own estimates in 1982 and lost virtually all of its bases and equipment. The forces of the various factions that make up the PLO remained deeply divided after that evacuation and through most of the mid-1980s. They often spent as much time fighting each other as preparing to fight any enemy. Since 1986, however, most of the various military elements of the PLO—except those of Abu Nidal, the 15th May Organization, and PFLP–General Command—have been brought back under the nominal authority of Yassir Arafat and the Executive Committee of the PLO.

Most elements of the PLO still operate individually under their own leaders, and all have relatively poor military training and equipment. Nevertheless, Palestinian forces have slowly reentered Lebanon.[154] Estimates of Palestinian active military strength vary sharply, but estimates in late 1988 indicated that there were about 11,000 to 16,300 full-time actives, with 5,600 to 8,000 Palestinian guerrillas in Lebanon, 2,500 in Syria, 500 in Algeria, 2,000 in Iraq, 2,000 in Jordan, 500 in the People's Democratic Republic of Yemen (PDRY), 500 in the Sudan, 100 in Tunisia, and 1,500 in the Yemen Arab Republic (YAR). Another 10,000 men had some form of serious militia or paramilitary status. There were small naval elements, and some 200 members of various PLO organizations had some kind of military flight training or experience, although none of the military elements of the PLO had an air component.[155]

The various Palestinian forces in Lebanon in 1988 deployed some 1,300 men in the Bekaa, 1,000 in the Mount Lebanon area, 800 near Tripoli and in the North, 2,500 near Beirut, and 3,000 in southern Lebanon.[156] Some are with the Druze near Aramun, Shueifat, Aitat, and Marrufiyehon; some are in the camps in Beirut, Sidon, and Tyre; and some are affiliated with Syria or the Party of God. PLO elements are again establishing a presence in el-Hilwe and Mieh Mieh near Sidon. These forces were significantly expanded in late 1988 and early 1989, but no reliable estimates of their new force strength are available.

The main factions within the Palestinian forces which are aligned with the PLO are:[157]

- Al Fatah (Pro-Arafat) with 1,500 active and 7,500 semi-active reserves and three brigades. Total manning is roughly 10,000, including forces outside Lebanon. These forces are supported by the Palestine Liberation Front/Abu Abbas Faction (200 men) and Arab Liberation Front (300 men).[158]
- Fatah (pro-Abu Musa dissidents) with 1,200–2,500 men.
- Democratic Front for the Liberation of Palestine (pro-Soviet, Hawatmeh) with 600–1,000 men and 8 battalions.
- Popular Front for the Liberation of Palestine (Habash) with 900 men and 6 battalions.
- Popular Front for the Liberation of Palestine (Talat Yaqub) with 100 men.
- Popular Front for the Liberation of Palestine—General Command (Jibril) with 500–800 men and 5–6 companies.
- Popular Struggle Front (Bahjat Abu Gharbiyah and Samir Ghusha) with 100–600 men.
- Palestine Popular Liberation Struggle (Abd al-Fatah and al-Ghanem) with 100 men.
- as-Saiqa (pro-Syria under Issan al-Qadi) with 600–1000 men and 5 battalions.
- Palestine Communist Party with 100 men.

The main factions within the Palestinian forces which are not clearly aligned with the PLO, or which are actively dissident, include:

- Abu Nidal Faction (Abu Nidal) with 800 men.
- 15th May Organization (al-Amri) with 100 men.
- Popular Front for the Liberation of Palestine, Special Command (Abu Muhammad), with 100 men.
- al-Fatah pro-Jordanian elements with 300 men.

These alignments are highly volatile, and Palestinian forces seem likely to remain divided. Even those elements which have been consistently loyal to the PLO have limited practical allegiance to it, except through their own leaders. The Al Fatah Uprising and Soviet-backed Democratic Front are particularly radical, although none of the present Palestinian forces have anything like the cohesion, strength, weaponry, and well-established military positions they had before the 1982 invasion.

It also seems unlikely that the Palestinian forces will emerge as a serious military threat to Israel unless they can form a more stable long-term coalition with the Amal, Hezbollah (Party of God), and/or Druze than now seems likely. The recent history of sporadic fighting between the Palestinians and the Druze, Hezbollah, and Amal raises doubts about the stability of any coalition. For example, serious fighting between the Shi'ites in the Amal and the Palestinians in the refugee camps of Sidon, Tyre, and Beirut broke out during October 1986 to January 1987 and became open warfare in February 1987. During the height of this fighting, the Amal ended in fighting their former Druze allies, as well as the Sunnis and Palestinians. An uncertain peace was enforced only by Syrian intervention.

Nevertheless, even a limited coalition of Palestinian forces and a faction such as the Amal could still present a serious threat to the Israeli-backed South Lebanon Army (SLA). The PLO helped the Amal against the Hezbollah in 1988, and the Amal have been far more tolerant of the PLO military buildup in southern Lebanon. The SLA only has 2,500 relatively low-grade active personnel and requires constant Israeli military backing.[159] This compares with up to 5,000 Amal and 1,000–1,500 Hezbollah troops in the area south of Sidon. The Hezbollah forces have often proved more effective than those of both Amal and the South Lebanon Army, although they have suffered severely from a lack of Iranian financing and support since Iran's cease-fire with Iraq in the summer of 1988.

As has been described earlier, Israel has increasingly been forced to provide support to the SLA in the form of armor and helicopters and to improve the defenses of its security zone along the border with Lebanon. There also seems little prospect that the UNIFIL forces in the area can ever provide Israel with real security. Israel is almost certain to face continuing low-level rocket or artillery attacks and infiltration attempts, and these could become far more serious if the Hezbollah should recover its strength and continue to grow in power.[160]

Most importantly, the massive popular uprising on the West Bank and in Gaza could either help lead to peace or revitalize the PLO's military option. The uprising is redefining the demands of the Palestinians in the occupied territories and is consuming a large part of Israel's troops and defense spending in internal security actions. The uprising also has moved the PLO and Palestinian movement in three different directions. One direction, under the leadership of Yassir Arafat, finally formally recognized Israel's right to exist on 14 December 1988, when Arafat formally and publicly accepted U.N. Resolutions 242 and 238. Another direction seems to be leading to a more militant Palestinian movement associated with the uprising on the West Bank and Gaza with growing Islamic undertones. A final direction is leading some extremist Palestinian groups into closer alignment with Syria and is leading them to take a hard-line military approach in dealing with Israel, which is in direct contradiction to the PLO's position that it has abandoned armed struggle for the peace process.

No one short of a prophet can predict the outcome and whether it is likely to bring peace, a stalemate, renewed fighting, or an awkward combination of all three. No one can predict how the various Palestinian military forces will interact with the Palestinian uprising in the occupied territories. Depending on the form such interaction takes, it could either help lead to a peace settlement or lead to a far more serious Palestinian threat to Israel.

Lebanese Force Developments Since 1982

Lebanon has been sharply affected by Arab-Israeli conflict, but its military forces have been shaped by very different pressures. Between early 1975 and late 1976, Lebanon began to be torn apart by open civil war. The Christians, aided by Syria, fought bitterly with the Sunni Muslims and their Palestinian allies. A cease-fire was established in October 1976, and held for about six years.

Syria remained in Lebanon as what the Arab League called the Arab Deterrent Force and kept a kind of peace in the north. Israeli-backed Christian and Shi'ite forces served as a buffer in the south. Syria, however, tilted toward the Muslims and Palestinians over time, and the PLO became progressively stronger and built up its forces and positions near the border of Israel. The Palestinians then made up about 11 percent of the population of Lebanon.

These developments helped trigger Israel's invasion of Lebanon in

June 1982. The aftermath of the resulting fighting led to the rise of Bashir Gemayel. His rise briefly seemed to indicate Lebanon would become a Christian-dominated and pro-Israeli state. Gemayel's assassination, however, led to the entry of a Western Multi-National Force (MNF) which gradually became involved in the revival of Lebanon's civil war and a renewed political struggle between Israel and Syria. Successful bombings of the MNF barracks produced large-scale casualties. The U.S. withdrew from the MNF, and all MNF elements left in March 1984.

Israel and Syria did sign a withdrawal agreement on 17 May 1983. The agreement was never fully implemented and was then violated. Lebanon continues to be partially occupied by Syrian troops and there are some 30,000 Syrian forces in Lebanon. Syria maintains troops in the Riyaq area of the Bekaa Valley and has special forces stationed at Matn, in the Tripoli area, and in the north and northeast. Israel withdrew the bulk of its forces from the south in 1985, but retained a 10 to 19 kilometer deep security zone north of the 1949 armistice line. It continues to train and arm the South Lebanon Army and keeps at least 100 full-time Israeli "advisors" in the area. In spite of past regional and Western efforts to settle the Lebanon crisis, the Israeli and Syrian occupations of Lebanon have become institutionalized and continues to have a broad destabilizing impact on the region.[161]

The past informal arrangements between Israel and Syria which limited the risk of a direct or indirect war before 1982 were tacitly reestablished after 1984 but are far less stable. Syria also became involved in struggles for influence in Lebanon with Iran and Iraq. Israel has done its best to frustrate any agreement between various Lebanese factions under Syrian auspices, initially in reaction to Syria's success in forcing Lebanon to terminate its agreement with Israel and then because of the fact that Israel's 1982 invasion triggered the rise of conflicting Shi'ite movements largely hostile to Israel and which continue to threaten Israel's position in the south.

The continuing civil war in Lebanon has not yet led to another round of fighting between Israel and Syria, but it continues to create new tensions in the area. Aside from creating a climate which allowed the rebirth of PLO forces within Lebanon, the conflict in Lebanon has helped paralyze progress toward a comprehensive Arab-Israeli peace settlement, and it has created the following problems within the country:

- There has been a steady increase in the conflicts between religious sects accompanied by increased reliance on military force rather than on the use of law and respect for human rights.

- Lebanon has become a center for covert operations and for various terrorist activities.
- Each Lebanese faction has continued to try to expand its foreign support and to exploit the crisis by building up its military forces.
- Syria has deployed 20,000 to 40,000 troops in Lebanon since 1984. In mid-1989, it had some 40,000 men in Lebanon under the command of General Said Bairak Dar of the army and General Ghazi Kanaan, who commanded a 3,000-man intelligence detachment. In combination with its Druze and Shi'ite allies, Syria controlled roughly 70 percent of Lebanon's territory. Syria also had ties to the Franjieh faction of the Christian Maronites, helping to further divide the country.
- The Israeli military presence in southern Lebanon continues to cause instability in the area and has triggered a new struggle between Israel and some factions of Lebanon's Shi'ites. Israel continues to have a large security zone in Lebanon and now uses the South Lebanon Army as its proxy in the area.
- The Palestinians have been caught in a grim struggle between Lebanon's Shi'ites and various factions of the Palestinian movement. This has turned into yet another bloody internal conflict with no clear end in sight.
- The United Nations Independent Force in Lebanon (UNIFIL) has 5,850 men and has been in existence since 1978, but it can do little to bring peace to the region.
- Arms continue to flow to Lebanon from many sources while the Lebanese Army remains weak and divided.
- During 1983 to 1987, Iranian influence in Lebanon increased through contacts between Iranian Revolutionary Guards and various Shi'ite sects. These contacts have decreased since Iran's cease-fire with Iraq in early 1988, but up to 500 Iranian Revolutionary Guards were still in Lebanon in late 1988. Iranian intervention helped fuel a struggle for control over the Shi'ites in Lebanon between the secular Amal and religious Hezbollah that further complicates any effort to reach a settlement in Lebanon.[162]
- There has been active Iraqi competition with Syria since the Iran-Iraq cease-fire in mid-1988. Iraq has supported Sunni factions, Lebanese Ba'athists, and Christian groups hostile to Syria. In late 1988, Iraq began to provide large numbers of weapons, including tanks, to various anti-Syrian forces, particularly the Maronites. By April 1989, these weapons included at least seven FROG-7 surface-to-surface missiles. This has added a new dimension to the Lebanese conflict, and Iraqi-Syrian efforts to dominate given military elements seem likely to continue.

- Changes have occurred in the balance of power between Christian factions. The end of Amin Gemayel's presidency on 23 September 1988 came without a clear successor. His attempt to make General Michel Aoun, the Maronite head of the Lebanese Army, the "President" led the Sunni factions in Parliament and the armed forces to openly break with the Christians. This soon resulted in a bloody new confrontation between the Christians and Syria. On 4 October, shortly after Gemayal left the presidency, Samir Geagea, the leader of the Lebanese Christian Militia, stripped Gemayel of his military support from the 3,500-man Katayeb militia. Geagea initially allied himself with Aoun, but a falling out between the two groups led Aoun to crush Geagea's forces in Beirut in March 1989.

During the late winter and spring of 1989, the struggle between General Aoun's efforts to "liberate" Lebanon under some form of Maronite control and Assad's efforts to prevent the creation of a Christian-dominated government led to a new political struggle between the Maronites and Syria. At the same time, Aoun tried to unify the Christian forces as a first step in unifying the country. During late February and early March 1989, Aoun used the support of three Christian brigades in the regular army to virtually crush most of the Lebanese forces' bases in Beirut, giving Aoun control over most of north and northeast Beirut. While Geagea's Lebanese forces remained in existence, Aoun established his power over all but the pro-Syrian Christian forces under Franjieh.

Aoun could not, however, extend this control to any other faction in Lebanon, and Syria increasingly made it clear it would not tolerate Aoun's claim to the presidency. Syria increased its deployments from 23,000 to 40,000 men, and during late March and April, it laid virtual siege to the Christian enclave in Beirut and northern Lebanon. The Christians fought back wherever possible but were generally outclassed and survived only because Syria chose not to commit its air force or make a direct all-out assault. Instead, Syria shelled the Christian part of Beirut and many other points in the Christian north to the point where it reduced many areas to rubble.[163]

This new escalation of the civil war seems so serious that it might well lead to either Syrian control of most of Lebanon or partition between the Christian and other sections of the country. Such a partition would inevitably create a permanent source of religious tension throughout the region. It would influence Sunni, Shi'ite, and Christian Arabs. It would almost inevitably force a continued Syrian and Israeli presence in Lebanon. At the same time, the crisis in Lebanon acts to undermine Palestinian moderates and worsen the Palestinian refugee problem. It has a negative influence on every Arab state as well as on the peace process.

It is almost impossible to discuss the national military forces of Lebanon in the normal sense of the term. There are no national forces in any real sense, and there has not been a real Lebanese defense budget for years. The U.S. has not issued unclassified estimates of Lebanese defense spending since 1983, when the Lebanese government was credited with spending $445 million a year on defense, with having 20,000 men in the armed forces, and with spending 8.2 percent of the GNP and 20 percent of the central government budget on military forces. This represented about 50 percent more expenditure than Lebanon had spent before the Israeli invasion in 1982 but was largely a response to a U.S. military aid effort which completely collapsed after the U.S. withdrawal from Lebanon. The most recent government data on military spending date back to 1986, when military spending was said to be $100 million. Lebanon owes the U.S. and France roughly $1 billion for prior arms deliveries, a sum which is highly unlikely to ever be paid.[164]

Since 1985, Lebanon has seen the power of its president and National Assembly erode to the vanishing point, and most of its "regular" military forces have come under the control of Maronite Christians (21 percent of the population), although there are still Sunni elements. This reached a crisis in September 1988, when the warring factions in Lebanon could not agree on a new president to replace Amin Gemayel, and the Maronite head of the Army, General Aoun, was selected by the outgoing Christian president as the "President." The remnant of the national forces almost splintered into ethnic factions, and the Christian and Muslim members of the National Assembly virtually ceased to cooperate in any form.[165]

In the period just before this split, the Christian-dominated "Army" was roughly equivalent to 10 light brigades with 15,000 men, 90 M-48A/5 medium tanks, 50 AMX-30 obsolete light tanks, 225–432 operational armored personnel carriers and other armored fighting vehicles (OAFVs), 59–70 major artillery weapons, 200 mortars, and a variety of small arms, light AA weapons, and TOW, Milan, and other antitank weapons.

Since the split over the presidency, four largely Christian brigades with roughly 15,000 men—the 5th, 8th, 9th, and 10th—have supported Aoun. Five other brigades, with some 18,000 men, have sided with various Moslem groups or have stayed neutral. The 3rd, 4th, and 6th brigades have disintegrated or split up. Most of the 3rd Brigade reinforced the 6th Brigade. About 1,500 Christians in the 4th Brigade moved to the Christian enclave.

The pro-Moslem forces are anything but united. The rest of the 6th Brigade is largely Shi'ite and is aligned with the Amal in West Beirut. The 1st Brigade is based in the Bekaa Valley and aligned with pro-Syrian Shi'ites. The 2nd Brigade is in north Lebanon and is composed of a mix of Moslem and Maronite troops under Syrian influence. The 7th Brigade is deployed in the Batroun region in the north, under the control of Christians under the influence of Suleiman Franjieh, who has ties to Syria. The 11th Brigade is largely Druze and is based in the Chouf.[166]

There has been fighting between the regular forces and both Christian and Moslem factions. One battle in February 1989 between the Army and the Christian Lebanese Forces under Samir Geaga was so intense that Aoun threatened to wipe out the Christian forces unless they halted fighting and withdrew.[167]

Repeated attempts to professionalize the army had only limited success even before the civil war divided it. The army had some good individual elements, but overall quality was poor to mediocre in terms of training, leadership, support, command and control, and maintenance. The officer and NCO corps of the Lebanese forces have suffered for decades from a wide variety of religious and family rivalries, competition for manpower from the various militias, and a heritage of sending ne'er-do-well sons of Maronite families into the army as a means of getting rid of them.

The 800-man Lebanese Air Force has never been combat capable and never could successfully operate its Mirage IIIs. The Mirage IIIs are the only modern fighter Lebanon has ever had. They are now in storage. The Air Force is now limited to a Maronite force with one active base along the Juniye-Jubayl highway and 6 obsolete Hunter F-70/T-66 aircraft, only 5 of which are operational. It also has 4 SA-342 attack helicopters with SS-11/12 air-to-surface missiles, 18 medium and 9 light transport helicopters, 8 training aircraft, and 2 transport aircraft. These helicopters and support aircraft have only limited operational capability.

The 500-man Lebanese Navy is based at Juniye and is also a largely Maronite-dominated force. In late 1988, it had one 38-meter patrol boat, three 20-meter patrol boats, and two 670-ton landing craft. It has always had only token military effectiveness, even in dealing with smugglers. A small customs force had one aircraft and five small patrol boats. There was also an 8,000-man Internal Security Force in the Ministry of the Interior which has been largely ineffective and which has often contributed to Lebanon's problems when it has attempted to take action. In late 1988, it was equipped with small arms and 30 Chaimite APCs.

There are several independent Christian militias. No accurate estimates exist of these forces, but they seemed to have had roughly the following strength in late 1988:

- Lebanese Forces Militia: 5,000–8,000 actives and 2,000–30,000 reservists. This force now is the dominant Christian force in Lebanon. It absorbed Camille Chamoun's militia by force in 1980, after fighting that killed 500 men. It is currently led by Samir Geagea, who seized control of Amin Gemayel's 3,500-man militia (Army of Metn) in October 1988 by threatening to attack it. It is affiliated with the South Lebanon Army and has been the main beneficiary of Iraq's effort to counter Syrian influence in Lebanon. Ironically, it has also gotten at least 50 U.S.-made APCs Iraq captured from Iran, large stocks of ammunition, and up to $200 million in aid. Exact equipment holdings are uncertain, but Iraqi aid raised them to around 100 T-34, T-55, M-48, and M-4 tanks, 20 AMX-13 light tanks, some OAFVs and M-113 APCs, 100 towed field artillery weapons, mortars, light antitank weapons and light anti-aircraft weapons, and three small patrol boats.[168]
- The Phalange: 800–1,000 actives and 5,000 reserves. Some main battle tanks, M-113 APCS, 120-mm mortars, and RPG-7s.
- Guardians of the Cedars (extreme right-wing): 700 men.
- Maradar Brigades (pro-Syrian Zehorta [Zghorta] Liberation Army): Christian forces under Sulayman Franjieh, with enclaves in northern Lebanon. Manpower is 400–500 actives, 600–1,000 reservists, and up to 1,700 men in the LAF 7th Brigade.
- South Lebanon Army (Israeli-backed): 60–75 percent Maronite and 25–35 percent Shi'ite. About 1,200–2,800 actives and 1,500 militia. Equipped with 40 M-4 and 30 T-54 tanks, 122-mm, 130-mm, and 155-mm artillery. The SLA is the successor to the force commanded by Hadad and is under General Antonine Lahd. It controls a zone of roughly 150,000–250,000 people along the Israeli border. About 50 percent of this zone is Shi'ite and 30 percent is Maronite.[169]

The Druze make up about 6 percent of the population of Lebanon and have some of the most effective forces in Lebanon. They are led by Walid Jumblatt and are concentrated largely in the Shouf Mountains. The Druze control one army brigade (the 11th, with 1,400 men) and have a Progressive Socialist Party (pro-Jumblatt) militia with 2,000–5,000 actives and 6,500–10,000 reservists.[170] This force has 50 T-34/54/55 medium tanks, BTR-60 and BTR-152 APCs, 122-mm and 130-mm artillery, some multiple rocket launchers, and mortars. It has 18 small patrol boats. The Druze are now actively trying to secure a separate enclave.

The Sunnis make up about 21 percent of the population of Lebanon and have a nominal strength of two army brigades. They are organized into six different militias, none of which have been highly effective but some of which are now receiving significant Iraqi aid:

- Al-Mourabitoun (Nasserite): This faction is led by Ibrahim Qulaylat and is located in urban coastal areas, mostly in Tripoli. It is Sunni fundamentalist, supports the PLO, and has had ties to the Hezbollah. It has 200–500 actives and influence over the 2nd Brigade (2,400 men) and the 12th Brigade (1,700 men) of the Lebanese Army.
- October 24 Movement (pro-Syrian secular group): Small.
- Islamic Unification Movement (Taweed or Tawheed Islami; Islamic Liberation Organization): founded in 1982. Led by Sheik Said Sha'aban. Sunni fundamentalist. Ties to the PLO and Iran. Anti-secular but poor relations with Shi'ites and Syria. Roughly 800–1,000 regulars. Centered in Tripoli, with some artillery and light armor, mortars, and light antitank weapons.
- Junudullah (PLO-financed Soldiers of God allied to Taweed): Several hundred.
- Popular Liberation Army (pro-Palestinian): Centered in Sidon.

The Shi'ites make up about 32 percent of the population (1 percent more are Alawites) and have emerged as a steadily greater force within Lebanon. They have a strength of two nominal army brigades and a number of different militias, of which the Hezbollah is the most effective. The main militias include:

- Amal (Disinherited, The Oppressed): Led by Nabih Berri. Pro-Syrian and secular. Positions in West Beirut and southern Lebanon. 4,500–5,000 active men, with some 5,000–10,000 reservists, 50 T-54 and some M-48 tanks, various armored cars and APCs, artillery and multiple rocket launchers, and light antitank and air-defense weapons. Strong influence over the 6th Brigade of the Army (1,500 men).[171]
- Al Amal al Islam (breakaway force with links to Iran's Revolutionary Guards): Founded 1982–1983 and led by Hussein Mussawi. Located near Baalbeck. Shiite fundamentalist; works closely with Iran and Hezbollah. 600–1,000 in active militia. Equipment includes 130-mm guns, mortars, rocket launchers, and anti-aircraft (AA) machine guns.

- Hezbollah (Party of God, Islamic Jihad): Pro-Iranian Shi'ite
  fundamentalist movement. Leaders include a range of mullahs
  and leading figures cooperating under a common name. Leaders are
  Muhammad Hussayn, Imaad Mougnieh, Hussein Musawi, Abbas
  Musawi, Subhi Tufayli, Muhammed Rad, Naim Qasim, and
  Muhammed Fennish. Forces deployed in West Beirut, Bekaa, and
  southern Lebanon. Forces include 3,500 actives and 25,000 in
  militia. Equipment includes AFVs, APCs, rocket launchers,
  antitank weapons, and light AA weapons.
- Islamic Resistance Movement: 400 actives.
- National Lebanese Resistance Front: A Syrian-backed organiza-
  tion, with Lebanese Communists and members of the Democratic
  Front for the Liberation of Palestine.[172]
- Islamic Jihad (special operations force): Antitank weapons.
- Alawi (Arab Democratic Party; Red Knights): Pro-Syrian forces
  located in Tripoli. Strength unknown.

The Amal benefited during 1988 and early 1989 from Iraq's defeat of
Iran and the resulting cut in Iranian aid to the Hezbollah. They have
also benefited from Syrian efforts to make the Amal a counterbalance
to the Iranian-supported Hezbollah and from PLO support. This led to
a major battle for dominance of parts of southern Lebanon in early 1989,
which the Amal-PLO coalition won. The Amal is now the dominant
Shi'ite faction in southern Lebanon and has about 1,000 regulars and
some 2,000 to 3,000 militia in the area. The Hezbollah have been at
least temporarily forced out of Tyre, a city it once threatened to
control.[173]

The future of Lebanon remains as unpredictable as ever.

Jordanian Force Developments Since 1982

Jordan is well aware of most of the lessons that have been discussed
relative to modern war. Nevertheless, there has been a steady decline
in Jordan's military capability relative to that of Israel and Syria
since 1967 and Jordan's loss of Jerusalem and the West Bank. Jordan not
only has lost the capability to act as a major regional military force, it
also has found it impossible to create a stable relationship with the
Palestinian movement and Syria. It had to fight a bloody struggle
with the PLO in 1970–1971 and came close to war with Syria. Since
that time, the threat from Syria, and from Palestinian pressure on
Jordan's internal stability, has often been as great or greater than the
threat from Israel.

Jordan has also had little luck in moving forward toward a peace with Israel. King Hussein's long effort to create a coalition with the PLO that would allow Jordan to negotiate a peace settlement virtually collapsed in 1986. The Palestinian uprising on the West Bank and in Gaza in 1987 then created a whole new movement independent of any ties to Jordan. It demonstrated that Jordanian ties to the West Bank created a growing risk of Jordanian involvement in a conflict with Israel, with little chance Jordan could win the loyalty and support of the Palestinians on the West Bank. King Hussein's decision to cut all ties between the Jordanian government and the local Palestinian government on the West Bank in mid-1988 was, at least in part, a formal recognition of these risks, although Jordan continues to try to work out a viable peace settlement with both Israel and the PLO.

At the same time, Jordan faces problems to the east. Jordan has developed strong ties to Iraq, but at least some Jordanian officers are now concerned about the size of Iraqi forces and Iraq's future political alignments. Jordan is forced to balance these with the need to minimize any hostile action by Syria and cannot risk becoming involved in the complex Syrian and Palestinian politics affecting the situation in Lebanon. Neither Saudi Arabia nor Kuwait has provided the high volumes of military aid Jordan needs to compete with its neighbors. The fall of oil prices in the Gulf since the mid-1980s has also led to a reduction in Saudi aid to Jordan and to massive cutbacks in the demand for expatriate Jordanian labor which may create a potential internal security threat.

Finally, Jordan has recently faced serious economic problems. Since 1984, Jordan's economic output has slipped to 2 to 3 percent, or less than the rate of population growth. Although the external debt ratio is only 12–14 percent, Jordan is now severely strapped for cash. It has lost most of the economic support it once received from the Arab world. Jordan mortgaged much of its defense spending on promises it would receive some $1.25 billion annually from 1978 on because of its status as a confrontation state with Israel, but such aid dropped to only $630 million in 1986 and dropped steadily thereafter. Jordan built up a $950 million military debt that it cannot repay. Saudi Arabia—the only nation that regularly paid its subsidy—made its last annual subsidy payment of $360 million in January 1989.[174] Iraq has done nothing to repay the over $800 million that it borrowed from Jordan, and remittances from foreign workers dropped by 32 percent in 1988.

While Jordan has tried to compensate, one result has been an increase in the annual budget deficit from 5 percent of GDP in 1983 to 14 percent in 1986. Excluding foreign grants, the budget deficit reached 23 percent in 1985 and 28 percent in 1986. The civil side of the external public debt also trebled between 1980 and 1986, reaching 60 percent of

GNP. The resulting strains have led Jordan to make major cutbacks in government spending and to place tight controls on the use of foreign exchange. Jordan has also reached an agreement with the International Monetary Fund (IMF) that allows it to seek rescheduling of its $6 billion foreign debt, although it is already behind in its $1.2 billion worth of payments.[175]

It is unclear, however, whether Jordan's people are willing to accept the kind of restraints on prices and spending Jordan needs to rebuild its economy. Major riots followed price rises in April 1989, and these had to be put down with the aid of troops, and an unknown number killed.[176] It is also unclear how Jordan's economy can recover without a peace with Israel that would allow free trade across the Jordan Valley. In spite of a new Arab Cooperation Council that includes Egypt, Iraq, and North Yemen, Jordan cannot maintain a meaningful pace of development by trading with other Arab states in the region. The end of the Iran-Iraq War also seems unlikely to do much to help revitalize Jordan's economy.[177]

Shifts in the Regional Balance of Power

The 1973 and 1982 wars have led to important changes in Jordan's forces, but they have demonstrated the potential cost to Jordan of any direct military encounter with Israel. Jordan has lacked the resources to act on many of the lessons it has learned from these two wars, and Israel and Syria have stepped up their military efforts at a rate that Jordan cannot hope to match. To put Jordan's military position in perspective, Jordan had 986 main battle tanks in late 1988.[178] This was 25 percent of Israel's tank strength (3,900) and 25 percent of Syria's strength (4,000). Although Jordan increased its total number of combat aircraft from 50 fighters in 1973 to 109 in 1988, it then had only 16 percent of Israel's combat aircraft strength (676) and 23 percent of Syria's (478). Jordan now has only 5 percent of Israel's total mobilizable manpower strength and 5 percent of Syria's.

The shift in the regional balance of power over time is equally clear when it is measured in terms of defense spending. According to ACDA estimates, Jordan's defense expenditures increased by only 36 percent in constant dollars between 1972 and 1982. In contrast, Israel's expenditures increased by 92 percent and Syria's by an incredible 302 percent. If one looks at the period between 1982 and 1986, Jordan's annual expenditures in constant 1984 dollars dropped by 10 percent and were roughly $720 million. Israel's military expenditures shifted from about $5,270 million to $5,110 million, a drop of only 5 percent, leaving a level about 7 times that of Jordan. Syria's military expenditures shifted from about $3,059 million to $3,680 million, a rise of 20 percent and a level about 5 times that of Jordan.[179]

It is more difficult to make comparisons of the recent trends in military spending. The IISS puts Jordanian military spending at $713.35 million in 1986, $745.5 million in 1987, and $762.8 million in 1988. These expenditure levels are about one-eighth those of Israel during the same period and one-fifth those of Syria.[180] These figures seem to be approximately correct but cannot be validated on the basis of national budget data.

The trends in arms-import data show somewhat similar patterns. Jordanian arms transfers rose from around $110 million per year in 1977 to around $1,100 million during 1981 to 1983 and dropped to $330 million in 1986. Israeli arms transfers dropped from around $1,100 million per year in 1977 to around $925 million during 1982 and dropped to $450 million in 1986. Syrian arms transfers rose from around $825 million per year in 1977 to around $2,600 million during 1982 and dropped to $1,100 million in 1986.

These figures do not reveal a clear comparative trend over time, particularly since Israel only has to import from 30–40 percent of its arms, while Jordan and Syria import over 90 percent. However, if the arms imports of each country are aggregated for the period from 1982 to 1986 to smooth out annual variations, and the Israeli figure is corrected to take account of Israel's military production capabilities, then Jordan imported around $3,360 million, Israel imported $11,000 million, and Syria imported $10,100 million. This indicates that Jordan's military investment has averaged around one-third that of Israel and Syria.[181]

Jordan's Resource Problems

Jordan also does not face an easy future. In the past, it has received a significant amount of arms and aid from the U.S. U.S. military deliveries dropped from $305 million in 1983, however, to $100 million in 1984, $139 million in 1985, and an estimated $73 million in 1986. Total U.S. MAP aid dropped from $39.9 million in FY1987 to $26.5 million in FY1988 and $10 million in FY1989. The end result is that Jordan has not been able to obtain the sale of a major weapons system from the U.S. since 1986. Even worse, Jordan owes the U.S. a total of $1.2 billion in past FMS loans, and the annual interest and principal on these loans runs about $67 to $71 million. While recent refinancing and the 30-percent devaluation of the dinar make it hard to calculate the full impact of Jordan's debt, Jordan was originally scheduled to pay about 7 times as much for past aid as it is now receiving.[182]

Jordan has also had problems in financing non-U.S. arms sales. Non-U.S. military deliveries dropped from $921 million in 1982 to $793 million in 1983 and $153 million in 1984. They rose to $440 million in 1985, but the cuts in U.S. deliveries offset much of this rise, and the fall in oil prices in the following year severely reduced Jordan's trade and expatriate income. The rise in the growth of Jordan's GDP slowed from 10 percent in the early 1980s to 4 percent in 1986. Per capita GDP has declined as a result, and unemployment has increased. Jordan's total debt has increased, and its debt service ratio has risen sharply.[183]

Jordan's manpower problems are different. The CIA puts the total Jordanian labor force at 580,000. It estimates that there are 639,000 males in the age group from 15 to 49 and that 456,000 are fit for military service. The IISS estimates that there are a total of about 163,000 males and 147,000 women in the age group from 18 to 22 years and about 195,000 males and 178,000 women in the age group from 22 to 32 years. Jordan had a total active military strength of about 82,500 in late 1988, of which a significant number were two-year conscripts. Jordan's total current organized military reserves include about 100,000 men, with 30,000 in Army combat units. This level of reserve strength in the Army combat units is very low, although service in the reserves theoretically entails an obligation up to age 40. Jordan seems to lack the financial resources to equip and train a large reserve force, although the desire to keep a tight political control over Jordan's armed forces is also a factor.[184]

Shifts in Jordanian Ground Forces

The Jordanian army has increased from 65,000 men in 1982 to 70,000 in 1989. It now has two armored divisions (with two tank, one mechanized infantry, and one air-defense brigade each), and two mechanized divisions (with one tank brigade, two mechanized, and one air-defense brigade each). There is one independent Royal Guards brigade and one special forces brigade with three airborne battalions. The major combat support formations include 16 independent artillery battalions and four more battalions in an independent field artillery brigade assigned to the General Staff. The four independent anti-aircraft battalions that used to exist in the Jordanian Army are forming the core of the divisional air-defense units.

The Jordanian Army is adequately equipped, although much of its equipment is obsolescent or heavily modified or rebuilt to try to keep it competitive with the equipment in neighboring forces. It has 200 M-47 and M-48A5 tanks (many up-gunned and modernized, but a significant number in storage), 218 M-60A1s and M-60A3s, 270 Khalid variants of the British Chieftain, and 291 upgraded Tariq variants of the Centurion. Jordan is also reported to have received 90 Chieftains, 60 M-

47s, 19 British Scorpion light tanks, and 35 M-113s that Iraq captured from Iran.[185]

Jordan's other armored vehicles include 140 obsolescent Ferret armored reconnaissance vehicles, 1,200 M-113 APCs, and 34 Saracen armored cars. Jordan also has about 50 BMP-1s it is using as part of a new reconnaissance unit. Jordan has some EE-11 Urutus from Brazil and more on order, but these are used by the PSD or national police.

Jordan has relatively modern antitank weapons. It has some 330 106-mm recoilless rifles, and it has 330 BGM-71A TOW crew-portable and 310 M-47 man-portable antitank guided missile launchers. This is one of the most modern and effective mixes of antitank weapons in the Arab world.

Jordan has significantly improved its artillery strength in recent years and has roughly 440 major artillery weapons. Jordan has 17 M-59 155-mm guns, 36 M-101A1 towed 105-mm howitzers, 38 M-114 and 20 M-44 towed 155-mm howitzers in reserve, and four M-115 203-mm towed howitzers (in storage). The weapons in its active forces are all self-propelled and include 234 M-109 155-mm and 103 M-110 203-mm self-propelled howitzers. It does not have multiple rocket launchers or surface-to-surface missiles. It does, however, have nearly 400 mortars, including 81-mm, 107-mm, and 120-mm weapons, and an unknown number of 112-mm APILAS rocket launchers.

The air-defense coverage of Jordan's army is still limited. The short-range weapons in its army include 100 M-163 radar-guided 20-mm Vulcan guns and 264 M-42 40-mm self-propelled anti-aircraft guns. These weapons lack range or guidance capability, however, and must rely largely on curtain fire. It has 36 self-propelled ZSU-23-4 radar guided AA guns, which are far more effective, but Israel has countermeasures to the radar on this weapon.

Jordan also has obsolescent SA-7B2 and 300 Redeye man-portable surface-to-air missiles, which are largely ineffective against Israeli and Syrian fighters with countermeasures. It has 40 SA-8s and 40 SA-13s mounted on vehicles and some man-portable SA-14s. These systems are less vulnerable to countermeasures. The SA-8 is an improved version whose radar and IFF capability have been upgraded significantly since 1982, and which is supposed to be able to locate and kill hovering helicopters and even be usable against armor. Jordan has received an advanced form of the SA-14 with hemispheric coverage similar to that of the Stinger and improved counter-countermeasure capability. According to some reports, Jordan also has some SA-13s and may have Javelins and Rapiers on order from the U.K. While any immediate order seems doubtful, these weapons could significantly improve its capability.

The Jordanian Air Force has all of Jordan's armed helicopters, as well as its combat aircraft, and many of its ground-based air defenses are devoted to the protection of air bases and fixed targets. It has grown from 7,500 men and 94 combat aircraft in 1982 to 11,000 men, 114 combat aircraft, and 24 armed helicopters. It is based at Amman, Azrak, H-4, H-5, Ja'afar, and Mafraq.

The fighter ground-attack aircraft in the Jordanian Air Force include four squadrons with 59 F-5Es and F-5Fs. Their ordnance includes Belouga cluster bombs and Durandal anti-runway and hard-point bombs. Maverick missiles are on order. The F-5Es and F-5Fs date back to May 1975 and are equipped with the APQ-135 radar. This radar is too limited to take full advantage of modern air-to-air missiles like the AIM-9P-4. Jordan's inability to obtain access to the funds and systems it needs to act upon its view of the lessons of the recent Arab-Israeli conflicts is illustrated by the fact that the F-5s have limited attack and no electronic warfare capability and do not have self-protection systems like rear-warning radars, chaff, and flare dispensers.

The Jordanian Air Force also has two interceptor squadrons with 35 Mirage F-1s (16 CJs, 17 EJs, and 5 BJs). Its air-to-air missiles include AIM-9P4 Sidewinders and R-550 Magiques. It is buying British versions of the Sidewinder with anti-flare and other IR countermeasure capabilities close to the AIM-9M. The Mirage F-1s have proved to present maintenance problems and have only limited ECM and ECCM capabilities. They do not have true look-down, shoot-down capability. The only self-protection system is a radar warning receiver, and the Mirage F-1 has an inadequate electro-mechanical gunsight.

Jordan also had a small other combat unit (OCU) with 15 F-5As and 5 F-5Bs, but it has recently sold 16 F-5A/Bs to Greece and is trying to sell four more. Jordan has also sold Greece 10 T-37 trainers and is trying to sell the remaining 7 and 2 C-130Bs.

Jordan has sought more modern aircraft, like the F-16, since the mid-1980s. It has been unable to obtain the agreement of the U.S. Congress to such sales, however, and only recently has found the funds for purchases from Western Europe.[186] Jordan may have begun to examine the option of buying Soviet aircraft like the MiG-29 after 1986, but its main interest has been in Western aircraft like the Tornado and Mirage-2000 jet fighters.[187] Jordan felt that the lessons of the 1973 and 1982 wars clearly demonstrated the overwhelming advantages of high-technology Western fighters and air munitions and also felt that the cost of setting up an entire new logistic support and training system for a Soviet-made aircraft would offset what was reported to be a much lower purchase cost than that for any Western fighter.

The purchase of advanced aircraft became even more critical in 1987, when Syria acquired its first MiG-29s. As a result, Jordan took the risk of going into debt to buy the aircraft, even though Saudi Arabia refused to finance them. French Prime Minister Chirac announced on 4 February 1988 that Jordan had bought 12 "M" variants of the Mirage 2000, with an option for 8 to 20 more. Each aircraft was reported to cost roughly $23 million. Buying the "M" variant meant, however, that the aircraft would have limited air-intercept avionics and no advanced EW or training-edge capability and would be limited largely to a laser rangefinder in terms of advanced avionics. Chirac also announced that 15 of Jordan's 32 existing Mirage F-1CJ/EJs would be modernized with modern air-to-ground and maritime attack aircraft using systems similar to the Mirage F-1CR in the French Air Force.[188]

In March 1988, new reports indicated that Jordan had also bought 8 Tornado interdictor-strike (IDS) aircraft with a package of weapons like the JP-233 and Skyshadow electronic warfare systems. The contract was said to be worth $708 million and delivery was said to be scheduled in three years, with an option to buy more. Financing was said to be provided with the assistance of the British government, with additional West German aid.[189] The Tornado sale was evidently intended to give Jordan a more advanced strike capability while building up a potential standardization on the Tornado by the Jordanian, Omani, and Saudi air forces. The sale collapsed in the spring of 1989, however, when West Germany refused to provide its share of the required credits. The exact details of Jordan's other orders are unclear at this writing, but it does have 14 C-101/5 COIN aircraft and trainers on order.[190]

Jordan has been very impressed with the performance of helicopters in the 1982 war and other recent fighting. Its helicopter force now includes 24 AH-1Ss with TOW antitank guided missiles, which Jordan bought in 1985. The AH-1Ss are effective U.S. combat helicopter designs. Jordan has concluded from Israel's experience in 1982 that armed helicopters need to operate in direct support of the army command to be most effective but that providing a maintenance and support base that is separate from the air force presents significant difficulties. Its other helicopters include 5 SA-316B Allouettes, 18 S-76s, 8 SA-342Ls, 4 Super Pumas, and 8 Hughes 500Ds. Jordan is purchasing a total of 12 Super Pumas, and this would double the troop-lift capability it had in 1985.

Jordan's ground-based air defenses include 14 batteries with a total of 126 Improved Hawk launchers. These are PIP-II versions of the Hawk, with optical tracking systems, improved ECCM, and higher power illuminators. They are, however, deployed in fixed sites, with fixed radars and support facilities. U.S. Army studies have shown that Jordan would need some 40 more Hawk fire units to provide adequate coverage of the country, but Jordan cannot afford them.

The rest of Jordan's ground-based air-defense force that can be used for air-base and point-target defense consists of the lighter short-range weapons obtained from USSR that have been discussed earlier. They include three batteries with 20–34 SA-8 vehicle-mounted surface-to-air missile fire units, three batteries with 12–20 SA-13 tracked vehicle-mounted surface-to-air missile fire units, and three batteries with 36 radar-guided ZSU-23-4 23-mm self-propelled AA guns. There are approximately 25 Soviet military advisors in Jordan.

Jordan is acquiring an improved air-battle management system from Westinghouse, but this system is severely limited in capability by funding constraints. Jordan is also buying two electronic warfare centers from Racal. Jordan now relies on two TPS-43 surveillance radars to provide medium- to high-altitude coverage of the northern and middle parts of the country and one more TPS-43 to cover the south. There is an obsolete Marconi radar to cover the northeast. These radars have 200 kilometers of coverage at medium altitudes against a MiG- or Kfir-sized target but only up to 23–48 kilometers of coverage at low altitudes. They have less than 15 kilometers of coverage against several key attack sectors. The TPS-43s are also relatively fixed in location and are vulnerable to suppression in any major attack. Jordan has 5 more TPS-63 gap-filler radars which provide 25–30 kilometers of coverage, but these are vulnerable to countermeasures and active suppression. This situation will improve in the course of 1989, however, as Jordan takes delivery on 5 Marconi S711 mobile radar systems.[191]

The transport and support aircraft in the Jordanian Air Force include a transport squadron with 6 C-130B/H and 3 C-212As, a VIP squadron with 2 Boeing 727s and 2 Mystere 50s, and 4 S-76 helicopters. There are 2 CN-235s and 1 C-212 on order. There is a force of training aircraft with 17 T-37Cs, 18 Bulldogs, 12 Warrior IIs, and 6 Senaca-IIs.

Jordanian training levels and maintenance are the best of those of any Arab state. Jordan has closely watched Israeli tactical and training developments, as well as those of the U.S., and has applied them wherever possible. It has been severely limited, however, by its lack of modern battle management, electronic warfare, and air combat systems.

The Jordanian Coast Guard

Jordan has a token Navy or Coast Guard to cover its 26 kilometer coastline on the Gulf of Aqaba. It has 250 men and 6 small coastal patrol craft. Only 2 are armed—a 12-meter Bertram-class Enforcer and a 9-meter Bertram. The Navy's only base is at Aqaba, within easy artillery range of Israel.

Jordanian Paramilitary Forces

Jordan also has some 6,500 personnel in its paramilitary forces. These include a 4,000-man Public Security Force and a civil militia or People's Army with up to 50,000 men and women. Jordan supports a 1,500-man brigade in the Palestine Liberation Army.

Future Trends

Jordan still has highly professional forces with considerable defensive capabilities, but it is not a match for either of its neighbors. Quite aside from its lack of major weapons, it has not been able to buy the advanced munitions and C^3I/BM systems it wants, although Jordanian planners have clearly been impressed by Israel's battle management and electronic warfare performance in 1982. Further, Jordan has not fought a major military action since 1967, while Israel has developed extremely high technology forces and has acquired a vast amount of expertise in using such systems. While Syrian forces are generally inferior to those of Jordan on a man-for-man basis, Syria has learned a great deal from its experience in 1973 and 1982 and has some units which are almost certainly equal in quality to those of Jordan. Whatever the political and social costs of the 1982 fighting may ultimately be for Israel and Syria, that fighting greatly strengthened both states as potential threats to Jordan.

Jordan is also highly vulnerable to air attack. All but one of Jordan's major population, industrial, political, and military centers are within 50 miles of the Syrian border and all are within 50 miles—or two minutes flying time—of Israeli air bases. The terrain in the Jordan Valley provides good terrain masking for low-altitude Israeli and Syrian attacks and leaves blind spots in the coverage of Jordan's radars.[192] Israeli aircraft regularly overfly Jordan, and Israeli ground forces can rapidly thrust across the Jordan River, although they might have major problems in advancing up the heights above the East Bank without taking major casualties.

Jordan normally deploys its four divisions as follows: The 4th Mechanized Division faces west from the Dead Sea to the Zarka River north of Salt; the 12th Mechanized Division faces west and north from the Zarka River, around Umm Qais, to Ramtha; the 5th Armored Division covers the area from Ramtha to the Iraqi border but is concentrated between Ramtha and the lava fields; and the 3rd Armored Division is in reserve, located centrally between Zarka City and Qatrana.

This means Jordan has only one and one-half active divisions to cover its entire northern border, while Syria has two whole corps, and at least five to six Syrian divisions are normally deployed within easy striking range of Jordan.[193] Jordanian and Syrian relations are now relatively amicable, but in 1980—when Jordan increased its contacts with Iraq and refused to strengthen its military ties to Syria—Syria accused Jordan of supporting the Muslim Brotherhood in Syria and deployed forces to the Jordanian border. These forces included three divisions, an air-defense brigade, and over 800 tanks.[194]

Egyptian Force Developments Since 1982[195]

Egypt's military role in the Middle East has undergone revolutionary changes since the mid-1970s. While the other confrontation states remained at war after 1973, Egypt sought peace. President Sadat first decided to oust his Soviet advisors, then to turn to the West for arms, and finally to seek a peace agreement with Israel. In 1978, the Camp David Accords changed Egypt from Israel's major military opponent to a nation primarily concerned with its own security and development. Egypt has kept strictly to the terms of its peace agreement with Israel.

Nevertheless, Egypt has been forced to maintain large forces. The failure of the other Arab states and Palestinians to negotiate a broader peace with Israel has forced Egypt to size its forces with at least some concern with the risk that another Arab-Israeli conflict might involve Egypt. At the same time, Egypt has had to shift its military planning to deal with the threat from Libya and the new problems posed by the instability in the Sudan and other surrounding states. This creates the risk that Egypt may have to use its military forces to deal with contingencies to the west, east, and south.

Resource Issues Affecting Egyptian Forces

Egypt does not face problems in providing adequate manpower for its forces. The CIA puts the total Egyptian labor force at about 15 to 17 million. It estimates that there are 12,203,000 males in the age group from 15 to 49 and that 7,949,000 are fit for military service. Roughly 520,000 reach military age annually. The IISS estimates that there are about 2,894,800 males and 2,568,600 women in the age group from 18 to 22 years and about 3,964,000 males and 3,931,000 women in the age group from 22 to 32 years.[196]

The main strain that Egypt's military effort puts on the country is its defense expenditures. According to U.S. government estimates, Egyptian military expenditures peaked in the period from 1973 to 1975, when they exceeded $7 billion in constant 1984 dollars. They then dropped to $3 to $4 billion during 1979–1981 and gradually rose back to around $6 billion in 1984–1985.[197] The burden of this increase, however, was offset by Egyptian economic growth. Egypt was spending nearly 32 percent of its GNP on military forces in 1973–1975 and only around 14 percent of its GNP by the mid-1980s. Similarly, Egypt was spending over 50 percent of all central government expenditures on military forces in 1973–1975, but only around 25 percent by 1986–1988.[198]

At this point, Egypt began to encounter a major economic crisis as a result of falling oil prices and direct and indirect revenues and a chronic over-dependence on imports.

To put this economic crisis in perspective, the fall of world oil prices in 1986 cut Egypt's oil revenues by over 50 percent. Other key sources of foreign exchange (tourism and worker remittances) were cut by foreign reaction to internal unrest, the loss of earnings in the Gulf that followed the fall in oil prices, and a lack of confidence in the Egyptian economy.

Egypt's balance of payments deteriorated and a large financing gap appeared in Egyptian fiscal year 1986/87 that continued into 1989. Egypt's foreign civil debt rose to $37 billion, and its total military debt was well in excess of $10 billion. The Egyptian GDP dropped from an average annual growth of 9 percent during 1974–1982 to less than 3 percent in 1986/87, and was only marginally more in 1987/88 and 1988/89.[199]

Egypt's foreign debt rose to $43 billion by the spring of 1989. Its debt to the U.S. rose to $10 billion, of which $4.5 billion was for foreign military sales (FMS) and other military "aid" in the form of high interest 12–14 percent loans. Egypt ceased to be able to pay back its debts to France and was on the threshold of being unable to pay back the U.S. Its long delays in implementing effective economic reform kept it from getting significant IMF and World Bank aid and also led the U.S. to suspend the payment of some $230 million in aid.[200]

These trends forced Egypt to cut back its defense expenditures to levels significantly below the levels necessary to pay for both so large an active force structure and force modernization. While precise figures are lacking, the IISS estimates that Egyptian military spending dropped to $5.22 billion in current dollars in 1986/1987 and to $4.57 billion in 1987/1988 and then rose to $5.64 billion in 1988/1989.[201] These figures, however, include U.S. aid and are measured in current dollars. The true value of Egyptian domestic defense expenditure is now far smaller than in the mid-1970s, although active manpower had not decreased, and Egypt now has far more expensive and more sophisticated equipment.

*The Impact of Egypt's Decision
to Turn to the West for Arms*

While Egypt has changed its forces to react to the lessons of the 1973 and 1982 wars, its force planning has been driven by other factors. One such factor is the scale of its arms imports. Egypt has also been able to keep its arms imports under reasonable control by regional standards.[202] Egypt imported $7.6 billion worth of arms from all sources during 1982–1986. Syria imported $10.8 billion, and Libya imported $10.2 billion. Israel imported only $3.7 billion worth of arms, but it received more aid than Egypt and had a massive domestic defense industry. As a result, Israel has been able to increase the quality and quantity of its weapons far more quickly than Egypt.

Another factor was the problem Egypt faced in shifting from Soviet to Western equipment. In 1978, when the Camp David Peace Accords were signed, Egypt's forces were still almost totally equipped by the Soviet Union, despite the fact that Egypt had broken its military ties to the U.S.S.R. some three years earlier. Much of this equipment had already begun to create major maintenance and operational-readiness problems because of Egypt's inability to obtain Soviet spare parts. This problem has grown steadily worse with time. Although the U.S. has provided substantial aid and Egypt received roughly $1.3 billion in grants during FY1986–FY1989, Egypt could not begin to replace the Soviet equipment in its force structure.

A comparison of Egypt's holdings of Soviet-made equipment in 1973 with those of 1987 (Table 4.4) shows how dependent Egypt became on obsolescent and increasingly inoperable Soviet equipment.

- The Soviet-made equipment still in Egypt's Army in 1988 included 1,599 T-54/T-55/T-62 medium tanks, 87 recovery tanks, 1,385 other armored vehicles, 125 self-propelled artillery weapons, and 1,680 antitank guns and missile launchers.
- The Soviet-made equipment in Egypt's air-defense forces in 1988 included 240 SA-2 launchers, 201 SA-3 launchers, 40 SA-6 launchers, 924 anti-aircraft guns, and more than 662 radars, of which 135 were 2-dimensional radars and 27 were 3-dimensional radars. The Soviet-made equipment in Egypt's Air Force in 1988 included 162 combat aircraft. These included 122 MiG-21MFs, 28 MiG-21 F13s, 9 MiG-21Rs for reconnaissance, 27 MiG-17s, 13 MiG-15s, 6 TU-16 medium bombers with Kelt missiles, 10 IL-28s, and 48 Soviet-made helicopters.
- The Egyptian Navy had the following Soviet-made equipment in 1973: 12 submarines, 4 destroyers, 10 submarine chasers, 18 missile

TABLE 4.4 Decline in Egypt's Military Force Strength Between 1973 and 1988[a]

Equipment Type	1973 Level	1987 Level	No. of Items Phased Out
Land Forces Equipment			
Medium tanks	2200	1599	601
Recovery tanks	220	87	133
Other armored vehicles	3590	1385	2205
Self-propelled artillery	549	148	401
Antitank guns/launchers	2885	1725	1160
Surface-to-surface missiles	65	0	65
Multiple rocket launchers	360	0	360
Artillery radars	10	0	10
Naval Forces Equipment			
Submarines	12	1	11
Missile boats	18	2	12
Torpedo boats	24	0	24
Destroyers	4	0	4
Anti-submarine helicopters	6	4	2
Sub-chasers	10	0	10
Minesweepers	12	4	8
Landing craft	13	3	10
Air Force Equipment			
Combat aircraft	600	162	438
Helicopters	260	39	221
Air Defense Force Equipment			
SA-2 launchers	480	240	240
SA-3 launchers	256	201	55
SA-6 launchers	60	40	20
2-dimensional radars	158	135	23
3-dimensional radars	48	27	21
Vertical measuring instruments	50	0	50
Shelka	123	117	6
AA guns	2124	924	1200

[a]The Soviet equipment listed for 1987 is operable but is without combat capability due to its low durability and the fact that it is no longer competitive with the Soviet equipment in threat forces.

patrol boats, 24 other patrol boats, 12 medium mine-sweepers, and 13 landing craft. The Soviet-made equipment still in the Egyptian Navy in 1988 included 8 missile patrol boats, 12 patrol boats, 1 submarine, and 3 landing craft medium.[203]

While other Arab states have added Western equipment to a Soviet-supplied force structure, Egypt is being forced to re-equip its force structure with equipment designed for a different training, support, logistics, and infrastructure system, and for different tactics. Although Egypt continues to obtain some critical parts from Soviet-bloc countries like Romania and Poland and Chinese versions of Soviet-designed equipment, it has not been able to obtain the massive flow of supplies it needs. The normalization of Egyptian-Soviet diplomatic relations in 1984 has not led to major deliveries of parts and munitions.

As a result, Egypt has been forced to retire much of its major Soviet-made equipment from its first-line combat units and now relegates it to low-grade defensive units, reserve status, spare part uses, or sale to other nations. Egyptian efforts to manufacture entire Soviet-designed equipment items in Egypt or to obtain Western technology to convert Soviet equipment have also had limited success.

Egypt has made some progress in building light systems like the SA-7, in adapting Soviet artillery to Western chassis, and in converting Soviet equipment to Western electronics. Even these efforts, however, generally result in technically inferior equipment with only one-quarter to one-third the operational life cycle of new Western-made systems. Further, Egypt has found that performance has rarely met design expectations. Further, the upgraded or modified Soviet-made equipment types that are in Egypt's forces are no longer competitive with the Soviet-made equipment in potential threat forces. Egypt has had more success in obtaining systems like French aircraft and light surface-to-air missiles and Spanish corvettes to supplement its purchases from the U.S. Egypt, however, has had very limited resources to buy such systems.

The Impact of U.S. Military Aid to Egypt

Egypt has, however, made significant progress in its conversion to U.S. equipment. It began to get major amounts of U.S. foreign military sales aid in FY1979, when it received $1.5 billion in FMS loans. It received $550 million more FMS financing in FY1981, $900 million in FY1982, $1,325 million in FY1983, $1,365 million in FY1984, $1,175 million in FY1985, $1,244 million in FY1986, and roughly $1,300 million annually in FY1987–FY1989. Since FY1985, all of this FMS financing has been in the form of grant aid.[204]

This aid has allowed Egypt to buy substantial amounts of U.S. military equipment. In late 1988, Egypt's army already operated 844 U.S.-made tanks, 1,361 other armored vehicles, and 532 TOW launchers. Egypt's air-defense forces had 72 Improved Hawk Launchers and 8 TPS-63 2D radars. Egypt's air forces had 75 U.S.-made combat aircraft including 35 F-4Es, 78 F-16s, plus 23 C-130H U.S.-made transport aircraft, and 15 U.S.-made CH-47C helicopters. Egypt had 101 other Western-made combat aircraft and 42 combat helicopters. The Egyptian Navy had acquired two Spanish frigates but had not yet acquired any U.S.-made ships.

These conversions, however, still fall far short of replacing Egypt's losses of Soviet equipment on a one-for-one basis. Egypt accepts the fact that its conversion to interdependence with the U.S. will not allow Egypt to reach its former level of military capability relative to its neighbors. Egypt still, however, will need increased U.S. aid to create an acceptable rate at which it can trade quality for quantity and must build a stronger defensive posture. Further, Egypt now faces the problem that U.S.-made equipment is far more expensive in constant dollars than the equipment Egypt received from the USSR and has follow-on support costs which are three to four times higher.

Egypt's Five-Year Defense Plans

Egypt's defense planners continue to face a difficult challenge. They must use U.S. aid to give Egypt an effective defense capability. They must find ways that Egypt can fully convert its maintenance, support, and training structure to use U.S. equipment and technology. They must respond to a continuing domestic economic crisis that began with the fall of oil prices in the mid-1980s and which is now driven by a serious shortfall of foreign capital and problems in industrial and agricultural output. And, they have had to maintain a much larger force structure than Egypt needs for prestige purposes, in order to ensure the political stability of the armed forces and to help provide employment and stability for Egypt's conscript-age manpower.

Egypt has sought to meet these challenges by shaping its forces according to the following principles:

- Emphasis on defensive forces and resource priority for those forces needed to deter a major attack on Egyptian soil.
- Creation of higher-technology forces, with fully adequate support, to reduce Egypt's need for larger numbers of modern weapons. Egypt is using quality as a substitute for quantity.
- Use of European and Chinese weapons systems and technologies to supplement U.S. deliveries, when these systems complement U.S.-supplied equipment and can be sustained at a reasonable cost.
- Limiting domestic military spending to support economic reform and development.
- Retention of select Soviet equipment as long as possible as the

"low" part of a "high-low" mix in Egypt's equipment. This mix frees resources to pay for more advanced Western technology and economic development.

- Modification of existing systems to support defensive missions rather than to buy large numbers of new systems overseas.
- Use of Egyptian reserves to save the cost of maintaining active manpower. This is made possible by Egypt's firm commitment to maintaining the peace and its ability to rely on defense and deterrence.
- Utilization of the U.S. aid to provide key high-technology systems for all services in those areas most likely to contribute to deterring war and providing territorial defense for Egypt.
- Minimal hard currency expenditures on military equipment, goods, and services.
- Minimal increases in foreign credits or loans for military imports and maximum reliance on U.S. aid.
- Development of Egypt's domestic arms industry to provide a steadily increasing amount of support equipment, spares, munitions, and arms so that Egypt may eventually make major reductions in its need for arms imports and aid.

Egypt has faced major internal bureaucratic and political problems in achieving these objectives, and its actions reflect a continuing political need to move slowly in rationalizing and reducing its force structure and its need to make purchases of high-tech military equipment for prestige purposes as well as effectiveness. Nevertheless, Egypt has succeeded in giving its defense plans a high degree of continuity and in creating reasonably well structured long-term plans.

Egypt has completed the implementation of its First Defense Five Year Plan (1983–87), which called for a force structure that depended on U.S. equipment, and has begun its second plan (1988–1992). The First Defense Five Year Plan (FY1983–FY1987) was implemented with minimal modification. These modifications allowed Egypt to allocate enough funds to obtain an armored brigade, start a limited program in the Navy, start upgrading its training centers, introduce an automated logistic system, and obtain spare parts for its land forces. The equipment levels and current orders which Egypt achieved under its First Defense Five Year plan are shown in Table 4.5. While Egypt's strength in terms of fully operational equipment is far lower than that Egypt maintained in 1973, it is clear that Egypt has made impressive progress in creating a U.S.- and Western-supplied force.

Egypt has made major progress in several key areas. Its Improved Hawk forces are becoming fully operational, the purchase of the E-2C

TABLE 4.5 Egypt's Major Military Equipment Strength in FY1988

Equipment Type	In Units	On Order	Total	Provided Through U.S. Aid
Land Force Equipment				
M-60 A3 Tanks	847	94	847	847
M-88 Recovery Vehicles	175	0	175	175
M-113 A2 Family	1,559	90	1,649	1,649
M-109 A2 155-mm SP Howitzers	148	48	196	196
TPQ-37 Artillery Radars	-	2	2	-
TOW Launchers	532	100	632	632
Swingfire Antitank Guided Missile Launchers (UK)	123	-	123	-
Milan Antitank Guided Missile Launchers (France)	124	-	124	-
Naval Force Equipment				
Submarines (Chinese)	4	-	4	-
Spanish Corvettes	2	-	2	-
Harpoon Missiles for Spanish Frigates	18	-	18	18
Light Missile Patrol Boats	12	-	12	-
Medium Missile Patrol Boats	6	-	6	6
Air Force Equipment				
F-16A	79	40	119	119
F-4E	33	-	33	33
Mirage 2000 (France)	12	-	12	-
CH-7 (Chinese)	60	-	60	-
CH-6 (Chinese)	45	-	45	-
Mirage 5 (France)	35	-	35	-
E-2C	2	3	5	5
Gazelle with HOT (France)	14	-	14	-
C-130	21	-	21	21
Helicopters	104	-	104	15

is enabling Egypt to replace much of its network of Soviet radars, and Egypt's C^{3}I contract with Hughes, or "Project 776," is the first step in integrating all of the elements of Egypt's new air-defense system. The buildup of an effective F-16 force is well underway, and Egypt's Army has benefited from substantial deliveries of U.S. equipment.

Egypt is steadily strengthening its training, support, and maintenance base. It is undergoing a successful transition from a period in which the major challenge was to decide what U.S. equipment to buy to a period in which U.S. equipment must be operated and supported by Egypt. Egypt is in the process of moving from "procurement push" to "support pull."

Egypt has reduced its force structure problems by reducing its overall forces and establishing clear priorities for using its own resources and U.S. aid. It has cut its military manpower significantly since 1974. In 1974, Egypt's total mobilization base was approximately 955,000 men. Its total active manpower was a little over 745,000. Since that time, Egypt has cut its mobilization base by 6 percent, to only 877,000 men, and has cut its total active manpower by 7 percent, to 695,000 men.

Even these cuts, however, disguise the real rate of change in Egyptian forces. In 1976, Egypt's force posture called for an active manning strength of 750,000. As a result of the Camp David Accords, Egypt reduced its active strength to about 575,000 and cut its peacetime active manpower requirements by over 23 percent.

Egypt's Second Defense Five Year Plan, which covers FY1988–FY1992, is making further reductions, although many key-force sizing and procurement decisions are still under consideration. Egypt faces extremely difficult choices between force quality and force quantity and often requires 2–6 years to fully acquire and convert to the major new U.S. equipment it can acquire at current aid levels. As a result, serious gaps will develop in Egypt's military capabilities because of lags in the time between Egypt's withdrawal of its Soviet-made equipment from service and the time when it will acquire U.S. equipment.

Egypt is seeking to solve some of these problems through improvements in its military industries, but it lost the external Arab funding and support it needed when it signed its peace treaty with Israel and was expelled from the Arab League. The Arab Industrial Organization that Egypt founded in 1975 with Kuwait, Qatar, Saudi Arabia, and the UAE promptly collapsed.[205] As a result, the high-technology and advanced-weapons production elements of Egypt's military industries were largely hollow shells until the mid-1980s. Egypt did produce most of its ammunition and assembled some sophisticated systems from the West, such as the Alphajet and Swingfire antitank missile. However, in spite of flashy arms shows and some interesting designs and modifications of Soviet equipment, Egypt's industries were grossly inefficient and had little useful output.

This situation has improved steadily since 1984, but Egypt has lacked the capital and organization to take advantage of its large pool of trained technical personnel and skilled manpower. Current plans will help to overcome this, as has the gradual resumption of Saudi support for Egypt's Arab Industrial Organization. Egypt is investing some $2 billion in coproduction of 555 U.S. M-1 tanks as a means of catalyzing the modernization of its industries, but it will need $4 to 6 billion more and considerable time before it can produce the amount of additional military equipment it really needs.[206]

Land Force Developments

Egypt's Army force plans clearly reflect Egypt's plans to create smaller, high-technology land forces which are structured for deterrence and defense rather than offensive capability. During 1988–1992, Egypt will couple major reductions in active and reserve manpower with an emphasis on creating a first-line tank force of about 847 medium tanks. This will be substantially smaller than the tank force of any of Egypt's major neighbors.

Egypt's total active Army manpower dropped from 313,000 in 1984 to 290,000 (180,000 conscripts) in 1987 and will be less than 250,000 in 1992.[207] Its trained reserve manpower pool dropped from 176,000 in 1984 to 161,000 in 1987 and will be less than 150,000 in 1992.[208] At the same time, Egypt will create smaller but more advanced technology antitank guided missile and artillery forces. Egypt will also improve the mechanization of part of its land forces, although this mechanization will only have its full effect after 1990.

The Egyptian Army now has two Army Corps: the 2nd and 3rd. These two Corps have a total major combat unit strength of four armored divisions (each with two armored and one mechanized brigade), five mechanized infantry divisions (normally with two mechanized and one armored brigade), three infantry divisions (with two infantry and one mechanized brigade), one Republican Guard armored brigade, three independent mechanized brigades, five independent infantry brigades, and two air-mobile and one paratroop brigade. The combat support units include fourteen artillery brigades, with two more forming, two heavy mortar brigades, seven commando groups, one FROG-7 surface-to-surface missile regiment, and one improved Scud-B surface-to-surface missile regiment.

The equipment in Army forces in mid-1988 included 2,425 main battle tanks: 1,040 T-54/55, 600 T-62s, and 785 M-60A3s. There were approximately 15 PT-76 light tanks, 200 BDRM-2 reconnaissance vehicles, and 220 BMP-1 and 150 BMR-600P mechanized infantry combat vehicles. There were also 3,275 armored personnel carriers. These included some 1,000 Walids (some being transferred to the National Guard), 200 Fahds, 1,075 BTR-50/OT-62s, and 1,000 M-113s.[209] About half of this mix of armor was composed of obsolescent or worn weapons.

Egypt's artillery strength included around 1,120 major towed weapons, some 200 self-propelled weapons, 300 multiple rocket launchers, and 21 surface-to-surface missile launchers. The towed artillery included 48 M-1931/1937, 400 M-1938, and 220 D-30 122-mm weapons. It also included 440 M-46 130-mm weapons and 12 M-1937 M-20 152-mm weapons. The self-propelled artillery included 140 M-109A2 155-mm howitzers and a number of D-30 122-mm guns placed on tracked armored vehicles. The multiple rocket launchers included VAP-8012 80-mm weapons, BM-21 and as-Saqr 18 and 30 122-mm weapons, BM-14 and BM-16 140-mm weapons, and BM-24 240-mm weapons. Egypt also had roughly 534 mortars, including 450 M-43 120-mm mortars, 60 M-43 160-mm mortars, and 24 M-1953 240-mm mortars. This artillery strength was adequate in terms of total numbers, but many types were obsolete, and Egypt had only about one-third of the number of self-propelled weapons needed to keep up with its armor in modern combat.[210]

Egypt has a similarly divided mix of antitank weapons. It now has over 1,000 obsolete Soviet-made AT-1 Snapper and AT-3 Swatter antitank guided missile launchers, and 1,400 obsolescent AT-3 Sagger launchers, many of which are difficult to recondition. It has 200 British-made Swingfire launchers, but these involved a first-generation guidance system that is very difficult to operate. Egypt's modern antitank guided weapons consist of 220 French-made man-portable weapons and 520 TOW launchers (52 mounted on M-901 variants of the M-113). Egypt ordered 180 TOW-II missile launchers with night sights and 7,511 TOW II missiles in 1988.

Egypt also has B-11 107-mm recoilless rifles, some old Soviet antitank guns, and large numbers of rocket launchers. Egypt is well aware that one of the lessons of both the 1973 and 1982 wars is that it needs antitank weapons with advanced guidance systems that do not require extensive operator training, but it cannot afford the systems it wants.

These same problems affect the army's air-defense weapons. Egypt is almost totally dependent on Soviet-supplied weapons or Egyptian modifications of these weapons. These include roughly 1,200 Soviet made SA-7 man-portable missile launchers and Egyptian-made Ayn as-Saqr variants of the SA-7. They also include some SA-9s. Egypt's towed anti-aircraft guns include 14.5-mm ZUU 2s and 4s, 460 ZU-23-2 and 45 Nile 37-mm guns, 150 M-1939 57-mm guns, and 300 S-60 57-mm guns. Its self-propelled weapons include 110 aging Soviet radar guided ZSU-23-4 23-mm guns and 40 ZSU-57-2 57-mm guns.

These forces will improve as the result of the flow of U.S. aid. By 1992, the Egyptian Army will be built around a cadre of 847 M-60A3 medium tanks, some 1,649 M-113 APC variants, 368 M-109A1 155-mm self-propelled howitzers, and 874 TOW and Improved TOW antitank guided missile launchers. Egypt will support this force with U.S. combat-support equipment, such as TPS-37 radars and computer systems for its artillery, and TOW and radar-guided 23-mm cannon conversions for its M-113s. Egypt will also coproduce up to 650 improved M-1 main battle tanks in the early 1990s.[211] These M-1 tanks will have the new 120-mm guns and will enable Egypt to keep pace with the advances in first-line tank technology taking place in neighboring states, as well as U.S. multiple rocket launchers to expand its artillery firepower.

Even so, roughly 30–40 percent of the Egyptian Army will consist of low-grade units relying primarily on Soviet equipment that is well over a decade old and for which most spare parts are virtually unobtainable. Egypt also faces the fact that some 80 percent of Libya's land and tactical air units are now deployed on the Western front against Egypt. Libya's total forces now have 3,290 tanks (496 T-72s, 1,000 T-62s, 1,800 T-54/T-55s, and 90 OF-40s).[212] It also has 900 BMP armored fighting vehicles, 3,290 APCs, 1,600 field artillery pieces, 700 multiple rocket launchers, 900 mortars, 2,400 antitank weapons, 120 surface-to-surface missiles, and 1,400 tank transporters. Libya continues to get new Soviet deliveries of T-72 tanks and is beginning to get significant numbers of the BMP-2 armored fighting vehicle. It also is getting significant deliveries of Czech Danias and BTR-60s.

Egypt will not be able to equal Libya's holdings of modern equipment. Egypt will almost certainly have to face an evolving Libyan tank threat with reactive and improved armor and upgraded guns and fire control and a massive armored fighting-vehicle threat which can only be countered with APCs. This is why Egypt is seeking aid in co-producing the M-1A1 tank. It is the only way Egypt can offset Libya's quantity with an edge in force quality.

Further, Egypt is seeking added armored mobility because it lacks the domestic resources to finance the proper deployment of its land forces from the Eastern to the Western front. While the details are highly sensitive, Egypt is forced to keep units in casernes first established by the British for the defense of the Suez Canal, when it urgently needs new and modern facilities near the massive Libyan deployments on Egypt's western border.

Air Force Developments

The Egyptian Air Force had 30,000 men in 1984. It had 25,000 men in early 1990, of which some 10,000 were conscripts. This limited cut in manpower reflected the need to respond to the far more demanding technical and maintenance requirements imposed by U.S. and European aircraft. It has gone from 676 combat aircraft in 1974 to roughly 440 combat aircraft. It still has large numbers of Soviet-made aircraft, but it is being rebuilt around a smaller mix of U.S.- and French-made aircraft plus a limited number of Chinese-made fighters.

Egypt still has one brigade of 9 obsolete Tu-16 bombers. It has 10 fighter ground-attack squadrons, with 2/33 F-4E, 1/16 Mirage 5E2, 1/15 Alphajet, 4/76 J-6, and 2/30 MiG-17. It has six brigades of air defense fighters with two squadrons per brigade. These include 2/33 F-16s, 1/16 Mirage 2000s, 2/42 Mirage 5Es, 5/84 MiG-21s, and 3/52 J-7s. It has a reconnaissance brigade with one squadron of 6 Mirage 5SDRs and one of 14 MiG-21Rs. There are 3 Mirage 2000Bs, 7 F-16Bs, 5 Mirage 5SDDs, 29 Alphajets, and 16 J-6s in Egypt's training forces, which have dual capability as combat aircraft.

Egypt has stressed modern air munitions for these aircraft but has not been able to cost-effectively modify its Soviet aircraft to use Western missiles. Its most advanced air-to-air missiles are the Aim-9L, R-330, R-550 Magic, and the Aim-7F. Its air-to-surface missiles include the AGM-65 Maverick, AS-30, and HOT. Its holdings of obsolete and low-capability Soviet-made missiles include the AA-2 Atoll, the AS-1 Kennel, and the AS-5 Kelt. Egyptian stocks of modern munitions are low, and most Soviet-made types are well beyond their useful life.

In spite of its limited resources, Egypt has reacted to the lessons of the 1982 war by acquiring five E-2C airborne early warning aircraft, two EC-130H electronic warfare aircraft, two Beech 1900 electronic intelligence aircraft, and four Commando electronic countermeasure helicopters. It has bought Teledyne-Ryan 324 remotely piloted vehicles and is working on a design of its own. It also has built up the attack strength of its helicopter force. It now has a total of 15 squadrons of helicopters, and two brigades with a total of four squadrons are equipped with 75 SA-342L attack helicopters. Half of these SA-342Ls have 20-mm guns and half have HOT antitank guided missiles.

Egypt's combat air strength is planned to drop from 530 combat aircraft in 1984 to 424 in 1992. Egypt will receive 81 F-16As, 4 F-16Bs, 3 E-2Cs, and 3 C-130Hs from the U.S. during 1988–1992. Its major holdings in 1992 will consist of 160 F-16s, 33 F-4Es, 61 Mirage 5s, 20 Mirage 2000s, 45 Alphajets, 60 Chinese F-7s, and 5 E-2Cs. This means Egypt will modernize its overall forces at about half the rate of its neighbors, but it will acquire significant first-line air technology and modern air-defense systems and improve its good dual capability in attack missions. Egypt hopes that this mix of advanced fighters, new helicopters, and E-2Cs can help compensate for the weakness of its navy. Egypt may, however, have to cut back its spending in order to save hard currency.

Egypt will be forced to maintain a high-low mix of fighters. The "high" side of the mix will include a buildup to 160 F-16s and 20 Mirage 2000s by mid-1995. These two types of fighters complement each other, although Egypt has had to cut back its plans to coproduce its Mirage 2000s because of its balance of payments crisis. Egypt plans to build advanced maintenance and training facilities to maximize the operational value of the F-16 and of F-16 engine and avionics repair depots. Egyptian Air Force planners are conscious of the training and support problems caused by the need to operate advanced fighters. It is steadily expanding its support effort and its ability to provide depot level and other major maintenance.

The "low" side of Egypt's operational air strength will include 45 Alphajet trainer-fighters, 53 Mirage Vs, 40 Chinese CH-6 (MiG-19 variants) which are used for training and will be phased out before 1990, 60 Chinese CH-7 (MiG-21 variants), and 33 F-4Es. The problems posed by the original condition of the F-4Es delivered to Egypt continue to reduce the value of these aircraft.

Egypt also maintains large numbers of fixed and rotary wing transport and support helicopters. Its main fixed-wing aircraft are two brigades (three squadrons) with 1 B-707, 1 B-737, 21 C-130H, 10 An-12, 5 DHC-5D, 3 Falcon 20, and Gulfstream III. Its rotary-wing aircraft include three brigades of helicopters: 1/15 CH-47Cs, 3/27 Mi-8s, 1/24 Commando, and 1/17 UH-12Es. This is a very small force to support Egypt's Army, Air Force, air-defense units, and Navy.

Air Defense Command Developments

Egypt's 80,000-man land-based air defenses now have some 50,000 conscripts, and large elements of this force have obsolete equipment, poor training, and low overall readiness. Nevertheless, the Air Defense Command is pivotal to Egypt's concept of deterrence. Egypt is being forced to phase out its Soviet-made surface-to-air missile systems far more quickly than it had originally planned. While these systems have had limited U.S. and French modification and there are some improved versions of the SA-2 in stock, Egypt realizes that its SA-2s and SA-3s are no longer suitable for first-line service. There are still 65 SA-2 and 60 SA-3 sites (400 SA-2 launchers and 240 SA-3 launchers), more to degrade medium- and high-altitude air attacks on area targets than as an effective means of active defense.[213]

Egypt will have to retain its SA-6s through 1992, although it has no medium-range missile systems on order which can act as a replacement. It has cut its active force from 84 to 60 launchers, and further cuts are planned. Israel proved in June 1982 that a technically advanced power can virtually ignore the SA-2 and SA-3 and, with virtual impunity, can strike against more modern variants of the SA-6 than are deployed in Egypt. Further, Libya already is acquiring aircraft with stand-off missile ranges.

By some point in the early 1990s, Egypt will have replaced roughly 780 Soviet SAM medium and heavy launchers with U.S.- and French-supplied surface-to-air missile defenses. It then will only have 12 Improved Hawk Batteries with 144 U.S.-made Improved Hawk launchers, plus 74 light Chaparral and 36 Crotale missile launchers. Unless it can also obtain 72 more I Hawk or Patriot launchers, this will create the same serious gaps between Egypt's force levels and its requirements.

Similar cuts will occur in Egypt's anti-aircraft guns. Egypt is trading 160 Soviet-made, self-propelled AA guns for 18 Amoun (Skyguard/ RIM-7F) systems with 36 twin 35-mm Skyguard guns and 36 quad surface-to-air missile launchers. Although Egypt will build up to 42 TPS-63 two-dimensional radars and 23 TPS-59 three-dimensional radars, this will compare with a peak strength of 158 Soviet two-dimensional radars and 48 three-dimensional radars. Although the U.S. systems are superior to the Soviet systems, this cannot compensate for a drop in major radar strength from 206 to 65, or 68 percent.

The end result is that Egypt cannot act fully on its interpretation of the lessons of the 1982 war and devote the technical resources to competing with developed states in the complex electronic warfare and SAM-suppression technologies which are already deployed in the area in large numbers. It should also be noted that Egypt will face a major high-technology threat on its western border. Libya is making massive changes in its ground-based air defenses in reaction to the U.S. raid during 1986. During 1986–1987, Libya has received 24 SA-5 missile launchers and at least 12 SA-13s and 8 SA-8s. It has received at least 17 advanced radar systems and is installing a new Xenit C^3I system. Libya will install at least 12 more SA-5s to help defend Tripoli during 1989 and seems to be getting substantial Soviet help in upgrading its electronic warfare capabilities.

Egypt also can only rely on high-technology air-defense weapons if these are fully integrated into an advanced command, control, communications, and intelligence (C^3I) system. Egypt has contracted with the Hughes Aircraft Company to study how it can best integrate its Improved Hawks, E-2Cs, F-16s, Mirage 2000s, etc., into such a system. This contract is called "Project 776" and is the first phase of what must be a continuing effort at air-defense integration.

In making this decision, Egypt will have to rely heavily on its peace with Israel. Egypt can maintain a balanced air-defense effort, but it cannot engage in advanced technological competition in C^3I

countermeasures and counter-countermeasures and must place high reliance on a limited number of E-2Cs, backed by possible reinforcement by the U.S. AWACS.

Naval Force Developments

Egypt now has a 20,000-man Navy and Coast Guard, with 12 submarines, 1 destroyer, 5 frigates, 41 patrol and coastal combatants, 9 mine-warfare ships, and 3 amphibious ships. It also has a small naval aviation component with 5 Sea King M-47 ASW and anti-ship helicopters and 12 SA-342 anti-ship helicopters. The Navy is based at Alexandria, Port Said, Mersa Matruh, Port Tewfig, Hurghada, and Safaqa. The Egyptian coastal defense force is manned by the Army but is under Navy control. It has SM-4-1 130-mm coastal guns and 30 Otomat and Samlet anti-ship missiles.

Egypt's naval forces are numerically impressive, but they are little more than a hollow shell. Two of Egypt's twelve submarines are aging Whiskey-class vessels that are not really operational. The other ten are six Soviet Romeos and four PRC-made Type-033 copies of the Romeo-class. Only the four PRC-made vessels are to be modernized. This is being done in Egypt with PRC assistance and began in October 1988. The modernized submarines will be given a Singer Librascope fire-control system and a combination of updated Mark 37 torpedos and Harpoon anti-ship missile launch capability.[214] The modernization will also add U.S. sonars and underwater operations equipment. Egypt also plans to provide U.S. variable-depth sonar and guns for its subchasers. The remaining six Soviet-made Romeos have token operational capability and are not in active service. The only prospect Egypt has for replacing them is the possible purchase of two ex-British Navy submarines of the Oberon class.

Egypt's major surface forces consist of one destroyer and five frigates. The destroyer is a British Z-class training ship. There are two Spanish-made El Suez-class frigates with 2 x 4 Harpoons, two PRC-made Al Zaffir frigates with CSS-N-2 (HY-2) missiles, and one British-made Tariq frigate, which is a training ship. Only the two El Suez frigates are modern designs, and they have comparatively limited ASW capability. The two PRC-made frigates—the *Najim al Zafir* and *El Nasser*—were obsolescent when constructed. Egypt sent the *Najim al Zafir* to the U.K. in 1988 to see if the two ships could be fitted with modern Western equipment.[215]

There are also 23 guided-missile patrol craft. These include six British-made Ramadan-class boats with 4 Otomat missile launchers, six October-class with two Otomat missile launchers, four PRC-made Hegu class with two CSS-N-2 missile launchers, and seven Soviet

Osa-Is with four SS-N-2A Styx missile launchers. The Hegu-class vessels are relatively limited capability designs, and the Osa-Is are obsolete.

The rest of Egypt's naval strength consists of eighteen patrol boats without guided weapons, which are suitable only for coastal defense and light-patrol missions, six SRN-6 Hovercraft minelayers, and six Soviet-made Yurka and T-301 mine countermeasure vessels which lack the sensors and equipment to deal with modern mines. There are three Soviet-made Polnocny-class medium landing ships, which can carry six tanks and 180 troops each, and three support ships and four tugs. Egypt is studying the conversion of two ships in Egypt to roll-on/roll-off status to use in moving troops and equipment to support friendly states, but funding is uncertain.

This is not a force that can deal with the threats in the region, and Egypt has been forced to steadily cut back on its operational activity and has already suffered serious losses of trained naval cadres. More than 60 percent of all Egyptian naval units reached the end of their useful life by 1986 because these were ex-Soviet vessels which could not be modernized and/or maintained in fully operational status. The most recent deliveries of these Soviet vessels occurred in 1967–68, and most of the weaponry and electronics on these ships are no longer operational. This includes the equipment on Egypt's destroyers, missile patrol boats, fast patrol boats, submarines, and sub-chasers. Egypt has acquired some vessels cheaply from the People's Republic of China through a "soft" loan. These PRC-made ships, however, lack the technology for modern naval warfare and have limited combat efficiency. They serve the purpose of keeping the Egyptian Navy at sea, but they do not solve its modernization problems.

Egypt is also well aware of the fact it lacks effective operational strength, air and missile defense for its ships, and modern naval electronics and munitions, and that it has had virtually no funds to improve its naval basing and infrastructure. It has taken the lessons of the Iran-Iraq War and the Falklands War to heart and is trying to find the funds necessary to create the ASW forces that can deal with the long-term threats to its Mediterranean and Red Sea waters. Even so, Egypt will be forced to severely limit the modernization of its naval forces and to give priority to land- and air-based air defense. Egypt's interdependence with the U.S. and peace with Israel allows it to take the risk of reducing its naval effort while concentrating on higher priority forces, but this does mean severe compromises in its naval capabilities.

These compromises could have serious consequences, given the growth of potential threats. Libya is introducing large amounts of high-quality naval equipment into its force structure. This equipment includes submarines, missile boats, coastal missiles and artillery, midget submarines with Chariot torpedoes, patrol and landing craft, and naval special forces which train for raids and sabotage missions. The development of Libyan naval forces seems more the product of Soviet than Libyan planning, but it is important to note that Libya's erratic leadership makes it a major and growing military threat. Libya is acquiring the ability to threaten Egypt's maritime lines of communication, and such a threat cannot be dismissed. Before Egypt broke with Libya, Qaddafi tried to order an Egyptian submarine based in Libya to attack the *Queen Elizabeth*, an action that forced Egypt to withdraw its ships from Libya.

Libya now has six Soviet F-class submarines, midget Yugoslav submarines, and Soviet and Italian mines it could to use in blocking Egyptian harbors. Libya's special forces routinely train in sabotage missions that could attack Egypt's oil rigs in El Alamein or be used in naval raids to outflank Egypt's land defenses against terrorism. Libya received one Koni-class frigate and two Natia class minesweepers during the last two years and will receive four Foxtrot submarines, four Yugoslav missile boats, and another Koni-class frigate during the next two years. This means Libya has received new warship tonnage at over seven times the rate of Egypt.

The Soviet 5th Naval Group is also normally stationed 28–30 miles off Al-Salun and routinely passes SIGINT, surveillance, and reconnaissance data to Libya. The Soviet cruiser *Slava* and the guided missile cruiser *Grozny* were deployed near Libya in January 1986 after the terrorist attacks on Rome and Vienna. Further, the Egyptian Navy also faces growing threats in the Red Sea. These include the Soviet naval facilities in Aden, the new Soviet naval base in Ethiopia's Dahlak Archipelago, and the potential linkage between Soviet naval forces and those of Ethiopia and Libya.

The only major recent improvement that has taken place in Egypt's naval capabilities is the acquisition of the E-2C by Egypt's Air Force. This will allow Egypt to use its aircraft more effectively in both air defense and maritime missions and provide advanced maritime surveillance to the Egyptian surface fleet. Unfortunately, however, the E-2Cs will have to be dedicated to air-to-air operations in many contingencies. Egypt currently lacks the ability to patrol and provide maritime surveillance for the Gulf of Suez, much less a broader operational area in the Red Sea. This is critical because of the number of ships and oil rigs in the area and the vulnerability of the Suez Canal. As several incidents illustrated in July 1984, it is comparatively easy to mine the Red Sea approaches to the canal and sinking one large ship could block the canal for at least a limited period and deny the Egyptian Navy the ability to reinforce from the Mediterranean to the Red Sea.

Missiles and Weapons of Mass Destruction

Like many of its neighbors, Egypt has not been able to escape the lessons of the 1982 war regarding the problems in penetrating air defenses or the pressures in developing long-range missiles and weapons of mass destruction which are a natural "lesson" of the Iran-Iraq War. It retains two surface-to-surface missile regiments with 12 FROG-7 free rocket launchers and 9 Scud B guided missile launchers from the equipment supplied by the USSR and has long had low-level research efforts in developing long-range guided missiles and nuclear weapons. It has had the capability to produce mustard and other chemical weapons since the early 1960s, and while it does not appear to have stockpiled such weapons, it seems to have gone on with its research efforts and developed the capability to produce nerve gas.

Egypt attempted to import the feedstock for nerve gas from Canada during 1988. This included highly specialized orders of fumigants, pesticides, arsenic, and strychnine for what seems to have been use in a poison gas production facility near or in the Beni Suef Air Base south of Cairo. The U.S. arrested two Egyptian military officers based at the Egyptian Embassy in Washington on 23 June 1988. They were arrested for conspiring with an Egyptian-born rocket scientist called Abdelkadr Helmy and other Egyptian agents to export 32 tons of rocket fuel chemicals, 432 pounds of carbon-fiber materials for nose cones and rocket motor nozzles, propulsion hardware, telemetry tracking equipment, equipment and materials for making rocket motor casings, and missile assembly plans for the Pershing II missile. These plans had been obtained from Messerschmidt in the FRG and an Italian firm.[216]

The full scale of Egyptian efforts to build-up a major deterrent using such weapons is difficult to determine. It is clear that Egypt has developed an improved version of the FROG called the Sakr 80. This is a TEL (transporter-erector-launcher) mounted system which is 6.5 meters long and 210 mm in diameter, weighs 660 kilograms, and has a maximum range of 80 kilometers and a 200-kilogram warhead. It can be mounted on both wheeled and tracked transporter-erector-launchers, and a variant is being studied that would hold four rockets per vehicle. Egypt claims there are two conventional warheads—one with 950 AP/AT bomblets and one with 65 antitank mines. It also claims it is developing an automatic survey and fire-control system for the rocket. This system could be used to deliver chemical weapons.[217] Egypt is also developing an improved copy of the Scud, which it has reverse engineered from a Soviet missile.[218]

What is more serious, however, is Egypt's possible cooperation with Iraq in paying for development and production of the "Badar 2000" long-range missile. This missile is reported to be a version of the Argentine Condor II or Alcran missile. Ranges have been reported from 480 to 900 kilometers. There are also reports that Egypt and Iraq are examining production of the Brazilian SS-300 Avibras with a range of 300 kilometers.

There are strong indications that Iraq is seeking to develop both chemical and biological warheads for these systems and may be reviving its nuclear weapons development effort. Egyptian acquisition of such systems would follow in the footsteps of Israel and Syria but is scarcely likely to help stabilize the situation in the Middle East.

Paramilitary Force Developments

Finally, Egypt maintains paramilitary forces which may ultimately do more to threaten its stability than help it. President Sadat originally established a large central security force to help ensure the loyalty of the regular forces. After his assassination, this force become the dumping ground for the lowest-grade conscripts. It was given miserable quarters, low pay, fed two meals a day, and often retained in service long beyond the normal time of conscription.

This led to large-scale riots in the force in early 1986. These riots were followed by a limited number of reforms and by cutting the force from roughly 500,000 to 300,000 men. It still exists, however, and is still very poorly trained, equipped, and paid. Its only practical purpose is to provide "jobs" for Egypt's least advantaged young men.

Egypt also has a 2,000-man Coast Guard with 38 small inshore patrol boats, a 12,000-man Frontier Corps, and a 60,000-man National Guard which is slightly better off than the Central Security Forces and which is being given Walid armored personnel carriers. These forces have little, if any, military value.

Looking Toward Peace or the Next War?

It is clear that in many ways the 1982 war has never really ended. Israel's northern border may be quiet, but the PLO is back in the area, and there is a new threat from the Shi'ite militias of the Amal and Hezbollah. Coupled to the growing divisions within the Christian factions in Lebanon and the growing Shi'ite radicalism in the rest of Lebanon, the border war between Israel and hostile elements in Lebanon seems likely to go on indefinitely and is probably likely to get worse. It does not, however, seem likely to lead to the kind of fighting that would involve major military action.

Given the PLO's shift to a search for peace with Israel, the struggle between Israel and the Palestinians seems much more likely to be a struggle between two competing forms of nationalism that ultimately leads to some form of political settlement than one that leads to prolonged war. It is possible that it could result in an enduring ethnic guerrilla struggle of the kind taking place in northern Ireland, but any such conclusion is now premature.

The short-term risk of war lies in another major conflict between Israel and Syria, and there is no question that both Syria and Israel are armed and ready for another round. Iraq and Lebanon have more than enough troubles of their own. It is possible that some elements of Jordan's forces might be dragged into such a conflict, but Jordan is all too conscious of the damage Israel could do and of the risk of any military dependence on Syria during or after a conflict.

As for Egypt, it is neither arming nor deploying for such a role. It is in the middle of conversion to U.S. arms and would now have to attack some 80 miles across the Sinai to even engage the IDF and do so along narrow and predictable lines of advance, without any forward-deployed heavy air defenses, with insufficient short-range air defenses in its ground units, without any forward stockpiles or pre-deployed logistic and C^3I system, and without any existing fortifications.

There are some Israelis that charge that Egypt's rapprochement with the Arab League in 1988 has weakened its commitment to peace. They cite a March 1988 exercise where Egypt practiced recovering the Sinai after an Israeli invasion as an example of provocative exercises and the fact that Egypt is now conducting joint exercises with Jordan. They also claim that although Egypt is sticking by the terms of its agreement with Israel and only has one mechanized division in the Sinai, it has a chain of fortifications and ammunition supply dumps in the Sinai that would allow it to build up to five divisions within 24 hours. These claims ignore the many real-world readiness problems in Egyptian forces, but they describe what is at least a theoretical Egyptian capability to join in another round of fighting.[219]

As for the causes of a future war, the main threat of war between Israel and Syria does not seem to be the risk that Syria would deliberately seek to destroy Israel—an action that could be suicidal given Israel's nuclear capabilities—but rather the risk that a war in Lebanon, a border or air incident or some crisis growing out of the Palestinian uprising, could escalate beyond control.

The only deliberate war scenario that seems to have credibility is that Syria might try to copy Egypt's experience in 1973 and try to create new political facts on the ground. It could conceivably launch some form of surprise attack across the Golan—where the IDF still keeps only one active and one rotational reserve division—or a flanking thrust through Lebanon or Jordan. Some Israeli sources have raised this specter as a threat ever since early 1985 and point to a number of threatening Syrian deployments since that time.

Syria keeps its best armored divisions in positions where they could support a sudden attack on the Golan. Syria also keeps three mechanized divisions and one armored division permanently deployed in or near the Golan, plus three independent artillery brigades, two independent armored brigades, and one independent mechanized brigade. Depending on the circumstances, two Syrian divisions could redeploy to attack through the Bekaa or through Jordan. Syria still keeps five independent brigades in the Bekaa under a headquarters element in Shutra and has recently deployed a new squadron of tanks near Mashrara close to the "red line" in southern Lebanon.[220]

This Syrian Army buildup is matched by the steady growth of Syria's air power and land-based air defenses. It is hard to know, however, whether this Syrian buildup is defensive and a search for political leverage or is really a preparation for another war. It is also hard to know whether Israel sees it as a serious threat or simply uses it as an added argument for more U.S. aid.

If Syria does attack, Israel seems more likely to wait for a Syrian attack than to preempt. Further, some Israeli experts privately state that Israel will rely on its air force rather than seek to dominate Syria on the ground. Israel may well seek to hold Syria at the present front-line and concentrate on strategic bombing. If so, it would launch an all-out attack to blast corridors through Syria's air defenses and then seek to hit hard enough at its economic infrastructure to create problems so serious that Syria would take years to recover.

Israel is also unlikely to take half measures in a future war. Many Israeli sources also feel that Israel should never again sacrifice a technical edge of the kind it had over Syrian air defenses in 1982 for so limited and pointless an objective. The thesis seems to be that Israel should seek to avoid a conflict, but strike as hard and decisively as it can if Syria should start one, and in a way that will achieve results long before either the U.S. or USSR can bring political or military influence to bear. There is also at least some talk about striking deliberately at Syria's now dominant Alawite minority as a means of destroying Syria's political unity and ability to recover.[221] The grim fact is that, in spite of all the political changes and peace efforts between 1967 and 1989, the next Arab-Israeli conflict may well be only a few years away. If so, the next war may be significantly more damaging to Syria than in 1973 and 1982. At the same time, the outcome may be distressingly close to that of past wars. Further, regardless of Israeli and Syrian plans, the outcome will probably be as indeterminate and as likely to lead to still further conflicts.

Notes

1. Based on data furnished by the Israeli Ministry of Defense in January 1989.

2. Data sheets provided by the U.S. Embassy in Tel Aviv in January 1989. These sheets showed defense spending as 21.0 percent of the budget in 1984 and interest payments as 14.5 percent; as 21.6 percent of the budget in 1985 and interest payments as 15.7 percent; as 19.8 percent of the budget in 1986 and interest payments as 13.4 percent; and as 17.2 percent of the budget in 1987 and interest payments as 12.5 percent.

3. The flow of U.S. aid does not coincide exactly with the flow of Israel's domestic expenditures because of different fiscal years. Israel claims that the true value of U.S. aid is much lower than that shown because Israel has had to repay a substantial portion as loans and because of inflation. Israel indicates that the value of U.S. aid in constant FY1977 dollars was $913 million in FY1978, $824 million in FY1979, $736 million in FY1980, $788 million in FY1981, $829 million in FY1982, $960 million in FY1983, $925 million in FY1984, $747 million in FY1985, $892 million in FY1986, $905 million in FY1987, and $873 million in FY1988.

4. See "So Much to Do, So Little Done," *Economist*, May 25, 1985, p. 69; "Israel Reports Least Immigration since '48, Amid Worry for Future," *New York Times*, January 7, 1986, p. A-4.

5. *Jane's Defence Weekly*, February 18, 1989, p. 249.

6. Based upon data sheets provided by the U.S. Embassy in Tel Aviv in January 1989.

7. *New York Times*, January 2, 1989, p. 1; *Armed Forces Journal*, November 1988, pp. 36–37.

8. Based on U.S. State Department, *Congressional Presentation for Security Assistance Program, FY1988*, pp. 159–160, and background information provided by the U.S. Embassy in Tel Aviv, January 1989.

9. Based on the IISS, *Military Balance, 1987–1988*, pp. 101–102; CIA, CPAS WF 87–001 (U), pp. 120–122; and "Overseas Study of Reserve Component Issues—Switzerland and Israel," Report by the Reserve Forces Policy Board, Office of the Secretary of Defense, June 4–12, 1988.

10. See Trevor N. Dupuy and Paul Martell, *Flawed Victory* (Washington: Hero Books, 1985), pp. 141–147; Richard A. Gabriel, *Operation Peace for Galilee* (New York: Hill and Wang, 1984), pp. 191–213; John Laffin, *War of Desperation* (London: Osprey, 1985), pp. 109–130; and Mark Urban, "Fire in Galilee," a three-part series in *Armed Forces*, March, April, and May 1986.

11. In early January 1986, Israel announced it was taking steps to fortify 30 settlements in the Golan Heights area and would improve the road system, fences, communications, and shelters in the area. Israel carried out similar improvements in the Galilee in 1985. *Jane's Defence Weekly*, January 18, 1985, p. 43.

12. "Overseas Study of Reserve Component Issues—Switzerland and Israel," Report by the Reserve Forces Policy Board, Office of the Secretary of Defense, June 4–12, 1988, pp. 14–19.

13. *Aviation Week*, October 3, 1988, p. 28; *Jane's Defence Weekly*, October 1, 1988, p. 753 and October 15, 1988, p. 915; *Washington Post*, September 20, 1988, p. A-1; *New York Times*, September 20, 1988, p. A-1; *Washington Times*, September 20, 1988, p. A-8; *Christian Science Monitor*, November 17, 1988, p. 14.

14. "Overseas Study of Reserve Component Issues—Switzerland and Israel," op. cit., p. 59.

15. Aharon Levran and Zeev Eytan, *The Middle East Military Balance, 1987–1988* (Boulder: Westview, 1988), pp. 310–311.

16. All air-defense artillery and surface-to-air missiles are under the command of the Air Force, which reports to the commander of the IAF.

17. IISS, *Military Balance, 1987–1988* (London: International Institute for Strategic Studies), pp. 101–102. Kenneth S. Brower, "The Middle East Military Balance: Israel versus the Rest," *International Defense Review*, 7/1986, pp. 907–913.

18. *Defense News*, July 11, 1988.

19. Ammunition is compatible with the U.S. M-256 and Rheinmetall guns.

20. *Jane's Defence Weekly*, May 13, 1989, p. 835.

21. Based upon *Jane's Defence Weekly*, February 25, 1989, pp. 296-297, and interviews in Israel.

22. *International Defense Review*, 6/1988, p. 610.

23. *International Defense Review*, 5/1988, p. 580.

24. *Jane's Defence Weekly*, October 15, 1988, p. 934.

25. The Jericho II is believed to have been derived from the French MD-620/660. It evidently is no longer deployed.

26. *Jane's Defence Weekly*, November 19, 1988, p. 1258; *Philadelphia Inquirer*, November 17, 1988, p. 21A.

27. Israel has the capability to deliver payloads at much longer ranges. Livermore Laboratories calculated that the Shavit or Comet booster used to launch the Offeq 1 (Horizon satellite) was capable of delivering a warhead to ranges of 3,000 miles. Separate work by the Department of Defense indicated that the maximum range would be as much as 4,500 miles. There is no fundamental difference between a satellite launch vehicle and an ICBM booster. U.S. officials note, however, that there are no current indications that Israel is developing the Shavit booster as an ICBM. See Stephens Broening, "Israel Could Build Missiles to Hit Soviets," *Baltimore Sun*, November 23, 1988, p. 1.

28. *Jane's Defence Weekly*, October 15, 1988, p. 934.

29. *Jane's Defence Weekly*, April 30, 1988, p. 829.

30. Israel has made structural improvements in 140 of its Phantoms, improved the avionics, and improved the radar, at a cost of $5 million per aircraft. It had planned to up-engine its F-4s with Pratt and Whitney PW-1120 engines but could not afford the cost of $10 million each. *Jane's Defence Weekly*, August 8, 1987, p. 21.

31. *Jane's Defence Weekly*, October 3, 1987, p. 725.

32. Brower, op. cit., 7/1986, pp. 910–911.

33. *Jane's Defence Weekly*, November 28, 1987, p. 1239.

34. *Insight*, November 16, 1987, p. 38.

35. *Jane's Defence Weekly*, November 19, 1988, p. 1261.

36. *Jane's Defence Weekly*, October 15, 1988, p. 959.

37. *Defense News*, April 4, 1988, p. 1.

38. *Defense News*, November 28, 1988, p. 17.

39. *International Defense Review*, 9/1987, p. 1204.

40. *Defense News*, April 4, 1988, p. 1.

41. *Washington Times*, November 4, 1988, p. A-11.

42. *Jane's Defence Weekly*, October 25, 1986, p. 929.

43. IISS, *Military Balance, 1987–1988*, pp. 101–102.

44. "Israel's Combat Helicopter," *Defence Update*, No. 67, pp. 8–40.

45. *Aviation Week*, June 9, 1986, p. 27. Israel now has fewer than 250 helicopters, and it is still forced to use the helicopter largely in the support role. About 1,000 troops, or 90 percent of Israel's casualties in 1982, were Medevaced by helicopter.

46. *International Defense Intelligence*, Vol. 8, No. 28, July 14, 1986, p. 1, and *Jane's Defence Weekly*, June 21, 1986, p. 1165.

47. Levran and Eytan, op. cit., p. 145.

48. Israel has sought to buy one assembled European design like the IKL 209/2000, with kits for follow-on submarines to be assembled in Israel. It has sought to obtain U.S. aid funding by having a U.S. contractor take the responsibility for prime contractor and then subcontracting to Israeli and European yards. The logical U.S. contractors—Bath, Ingalls, and Todd—have been reluctant to take the risk for cost escalation in a deal with such a low profit margin and where they have so little real control. *Proceedings*, March 1987, p. 53, and *Jane's Defence Weekly*, April 30, 1988, and May 14, 1988, p. 933.

49. *Defense News*, March 27, 1989, pp. 3 and 42.

50. *Jane's Defence Weekly*, April 30, 1988, and May 14, 1988, p. 933.

51. Michael Vlahos, "Middle Eastern, North African, and South Asian Navies," *Proceedings*, March 1989, pp. 148–149.

52. Defense Security Assistance Agency, *Foreign Military Sales and Security Assistance Facts, 1987*, pp. 24–25.

53. See "So Much to Do, So Little Done," *Economist*, May 25, 1985, p. 69; "Israel Reports Least Immigration Since '48, Amid Worry for Future," *New York Times*, January 7, 1986, p. A-4.

54. See U.S. Arms Control and Disarmament Agency, *World Military Expenditures and Arms Transfers, 1985* (Washington: GPO, 1985), p. 66, and *Defense Week*, April 16, 1986, p. 5.

55. This level of debt payment will not be paid off until FY1996. By that time,

Israel will have paid a total of $5.4 billion on the principal and $14.0 billion in interest.

56. The main sources for the comments on the Lavi and debates over Israel's military industry include *Defense Week,* April 21, 1986, May 5, 1986, p. 15, and June 2, 1986, p. 13; Leonard Silk, "Military Costs an Israeli Issue," *New York Times,* June 4, 1986, p. D-2, August 31, 1987, p. A-1; *Wall Street Journal,* August 31, 1987, p. 13, and December 17, 1987, p. 26; *Jane's Defence Weekly,* August 29, 1987, p. 361, September 12, 1987, pp. 512 and 544; October 3, 1987, p. 725; February 27, 1988, p. 356, June 11, 1988, p. 1150, June 25, 1988, p. 1295; *Armed Forces Journal,* October, 1987, p. 40; *Aviation Week,* September 7, 1987, pp. 15 and 23–25, September 14, 1987, pp. 22–23; *Washington Post,* September 1, 1987, p. A-14, December 15, 1987, p. A-25.

57. See Thomas L. Friedman, "Skirmish Over Israel's New Jet," *New York Times,* July 20, 1986, and Friedman's reports in the editions of August 31, 1987, p. A-1, September 2, 1987, p. A-2, and September 3, 1987, p. A-10; and *Aviation Week,* September 7, 1987, p. 15.

58. *Aviation Week,* September 7, 1988, pp. 23–27.

59. *Jane's Defence Weekly,* June 11, 1988, p. 1150, June 25, 1988, p. 1295, and February 27, 1988, p. 356.

60. Ibid.

61. *Jane's Defence Weekly,* February 20, 1988, p. 301.

62. *Washington Times,* November 4, 1988, p. A-11.

63. General T.R. Milton, "Israel's First Line of Defense," *Air Force,* May 1986, pp. 62–69; *Defense News,* June 16, 1986, pp. 1 and 15; *Los Angeles Times,* April 28, 1986; *Wall Street Journal,* April 29, 1986, p. 34; and *Chicago Tribune,* June 5, 1986, p. I-5.

64. *Jane's Defence Weekly,* March 12, 1988; May 14, 1988, p. 933; June 18, 1988, p. 1236.

65. Ibid.

66. "Replaying a Bad Dream," *Newsweek,* October 6, 1986, p. 32; Thomas L. Friedman, "Israeli Raid: New Tactic," *New York Times,* September 26, 1986, p. A-8; "Israel Says Iranians Train Guerrillas in Lebanon," *New York Times,* September 22, 1986, p. A-4; William Drozdiak, "Shamir Accuses Syria in Attacks," *Washington Post,* September 25, 1986, p. A-28; Ihsan A. Hijazi, "Palestinian Resurgences Seen in Southern Lebanon," *New York Times,* September 25, 1986; "Israel to Use Helicopters to Back Lebanese Militia Allies," *Washington Times,* September 22, 1986, p. 8.

67. *New York Times,* December 10, 1988, p. 1.

68. See Dupuy and Martell, op. cit. Also see Ze'ev Schiff, "The Israeli Defense Forces After Lebanon: Crisis, Change, and Uncertainty," *Middle East Insight,* Vol. 4, No. 3, 1985, pp. 15–23, and William Claiborne, "Israeli Studies Lessons of Lebanon War: Some See Soldier's Will to Fight Dulled," *Washington Post,* March 31, 1986, p. A-1.

69. Ariel Levite, "New IDF Plan Prompted by Riots," *Armed Forces Journal,* February 1988, p. 34.

70. *Jane's Defence Weekly,* January 15, 1988, p. 80.

71. *Jane's Defence Weekly,* June 25, 1988, p. 1273.

72. *New York Times,* January 29, 1989, p. E-2.

73. *Washington Post,* February 28, 1988, p. A-29, and March 7, 1988, p. A-23.

74. Israel has reported that the additional costs to the IDF of dealing with the uprising on the West Bank reached $237 million between December 1987 and June 1988. It could get only a $156 million supplement to the defense budget. The IDF stated, however, that it had saved $60 million because reserve forces had to cancel their training for duty in dealing with the uprising. *Jane's Defence Weekly,* June 25, 1988, p. 1273.

75. *Washington Post,* January 30, 1989, p. A-11.

76. Their main reason for concern was Egypt's nuclear weapons effort. A number of German and other Western scientists were recruited by Egypt for this effort. Egypt never properly organized its research and development effort, however, and Israel assassinated several of the scientists and led others to leave the project.

77. The Machon-2 reactor, which France provided to Israel, has never been publicly described or subject to inspection. Some sources refer to a six-floor nuclear weapons facility underneath the reactor.

78. Norway protested the lack of inspection rights after the details of Israel's nuclear weapons efforts leaked in the *Sunday Times* in 1986. After repeated protests, Israel agreed to allow Norway to inspect the "residual" stocks of heavy water but not to allow verification of how the rest had been used. The agreement was face-saving for Norway, but meaningless. *New York Times,* March 17, 1988, p. A-31, and June 11, 1988, p. A-4.

79. Egypt used poison gas during its civil war in the Yemens in the mid-1960s, and Israel was well aware of the fact that Egypt was studying the production of nerve gas and mustard gas at the time.

80. There are reports that Prime Minister Eshkol did not support the bomb project, that little work took place on the bomb project between 1963 and 1968, and that Professor D.E. Bergman, the one member of Israel's Atomic Energy Commission who had not resigned in 1957, was dismissed as head of the commission in 1966 for his support of the weapons project. This may be true, but it does not explain the amount of Mossad activity that went on to get material for weapons production during this period. Further, CIA sources reported that Israeli fighters were practicing the special lob-and-turn delivery methods typical of nuclear bomb deliveries as early as 1964.

81. Helena Cobban, "Israel's Nuclear Game," *World Policy Journal* (Summer, 1988), pp. 424–425.

82. Israeli scientists made claims about a laser-enrichment capability in 1974, but it is unclear when—if ever—this became operational.

83. Israel has skillfully manipulated the uncertainties surrounding its nuclear effort to have the best of both worlds: deterrence without formal declaration. The revelations of the details of the Israeli nuclear effort by Mordechai Vanunu (an Israeli who had worked at Dimona for nine years and who left the country with large numbers of classified papers and photos) in the London *Sunday Times* indicate, however, that the Israeli effort was considerably more advanced at this time than many Western experts thought. See the *Sunday Times,* October 5, 1986, pp. 1–3, and October 12, 1986, pp. 1 and 12.

84. *Time*, April 12, 1976, pp. 39–40.

85. Cobban, op. cit., pp. 424–425.

86. *International Defense Review*, 7/1987, p. 857.

87. Jeff Abramowitz, "CW Changes the Rules of War in the Middle East," *Jane's Defence Weekly*, November 7, 1987, pp. 1063–1069.

88. For recent reporting on the Israeli nuclear effort, see the *Sunday Times*, October 5, 1986; *Washington Times*, October 6, 1986; *Boston Globe*, October 14, 1986; *New York Times*, October 27, 1986; and *Washington Post*, October 31, 1986. Recent BBC and ITV reporting efforts seem to give more credibility to the idea that Israel has some form of relatively short-range nuclear armed missile. Ranges of anywhere from 75 to 930 NM have been reported, with accuracies of anywhere from 0.1 km to radar correlator guidance packages capable of CEPs (circular errors of probability) of 100 meters.

89. *Aviation Week*, December 7, 1987, p. 32, and March 21, 1988, p. 18.

90. *Economist*, August 1, 1987, p. 41; *Washington Times*, July 24, 1987, p. A-9, and April 4, 1988, p. 17; *International Defense Review*, 7/1987, p. 857, and *New York Times*, July 29, 1987, p. A-10.

91. *Washington Times*, April 4, 1988, p. 17.

92. Israel has the capability to deliver payloads at much longer ranges. Livermore Laboratories calculated that the Shavit or Comet booster used to launch the Offeq 1 (Horizon satellite) was capable of delivering a warhead to ranges of 3,000 miles. Separate work by the Department of Defense indicated that the maximum range would be as much as 4,500 miles. There is no fundamental difference between a satellite launch vehicle and an ICBM booster. U.S. officials note, however, that there are no current indications that Israel is developing the Shavit booster as an ICBM. See Stephens Broening, "Israel Could Build Missiles to Hit Soviets," *Baltimore Sun*, November 23, 1988, p. 1.

93. Israeli chemical protection uniforms exist which cover the entire soldier and allow full use of weapons and supplies in a chemical environment. Israel faces special problems, however, because such gear has to be used in a climate that can be far hotter than that of most of Western Europe.

94. Abramowitz, op. cit., pp. 1063–1069.

95. *Jane's Defence Weekly*, April 23, 1988, p. 785.

96. *Jane's Defence Weekly*, April 8, 1988, p. 587; *Washington Times*, April 3, 1989, p. A-9.

97. *Aviation Week*, December 7, 1987, p. 32, and March 21, 1988, p. 18.

98. *Washington Times*, April 3, 1989, p. A-9.

99. The U.S. will fund 80 percent of the development cost and has agreed that Israel can pay 10 percent of its share out of FMS credits.

100. *Washington Times*, December 23, 1987, p. A-8, and June 28, 1988, p. A-6; *Washington Post*, June 29, 1988, p. 1.

101. For excellent reporting on the issues involved in the creation and planning of Israel's nuclear forces, see Peter Pry, *Israel's Nuclear Arsenal* (Boulder: Westview/Croom Helm, 1984); *Sunday Times*, October 5, 1986, pp. 1–3, and October 12, 1986, pp. 1 and 12; Martha Wegner, "Recipe for an Israeli Nuclear Arsenal," *Middle East Report*, November-December,

1986, pp. 9–14; Leonard Spector, *Going Nuclear* (Cambridge: Ballinger, 1987), pp. 140–148; and Cobban, op. cit., pp. 416–433. Much of the material briefed by the CIA can be found in "Prospects for Further Nuclear Proliferation," a CIA White Paper dated September 4, 1984. A good history of much of Israel's espionage effort to acquire a major nuclear capability can be found in Herbert Krosney and Steve Weissman, *The Islamic Bomb* (New York: Times Books, 1981).

102. See Claiborne, op. cit., p. A-1.

103. See Martin Sieff, "Israeli Officer Blasts Army Bureaucracy, Reduced Readiness," *Washington Times*, June 3, 1986, p. A-6.

104. *Armed Forces Journal*, January 1988, p. 26, and *Jane's Defence Weekly*, November 28, 1987, p. 1249.

105. *Wall Street Journal*, April 14, 1988, p. 26; *Chicago Tribune*, October 2, 1988, pp. 5–16.

106. CIA, *The World Factbook, 1987*, CPAS 87 WF-001 (Washington: GPO, 1988), pp. 236–238.

107. IISS, *Military Balance, 1987–1988*, p. 113.

108. ACDA, *World Military Expenditures and Arms Transfers, 1987* (Washington: GPO, 1988), p. 79.

109. IISS, *Military Balance, 1987–1988*, p. 113.

110. *Los Angeles Times*, May 26, 1986, p. I-8. Also see "A Man with Ambitions Too Big for His Country," *Economist*, May 3, 1986, pp. 37–38, and "Syrian Trade: Going West," *Economist*, June 7, 1986, pp. 84–85, for a good summary description of Assad's economic problems.

111. ACDA, op. cit., p. 121.

112. Syria has a total debt with the USSR that some sources estimate as being as high as $15 to $19 billion. Syria also has experienced serious credit problems in getting additional arms from the USSR since 1986 and has had serious differences with the USSR over payment terms, Syrian policies in Lebanon, Syrian treatment of the PLO, the Soviet rapprochement with Egypt, and Soviet efforts to improve its ties with Israel. *Washington Times*, July 15, 1988, p. A-8.

113. Central Intelligence Agency, *Handbook of Economic Statistics, 1988*, Washington, CIA CPAS 88-10001, September, 1988, p. 187.

114. *RUSI Newsbrief*, February, 1986, pp. 3–4.

115. CIA, *Handbook of Economic Statistics, 1987* (Washington: GPO, CPAS 87-10001, 1987), p. 117.

116. CIA, op. cit., pp. 117–118.

117. *Jane's Defence Weekly*, April 30, 1988.

118. Jim Hoagland and Patrick E. Tyler, "Reduced Soviet Arms Flow Weakens Syrian Military," *Washington Post*, September 25, 1987, p. A-1; *San Francisco Chronicle*, July 29, 1987, p. 1E.

119. These estimates are based on the IISS, *Military Balance*.

120. The reader should remember that the Israeli-Syrian border is only 70 kilometers long and has only limited lines of armored advance. The average height is 3,000–5,500 meters with peaks of 9,300 meters in the far north. It is rough rock-strewn terrain with many volcanic hillocks. Temperatures

range from 50 degrees Centigrade in the summer to below freezing in the winter.

121. The normal Syrian tank battalion has 31 tanks, 10 per company in platoons of three, plus a command tank at the battalion HQ, which also has 2–3 BMP-PUs or BTR-50s. The tank battalions attached to mechanized infantry units have 40–44 tanks with four three-tank platoons per company. A T-72 tank battalion has 141 men, and a T-55/62 battalion has 160. Soviet advisors supervise training and maintenance at the battalion level. Nevertheless, Syrian technical support remains very limited at the battalion level, and repairs are conducted at base depots at El Kisweh, Al Kuteifa, and Qatana. There is a serious shortage of skilled Syrian technicians and maintenance personnel, and Cuban technicians have been attached to maintenance depots in the past. Syria has continued to abandon armored vehicles for service reasons that IDF units could rapidly repair in the field.

122. *New York Times,* June 6, 1986, p. 11; *Washington Post,* June 11, 1986, p. 36, and *Defense Week,* April 14, 1986, p. 5.

123. Israeli reports of improved training in 1988 differ sharply with the information of British, French, and U.S. sources.

124. While press reports of up to 30 units appeared in 1982, the Syrian order-of-battle seems to have had only ten airborne and special forces units.

125. J. M. Moreaux, "The Syrian Army," *Defense Update,* No. 69, pp. 29–30.

126. The following comparisons are based on the 1982–1983 and 1987–1988 editions of the IISS *Military Balance.* Estimates differ sharply in other sources.

127. A significant number of Syrian tanks are in storage, used as reserves or as static defenses. Some estimates of this portion of Syria's tank force go as high as 1,200 tanks.

128. One U.S. source feels it is possible that Republican Guard forces may have had such upgrading.

129. The AT-6 is not believed to be deployed in Syrian forces.

130. Moreaux, op. cit., p. 31.

131. *Jane's Defence Weekly,* April 2, 1988, p. 614, April 30, 1988, p. 853.

132. *New York Times,* June 6, 1986, p. 11; *Washington Post,* June 11, 1986, p. 36, *Defense Week,* April 14, 1986, p. 5.

133. Syrian units deploy as close as 10 kilometers from the front line versus 20–25 kilometers for Soviet units.

134. *Jane's Defence Weekly,* July 26, 1982, p. 92.

135. The analysis in this section is based largely on various interviews. Also see *Jane's Defence Weekly,* July 26, 1986, p. 92, April 2, 1988, p. 613, April 30, 1988, p. 853; *Washington Post,* June 23, 1988, p. 33, September 7, 1988, p. A-25; *Los Angeles Times,* July 14, 1988, p. I-1; *Washington Times,* September 18, 1987, p. 2; *New York Times,* June 22, 1988, p. A-6.

136. Major General Avihu Ben-Nun, commander of the Israeli Air Force, claimed in 1988 that Syria was spending 75 percent of its total defense budget on its Air Force and air defenses in an effort to reach strategic parity with Israel. This is highly doubtful, but this is a very high priority area of investment. *Jane's Defence Weekly,* July 30, 1988, p. 161.

137. Significant numbers of older Syrian combat aircraft are in storage.

138. Israel easily shot down two of these MiG-23s on November 19, 1985. *New York Times*, November 20, 1985, p. A-1.

139. These aircraft began to be delivered in 1987. They were originally scheduled to begin delivery in 1986, but the delivery was delayed when the Soviets insisted on prior payment. Delivery of all 24 aircraft was complete in late 1988.

140. Brigitte Sauerwein, "MiG-29 at Farnborough," *International Defense Review*, 10/1988, p. 1243.

141. Israel first shot down a Syrian RPV on June 13, 1986. *Washington Post*, May 30, 1986, p. 9, and *Jane's Defence Weekly*, August 10, 1986, pp. 260–261.

142. Tony Banks, "Syria Upgrades Forces Facing Golan Heights," *Jane's Defence Weekly*, April 12, 1986, pp. 660–661; Joseph S. Bermudez, "The Syrian Missile Threat," *Marine Corps Gazette*, January 1985, pp. 54–62; *Defense Week*, April 14, 1986, p. 5; *Washington Post*, June 11, 1985, p. 36; Department of Defense, *Soviet Military Power, 1986* (Washington: GPO, 1986), pp. 133–134; CIA, *Handbook of Economic Statistics, 1985* (Washington: GPO CPAS-85-10001, September, 1985), pp. 118–124; and Urban, "Fire in Galilee," Parts Two and Three, *Armed Forces*, April and May, 1986.

143. IISS, *Military Balance, 1987–1988*; and "Israel's Combat Helicopters," *Defence Update*, No. 67, pp. 11 and 37.

144. Light armament includes optional machine guns and rocket pods without advanced fire-control systems or other heavy weapons.

145. *Jane's Defence Weekly*, June 29, 1986, p. 1240.

146. *Jane's Defence Weekly*, October 12, 1985, pp. 793–794.

147. See Urban, "Fire in Galilee," Parts Two and Three, *Armed Forces*, April and May, 1986.

148. *Jane's Defence Weekly*, June 29, 1986, p. 827.

149. *Proceedings*, March 1987, p. 54.

150. *Jane's Defence Weekly*, May 21, 1988; *New York Times*, August 28, 1988, p. A-1.

151. *Washington Times*, September 25, 1988, p. 1A.

152. See Joseph S. Bermudez, "Syrian Command Structure," *Jane's Defence Weekly*, October 25, 1986, pp. 972–976.

153. *Washington Times*, July 21, 1986, p. 3A; *Jane's Defence Weekly*, June 28, 1986, pp. 1228 and 1240.

154. *Los Angeles Times*, June 21, 1986, p. I-6; *Jane's Defence Weekly*, January 18, 1986; "Replaying a Bad Dream," *Newsweek*, October 6, 1986, p. 32; Friedman, "Israeli Raid: New Tactic," p. A-8; and "Israel Says Iranians Train Guerrillas in Lebanon," *New York Times*, September 22, 1986, p. A-4; Drozdiak, op. cit.; Hijazi, op. cit.; "Israel to Use Helicopters to Back Lebanese Militia Allies," *Washington Times*, p. 8, September 22, 1986.

155. Based on estimates in the JCSS, *Military Balance in the Middle East, 1986*, pp. 325–326, and discussions with U.S. officials.

156. Palestinian civilians make up about 11 percent of the population of Lebanon.

157. Based on IISS and JCSS estimates, and Maxine Polack, "Seeking Unity Among the Splinters," *Insight*, October 12, 1987, pp. 36–38.

158. Fatah is the Arabic acronym of Harak at al-Tahir al Filistini. It was founded in 1957.

159. There are strong indications that Iran has steadily increased its financial, training, and weapons support of the Party of God during the last year, as well as Syria, and that the Party of God has a major training camp near Ba'albeck. The Party of God has launched at least one four-point attack against the SLA and is steadily improving in military capability. This presents Israel with serious problems because any reprisal attacks on Shi'ite villages and facilities tend to increase the power of the Party of God relative to the Amal and risk alienating the Amal even more.

160. *Washington Times*, September 22, 1986, p. 8; *New York Times*, September 25, 1986, p. A-11, September 26, 1986, p. A-8, October 5, 1986, p. E-3.

161. Adapted from CIA, CPAS WF 87-001 (U), p. 139.

162. The situation is very unstable at this writing, as are all alignments in Lebanon. Iran came into conflict with many of the factions in the Hezbollah in late 1988, when it tried to end the hostage crisis that was cutting it off from access to the West. It reduced its number in the Revolutionary Guard to about 500 men and its subsidies of the Hezbollah from about $10–11 million to $1 million. *Washington Times*, September 30, 1988, p. A-9.

163. *Jane's Defence Weekly*, November 8, 1988, p. 1141.

164. IISS, *Military Balance, 1988–1989*, p. 104.

165. *Washington Post*, September 22, 1988, p. A-35, 1988, September 23, 1988, p. A-1, September 24, 1988, p. A-1; *Washington Times*, September 23, 1988, p. A-1, September 26, 1988, p. A-9; *New York Times*, September 24, 1988, p. A-1; *Baltimore Sun*, August 15, 1988, p. 2A.

166. James Bruce, "Will Geagea Push Lebanon into Partition?" *Jane's Defence Weekly*, pp. 1140–1142.

167. Ibid., *Washington Post*, October 25, 1988, p. A-19; *Philadelphia Inquirer*, February 18, 1989, p. 1.

168. *Jane's Defence Weekly*, September 26, 1987, pp. 697–698; *Defense and Diplomacy*, April 1989, pp. 56–57; *International Defense Review*, 6/1988, p. 611; *Los Angeles Times*, October 5, 1988, p. I-9; *Jane's Defence Weekly*, November 5, 1988, p. 1141.

169. The SLA is heavily subsidized by Israel. It pays the salaries of the SLA and provides training and equipment. SLA members earn $150–200 a month, and their relatives receive permission to work in Israel. *Jane's Defence Weekly*, September 26, 1987, pp. 697–698.

170. *International Defense Review*, 6/1988, p. 611.

171. Ibid.

172. Active in the southern border area. *Jane's Defence Weekly*, September 26, 1987, pp. 697–698.

173. *Washington Times*, February 8, 1989, p. A-9; *New York Times*, January 12, 1989, p. A-3; *Philadelphia Inquirer*, January 12, 1989, p. 10A.

174. *Washington Post*, March 14, 1989, p. A-21.

175. *New York Times*, April 17, 1989, p. D-10.

176. *Washington Post*, April 20, 1989, p. A-29.

177. *Chicago Tribune*, October 2, 1988, p. F-5, and U.S. Department of Commerce, *Foreign Economic Trends: Jordan*, FET 88-38, April, 1988.

178. This includes approximately 200 relatively low quality M-47s and M-48s.

179. These estimates are very uncertain. They take account of both national defense budgets and arms transfers as reflected in IISS and ACDA data and are adjusted by the author.

180. IISS, *Military Balance, 1987–1988* and *1988–1989*.

181. Author's extrapolation based on discussions with Israeli defense officials and the data in ACDA, op. cit., pp. 129–130.

182. Congressional Presentation for Security Assistance Programs, FY1988, pp. 164–167, and information provided by the Defense Security Assistance Agency.

183. Ibid.

184. Based on the IISS, *Military Balance, 1987–1988*, pp. 101–102, and CIA, CPAS WF 87-001 (U), pp. 120–122.

185. *Chicago Tribune*, August 18, 1988, p. I-4.

186. Hussein said in April 1986 that "we can no longer look to the United States to be our major weapons supplier. We must diversify our sources and our relations. Sensible working relations can continue between my country and the United States, but such relations will, of necessity, be limited in view of this . . . snub." *Jane's Defence Weekly*, April 6, 1988.

187. Jordan initially denied an interest in the MiG-29 after reports surfaced in the press. These same reports said Moscow would sell Jordan the SA-11 Gadfly and SS-23 Scarab. It later became apparent that the Soviets had made some form of offer. At this writing, Soviet sales to Jordan since the first Soviet sale in 1981 have been limited to the SA-8, AS-13, SA-14, and ZSU-23-4. *Jane's Defence Weekly*, August 8, 1987, pp. 206–207, and February 20, 1988, p. 311.

188. *Jane's Defence Weekly*, February 12, 1988, p. 239, and February 20, 1988, p. 311; *Aviation Week*, February 15, 1988, p. 21.

189. The purchase was reported at a time Jordan was ready to provide some 3,000 troops to Saudi Arabia to help compensate for its loss of Pakistani forces and to provide additional security forces to deal with any potential Iranian threat to the annual Haj in Mecca. *Jane's Defence Weekly*, February 20, 1988, p. 311.

190. *Wall Street Journal*, September 13, 1988, p. 32; *Aviation Week*, March 7, 1988, p. 29.

191. *Jane's Defence Weekly*, October 15, 1988, p. 934.

192. Jordan is also highly vulnerable to attack on its central water facility and a tunnel which carries virtually all of the water to its Jordan River Valley farms.

193. The Syrian divisions normally include a mechanized corps with the 5th Mech, 7th Mech, and 9th Armored divisions, and an armored corps with the 10th Mech, 1st Armored, and 11th Armored divisions. The 3rd Armored Division could also deploy against Jordan.

194. See Anthony H. Cordesman, *Jordanian Arms and the Middle East Balance, Update* (Washington: Middle East Institute, 1985), p. 6.

195. The primary sources for the following description of Egypt are interviews in Egypt; various editions of the IISS, *Military Balance*; JCSS, *Middle East Military Balance*; the *Journal of Defense and Diplomacy*, November, 1988, pp. 28–33; and Gerard Tube, "Egypt: Arms Manufacturing Base for the Arab World," *International Defense Review*, 1/1988, pp. 73–76.

196. Based on the IISS, *Military Balance, 1988–1989*, pp. 101–102, and CIA, CPAS WF 87-001 (U), pp. 71–72.

197. ACDA, op. cit., pp. 129–130.

198. Estimates based on the trends in ACDA, op. cit., p. 57.

199. State Department, *Congressional Presentation for Security Assistance Programs, FY1988* and *FY1989*. See country sections for Egypt.

200. *Washington Post*, March 8, 1989, p. A-26; March 15, 1989, p. A-26; *Economist*, April 1–7, 1989, pp. 34–35; *U.S. News and World Report*, April 10, 1989, p. 44.

201. IISS, *Military Balance, 1988–1989*, p. 98.

202. ACDA, op. cit., pp. 129–130.

203. Two Soviet Skory-class destroyers were not operational, as was one Soviet W-class submarine.

204. Defense Security Assistance Agency, *Foreign Military Sales and Security Assistance Facts, 1987*, pp. 24–25.

205. The industry was founded with $1.04 billion, of which $262 million has been frozen in banks since 1979.

206. *Jane's Defence Weekly*, April 9, 1988, pp. 681–682; *Washington Times*, March 4, 1988, p. A-3, and April 4, 1988, p. A-8; Tube, op. cit., pp. 73–76.

207. Based on interviews in Egypt. The IISS shows a total active manning of 320,000 for 1988–1989.

208. The total Egyptian Army reserve pool is around 500,000 men, but this simply reflects the number of men with a legal obligation to serve, not the number that are trained and which would be called up in war.

209. IISS, *Military Balance, 1988–1989*, pp. 98–99.

210. Estimates are based largely on the IISS, *Military Balance, 1988–1989*, pp. 98–99.

211. *New York Times*, November 2, 1988, p. A-13; *Washington Times*, November 2, 1988, p. 9.

212. Reports of large numbers of modified Soviet tanks are not true. For example, the Ramses II modification of the T-54/T-55 existed only in prototype form in 1988, and there were no plans for production. *International Defense Review*, 2/1988, pp. 1985–1987.

213. *International Defense Review*, 1/1988, p. 75.

214. Vlahos, op. cit., pp. 148–149.

215. Ibid.

216. *Washington Post*, August 20, 1988, p. A-1; *New York Times*, June 25, 1988, p. 1.

217. *Jane's Defence Weekly*, March 12, 1988, pp. 462–463.

218. *Atlanta Constitution*, October 5, 1988, p. 17A.

219. *Washington Times*, April 4, 1988, p. A-8.

220. *Jane's Defence Weekly*, June 28, 1986, p. 1240; *Washington Times*, June 26, 1986, p. 9A.

221. For typical reporting, see Leslie H. Gelb, "Israelis Say Syria Might Seek a War," *New York Times*, July 20, 1986, p. 3; and Simon O' Dwyer-Russell, "Fears Grow Over Golan War," *Jane's Defence Weekly*, June 28, 1986, p. 1240.

5

CONCLUSIONS

The Special Conditions of the Arab-Israeli Conflicts

One must be careful about generalizing too much from the lessons of the Arab-Israeli conflicts. As the previous chapters have shown, the lessons of one war are not necessarily the lessons of the next. Further, modern war is simply too complex to reduce it to a short list of simple lessons. Israel has succeeded in large part because it sought excellence in every relevant aspect of military performance and did not concentrate on only a few selected areas. The Arabs often failed because they could not match Israel's overall excellence and not because they lacked broad competence or experienced failures in a few critical areas.

It is also dangerous to generalize about the Arab-Israeli conflicts without considering the broader lessons described in the other volumes of this series. The Arab-Israeli conflicts have taken place in a very small area with unique terrain and weather conditions. Israel is only about the size of the state of Massachusetts. If one exempts the occupied territories, Israel has a total land area of only 20,770 square kilometers. Its land boundaries are only 1,036 kilometers long, and it has only 273 kilometers of sea coast.

The entire West Bank is roughly the size of Delaware and has only about 5,640 square kilometers; the Gaza strip has only 380 square kilometers. Modern combat aircraft can cross the length of Israel in a matter of minutes, and the entire Golan Heights area is so small that it is almost impossible to find any historical parallel for the engagement of similar amounts of armor and air power in such a limited area.

While a number of the Arab-Israeli engagements have been fought under cloud cover, the vast majority have been in relatively clear territory. They have been fought in either arid mountain areas in the north or in a mixture of mountain and desert in the south. These weather and terrain conditions do not parallel those in Europe or Asia.

The major nations in the Arab-Israeli conflicts have also been able to fight from very short lines of communication. Israel draws at least one advantage from its small size: It is able to rapidly redeploy and concentrate its forces and can draw immediately on virtually any facility in the country to equip and support its troops. Jordan and Syria are in a somewhat similar position, since virtually all their forces and facilities are relatively near the Israeli border. Egypt has considerable strategic depth, but until the Camp David Accords of 1978, it had spent over 25 years concentrating virtually all of its military bases and facilities to fight along the Suez Canal front or in the Sinai.

All of the commanders in the Arab-Israeli conflicts have faced special imperatives in space and time and in deploying very high concentrations of land and air power into very small fronts. There are, in fact, many U.S. war games that do not allow concentrations of armor which were typical of the 1973 and 1982 conflict. All of the commanders have faced the problem of dealing with tactical preemption or surprise because the forces on both sides have been kept constantly on a near-wartime footing. All of the commanders have operated with highly detailed knowledge of the capabilities of the individual units and commanders on the opposing side, and all of the commanders have lived for their entire adult lives with a detailed knowledge of the terrain where they may have to fight. While these conditions are not unique, they are certainly different from the conditions that shape command in most other conflicts in the world.

The Arab-Israeli conflicts have also involved a wide range of weapons systems and technologies, and the analysis of the fighting in 1973 and 1982 has shown that the way in which these weapons and technologies impact on the battle is highly situation-specific and changes rapidly over time. One of the key lessons about the lessons of modern war is that any given weapon and technology must be examined in terms of as many case studies as possible, that the special conditions of these case studies need to be clearly understood, and that any application of such lessons to other conditions must take these differences fully into account.

The Problem of Grand Strategy

Nevertheless, there are some consistent patterns in the conduct and outcome of the fighting. For example, the Arab-Israeli wars of 1956, 1967, 1973, and 1982 all have one thing in common: Israel won a major victory on the battlefield which it could translate into a temporary gain in security, but not into the kind of victory that decisively altered the politics of the region. While war often served as an extension of politics by other means, even the most dramatic victories simply laid the groundwork for another arms race and future combat.

It is worth noting that the most critical single action that occurred to change the military balance and strategic realities in the region was Anwar Sadat's decision to seek peace and to do so at great personal risk and cost. Similarly, the Camp David Agreement has done more to improve Israel's security position than any of its military victories.

In contrast, Israel's military victory in 1982 proved to be so lacking in grand strategic purpose that it eventually turned into a strategic defeat. While Israel can scarcely be blamed for failing to change the political structure of an entire region by force of arms, virtually all the major actors involved in the wars under study can be blamed for their willingness to engage in war with only a dim or unrealistic picture of the outcome they wanted from the conflict.

The Importance of Training, Maneuver, and Innovation

Another consistent lesson of the Arab-Israeli conflicts is that force quality is often more important than quantity. It is always tempting to predict the outcome of war in terms of force ratios. The Arab-Israeli experience indicates, however, that a combination of superior training, maneuver capability, and tactical and technical innovation can decisively offset sheer mass. Even at their worst, the Israeli Defense Forces were consistently able to outmaneuver and out-innovate their Arab opponents.

It is important to note, however, that Israel's superiority in force quality was not the result of some inherent ethnic superiority or of any inherent superiority of Western tactics and technology. Israel succeeded because it stressed the right operational aspects of force quality. It constantly adapted its training at every level, from the private to commander, to stress realism, operational challenges, and innovation. It borrowed training techniques from every available source, and it created many techniques of its own. The IDF is probably the only force in the world to be able to give its reserves consistently realistic combat training.

Similarly, Israel adopted the best tactics it could find regardless of source. It did not model itself on any given army and looked closely at the strengths of Soviet tactics as well as their weaknesses. Unlike many Western armies, it also constantly tested its mix of maneuver, firepower, and supply rather than organizing and training these elements in partial separation from each other.

Israel has also been constantly forced to break down the usual command and organizational barriers that block the effective integration of the elements of combined arms and combined operations. While many military forces have been allowed to evolve in relatively fixed compartments and along highly stratified bureaucratic lines, Israel has been forced into change in order to survive. This has affected the evolution of every element of its combat arms and of its C^3I. The result has scarcely achieved 100 percent efficiency, but it probably is more efficient that that of any other land or air force in the world.

In contrast, Israel's Arab opponents have often shown great tactical skill of their own and have steadily improved their own use of maneuver, tactics, and technology. Jordan, however, has lacked the resources to compete with the modernization of Israeli forces, and Egypt and Syria have suffered severely from a heritage of highly structured and rigid bureaucratic compartmentalization and from the adoption of Soviet defensive tactics with only limited emphasis on the offensive portions of Soviet doctrine. This combination of internal bureaucracy and relatively slow use of mass has left the key Arab forces exceptionally vulnerable to Israel's strengths.

Egypt and Syria have also only been able to achieve limited and sporadic realism in their operational training. Given units and combat elements have reached or surpassed the average proficiency of Israeli forces, but the overall training quality of land and air forces has been poor to mediocre. Forces have been expanded too quickly to preserve force quality. Command selection has been driven by internal politics and without sufficiently demanding emphasis on training and exercise performance. Junior officers and NCOs have had far too little training, and far too little use has been made of that training when it has occurred. Innovation is not given sufficient emphasis, and it is often discouraged.

There has tended to be a "set piece" character to Egyptian and Syrian exercises, military plans, and operations. Far too often, forces have been trained and organized for one scenario or one attack. This has often worked when Arab forces have been able to seize the initiative—as occurred at the start of the 1973 conflict—but it has left them over-rigid and vulnerable once Israel has struck at the basic operational concept. This also helps to explain why Arab armies have tended to fight better while on the defensive than on the attack. The issue has never been courage. It has always been one of competence and flexibility, particularly at higher levels of command.

It is also worth pointing out that Israel's superiority in training, maneuver, and innovation has been made possible by the fact it has never deeply politicized its forces. Israel's worst moments have occurred—as during the initial reaction to the Arab attack in 1973 and the expansion of the war in 1982—when the political system has delayed for political reasons or has attempted to ignore military reality in the name of political goals. The rest of the time, Israel has been able to preserve a relatively free flow of honest information in both directions, from the lowest levels of command to the highest.

In contrast, the Arab forces have found it difficult to be realistic in evaluating their training, organization, and modernization. The politics of commanders have been critical to advancement both in dealing with a given military service and in dealing with the state's concern with loyalty and internal security. Plans are generally distanced from training and operations. Insufficient effort goes into ensuring technical competence. The bureaucratic life of a given service, and given element within that service, is allowed to be more important than military competence.

This experience leads to three major lessons:

- The first is that training, maneuver, and innovation are all parts of a single process that must be encouraged as much as possible and which must be kept tied to operational need. Improving force quality involves far more than acquiring equipment. It requires a system that is focused on the "demand pull" of the key operational aspects of the art of war.
- The second is that military forces tend to be their own worst enemy. They tend to fall into the trap of becoming complex bureaucratic structures with their own subculture, and they tend to reward the ability to operate according to the rules of that structure rather than military proficiency per se.
- The third is that freedom of communication at all levels within the armed forces and command process is essential. The two-way flow of realistic information from top to bottom in any military service is an essential condition for success. So is the ability to break down the barriers of communication between areas like the political leadership, operations, planning, training, and intelligence.

The natural tendency to organize forces into efficient compartments and functions can be a powerful threat to their military effectiveness unless the personnel in each compartment are forced to cross those barriers and lines of authority as part of their normal duties.

The Need for the Proper Balance of Arms

For all the various lessons regarding individual tactics and technology scattered throughout this book, the key lesson is that a successful force must achieve the proper balance of arms. Both Arab and Israeli successes generally occurred because of a superiority in this balance. Arab and Israeli failures generally occurred when it did not exist.

While the 1967 Arab-Israeli conflict may have been dominated by the tank and by Israel's surprise attack on unsheltered Arab airfields, the 1973 and 1982 conflicts do not reveal any branch of combat arms as dominant. The classic need for a balanced approach to both combined arms and combined operations emerges in both conflicts.

Similarly, no clear trade-offs emerge between attrition, mobility, and protection. The side performed best that made the best use of all three in a given condition. Attrition or firepower could not substitute for maneuver and protection. Maneuver could not dominate over firepower and protection. What counted was the ability to use the best possible combination suited to the operational mission of the forces on a given side.

Technology Transfer

Israel consistently did far better than its Arab neighbors in rapidly transferring and altering military technology. This partly was a result of the fact that Israel paid far more attention to the merits of technology and was willing to allocate the resources to use it effectively. In many cases, however, Egyptian and Syrian forces simply did not organize effectively to use the weapons and technology they deployed. They emphasized sheer mass without proper regard to force quality, and they did not adopt the kind of manpower management and pay policy necessary to get the kind of officer corps and other ranks necessary to operate advanced military systems.

Egypt and Syria also often failed to see modern technology as requiring the integration of major weapons into logistic and support systems that could provide the proper mix of munitions, maintenance, repair and recovery capability, sensors, and battle management systems. Israel clearly saw the value of a systematic approach to fully integrating major weapons into its forces and of acquiring the proper sustainability. The value of the proper amount of technical support was demonstrated again and again in the fighting in 1973 and 1982. Israel constantly benefited from this support. The Arab forces performed far better when they had it than when they did not.

Israel also gained an additional advantage because its training was far more realistic and demanding, particularly at the combined-arms and combined-operations levels. Far too often, Egyptian and Syrian forces went through set piece exercises and avoided the kind of training that really test unit and command performance. The politization of their command structure also often interfered with the kind of realism required.

Arab forces did, however, suffer from external problems. They lacked access to many of the most advanced Western weapons and technology. The U.S. denied weapons to states hostile to Israel, and Europe often sharply restricted the sale of such systems. The USSR seriously restricted the availability of many key systems, and did not organize effective advisory efforts, particularly in providing training in offensive warfare.

The Cost of Technology and Force Modernization

Israel's experience in recent combat has shown again and again that when high-technology forces are tailored to the demands of their mission, they can outperform much larger forces of lower quality. It has shown the advantage of high-performance aircraft and land-weapons systems and of modern sensors and battle management systems. In fact, Israel's experience is an interesting challenge to anyone who feels that low-cost and moderate-performance systems can be effective against threats like Warsaw Pact forces.

Both Israel and its Arab neighbors, however, have had increasing problems in coping with the rise in cost of modern weapons and technology. In spite of massive external aid, Israel and Syria both face major financial limits on their ability to react to the lessons of past wars and to give their forces the combination of readiness and modernization that each nation desires.

The resulting problems are particularly striking in the case of Israel. While the Lavi crisis is symptomatic of problems that were driven by Israel's political and economic needs, Israel still would have come to the point where it could not fund the force quality it wants, in spite of force cuts and a reliance on mobilization. Jordan, Egypt, and Syria encountered similar problems even earlier. The problem of force cost is just as serious in the Middle East as it is in the West and the East.

The Trend Toward Acquiring Weapons
of Mass Destruction

The final—and grimmest—lesson that has grown out of the most recent Arab-Israeli conflict is one with unfortunate similarities to the lessons of the Iran-Iraq War: The arms races in the Third World are now becoming focused on the search for weapons of mass destruction. This search is not entirely new. Israel first began examining nuclear options in the 1950s, and Egypt used poison gas against the Royalists during the Yemeni civil war in the 1960s. Israel acquired a significant stockpile of nuclear weapons by 1967. Egypt and Libya sought both nuclear weapons and long-range delivery systems, and Egypt and Syria were heavily equipped with chemical defense gear when they attacked in 1973.

Nevertheless, the search for weapons of mass destruction described in earlier sections of this volume has been transformed into a major regional arms race by several new developments.

- the revelation that Israel has acquired over 100 nuclear weapons and is developing missiles with IRBM ranges;
- Syria's response to Israel in the form of the development of a capability to produce and deliver nerve gas and other chemical weapons;
- Soviet use of chemical weapons and biotoxins in Afghanistan;
- India and Pakistan's development of nuclear weapons;
- Iraq and Iran's use of poison gas in their war and Iraq's use of poison gas against its rebellious Kurds; and
- Libya's use of gas during the final phases of its war in Chad and construction of a large chemical warfare plant.

The end result has been a surge in the arms race in the search for weapons of mass destruction in the Middle East which has driven virtually every nation with a major technology base, or large amounts of oil money, to begin some form of effort to acquire weapons of mass destruction or of suitable delivery systems. The Middle East arms race interacts with other arms races, such as the efforts of Argentina and Brazil to develop long-range missiles and at least develop the capability to make nuclear weapons, similar efforts at proliferation in Asia, South Africa's nuclear weapons effort, and the search of various Western firms and the PRC to enter the market for missiles, nuclear components, and the equipment needed for chemical and biological weapons.

It is true that most of these efforts are still in their early stages, and the full nature of the trends in each country is still uncertain. Past estimates of the rate of proliferation of weapons of mass destruction have been notoriously over-pessimistic, and estimates of the effects of the use of such weapons—particularly chemical and biological agents—tend to be grossly exaggerated. Nevertheless, Table 5.1 shows that this new arms race is all too real.

It is also important to understand that many of the nations in the Middle East are extremely vulnerable. Many are literally "one-bomb"

TABLE 5.1 The Race for Weapons of Mass Destruction

NORTH AFRICA

Mauritania
• No resources of its own and no signs of any development activity.

Morocco
• No indications of any organized activity.

Algeria

  Delivery Systems
  • 18 Su-20 Fitter C fighter ground attack.
  • 60 MiG-23BM fighter ground attack.
  • Multiple rocket launchers and artillery.

  Chemical Weapons
  • Basic technology and industrial infrastructure for production of nerve, mustard, and cyanide gas present in country.
  • No indications of any organized activity.

  Biological Weapons
  • Moderate research capability.
  • No indications of any organized activity.

  Nuclear Weapons
  • Limited research capability.
  • No indications of any organized activity.

Libya

  Delivery Systems
  • Possible purchase of PRC-made M-9 missile with 125–375 mile range.
  • 48 FROG-7 rockets with 40-km range.
  • 80 Scud B with 190-mile range.
  • Considering Brazilian Orbita MB/EE missile with 600-km (375-mile) range?
  • Considering OTRAG missile?
  • 6 Tu-22 bombers.
  • 58 Mirage 5 fighter ground attack.
  • 14 Mirage F-1D fighter ground attack.
  • 44 MiG-23BM Flogger F and 14 MiG-23U fighter ground attack.
  • 90 Su-20 and Su-22 Fitter E, J, and F fighter ground attack.
  • Tube artillery and multiple rocket launchers.

  Chemical Weapons
  • Nerve and mustard gas production in industrial park. Plant built with some Japanese corporate assistance.
  • May have used poison gas or CS gas in final phases of war against Chad.
  • Unconfirmed reports of shipments of chemical weapons to Syria and Iran do not seem valid.

(continues)

TABLE 5.1 *(continued)*

Libya (continued)

Biological Weapons
- Limited research capability.
- Some research activity but scale unknown. No evidence of production capability.

Nuclear Weapons
- Has actively sought to create a development and production capability but no evidence of any real progress or success.

Chad
- No resources of its own. Libya may have used poison gas in Chad during final phases of fighting in 1987.

Tunisia
- No indications of any activity.

Egypt

Delivery Systems
- Possible cooperation with Iraq in paying for development and production of "Badar 2000" long-range missile. This is also reported to be a version of the Argentine Condor II or Alcran missile. Ranges for the Condor II have been reported of 480 to 900 kilometers. Egypt may also be interested in the Brazilian SS-300 Avibras with a range of 300 kilometers.Egyptian officers were arrested for trying to smuggle carbon materials for a missile out of the U.S. in June 1988.
- 9 Scud B with 170-km range.
- 12 FROG 7 rockets with 40-km range.
- 9 Tu-16 bombers.
- 32 F-4E fighter ground attack.
- 54 Mirage 5 fighter ground attack.
- 14 Mirage 2000EM fighter ground attack.
- SAKR-80 rocket with 50-km range and other multiple rocket launcher weapons.
- Tube artillery.

Chemical Weapons
- Produced and used extensive amounts of mustard gas in Yemeni civil war in 1960s, but agents may have been stocks British abandoned in Egypt after World War II. Effort was tightly controlled by Nasser and was unknown to many Egyptian military serving in Yemen.
- Completed research and designs for production of nerve and cyanide gas before 1973.
- Unconfirmed reports of recent efforts to acquire feedstocks for nerve gas. Some efforts to obtain feedstocks from Canada.
- Industrial infrastructure present for rapid production of cyanide gas.

Biological Weapons
- Major laboratory and technical base.
- No evidence of any organized activity.

(continues)

TABLE 5.1 *(continued)*

Egypt (continued)

Nuclear Weapons
- Low-level research effort. No evidence of more than basic research since the 1960s.

LEVANT

Israel

Delivery Systems
- Jericho I missile with up to 452–650-km range and possible nuclear warhead.
- Jericho IIB missile under development with IRBM (820–1,450-km?) range.
- F-16 and F-4E fighter-bombers capable of long-range refueling and of carrying nuclear and chemical bombs.
- 160 Lance missiles with 130-km range.
- MAR-290 rocket with 30-km range.

Chemical Weapons
- Nerve gas production facility in the restricted area in the Sinai near Dimona, established in 1982.
- Extensive laboratory research into gas warfare and defense.
- Development of defensive systems includes Shalon Chemical Industries protection gear, Elbit Computer gas detectors, and Bezal R&D aircrew protection system.

Biological Weapons
- Extensive research into weapons and defense.
- No evidence of any active production effort.
- Warhead delivery capability for bombs, rockets, and missiles but none believed to have been equipped with chemical gas.

Nuclear Weapons
- Estimates differ sharply.
- Believed to be well over 100 nuclear weapons assemblies, with some weapons with yields over 100 Kt and some with possible ER variants or variable yields.

Syria

Delivery Systems
- 36 SS-21s with 60–75-mile range. Believed to have chemical warheads.
- 18 Scud Bs with 170-mile range. Believed to have chemical warheads.
- 18–28 Su-24 long-range strike fighters may be on order.
- 50 MiG-23BM Flogger F fighter ground attack.
- 19 Su-20 fighter ground attack.
- 28 Su-17 fighter ground attack.
- 24 FROG-7 rockets.
- Possible order for PRC-made M-9 missile (175–375-mile range).
- Multiple rocket launchers and tube artillery.

Chemical Weapons
- Major nerve gas and other chemical agent production facility north of Damascus.
- Unconfirmed reports of sheltered Scud missiles with nerve gas warheads.

(continues)

TABLE 5.1 *(continued)*

Syria (continued)

Chemical Weapons (continued)
- Shells, bombs, and warheads for multiple rocket launchers.
- FROG warheads under development. Reports of SS-21 capability to deliver chemical weapons are not believed by U.S. or Israeli experts.

Biological Weapons
- Extensive research effort.
- Some indications of production of botulin and other agents.

Nuclear Weapons
- Ongoing research effort.
- No evidence of major progress in a development effort.

Jordan

Delivery Systems
- 32 Mirage F-1D fighter ground attack.
- May be buying Tornado or Mirage 2000 fighters with long-range strike capability.

Chemical Weapons
- Technology base is present but no signs of development activity.

Biological Weapons
- Technology base is present but no signs of development activity.

Nuclear Weapons
- No indications of any effort.

Lebanon

- No confirmed indications of activity.
- Maronite Christians began exploring possible purchase of poison gas in 1984.
- Hezbollah may have tried to produce an agent called "metallic nitrogen" (probably nitrogen mustard gas) at a laboratory in West Beirut.

GULF

Iran

Delivery Systems
- Scud B (R-17E) missiles with 230-km range.
- Possible order for PRC-made M-9 missile (175–375-mile range).
- Iranian made IRAN 130 missile with more than 150-km range.
- Iranian Oghab rocket with more than 40-km range.
- F-4D/E fighter bombers.
- HY-2 Silkworm missiles.
- Multiple rocket launchers and tube artillery.

(continues)

TABLE 5.1 *(continued)*

Iran (continued)

Chemical Weapons
- Production of nerve gas has started or is nearing completion.
- Stockpiles of cyanide and mustard gas weapons.
- Substantial assistance in some aspects of production may have been provided by Japanese companies.

Biological Weapons
- Extensive laboratory and research capability.
- Active research effort may have begun in 1987.

Nuclear Weapons
- Has revived nuclear weapons production plant begun under Shah.
- Significant West German and Argentine corporate support in some aspects of nuclear weapons effort.
- Stockpiles of uranium.

Iraq

Delivery Systems
- Tu-16 and Tu-22 bombers.
- Acquiring MiG-29 fighters.
- Mirage F-1, MiG-23BM, and S-20 fighter attack aircraft.
- Extended-range Scuds and other missiles called Al-Hussein (390-km) and Al-Abbas (540-km). Some reports of ranges up to 800 kilometers.
- Possible cooperation with Egypt in paying for development and production of "Badar 2000" long-range missile. This is also reported to be a version of the Argentine Condor II or Alcran missile.
- FROG 7 rockets with 40-km range.
- Multiple rocket launchers and tube artillery.

Chemical Weapons
- Massive production facilities and stockpiles of mustard, nerve, and cyanide gas.

Biological Weapons
- Major research effort. Production has begun of at least one highly lethal agent. Degree of weaponization unknown.
- Laboratory capability to make anthrax, botulin, tularemia, and other biological agents.

Nuclear Weapons
- Osirak reactor was probably designed for weapons production. No major production capability since Israel destroyed most of Osirak, but considerable research. Has major stockpiles of uranium and possibly some illegal enriched material. Interested in laser isotope separation.

(continues)

TABLE 5.1 *(continued)*

Saudi Arabia

Delivery Systems
- PRC-made CSS-2 surface-to-surface missiles with IRBM ranges (up to 1,800 km).
- 34 Tornado strike fighters.

Chemical Weapons
- Low-level research effort began in 1984. No evidence of efforts to acquire actual agents.
- Plastics plants and oil facilities provide much of the equipment needed for production of chemical weapons.

Biological Weapons
- No indications of organized effort.
- Laboratory capability to make simple biological agents.

Nuclear Weapons
- Slight indications of financial ties to the Pakistani nuclear weapons effort, but no serious evidence of such ties.

Kuwait
- Acquiring A/F-18 with advanced long-range strike capability.
- No indications of any interest in weapons of mass destruction.

Bahrain
- No indications of any interest in weapons of mass destruction.

Qatar
- No indications of any interest in weapons of mass destruction.

UAE
- No indications of any interest in weapons of mass destruction.

Oman
- No indications of any interest in weapons of mass destruction.

RED SEA

North Yemen

Delivery Systems
- 15 Su-22 fighter ground attack.
- 65 BM-21 multiple rocket launchers.
- Tube artillery.

Chemical Weapons
- May have limited stockpiles of mustard gas captured from Egypt in the 1960s.

Biological Weapons
- No indications of organized effort.

(continues)

TABLE 5.1 *(continued)*

North Yemen (continued)

Nuclear Weapons
- No indications of organized effort.

South Yemen

Delivery Systems
- FROG-7.
- Scud B.
- 5 Su-20/Su-22 fighter ground attack.

Chemical Weaponso
- No indications of organized effort.

Biological Weapons
- No indications of organized effort.

Nuclear Weapons
- No indications of organized effort.

Sudan
- No indications of organized effort.

Ethiopia

Delivery Systems
- 40 MiG-23 fighter ground attack.
- 78 MiG-21 fighter ground attack.
- BM-21 122-mm multiple rocket launchers and tube artillery.

Chemical Weapons
- Possible limited use of chemical weapons supplied by Soviets or Cuba against Eritrean People's Liberation Front (EPLF) in Eritrea.

Biological Weapons
- Reports of use of mycotoxins or other toxins supplied by Soviets or Cuba seem to be untrue.

Nuclear Weapons
- No indications of organized effort.

Djibouti
- Nature of French stockpiles, if any, is unknown.
- No local effort or capability.

Somalia
- No local effort or capability.

(continues)

TABLE 5.1 *(continued)*

OTHER RELATED

Turkey

Delivery Systems
- 95 F-4E fighter ground attack.
- 100+ F-104 fighter ground attack.
- Tube artillery.

Chemical Weapons
- Fully capable in terms of technology and industrial infrastructure.
- No indications of organized effort.

Biological Weapons
- Fully capable in terms of technology and industrial infrastructure.
- No indications of organized effort.

Nuclear Weapons
- No indications of organized effort.

India

Delivery Systems
- 40 Mirage 2000H fighter ground attack.
- 44 MiG-29 fighter ground attack.
- 95 MiG-23BN Flogger H fighter ground attack.
- 24 MiG-27 Flogger D/J fighter ground attack.
- 120 BM-21 122-mm multiple rocket launchers.
- Tube artillery.
- Prithvi and longer-range missiles under development. (The Prithvi is a 150-km range missile with a one-ton warhead and inertial navigation. It is scheduled to be ready by 1993.)
- SLV-3 space vehicle could be adapted into long-range surface-to-surface missile with 1,000–1,550-mile range. Longer range ASLV and PSLV boost vehicles are in development.

Chemical Weapons
- No evidence of stockpiling. Research complete on production of nerve, mustard, and cyanide gas. Rapid deployment and stockpiling capability for cyanide gas. Status of nerve and mustard gas production capability unknown, but all basic industrial infrastructure is present.

Biological Weapons
- Research effort. Laboratories actively involved in development of biological agents. No evidence of production.

Nuclear Weapons
- Active nuclear weapons development and production effort in spite of denials. Research into fusion weapons, but initial production is likely to be fission weapons in the 100-Kt range and possibly enhanced radiation weapons.

(continues)

TABLE 5.1 *(continued)*

Pakistan

Delivery Systems
- 39 F-16 fighter ground attack.
- 16 Mirage IIIEP fighter ground attack.
- 50 Mirage 5PA3 fighter ground attack.
- BM-21 12-mm multiple rocket launchers.
- Tube artillery.

Chemical Weapons
- No evidence of stockpiling. Research complete on production of nerve, mustard, and cyanide gas. Rapid deployment and stockpiling capability for cyanide gas. Status of nerve and mustard gas production capability unknown, but all basic industrial infrastructure is present.

Biological Weapons
- Research effort. Laboratories actively involved in development of biological agents. No evidence of production.

Nuclear Weapons
- Active nuclear weapons development and production effort nearing completion in spite of denials. Research into enhanced radiation and fusion weapons, but initial production is likely to be fission weapons in the 100-Kt range.

Afghanistan
- No local effort or capability.
- USSR may have used lethal chemical weapons, and there are highly uncertain reports of the use of biological agents. Long-range delivery systems are reported to have included artillery, helicopters, fighter-bombers, and bombers.

NOTE: The above data are estimates based on press reports and other unclassified sources and do not represent official positions of the U.S. government. See *New York Times*, July 3, 1988, p. 3; *Christian Science Monitor*, July 15, 1988, p. 1; "A Deadly New Missile Game," *Time*, July 4, 1988, p. 38; *Washington Post*, March 27, 1988, p. C-1, and April 5, 1988, p. A-1; and "Ballistic Missile Proliferation Potential of Non-Military Powers," CRS-87-654 SPR, August 6, 1987, and working updates by the CRS.

countries. A single nuclear hit on a capital would kill so much of the population and leadership that the country could not hope to recover in its prewar form, if it could recover as a national entity. Most are very vulnerable in the sense they could not recover for years from a single ground burst on their capital. While chemical and biological agents are far less lethal than nuclear weapons, they too can be used selectively to achieve devastating results. The panic alone resulting from an urban attack could kill thousands, while strikes on key air bases and casernes could paralyze national military forces. Attacks on key oil, power, desalinization and other water facilities, communications, and other strategic targets could have critical effects on the national economy and life of large segments of the population.

Finally, other weapons can also cause the most serious damage in the region. Long-range missiles and aircraft with precision-guided warheads or highly lethal killing mechanisms like fuel-air explosives could often achieve the same lethality against fixed- and highly sensitive targets like oil, power, desalinization and other water facilities, and communications targets. Careful selection of long-range precision killing mechanisms could well be as devastating—or prone to trigger massive conflicts—as the use of weapons of mass destruction. This prospect is particularly chilling because the past of the Middle East is such a miserable prologue to its future.

SOURCES AND METHODS

No effort to describe a process as complex as war can ever hope to be complete. This is particularly true when much of the material on the conflicts under study is still classified and where so many of the sources available on the war are in conflict. This volume draws heavily on interviews with both Arab and Israeli sources, many of which were involved in senior positions in the conflicts under study. It also makes extensive use of academic, press, and magazine sources and of research conducted in Israel, Egypt, and Jordan.

The reader should be aware, however, that senior officers and officials involved on the same side disagreed on key points relating to the same battle. In many cases figures and data have had to be adjusted on a "best guess" basis because of the differences between supposedly authoritative sources. While any given data and figures may initially seem authoritative, they only continue to seem authoritative until one turns to the next source.

The senior commanders on both the Arab and Israeli sides in both the 1973 and 1982 conflicts often became involved in personal conflicts with their rivals. Many indulged in exchanges of postwar charges and counter-charges with their colleagues regarding many of the details dealt with in this book. Judgments have had to be made throughout this book as to which report was right, many based on private interviews. It became all too clear, however, that if truth is the first casualty of war, then history is the first casualty of peace. No one outside the actual commands involved can be certain as to which interpretation of many issues is right.

The reader should also be warned that interview after interview revealed how impressionistic most lessons learned in combat really are. Participants in war are scarcely objective observers of the details of tactics and technology. They operate on the basis of limited and constantly changing knowledge, and their priority is combat and command, not recordkeeping and analysis. While some data can be reconstituted after the fact, much cannot. Once again, this forces any analyst into making judgments and informed guesses on the basis of inadequate data and sharply conflicting viewpoints.

These conflicts between sources were particularly severe in the case of the data and figures on the 1973 war because so many authors, official and otherwise, rushed reports into print. Their reports and conclusions were later proved to be wrong, or at least highly uncertain, by Egyptian and Israel examination of captured and damaged equipment and by efforts at more systematic collection of the data available.

The 1982 conflict presented the special problem that Israel made extensive use of electronic warfare and advanced air-defense suppression techniques and conducted a major disinformation campaign after the war to disguise the true nature of the mix of tactics and technology it actually used. Israel was still declassifying some key technology used in the war in late 1988. Similar problems affect the ability to provide an accurate coverage of intelligence and targeting techniques. For other reasons, a great deal of conflicting data emerged on Israeli success in using helicopters, some of which seems to have been deliberately exaggerated in an attempt to give the helicopter more prominence in Israeli force planning.

A basic problem that is repeated in many of the written sources used in this work is the tendency of postwar analysts to focus on their area of interest and to exclude the importance of other factors in the conflict. Much, if not most, of the specialized technical literature on given types of weapons and operations is filled with special pleading, arguments for given weapons and technologies, or analysis which focuses solely on the area of tactics and technology under study. Many writers add a strong service or national bias to this problem.

Finally, the analysis of the the events and lessons for the period between 1982 and 1989 has presented the inevitable problem of trying to analyze history in "real time." All of the governments involved try to classify much of the material presented. While the use of computer data bases allows the rapid cross-correlation and checking of media reporting, it does not substitute for access to classified data. This is particularly true of the description of Egyptian, Israeli, and Syrian efforts to deploy nuclear, chemical, and biological weapons.

The authors of this book fully recognize these limitations. The "fog of peace" is just as much a problem in understanding conflict as the "fog of war" and is just as unavoidable. In practice, therefore, the reader should be aware that any given lesson in this book requires careful analysis of other sources before it can be taken for granted. At the same time, we believe that the mix of interviews, data bases, and written sources upon which this book is based represent a valid starting point for what is ultimately an impossible process—understanding the overall nature of modern conflicts.

BIBLIOGRAPHY

Adan, Avrahham (Bren), *On the Banks of the Suez*, San Francisco, Presidio, 1980.

Albrecht, Gerhard, *Weyer's Warships of the World 1984/85*, 57th ed., Annapolis, Md., Nautical & Aviation Publishing Co., 1984.

ARCO Series of Illustrated Guides, New York, Salamander Books, ARCO.

———, *The Israeli Air Force*.

———, *Military Helicopters*.

———, *The Modern Soviet Air Force*.

———, *The Modern Soviet Navy*.

———, *The Modern U.S. Air Force*.

———, *The Modern U.S. Navy*.

———, *Weapons of the Modern Soviet Ground Forces*.

Arlinghaus, Bruce, *Arms for Africa*, Lexington, Mass., Lexington Books, 1983.

Army, Department of, *1985 Weapon Systems*, Washington, D.C., Government Printing Office, 1985.

———, *Soviet Army Operations*, IAG-13-U-78, April 1978.

Army Armor Center, Threat Branch, *Organization and Equipment of the Soviet Army*, Fort Knox, Kentucky, January 1981.

Asher, Jerry, and Eric Hammel, *Duel for the Golan*, New York, Morrow, 1987.

Ayoob, Mohammad, ed., *The Middle East in World Politics*, London, Croom Helm, 1981.

Badri, Magdoub, and Zohdy, *The Ramadan War, 1973*, New York, Hippocrene, 1974.

Banks, Tony, "Syria Upgrades Forces Facing Golan Heights," *Jane's Defence Weekly*, 12 April, 1986, pp. 660–661.

Barker, A.J., *Arab-Israeli Wars*, New York, Hippocrene, 1980.

Bass, Gail, and Bonnie Jean Cordes, *Actions Against Non-Nuclear Energy Facilities: September 1981–September 1982*, Santa Monica, Calif., Rand Corporation, April 1983.

Bavly, Dan, and Eliahu Saltpeter, *Fire in Beirut*, New York, Stein and Day, 1984.

Baylis, John, and Gerald Segal, eds., *Soviet Strategy*, Totowa, N.J., Allanheld, Osmun & Co., 1981.

Be'eri, Eliezer, *Army Officers in Arab Politics and Society*, New York, Praeger Publishers, 1970.

Ben Horin, Yoav, and Barry Posen, *Israel's Strategic Doctrine*, Santa Monica, Calif., Rand Corporation, September 1981.

Ben Porat and others, *Kippur, Special Edition*, Tel Aviv, 1973.

Bermudez, Joseph S., "The Syrian Missile Threat," *Marine Corps Gazette,* January, 1985, pp. 54–62; *Defense Week,* April 14, 1986, p. 5.

Bertram, Cristoph, ed., *Third World Conflict and International Security,* London, Macmillan, 1982.

Betts, Richard K., *Surprise Attack,* Washington, D.C., Brookings Institution, 1982.

Bishara, Ghassan, "The Political Repercussions of the Israeli Raid on the Iraqi Nuclear Reactor," *Journal of Palestine Studies,* Spring 1982, pp. 58–76.

Blechman, Barry M., and Stephan S. Kaplan, *Force Without War,* Washington, D.C., Brookings Institution, 1978.

Bloom, James J., "From the Litani to Beirut: A Brief Strategic Assessment of Israel's Operations in Lebanon, 1978–1982, *Middle East Insight,* November/December 1982.

———, "Six Days Plus Ten Weeks War," *Middle East Insight,* January–February 1983.

Brassey's Defense Yearbook (later *RUSI and Brassey's Defense Yearbook*), London, various years.

Brower, Kenneth S., "The Middle East Military Balance: Israel versus the Rest," *International Defense Review,* 7/1986, pp. 907–913.

Bussert, Jim, "Can the USSR Build and Support High-Technology Fighters?" *Defense Electronics,* April 1985, pp. 121–130.

Campbell, John C., "The Middle East: House of Containment Built on Shifting Sands," *Foreign Affairs,* Summer 1981, pp. 593–628.

Carus, W. Seth, "The Military Balance of Power in the Middle East," *Current History,* January 1978.

———, "The Bekaa Valley Campaign," *Washington Quarterly,* September 1982.

Carver, Michael, *War Since 1945,* London, Weidenfeld and Nicholson, 1980.

Chalian, Gerald, *Guerrilla Strategies,* Berkeley, University of California Press, 1982.

Chicago Tribune, various editions.

Christian Science Monitor, various editions.

CIA, *Handbook of Economic Statistics, 1985,* Washington, GPO, CPAS-85-10001, September 1985.

Claiborne, William, "Israeli Studies Lessons of Lebanon War: Some See Soldier's Will to Fight Dulled," *Washington Post,* March 31, 1986, p. A-1.

Clarke, John I., and Howard Bowen-Jones, *Change and Development in the Middle East,* New York, Methuen, 1981.

Clemens, Walter C., Jr., *The U.S.S.R. and Global Interdependence,* Washington, D.C., American Enterprise Institute Studies in Foreign Policy, 1978.

Combat Fleets of the World 1986/87, Their Ships, Aircraft, and Armament, A.D. Baker III, ed., Annapolis, Md., Naval Institute Press, 1986.

Congressional Presentation for Security Assistance Programs, Vols. 1 and 2, Fiscal Year 1987, U.S. State Department.

Congressional Research Service, Library of Congress, *Soviet Policy and the United States Response in the Third World*, Washington, D.C., Government Printing Office, 1981.

Conway's All the World's Fighting Ships 1947–1982, London, Conway Maritime Press, 1983.

Cordesman, Anthony H., *Jordan and the Middle East Balance*, Washington, D.C., Middle East Institute, 1978 and 1985.

——, "Lessons of the Iran-Iraq War," *Armed Forces Journal*, April–June 1982, pp. 32–47, 68–85.

——, "The Sixth Arab-Israeli Conflict: Military Lessons for American Defense Planning," *Armed Forces Journal*, August 1982.

——, "U.S. Middle East Aid: Some Questions," *Defense and Foreign Affairs*, June 1986, pp. 15–18.

Croan, Melvin, "A New Afrika Korps," *Washington Quarterly*, no. 3 (Winter 1980), pp. 21–37.

Davis, Jacquelyn K., and Robert L. Pfaltzgraff, *Power Projection and the Long-Range Combat Aircraft*, Cambridge, Mass., Institute for Foreign Policy Analysis, 1981.

Defence Update, "Helicopter Special," Number 60, March 1985.

Defense and Foreign Affairs, various editions.

——, "France's Special Operations Forces," June 1985, pp. 32–33.

Defense News, various editions.

Dupuy, Trevor N., *Elusive Victory: The Arab-Israeli Wars, 1947–1974*, New York, Harper and Row, 1978.

——, and Paul Martell, *Flawed Victory*, Washington, Hero Books, 1985.

Economist, various editions.

——, *EIU Regional Review: The Middle East and North Africa, 1985*, Economist Publications, London, 1985.

——, *EIU Regional Review: The Middle East and North Africa, 1986*, London, Economic Publications, 1986.

El-Edroos, Brigadier S.A., *The Hashemite Arab Army, 1908–1979*, Amman, Publishing Committee, 1980.

Eshel, David, *Born in Battle* Series, nos. 1, 3, 12, and 16, Tel Aviv, Eshel-Dramit, 1978.

—— *The Israeli Air Force*, Tel Aviv, Eshel-Dramit, 1980.

——, *The Israeli Commandos*, Tel Aviv, Eshel-Dramit, 1979.

—— *Israel's Armor*, Tel Aviv, Eshel-Dramit, 1978.

——, *The Lebanon War*, Tel Aviv, Eshel-Dramit, 1982.

——, *Peace for Galilee*, Special edition of the *Born in Battle* Series, Tel Aviv, Eshel-Dramit, 1982.

——, *The U.S. Rapid Deployment Forces*, New York, Arco Publishing, Inc., 1985.

——, *The Yom Kippur War*, Tel Aviv, Eshel-Dramit, 1978.

Evron, Yair, *An American-Israel Defense Treaty*, no. 14, Tel Aviv, Center for Strategic Studies, Tel Aviv University, December 1981.

Feldman, Shai, "A Nuclear Middle East," *Survival*, 23, no. 3, May–June 1981, pp. 107–116.

————, *Israeli Nuclear Deterrence, A Strategy for the 1980s*, New York, Columbia University Press, 1982.

————, and Heda Rechnitz-Kijner, *Deception, Consensus and War: Israel in Lebanon*, Tel Aviv University, Jaffee Center for Strategic Studies, Paper no. 27, 1984.

Financial Times, London and Frankfurt.

Friedman, Thomas L., "Skirmish Over Israel's New Jet," *New York Times*, July 20, 1986.

————, "Israel Says Iranians Train Guerillas in Lebanon" *New York Times*, September 22, 1986, p. A-4.

————, "Israeli Raid: New Tactic," *New York Times*, September 26, 1986, p. A-8.

Furling, R.D.M., "Israel Lashes Out," *International Defense Review* (Geneva) 15, no. 8, 1982, pp. 1001–1003.

Gabriel, Richard A., *Operation Peace for Galilee*, New York, Hill and Wang, 1984.

————, "Lessons of War: The IDF in Lebanon," *Military Review*, August, 1984.

Gelb, Leslie H., "Israelis Say Syria Might Seek a War," *New York Times*, July 20, 1986, p. 3.

Golan, Galia, "The Soviet Union and the Israeli War in Lebanon," Research Paper 46, Jerusalem, Soviet and East European Research Center, 1982.

Green, Richard, ed., *Middle East Review, 1986*, London, Middle East Review Company, 1986.

Grimmett, Richard F., *Trends in Conventional Arms Transfers to the Third World by Major Supplier, 1978–1985*, Washington, CRS Report 86–99F, May 9, 1986.

Gunston, Bill, *Modern Airborne Missiles*, New York, ARCO, 1983.

————, *Modern Soviet Air Force*, New York, ARCO, 1982.

————, and Martin Streetly, "Su-24 Fencer C; Major Equipment Change," *MERIP Reports*, various editions.

Handel, Michael I., *Israel's Political Military Doctrine*, Cambridge, Harvard, 1973.

Hanks, Robert, *The U.S. Military Presence in the Middle East: Problems and Prospects*, Cambridge, Mass., Institute for Foreign Policy Analysis, 1982.

Harkabi, Yehoshafat, "Reflections on National Defence Policy," *Jerusalem Quarterly*, no. 18, Winter 1981, pp. 121–140.

Heikel, Mohammed, *The Road to Ramadan*, New York, Quadrangle, 1975.

Heller, Mark, Dov Tamari, and Zeev Eytan, *The Middle East Military Balance*, Jaffe Center for Strategic Studies, Tel Aviv University, 1985.

Herzog, Chaim, *The Arab-Israeli Wars*, New York, Random House, 1982.

Hijazi, Ishan A., "Palestinian Resurgence Seen in Southern Lebanon," *New York Times*, September 25, 1986.

Hunter, Shireen, ed., *Political and Economic Trends in the Middle East*, The Center for Strategic and International Studies, Boulder, Colo., Westview Press, 1985.

Hurewitz, J. C., *Middle East Politics: The Military Dimension*, New York, Praeger Publishers, 1969.

International Defense Review, Switzerland, Geneva, various editions.

International Defense Review, Special Series, various editions.
International Institute for Strategic Studies, *The Middle East and the International System,* Parts I and II, Adelphi Papers no. 114 and 115, London, 1975.
————, *The Military Balance,* London, various years.
International Journal of Middle East Studies, New York.
The Jaffe Center for Strategic Studies, *The Middle East Military Balance,* Tel Aviv, Tel Aviv University, various years.
Jane's, *All the World's Aircraft,* London, various years.
————, *Armour and Artillery,* London, various years.
————, *Aviation Annual,* London, various years.
————, *Combat Support Equipment,* London, various years.
———— *Defense Review,* London, various years.
————, *Fighting Ships,* London, various years.
————, *Infantry Weapons,* London, various years.
————, *Military Annual,* London, various years.
————, *Military Communications,* London, various years.
————, *Naval Annual,* London, various years.
————, *Naval Review,* London, various years.
————, *Weapons Systems,* London, various years.
Jenkins, Brian Michael, et al., "Nuclear Terrorism and Its Consequences," *Society,* Vol. 17, no. 5, July–August 1980, pp. 5–25.
Jones, Rodney W., *Nuclear Proliferation: Islam, the Bomb and South Asia,* Washington Paper no. 82, Center for Strategic and International Studies, Beverly Hills, Calif., Sage Publications, 1981.
————, ed., *Small Nuclear Forces and U.S. Security Policy,* Lexington, Mass., Lexington Books, 1984.
Jordan, John, *Modern Naval Aviation and Aircraft Carriers,* New York, Arco, 1983.
Joyner, Christopher C., and Shahqat Ali Shah, "The Reagan Policy of 'Strategic Consensus' in the Middle East," *Strategic Review,* Fall 1981, pp. 15–24.
Jureidini, Paul, and R.D. McLaurin, *Beyond Camp David,* Syracuse, N.Y., Syracuse University Press, 1981.
Kaplan, Stephen S., *Diplomacy of Power,* Washington, D.C., Brookings Institution, 1981.
Karsh, Efraim, *The Cautious Bear,* Boulder, Colo., Westview Press, 1985.
————, *Soviet Arms Transfers to the Middle East in the 1970s,* Tel Aviv, Tel Aviv University, 1983.
Keegan, John, *World Armies,* New York, Facts on File, 1979.
————, *World Armies,* 2nd ed., London, Macmillan Pub., 1983.
Kerr, Malcolm, and El Sayed Yassin, eds., *Rich and Poor States in the Middle East,* Boulder, Colo., Westview, 1982.
Khalidi, Rashid, *Under Siege,* New York, Columbia, 1986.
Khalidi, Walid, *Conflict and Violence in Lebanon,* Cambridge, Harvard Center for International Affairs, 1984.
Klare, Michael T., *American Arms Supermarket,* Austin, Texas, University of Texas Press, 1984.

Klieman, Aaron S., *Israel's Global Reach*, London, Pergamon-Brassey's, 1985.

Korb, Edward L., ed., *The World's Missile Systems*, 7th ed., Pamona, Calif., General Dynamics, Pamona Division, 1982.

Kronsky, Herbert, and Stephen Weissman, *The Islamic Bomb*, New York, Times Books, 1981.

Kurian, George, *Atlas of the Third World*, New York, Facts on File, 1983.

Laffin, John L., *The Dagger of Islam*, London, Sphere, 1979.

———, *War of Desperation*, London, Osprey, 1985.

Lambeth, Benjamin S., *Moscow's Lessons From the 1982 Lebanon Air War*, Santa Monica, Rand Corporation, 1984.

Leites, Nathan, *Soviet Style in War*, New York, Crane, Russak & Co., 1982.

Leltenberg, Milton, and Gabriel Sheffer, eds., *Great Power Intervention in the Middle East*, New York, Pergamon Press, 1979.

Luttwak, Edward, and Dan Horowitz, *The Israeli Army*, New York, Harper and Row, 1975.

McLaurin, R.D., "U.S. Strategy in the Middle East and the Arab Reaction," *Journal of East and West Studies*, XI, 2, Fall–Winter 1982.

Macksey, Kenneth, *Tank Facts and Feats*, New York, Two Continents Publishing Group, 1974.

Middle East Economic Digest, London.

Middle East Insight, various editions.

Middle East Journal, Washington, D.C., Middle East Institute, various editions.

Middle East Review, 1985, World of Information, Saffron Walden, England, 1985.

———, *1986*, World of Information, Saffron Walden, England, 1986

Milton, General T.R., "Israel's First Line of Defense," *Air Force*, May, 1986, pp. 62–69.

"Modern Inter-Arms Concepts, IDF Organization, the Yom Kippur War and After," *Defence Update*, No. 69, pp. 32–63.

Moreaux, J.M., "The Syrian Army," *Defence Update*, No. 69, pp. 26–43.

Natkiel, Richard, *Atlas of the 20th Century*, New York, Facts on File, 1982.

Navy, Department of, Office of the Chief of Naval Operations, *Understanding Soviet Naval Developments*, Washington, D.C., Government Printing Office, April 1985.

Neff, Donald, *Warriors at Suez*, New York, Linden, 1981.

———, *Warriors for Jerusalem*, New York, Linden, 1984.

———, *Warriors Against Israel*, Battleboro, Amana, 1988.

Neuman, Stephanie, *Defense Planning in Less-Industrialized States*, Lexington, Mass., Lexington Books, 1984.

Newhouse, John, "The Diplomatic Round, Politics and Weapons Sales," *New Yorker*, June 9, 1986, pp. 46–69.

New York Times, various editions.

Novik, Nimrod, *Encounter with Reality; Reagan and the Middle East*, Boulder, Colo., Westview Press, 1985.

Noyes, James H., *The Clouded Lens*, Stanford, Calif., Hoover Institution, 1982.

O'Dwyer-Russell, Simon, "Fears Grow Over Golan War," *Jane's Defence Weekly*, 28 June, 1986, p. 1240.

Peres, Shimon, *Military Aspects of the Arab-Israeli Conflict*, Tel Aviv, UPP, 1975.

Perlmutter, Amos, *Military and Politics in Israel, Nation Building and Role Expansion*, New York, Praeger, 1969.

———, *Politics and the Military in Israel, 1967–1977*, London, Cass, 1978.

———, "Begin's Rhetoric and Sharon's Tactics," *Foreign Affairs*, Fall, 1982.

Pierre, Andrew J., "Beyond the 'Plane Package': Arms and Politics in the Middle East," *International Security 3*, no. 1, Summer 1978, pp. 148–161.

———, *The Global Politics of Arms Sales*, Princeton, N.J., Princeton University Press, 1982.

von Pikva, Otto, *Armies of the Middle East*, New York, Mayflower, 1979.

Pry, Peter, *Israel's Nuclear Arsenal*, Boulder, Colo., Westview Press, 1984.

Ra'anan, Uri, *The USSR Arms the Third World*, Cambridge, Mass., M.I.T. Press, 1969.

Rabinovich, Itamar, *The War for Lebanon, 1970–1983*, Ithaca, N.Y., Cornell University, 1984.

Randall, Jonathan C., *Going All The Way*, New York, Viking Press, 1983.

Richards, Martin, "The Israeli-Lebanon War of 1982," *Army Quarterly*, January, 1983.

Roberts, Hugh, *An Urban Profile of the Middle East*, London, Croom Helm, 1979.

Royal United Services Institute/Brassey's, *International Weapons Development*, 4th ed., London, Brassey's, 1981.

Rubenstein, Alvin Z., *Red Star Over the Nile*, Princeton, Princeton University Press, 1977.

Safran, Nadav, *Israel: The Embattled Ally*, Cambridge, Belknap/Harvard, 1982.

———, *From War to War*, New York, Pegasus, 1969.

Sayigh, Yezid, "Israel's Military Performance in Lebanon, June 1982," *Journal of Palestine Studies*, Fall, 1983.

———, "Palestinian Military Performance in the 1982 War," *Journal of Palestine Studies*, Summer, 1983.

Schiff, Ze'ev, "The Israeli Defense Forces After Lebanon: Crisis, Change, and Uncertainty," *Middle East Insight*, Volume 4, Number 3, 1985, pp. 15–23.

———, "The Green Light," *Foreign Policy*, Spring 1983.

———, *A History of the Israeli Army*, New York, Macmillan, 1985.

———, "The Palestinian Surprise," *Armed Forces Journal*, February, 1984.

———, and Hirsch Goodman, "The Road to War: Ariel Sharon's Modern Day Putsch," *Spectrum*, April/May 1984.

———, *Earthquake*, Jerusalem, 1973.

———, and Ehud Ya'ari, *Israel's War in Lebanon*, New York, Simon and Schuster, 1984.

Schmid, Alex P., *Soviet Military Interventions Since 1945*, New Brunswick, N.J., Transaction, Inc., 1985.

Schrage, Daniel P., "Air Warfare: Helicopters and the Battlefield," *Journal of Defense and Diplomacy*, Vol. 3, No. 5, pp. 17–20.

Schultz, James B., "New Strategies and Soviet Threats Spark EW Responses," *Defense Electronics*, February, 1985, pp. 17–21.

Sella, Amon, *Soviet Political and Military Conduct in the Middle East*, London, Macmillan, 1981.

Senger, F.M., von, and F.M. Etterlin, *Tanks of the World 1983*, Annapolis, Md., Nautical & Aviation Publishing Co., 1983.

Shamir, Yitzhak, "Israel's Role in a Changing Middle East," *Foreign Affairs*, Spring 1982, pp. 789–802.

El-Shazly, Lt. General Saad, *The Crossing of Suez*, San Francisco, American Mideast Research, 1980.

Sieff, Martin, "Israeli Officer Blasts Army Bureaucracy, Reduced Readiness," *Washington Times*, June 3, 1986, p. A-6.

Silk, Leonard, "Military Costs an Israeli Issue," *New York Times*, June 4, 1986, p. D-2.

SIPRI, *World Armaments and Disarmaments; SIPRI Yearbook 1985*, London, Taylor & Francis, 1985.

Snyder, Jed C., and Samuel F. Wells, Jr., eds., *Limiting Nuclear Proliferation*, Cambridge, Mass., Ballinger Publishing Co., 1985.

Stauffer, Thomas R., *U.S. Aid to Israel: The Vital Link*, Middle East Problem Paper no. 24, Washington, D.C., Middle East Institute, 1983.

Stockholm International Peace Research Institute, *Tactical Nuclear Weapons: European Perspectives*, New York, Crane, Russak & Co., 1978.

———, *World Armaments and Disarmament: SIPRI Yearbook*, various years (computer print out for 1982), London, Taylor and Francis, Ltd.

Sweetman, Bill, "New Soviet Combat Aircraft," *International Defense Review*, 1/1984, pp. 35–38.

Timermann, Jacobo, *The Longest War*, New York, Knopf, 1982.

Urban, Mark, "Fire in Galilee," a three-part series in *Armed Forces*, March, April, and May 1986.

U.S. Arms Control and Disarmament Agency, *World Military Expenditures and Arms Transfers*, various editions, Washington, D.C.

U.S. Central Intelligence Agency, *Handbook of Economic Statistics*, various editions.

———, *World Factbook*, Washington, D.C., Government Printing Office, various years.

U.S. Congress, House of Representatives, Committee on Foreign Affairs, *Proposed Arms Sales for Countries in the Middle East*, 96th Cong., 1st Sess., 1979.

U.S. Defense Security Assistance Agency, *Foreign Military Sales, Foreign Military Construction Sales and Military Assistance Facts*, Washington, D.C., Government Printing Office, various years.

U.S. Department of Defense, *Soviet Military Power*, Washington, D.C., Government Printing Office, various years.

———, *Foreign Military Sales, Foreign Military Construction Sales and Military Assistance Facts*, September 1984.

U.S. News and World Report, various editions.

van Creveld, Martin, *Military Lessons of the Yom Kippur War: Historical Perspectives*, Washington Paper no. 24, Beverly Hills, Calif., Sage Publications, 1975.

——, "Not Exactly a Triumph," *Jerusalem Post Magazine*, December 10, 1982.

Van Dam, Nikolaos, *The Struggle for Power in Syria*, London, Croom Helm, 1981.

von Pikva, Otto, *Armies of the Middle East*, New York, Mayflower Books, 1979.

Wall Street Journal, various editions.

War Data, special editions of the *Born in Battle* Series, Jerusalem, Eshel-Dramit.

Washington Post, various editions.

Washington Times, various editions.

Weissman, Steve, and Herbert Krosney, *The Islamic Bomb*, New York, Times Books, 1981.

Weizman, Ezer, *On Eagle's Wings*, New York, Macmillan, 1976.

Whetten, Lawrence L., *The Canal War: Four Power Conflict in the Middle East*, Cambridge, MIT, 1974.

White, B.T., *Wheeled Armoured Fighting Vehicles in Service*, Poole, Dorset, Blandford Press, 1983.

World of Information, *Middle East Review*, London, various years.

Yaacov, Bar-Simon-Tov, *The Israeli-Egyptian War of Attrition, 1969–1970*, New York, Columbia, 1980.

Index